LANDMARK COLLECTOR'S LIBRARY

COLWYN BAY
ITS HISTORY ACROSS THE YEARS

Ivor Wynne Jones
Norman Tucker

LANDMARK COLLECTOR'S LIBRARY

COLWYN BAY
ITS HISTORY ACROSS THE YEARS

Ivor Wynne Jones
Norman Tucker

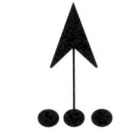

Landmark Publishing

Published by
Landmark Publishing Ltd,
Ashbourne Hall, Ashbourne, Derbyshire DE6 1EJ, England
Tel: (01335) 347349 Fax: (01335) 347303
e-mail: landmark@clara.net
web site: www.landmarkpublishing.co.uk

British Library Cataloguing in Publication Data:
a catalogue record for this book is available from the British Library

ISBN 1-84306-014-0

Colwyn Bay: its history across the years
Book 1 - *Colwyn Bay, its origin and growth* (revised),
© Ivor Wynne Jones and Conwy County Borough Council, 2001
Book 2 - *Colwyn Bay, a 21st century overview,*
© Ivor Wynne Jones, 1995, 2001

Photographs from Colwyn Bay Library archives

The rights of the copyright owners to this work has
been asserted by them in accordance with the Copyright,
Design and Patents Act, 1993.

All rights reserved. No part of this publication
may be reproduced, stored in a retrieval system,
or transmitted, in any form or by any means,
electronic, mechanical, photocopying, recording
or otherwise, without the prior permission of
Landmark Publishing Ltd

Printed in Great Britain by MPG Ltd, Bodmin, Cornwall
Designed by Able Design
Cover by James Allsopp

Front cover: The original pier pavilion, Colwyn Bay pier
Back cover: The Colwyn Bay Hotel and West Promenade
Page 2: The Colwyn Bay Hotel
Page 3: The yard and workshop of wheelwright Joseph Evans, beside the River Colwyn, at Llawr Pentre, Old Colwyn, photographed in the late 1880s

CONTENTS

BOOK 1
Colwyn Bay, its origin and growth
by Norman Tucker, revised by Ivor Wynne Jones

PART 1 FROM THE EARLIEST TIMES TO THE AGE OF ELIZABETH I

1	Origins	10
2	Prehistoric and Roman Times	22
3	Welsh and Saxons	27
4	The Great Seneschal	34
5	The English Conquest	40
6	The Age of the Tudors	53
7	The Conways of Bryn Euryn	60

PART 2 THE RISE OF THE MODERN COMMUNITY

8	The Dawn of Modern Times	71
9	The Coaching Era	77
10	The Vestry Books	86
11	The Coming of the Railway	100
12	The Birth of a Resort	111
13	Expansion and Development	123
14	Colwyn Bay's Religious Institutions	137
15	Education	146
16	From Urban District to Municipal Borough	153

PART 3 ANCIENT PARISHES AND VILLAGES

17	Llandrillo-yn-Rhos, or Rhos-on-Sea	167
18	Llysfaen	181
19	Mochdre	191
20	Llanelian	193

BOOK 2
Colwyn Bay, a 21st Century overview
by Ivor Wynne Jones

21	A 21st Century Overview	202
	End notes	243
	Abbreviations in the text	249
	Index	250

The second (above) and third (below) pavilions on the pier

FOREWORD

COLWYN BAY is a name created as recently as 1872, yet when commissioned to write the history of his adopted town in 1949, in celebration of the forthcoming 1951 Festival of Britain, journalist Norman Ralph Friedel Tucker was able to trace its story back to pre-Roman days. It was a journey through time which delayed publication of *Colwyn Bay, its origin and growth* until 1953, when Professor Arthur H.Dodd, in his original Foreword, said a reader knowing Colwyn Bay as a place where everything he saw was new, save for sea, sky and mountains, would be surprised to find he was halfway through the book before the pattern or even the name of the town came into the picture.

That was not quite what Norman Tucker had intended. Born in Swansea, he was five years of age when his parents moved to Colwyn Bay in 1899. His writing career began in 1910, when he joined the Colwyn Bay-based *Welsh Coast Pioneer* as a trainee reporter. In March 1914 he emigrated to Canada, and soon afterwards joined the staff of the *Toronto Evening Telegram*. The sudden death of a sister in 1922 necessitated his returning to Colwyn Bay with his mother, who was staying with him in Canada. He subsequently edited the *Llandudno Advertiser* before returning to what had become the *North Wales Pioneer*, as head of its Colwyn Bay office, situated over Lloyds Bank (at the corner of Conwy Road and Llewelyn Road). He retired in 1956, but should have left some eighteen months earlier, when I was appointed to take over his role – but leaving after just a few weeks to join the *Liverpool Daily Post*, though staying in Colwyn Bay, eventually to become the paper's Chief Welsh Correspondent. We remained good friends until his death in 1971, when I was chosen to inherit his personal annotated copy of *Colwyn Bay, its origin and growth,* inscribed: "knowing this book will be useful and valued."

When my own *Colwyn Bay, a brief history,* was published, in 1995, I explained: "Rather than repeat [Norman Tucker's] work, this book is designed to be complementary, adding what he never got around to saying, material which came to light after his death, or extracts from the notebooks of a journalist who has enjoyed being present at anything of any note that has taken place in Colwyn Bay during the past 40 years." Norman Tucker had actually read most of my book when I showed him the original typescript, before depositing it at Colwyn Bay Library in 1959 for use as a reference tool.

Both books are now published in one comprehensive volume, spanning two millennia of history and a century of combined journalistic involvement in the life of the town. Between one set of covers *Colwyn Bay, its history across the years* helps redress the imbalance noted in 1953 by Professor Dodd.

The strange contract between the old Colwyn Bay Borough Council and Norman Tucker required him to deliver his book in instalments, for monthly printing and storage as uncut sheets. The Festival of Britain came and went, with the author's only just entering the 19th century. Readers will detect he had to rush through the all-important Victorian period and the 20th century. It was the end of 1951 before Norman Tucker finished the book – by which time the Council had lost interest, and questioned whether the money could be found for publication.

King George VI died in February 1952, presenting the Council with an unexpected alternative target to celebrate – the 1953 Coronation of Queen Elizabeth II – and more weeks of discussion as to whether they could afford it. During that debate Norman Tucker wrote four additional chapters and a concluding note. There was much more he wanted to write about the 19th and early 20th centuries, to match the depth of his earlier chapters, but the Council refused to allow him to make amendments to any of the sheets printed and stored during the previous three years (by two different printers). *Colwyn Bay, its origin and growth* was published on 16 June 1953 — a fortnight after the crowning of Queen Elizabeth (who received a specially bound copy).

As owner of his personal annotated copy I found myself with the onerous task of incorporating, in this new edition, the amendments Norman Tucker would have liked to write half-a-century ago – including some deletions. Some revisions, such as names and dates, were simple. Others required an element of research and rewriting from what are nothing more than marginal notes. It also seemed sensible to do a minimum amount of updating where that would not interfere with the original text. Place names such as Conwy, Caernarfon and Llangystennin are now spelled according to modern standard orthography, but obsolete versions are retained where they are essential in their historical context. In 1953 the Council refused Norman Tucker time to compile an index, and that deficiency is now addressed, with a common index for both his and my sections of this new book.

Colwyn Bay has enjoyed the benefits of an outstanding public library since April 1905. It was Librarian Ifor Davies who, in 1949, persuaded the Council to commission Norman Tucker's original book, and it was Librarian Gillian Fraser who arranged for the successor Council to publish my 1959 manuscript, which had been in the library for 36 years. Special credit is due to today's staff, led by County Librarian and Archivist Rona Aldrich, for being able to unearth most of the illustrations used for both books, to illustrate this much-revised edition.

Ivor Wynne Jones

BOOK 1

PART ONE

FROM THE EARLIEST TIMES TO THE AGE OF ELIZABETH I

This painting of the foot of Rhos Road is by the late F. W. Pike, and depicts a scene in the early 1890s. A corner of Combermere Lodge is seen on the left of the picture. On the right is the cottage occupied by Messrs. Wynne Davies which had its western portion sheared off when Rhos Road was widened. (Courtesy E. R. Jackson).

ORIGINS 1

*"When I passed through in 1857, there was
a solitary cottage, a toll bar, where there is
now a flourishing seaside town."*[1]

A SCEPTIC might contend that a town so recent in origin as that to which Archdeacon Thomas referred, could lay no claim to history. To refute this it is but necessary to glance at the homely hill of Bryn Euryn keeping watch, like some tutelary spirit, over the new town at its feet. Around the crest, curve lines of rain-washed rubble which testify to ancient Britons' once occupying a hill-fort there.

Before one investigates the prosaic annals of a town's growth there seems justification for adding colour by introducing a few picturesque episodes from the archives of the years. A writer, surely, is entitled to paint his picture with the brush of imagination provided he uses the pigments of fact. Out of the mists and the silence emerge shadowy forms - Ordovices in their hill fort on Bryn Euryn - Suetonius Paulinus at the head of his XIV and XX Legions, marching on Mona to slay the druids and hew down the sacred groves. The monk Gildas vituperating King Maelgwn Gwynedd who (Pennant avers) had a palace on Bryn Euryn. Cistercian monks labouring on their sea-weir before Rhos Fynach. Llewelyn the Great's seneschal dwelling in his "chiefest manor-house" - Llys Euryn. Giraldus Cambrensis and Archbishop Baldwin on their Crusade recruitment, journeying this way from Conwy to Rhuddlan. Poor harassed John Leland, King Henry VIII's Antiquary, gazing upon "the marsh often overflowen," where now Llandudno Road crosses to Penrhyn Bay.

Nor must Edward Lhwyd be overlooked. We owe a debt to the doughty scholar who left behind his meticulous observations in so quaint a medley of Welsh, English and Latin. Assuredly Lhwyd must not be omitted, for he it is who gives a clue to the origin of the Borough's name. Llysfaen, he tells us, lies a mile and a half from "Avon Golwyn" on the boundary of Llandrillo.[2]

That was penned in the sixteen-nineties, so we know that "Colwyn" originates from the unpretentious brook which flows beside Beach Road. The place must have taken its name from the stream; not the stream from the place, for there would not be so much as a hamlet there in Lhwyd's day. As late as 1772, when the Poor Rate payment of each inhabitant was recorded, Colwyn could boast only 29 persons, and most of these were on farms. Llanelian, far more ancient, barely merited the name of hamlet, for Lhwyd comments *"there are by ye Church but 4 or 5 houses."* The name of Colwyn occurs in the Llanelian parish register of 1652, and in 1685 when the Rural Dean conducted a visitation, and the total of men, women and children in "Colwun" township amounted to 20.

So it is apparent that Old Colwyn, despite its appellation, is not so very old! A map, of as recently as 1832, makes no reference to Colwyn, though it gives Tan-y-Lan. "Old" Colwyn acquired its designation in the 19th century to differentiate between it and the new watering-place which was termed for a brief while "New" Colwyn.

It is Lhwyd who informs us there was a gorse beacon at Llysfaen and another on Llanelian Mountain. He mentions that "the Plas" at Llysfaen was also known as "Y Plas yr Escob"- the Bishop's Hall - which suggests my Lord of St. Asaph had a dwelling in what is now the Borough. The late Rev. T. Llechid Jones, Rector of Llysfaen, considered the hall might have belonged to the Bishop of Bangor, as Llysfaen is said to have been part of the land given by Edward I to the prelate who christened the first Prince of Wales. On the other hand it is known that the Bishop of St. Asaph held lands in Llysfaen. St. Asaph was burnt on more than one occasion; it may be that the bishop thought it expedient to have a convenient country retreat.

THE FIRST COLWYN

When dealing with a history of Colwyn Bay curiosity is naturally aroused by the origin of the name. Months of searching failed to bring to light any mention of Colwyn earlier than the seventeenth century – with one exception. As far back as 1334 it occurs in a *Survey of the Honour of Denbigh*, a Latin document made by command of Edward III (and published in 1914 with an English introduction by Professor Paul Vinogradof and Francis Morgan). There is a reference to the "vill" or township of COLOYNE. Close by are other familiar names - though in unfamiliar garb. Rue is mentioned and so is Moghedreue, now providentially abbreviated to Mochdre. Penmaen and Lassemain are marked but these were already recorded in the reign of Edward I. Strangely enough the greatest importance seems to attach to two townships now rarely mentioned.

LOYDCOYD AND TEUNNAN

The little isolated school south of Bryn-y-maen perpetuates the name of Llwydcoed township, while Twnan is retained in the names of farms between Llysfaen and Dolwen.

The *Survey* affords a picture which is both illuminating and strange. It depicts a land where serfs were an accepted part of the community; where, instead of rates and taxes, the lord took his payment in produce; a hen at Christmas-tide perhaps, or labour at the plough, or in the harvest field. Words familiar to them sound uncouth to our ears. There was "tunc" to be paid in lieu of stipulated supplies in kind. If a vassal's daughter married he had to pay the lord a fee called "amorbyr" according to the custom of the times. There were payments to the King's chief civil officer in the district who went by the name of Raglot.[3]

Nativus, a native, was a term frequently used, denoting a bondman. The payments were usually made on some holy day, chiefly at that known as the Feast of the Exaltation of the Holy Cross. There was a festival on this occasion for which wooden pavilions were raised, and for these, men might contribute labour or wood as part of their tribute. The contributors had to be responsible for food for the Raglot's horse and groom, for the upkeep of the lord's dogs, the support of his pages, details of which will be found set forth with meticulous care in the *Survey*.

Every family was listed. This area was divided into "vills" or townships (often termed "towns") and many familiar names, such as Colwyn, Rhiw, or Mochdre, were then in use. Those which occur most frequently in old records are Penmaen and Llysfaen (almost invariably united). These evidently constituted a separate manor. Here are extracts:

"In Penmaen and Lassemayn, two vills added late to the Honour, the 'custumarius' if he had two hens gave one to his lord; if he had only one cock and one hen he gave nothing. The villata of Moghedreue, also, in the commote of Ughdulas, included three progenies of free tenants, and one progeny or lectum which was said to be neither purely free nor purely servile."

With the exception of Dinerth, Llysfaen, and Creuddyn, the writer has not been able to trace our familiar place-names farther back than the Edwardian Conquest. Earlier than that it is difficult to comprehend the tribal system which prevailed. The tendency was loyalty to blood rather than territory. Where large families were concerned the division of land among progeny after several generations became so involved that, economically at all events, the new order came in time to save the system from chaos. The word "Gwely," or (mutated) "wely," figures prominently in records. "Gwely" for "bed" was extended to imply "family," and later the territory occupied by a family.

Edward I, having created the counties of Caernarvon, Merioneth and Anglesey (the original Principality), also formed the lordships of Denbigh, Ruthin, Chirk, and Bromfield-and-Yale. We are concerned only with Denbigh Lordship, or Honour. It might well be imagined that in those troublesome times the land was occupied by inhabitants (possibly nomadic) about whom little was known.

The *Survey* proves the contrary. The whole Honour was divided into townships, measured and named, and a systematic check was kept on the inhabitants, and on what they produced. It will be seen that local townships of the Lordship of Denbigh, in Plantagenet days, practically coincide with our present wards.

The *Survey* sets forth in detail each "villata" (township) in this area. It shows the "villata de Rue" was distinct from the "villata de Coloyne" (also spelt Coleyne), so it is obvious that Colwyn Bay's early name was Rhiw, and that Old Colwyn was the original Colwyn township. Also mentioned are Penmaen, Lassevayn, Tuennan, Moghedreue and Dynerth.

Of particular interest is the "villata Loydcoyd cum Hamellis de Whleptre et Dynerth." This Whleptre must be the land of Edward Conway of Bryn Euryn which, in 1572, was called "Gwleptre"[4] so the name evidently was applied to some hamlet between Dinerth and Bryn-y-maen which has ceased to exist. When one recollects how rapidly cottages have disappeared within memory, it is easy to imagine the wattle-and-daub dwellings vanishing without trace.

EARLY MAPS

Maps of early cartographers give little detail which might assist in building up a picture of the past, yet reference to the few local names inserted may be of slight assistance.

Year	Cartographer	Names
1577	C. SAXTON	Llandrighlo, Penrin, Dasart, Llanelian, Llangustennyn.
1610	J. SPEEDE	Llandrighla, Penryn, Brynyryn, Llanelian, Llangustennyn, Eglosrosse. (In his Denbighshire map Speede marks only Dasart which adjoins Llansanfraid.)
1646	JANJANNSON	Penryn, Brynyryn.
1675	J. OGILBY	Crosworth.
1777	EMANUEL BOWEN	Creyddyn Head, Llandrighla, Bochdre, Crosworth, Llysvain, Llan Elion
1805	J. STOCKDALE	Llandrighla, Bochdre, Llan Eligon.
1805	J. CARY	Llandrighla, Bochdre, Llan Eligon, Llysvain, Crostworth
1811	T. TELFORD	Colwin, Penmaen Rhos, Mochdref.

Cary's map shows two roads - one from Betws, through Dolwen, to Conwy Ferry, passing through Groesffordd (which he terms Crostworth), which is the cross roads south of Bryn Eisteddfod; the other from "Abergeley." Dasart would be Dyserth. The Church at Llansanffraid, according to Browne Willis, sometimes went by that name. Rhys (the unfortunate son of Gruffydd Goch of Graianllyn) who was slain by an arrow from Conwy Castle is described as "Rector of Disserth."

PAST RECORDS

To seek the secrets of the past it is necessary to probe into the records of Llysfaen or Llandrillo-yn-Rhos (Dinerth, to use a more ancient name). The name Rhos - indicating moorland or high plain - has lost its significance though it persistently occurs in this neighbourhood: Penmaen Rhos, Llandrillo-yn-Rhos, Betws-yn-Rhos, Eglwys Rhos. In medieval times Rhos was the name of the cantref (an area of approximately a hundred townships) which extended from the Clwyd to the Conwy along the coast. It was debatable land. Across it hostile forces surged to and fro, ever since the Roman legions marched this way from Deva. In many an old record the names

Groes Mill, beside the Old Highway, just west of Eirias Park entrance. Parts are still recognisable

of townships of Penmaen and Llysfaen appear linked together and, indeed, geographically they are one. Stand on Colwyn Bay pier and, forgetting for a moment the encroaching houses, note the long ridge sloping from its peak at Llysfaen Marian, in an unbroken line against the sky until it drops abruptly to the ocean. A natural bastion! It was a desirable base for any invading general intent on essaying the passage of the Conwy, that broad moat between their advance and the almost impregnable fastness of Snowdon. Little wonder Edward I bestowed "Penmeyn and Lessemyn" on one of his follower, to be held by the service of one knights fee.[5]

Penmaen Rhos! The name speaks for itself. "The stone headland in Rhos". The first spot where the uplands unite with the ocean. After the invaders had marched along the flat coastal road from Chester, and across the far-famed Morfa Rhuddlan, this promontory must have loomed massive and menacing before the warriors' eyes. It was not merely a landmark but a place of military importance right across their path. Even in the peaceful days of the eighteenth century travellers demurred at passing that way. Much of the headland has been quarried away; the perilous rock-road, cut into its face, has vanished; but its terrors survive in traveller's tales. One can detect the elation of Thomas Pennant when he writes of the "fine coach-road" which had just been "formed far beyond this precipice"⁶ to cope with the traffic between Chester and Bangor, which was making itself felt in the 1770s. Luckless coach-road! Much of that too has been blasted away, though some traces remain, grass-grown and ignored.

An irrefutable fact which must not be forgotten is that the area covered by the Borough lay right athwart this ancient coastal route in North Wales, and princes, priests and peasants must have passed through what is now Colwyn Bay. Which way did they come? By way of Rhyd-y-Foel and Llysfaen, or around Penmaen headland? Most incidents point to Penmaen.

If, as is often said, the Old Highway at the foot of Pwllycrochan Woods is of Roman Origin, the fact would assist materially in building up the picture of the past. That it does not conform to the popular conception of a "Roman Road" need not cause disquietude. Their roads were not invariably straight, and in outpost territory (as this would have been regarded) their engineers probably made use of a British track - possibly the one connecting Pen-y-corddin Mawr with Bryn Euryn.

"*The straightness of Roman roads,*" Thomas Codrington reminds us, "*has been, perhaps, too much insisted upon. There is no doubt that the Romans made use of the older tracks, and that they sometimes improved them in places without laying them out afresh in the Roman manner.*"

Roman buildings, implements or coins have been found at Prestatyn, Abergele, Pentregwyddel (Llanddulas), Llysfaen, Bryn Euryn, Nant Sempyr, Penrhyn Bay and Little Orme. This suggests, even if it does not prove, a definite route down the coast through this area. If it can be established that a hard-surfaced road existed before the eighteenth century, there is a probability of its being Roman in origin. This, surely, the Old Highway can claim! The "griste water myll,"⁷ belonging to the farm called "Fferme y Rhiw," stood where the road crossed Eirias Dingle in Elizabethan times. The Elizabethan adventurer Captain Tom Price, Plas Iolyn, records that he went from" Y Groes yn Eirias" to Conwy. As if to corroborate this route, while. Arthur Roberts⁸ was digging in his garden at Ystrad, Seafield Road, beside the Old Highway, in 1943, he picked up a tiny silver Elizabethan coin, a three-halfpenny piece dated 1561. A similar coin of the same date was picked up by Moses Williams when digging in his garden at 2, Nant-y-Glyn Cottages, in March 1947. A map of 1720, now at Gwydir Castle, clearly shows the Old Highway running from Conwy ferry through "Bochdre" to Groes-yn-Eirias.

In Thomas Telford's autobiography (1838), published after his death, the editor, John Rickman, writes:

"*From the date of the provincial military roads made in Britain and elsewhere by the Romans, skilful road-making sunk into the general oblivion of the dark ages, and was not revived until the beginning of the last century, when, under the name of Turnpikes, good roads began to be made between large towns.*"

Dr. Trevelyan writes:

"*The importance of Roman roads after the makers had gone, lay in this: no one made any more hard roads in the island until the turnpike movement of the eighteenth century. Or again: In the middle ages roads were little more than riding-ways. To travel by land meant to walk or ride.*"

Llewelyn the Great, in his charter to the monks of Aberconwy Abbey, alludes to "the public road"⁹. Might it not be a portion of this? It is important to stress the part this thoroughfare has played in the growth of the district. There seems to have been a definite coastal route or track from the ealiest occupation of the land.

For more than 2,000 years communication must have existed between points which would have required travellers to pass through the site of modern Colwyn Bay - Richard II was ambushed at Penmaen Head, and there is a certain continuity about the route which is convincing:

BRITISH — Pen-y-Corddin Mawr and Bryn Euryn hill-fort.
ROMAN — Prestatyn and Abergele, Nant Sempyr and Little Orme.
PRE-CONQUEST WELSH — Strongholds at Rhuddlan and Deganwy.
NORMAN — Robert of Rhuddlan's castles at Rhuddlan and Deganwy.
EDWARDIAN — Royal castles at Rhuddlan and Conwy.

ROYAL BAGGAGE

Regular traffic between Rhuddlan Castle and Conwy Castle is implied by entries contained in the account of the expenses incurred in the building of Rhuddlan in 1281-2. Roads were then in existence, for there is an entry for wages of two men "mending the road by which the hay was carried from the meadows." There occur the following items: [10]

"For the reparation of a cart of the King's conveying a pipe of honey from Aberconwy to Rothelan .... 1s 4d.
For one cart with four horses, hired to convey the Queen's bagge from Rothelan to Aberconwy .... 2s 0d.
Thursday, the 1st day of April, paid for the carriage of figs and raisins from Rothelan to Aberconwy .... 8d.
For the carriage of the King's fruit from Rothela to Aberconwy .... 1s 0d.
11th day of May, paid for the carriage of cheese from Rothelan to Aberconwy ...... 4d.
For the passage of the Lady Joan, the King's daughter, at Aberconwy .... 2s 0d.
For the carriage of the baggage of the King's daughter from Aberconwy to Rothelan .... 3s.8d.
Paid to a boy carrying letters of the King to Aberconwy for his expenses .... 3d."

There was obviously a road between the two royal castles, and it is difficult to imagine it could have been other than the Old Highway. Though no proof has yet been produced to establish the Old Highway as a road of Roman origin, the writer, personally, is convinced it was the military highway used by Edward I. The map of 1720 establishes it as being of pre-turnpike origin, and its creation must have called for greater organization than any local body would have attempted. One feels justified in assuming that the hundreds of "hatchet-men" Edward employed to clear the woods along his line of march, from Flint to Rhuddlan, thence to the Conwy, used their axes to hew a way for the invading army through the forest now known as the Pwllycrochan Woods. Morris gives the number at 700 to 1,000 woodmen employed in September 1277 on the district between Rhuddlan and the Conwy River. There were also 100 to 150 mechanics.[11]

NOMENCLATURE

Modern spelling of place names is adopted for there is no consistency in the archaic forms. Their infinite variety is amusing, and, where Llysfaen is concerned, there might well have been a contest among cartographers and chroniclers to see how many variants could be produced. Eirias appears as Erias or Eirios; Llandrillo as Llandrighla or Llandrighlo; Penmaen as Penmayne or Penmain; Mochdre as Bochdre, Mochdref or Moghedreue; Rhiw as Rue or Rew; Dinerth as Dinarth, Dynarth or Dynnerth; Rhos as Ros or Roos; Bryn Euryn as Bryneurin or Brynyryn.

Llysfaen offers the widest assortment. Browne Willis has it Lys-Vaen; Lhwyd prefers Lhysvaen or Lhys-Vaen; the *Calendar of Inquisitions* gives Lessemayn or Lessemeyn, while the *Calendar of Wynn Papers* provides an even more varied assortment in Llysvayne, Llysmayne, Llystvayne, Llysvaine or Llyswayn. For originality the prize must go to Llanrwst which in the *Survey* is transformed into Thlan Ourost.

Other examples could be quoted but these will suffice. It might be mentioned that Pwllycrochan was almost consistently spelt Pwllycrochon until the arrival of the Erskine family. There were, however, exceptions. The 1693 tombstone in Llandrillo Church uses "a" as does a map of 1720. Why the spelling was altered is not apparent.[12]

THE LANDSCAPE

Vague references are found not infrequently to a sixth century subsidence along this coast, but there seems little point in dwelling on this when so great an authority as Dr. F. J. North says concisely:

"There is nothing but legend to vouch for a fifth century inundation." Dr. North, contributing a supplement to the Llandudno, Colwyn Bay and District Field Club, adds: *"It is true that there was once land in the region concerned, and that the coast line did once lie further to the north, but those conditions obtained at a period much more remote than the days during which Helig is supposed to have lived."*

There is, nevertheless, considerable evidence that the sea has persistently encroached. Even to-day it is possible, at low water to come upon tree roots in the sand at Rhos-on-Sea[13] or Old Colwyn. Not many years ago a workman in the employ of the Borough Council, fixing iron steps from the promenade at Rhos-on-Sea, uncovered a tree root in a hollow of which was a hoard of nuts. A sample of the wood was identified as oak. Colwyn Bay's choice of an oak for its coat of arms was appropriate. The country was thickly wooded. Leland (c1530) says there was *"Meately good wood aboute Conwey Abbay."*

TRACES OF A LOST MORFA

A photograph taken on the foreshore below the original Colwyn Bay railway station, some time in the 1880s, shows a fringe of turf between the embankment and the shingle - the last tattered remnant of a morfa which had gradually disappeared. When one considers the sequence of the low land at Morfa Conwy, Maesdu, Penrhyn Bay and Morfa Rhuddlan, it is not difficult to accept the statement that this coastal strip once extended almost to the Point of Ayr. The land between the Ormes is still known as Morfa Rhianedd or "Maiden's Marsh" - a designation once applied to the entire area. It is an ancient name; Taliesin in the sixth century wrote of "Morfa Rhianedd," and in the twelfth century Gwalchmai termed it "Morfa Rhianedd Maelgwn."

Browne Willis speaks of the disappearance of Gronant Moor, possessed by the See of St.Asaph by virtue of a grant made by the Black Prince to Llewelyn ap Madoc, elected Bishop A.D. 1357. In 1397 Bishop Trevor (of Llangollen Bridge fame), obtained from Richard II an abatement of the Quit Rent of Gronant-is-y-Mor at the rate of 1/- an acre *"for every Acre destroyed by the Sea."* If that was happening in the Prestatyn area it is conceivable the same process was continuing nearer here. Pennant (circa 1773) says:

"A few miles to the west of Gronant Moor under the parish of Abergeleu, in Denbighshire, are to be seen at low water, very remote from the shore, bedded in the sand, immense numbers of oak trees, a forest before this event. Lastly in the church-yard wall of Abergeleu is a dateless

Fragment of the Morfa beneath Colwyn Bay station before the east promenade was begun. View taken probably in the 1880s

epitaph, in Welsh signifying that the person who was interred there lived three miles to the north of that spot, a tract now entirely possessed by the sea." Saxton's map shows Abergele considerably farther inland than it now is.

A GREAT STORM

In February, 1606, a meeting of local magistrates was called at Abergele to consider what steps could be taken to repair a breach of the sea bank between Abergele and Foryd where much damage had already been caused to the surrounding country.[14] Doubtless this was connected with the same storm that caused even greater damage round the coasts of Glamorgan where, in the spring of 1606, South Wales and the Border were brought together by a common disaster. The conditions moved the Speaker of the House of Commons to open a subscription list for the relief of the sufferers.[15] The damage had not been fully repaired in 1635[16] or even in 1638[17]. An advertisement in *The Star* of 1798 shows Abergele was then fighting the incoming tides.

A large monolith below low-water mark, off Llandrillo shore, is known as Maen-y-Hensor, or, alternatively, Maen Rhys (Rhys's stone). Rhys was, according to legend, a chief shepherd of Prince Owain Gwynedd (circa 1137) and it is said it was his custom to blow his shepherd's horn from this stone. Another large boulder, near the Dingle, also goes by the name of Maen Rhys.

In 1923 the writer interviewed the late John W. Lloyd, of the Marine Hotel, Old Colwyn, who was born at Tan Lan, Llanelian, in 1844. Lloyd's mother was reared at Aberhod, now a restaurant beside Rhos Promenade, but then an isolated farm of about fifty acres. In his mother's day, said Mr. Lloyd, cows grazed on land which stretched between the farm house and the sea[18]. If the map prepared for Robert Davies in 1763 is consulted, it will be seen that Aberhod stands well back from the shore. In the Vestry Books of Llandrillo-yn-Rhos parish, circa 1772, the name is given "Aberhodni," but this may have no significance for spelling throughout is erratic. The Tithe Commutation Schedule of 1846 spells it "Aberhodney."

EROSION AT COLWYN

At Old Colwyn, before the Promenade was built, erosion proceeded rapidly. It is recorded that large tracts of beach were lowered as much as six feet in the six years ending 1907[19]. *"The ancient lost land north of Colwyn was protected by Muriau or walls, signs of which may still be seen on a very low ebb of the tide in the shape of a long line of surf as the waves break upon them,"* writes Mr William Ashton. *"The walls are said to run out about a mile from the shore for about four miles in a west-to-east direction."* Ashton adds that tradition claims there were thirty gates in the dyke between Gogarth and the Point of Ayr. Tradition does not explain why men undertook such colossal labour when there were few inhabitants to dispute possession of a fertile hinterland.

The Rev. Robert Williams in his *History of Aberconwy* (1835) writes:

"In 1818, when lowering the churchyard on the south side of the church (Llandrillo), an immense quantity of bones were discovered heaped together confusedly; they were most probably conveyed from the church-yard of the original church, which was situated considerably lower down at the time it was destroyed by the sea. At a very low ebb, and when a strong south-west wind prevails, the waves may be distinctly seen breaking upon a sarn or causeway, which runs into the sea from Great Orme's head, about four miles below Llandrillo church; and it is still called the muriau or the walls."

The mystery of this alleged dyke has not been satisfactorily solved. The Rev.T. E. Timothy in his *Souvenir of Llandrillo* writes:

"When the sewage pipes in connection with the Drainage Scheme carried out by the Colwyn Bay Urban District Council in 1907 were being laid, the Contractor, at a spot near the lowest water mark, had to cut through a wall about six feet in width - evidently an old stone dyke erected to withstand the sea."

Ashton also makes reference to this:

"It is worthy of note that when, in 1907, a new sewer outfall was being laid by the Colwyn Bay U.D.C. midway between the Little Orme and Rhos Pier, a massive stone wall about 12 feet in diameter, with holes in which iron stauncheons had apparently been fixed, was encountered below L.W. about 680 yards seaward of the seawall. The spot is opposite the old farm which stands just above H.W. mark and which is known as 'Rhyd-y-cerrig-gwynion; 'the ford of the white stones."

Ford implies a river hard by. This walling may have been part of an old coast road, or more probably of a harbour in the estuary of the old Conwy river prior to the 6th century. The ancient course probably silted up very gradually. An old man living near Pabo told the writer (in 1914) that his grandmother, born in 1815, could remember flat boats, laden with coal, coming to Mochdre from Glan Conwy. Tradition assigns as the site of the name of Dinerth (a fort), the ancient name of the Colwyn parish (sic), a knoll, a mile or so inland, between Rhos and Conwy, where vessels sailed up the old river to unload cargo[20].

Even if the dyke with its thirty gates - the purpose whereof is not stated - is relegated to legend, there is ample proof that the ocean had made severe inroads on our coast, a practice from which it has by no means desisted, as Colwyn Bay knows to its cost!

RIVER BED MARSH

Before leaving the physical features of this area some attention must be paid to the Mochdre Valley. Was this the original mouth of the Conwy River? The question is repeatedly asked; it is doubtful whether a fully satisfactory answer will be forthcoming. Those early cartographers, Saxton in 1577, and Speed in 1610, both show the Afon Ganol as a small but distinct river entering the sea between Llandrillo and the Little Orme (Rhiwledyn). Leland, who wrote of this area in Henry VIII's reign, affords a slight clue.

"This Commote (Credine) partely by Conwey ryver, partely by the Se, yn a maner insulatid,

and one way owte of Denbigh land; the way is over a made causey, over a marsch often overflowen."[21]

This "made causeway" must be that near Glan Conwy Corner, known as Sarn-y-Mynach (Monk's Causeway) on account of its connection with the Abbey of Aberconwy, founded by Llewelyn the Great. Mention of this "causey" seems proof that no river flowed through the Mochdre valley in Leland's time or else he would have referred to ferry, ford or bridge. Evans, writing in 1800, says there were persons living in the neighbourhood *"who say they can remember when the present marsh, which forms the communication, was usually washed over at high tides."* It is said the Romans were the only people in early times to make causeways and that the name "sarn," like "caer" or "castra," is an indication of their presence. In other words, if the Conwy river flowed down this eastern branch it did so before Roman times. This contention might be supported - if importance can be attached to legend - by the story of Maelgwn Gwynedd, in his capital at Deganwy, causing his bards and minstrels to swim the Conwy river to Conwy Mountain for the first Eisteddfod. When the foundations were excavated for Colwyn Bay Crematorium, in the late 1950s, sea sand and gravel was found.

AN OLD LAWSUIT

Further reference to this marsh is contained in a lawsuit of 1687. Its preamble describes *"one part of the marsh called Morfa Dinerth containing 34 acres of land, lying in Dinerth Township, between a certain stream dividing the Counties of Denbigh and Caernarvon."* It is presumed this marsh was then in the nature of a common and the sea overflowed it at most spring tides. The account proceeds:

"There is a channell on the West side of the marsh that divides the Counties of Denbigh and Caernarvonshire; at the lower end of which channell of water adjoining to the sea was, as is reputed, a creake wherein Boats and Shipps of 20 or 30 tun might at a certain time of flowing water gett in there and soe lye safe from storms, and soe it hath ever continued from beyond living memory till 1687."

This lawsuit was brought by Robert Davies, of Bryn Euryn, grandson of the Robert Davies who married the daughter of Sir Peter Mutton, who bought Bryn Euryn from Rheinallt Conway in 1629 – Miss Mutton taking Bryn Euryn with her as her dowry. The suit of 1687 was against William Pugh, of Penrhyn (Old Hall) because Pugh had built *"a bridge upon the creake and stopped the sea from overflowing and also all boates and small vessells from getting in there for shelter in stormy weather."* It was in this creek that an Elizabethan ancestor of Mr. Pugh *"kept a small pinnace,"* mentioned in the trial of Williams and Yorke for conspiracy against the Crown. If there was a *"channel on the West side of the marsh,"* and if another branch entered the sea near the foot of what is now Rhos Road, it seems obvious how the main stream came by its name. Afon Ganol means Middle River. The county boundary followed the original course of this until it joined the ocean. Where Odstone has been built, ancient masonry (which now forms a rockery) may have been the culvert over which a farm road passed across the Afon Ganol's mouth. The masonry is also said to be part of an old quay, an extension of which was found reaching towards the sea when foundations were dug for the present sea wall completed in 1956. The map of 1720 shows the Afon Ganol broadening into a lake near its mouth. The outlet to the sea is so straight as to appear artificial.

The nature of the marsh has materially altered. The manner in which Dinerth Road and Llangwstenin Road follow the configuration of the land suggests their course was influenced by the marsh across which there was no straight road until the "Vicar's Road" - as it was termed - was made in the 19th century by the Vicar of Llandrillo. It is now Llandudno Road – the shop at the intersection with Llanrhos Road is still known as "Toll Bar." Prior to that, anyone journeying from Rhos-on-Sea to Penrhyn Bay would have to wait for low tide and go by way of the shore to Morfa Road.

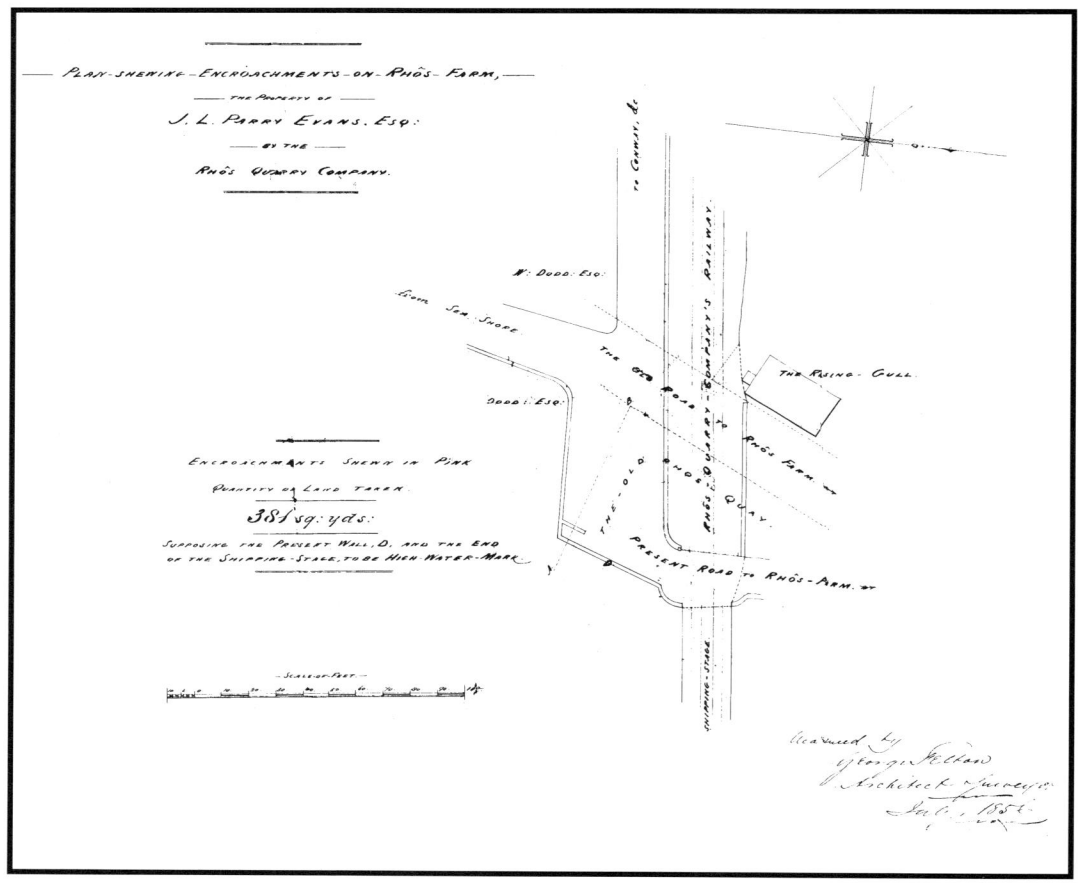

This plan, formerly belonging to the late Miss Parry-Evans shows the foot of Rhos Road in 1855. "The Rising Gull" cottage is demolished, and the Quarry Company's railway and shipping stage has also dissapeared. "Rhos Farm" is Rhos Fynach. Particular interest attaches to the site of "The Old Rhos Quay"

CAUSES OF CHANGE

There were three main causes for the change in the character of the marsh. The first was the building of an old sea wall near Penrhyn Bay, said to have been undertaken by General Owen Williams, of Craig-y-don, Anglesey; next the constructing of the railway, particularly the branch line to Llanrwst opened in 1863; and last, the creation of the Rhos Golf Links. The meanderings of the original water courses are still discernible in the links. The present straight cut is obviously artificial. Williams, who published his Aberconwy in 1835, refers to the "late drainage" of the marsh. Llewelyn the Great in his charter to the monks of Aberconwy Abbey speaks of "the water which flows down through the ditch itself as far as Aberdowyth."

That this was the Afon Ganol scarcely admits of doubt. Until the closing decades of the 19th century a stream flowed down what is now the lower portion of Penrhyn Avenue, thus making the Abbey Road locality an island. This isolation may have induced the monks of the Abbey to build the original Rhos Fynach, and (perhaps) caused St.Trillo to erect his cell at the spring which perpetuates his name. The farm at the western end of Abbey Road (now demolished) was known as Rhyd Farm, or more correctly, Rhyd-y-cerrig-gwynion - the Ford of the White Stones. Evidently this name was used in Leland's time - though the farm was not built until the eighteenth century. Leland describes the bay as a good "road" for great ships. *"There is northward in Credine a bay or rode very goode for shippis, and that greate, caullid Carrig Gonnyon Anglice White Stonys."*

Archdeacon Thomas observes: "Rhyd y Cerrig Gwynion, the Ford of the White Stones, still preserves the name of the causeway by which it was approached; as in another part does Pensarn, in Abergele."[22] The Bodysgallen Roll for 28 May 1608 refers to the drowning of Hughe Benett at Rhyd y Kerrig Winion. The name occurs again in the Welsh Port Books 1550-1603,[23] when the list of landing places in Caernarvonshire in the reign of Henry VIII includes Aber Kerrik Gwynyon. This seems to place it at the mouth of the Afon Ganol.

In *Old Price's Remains* there is a tantalizing reference. Writing about Robert Foulkes, who dwelt in the Rising Sun Inn (beside the Old Highway) the Rev. J. Price observes: *"It was he who remembered men who should say that they had seen vessels in the aforesaid River Afon Ganol, under Llandrillo Church."* One is left wondering what "under" the church signifies! The Afon Ganol is a stream which mastered the difficult task of flowing simultaneously in two directions. While the better-known portion empties at Penrhyn Bay, another branch turns westward and joins the Conwy River near Glan Conwy Corner. The building of the Chester and Holyhead railway, in 1848, confined this portion to artificial ditches, but sufficient water remains to hint at its former freedom. The reader is perplexed rather than satisfied by a brief reference of Thomas Roscoe who published his *Wanderings in North Wales* in 1836.

On returning to Conwy by the Little Orme's Head, I entered Denbighshire, and traversed a small but lovely vale, richly wooded, and embosomed in swelling hills. A small stream, which unites, at some distance below, with the Conwy, meanders fantastically through the hollow, tempting the angler from his road; and its course, sometimes visible sometimes concealed by golden copses, conducts the eye up to the vale until it is lost among the hills.

What small stream is this that unites with the Conwy? Might it not be this branch of the Afon Ganol, which is supposed to have allowed small boats to voyage as far as Mochdre? At least there is something tangible on which to build. And where was the The Ship inn mentioned in the Llangystennin Vestry books (which would hardly refer to the one at the Llandrillo vicarage door)? Some people hold that Mochdre means Moch-trai - Quick-tide. The writer has talked to a man whose father carried bags of coal to his cottage near Pensarn bridge. He rowed them to his garden before the Llanrwst railway line was constructed. Old residents claim boats once reached Mochdre. Perhaps there is reason for their belief.

APPENDIX - THE WESTERN BOUNDARY

Originally the county western boundary forked on reaching the low land north of Llandrillo Church. One portion went eastward to unite with the shore at the foot of Rhos Road; the other turned some hundred yards to the west of Rhyd Farm to follow the line adopted today. Thus a detached tract of land known as Morfa Llandrillo, measuring 119 acres, was cut off from Denbighshire. It was regarded as part of Eirias (then in Caernarvonshire). In 1879 there was a readjustment of boundaries, particularly where the detached portions of the Creuddyn hundred was concerned. At this time this "island" was included in Denbighshire, and, also at that date, in the civil parish of Llandrillo-yn-Rhos. In different parts of the present borough other areas were transferred to the civil parishes of Eirias and Llysfaen. It is difficult to describe the transfers in words; those interested in detail should consult the Ordnance Survey map of c1880.

Prehistoric and Roman Times

Links with neolithic man have been encountered from time to time. Colwyn Bay had barely come by its name when a visitor in 1868 picked up a curious pebble on the shingle bordering the strip of sward at the edge of the beach. This was later identified as a stone celt which, according to Chancellor Ellis Davies, "was almost certainly made at the Graig Lwyd neolithic factory, Penmaenmawr." It was presented to St. Asaph Cathedral library.[24] A bronze celt was also found in a field near Colwyn Bay.[25]

TUMULI

Situated two fields to the north-east of Glan-y-Gors Farm, in Llanelian Parish, is a fine tumulus, measuring 120 paces in circumference by 6 feet in height. About a hundred yards to the NNE a smaller tumulus of about 50 paces in circumference and 2ft 6ins high. Two more tumuli were found about a mile away in a field of an adjoining farm. They lie about 630 yards to the southwest of Gloddaeth Farm on the left-hand side of the road which leads from Llanelian village to Tal-y-Cafn. One measures about 70 paces and is 2ft 6ins high but was partly destroyed by roadmen. The central part contained a cist over which a cairn had been raised. Inside the cist was an urn containing cremated bones. This was brittle and fell to pieces when touched.[26] A tumulus stands on the highest point of the moor (1,093 ft.) known as Mynydd Llanelian (Llanelian Mountain), to the south west of Tyn-y-Ffridd. The mound is called "Twr Jiwbili," of which Venables-Williams writes:

"At the extreme South corner of the Parish are to be seen the remains of a Tower, erected like the larger one on Moel Fammau, on the Vale of Clwyd Mountains, in 1810, to commemorate the Jubilee of George III. It is said to have been from twenty-five to thirty feet high, but judging by the circumference of the base, it could not have been above ten or fifteen feet high. It was built partly of peat, partly of sods, upon a base of unprepared stones." [27]

MONOLITH

On the crest of the hill known as Blackberry Mountain, in Nantyglyn Valley, in one of the fields belonging to historic Glyn Farm, reposes the remnant of a huge monolith. Though once obviously upright, it now lies upon its side. From its position it may have been a "Maen Nawdd" or Stone of Refuge. It is said to have divided the jurisdiction of Gloddaeth from that of Bryn Ffanigl. *"Towards the end of the Feudal period,"* writes the Rev. W. Venables-Williams, *"an offender against the Law could fly to one of these and claim the protection of the lord in whose district it was situated."* Higher up Nantyglyn Valley at a farm called Bryn-y-Maen was a ruin and a well called Ffrith St. Crysto.[28] This is now incorporated in the reservoir.

MYNYDD MERCI

Mynydd Merci, near the borders of Llansanffraid, is considered by Venables Williams, to be possibly *"so called from Mercuri (Mercury) whom the Romans worshipped - a Cultus (worship) introduced by them into Wales."* The Rev. Meredith J. Hughes wrote:

"I have previously traced here the lines of an extensive British hill-camp, and my conjecture is that some of these lines were made use of in delineating the geometrical design of Ilium. It is to be regretted that the lines cannot be accurately traced owing to various causes, chiefly the fact that much of the land is under cultivation."[29]

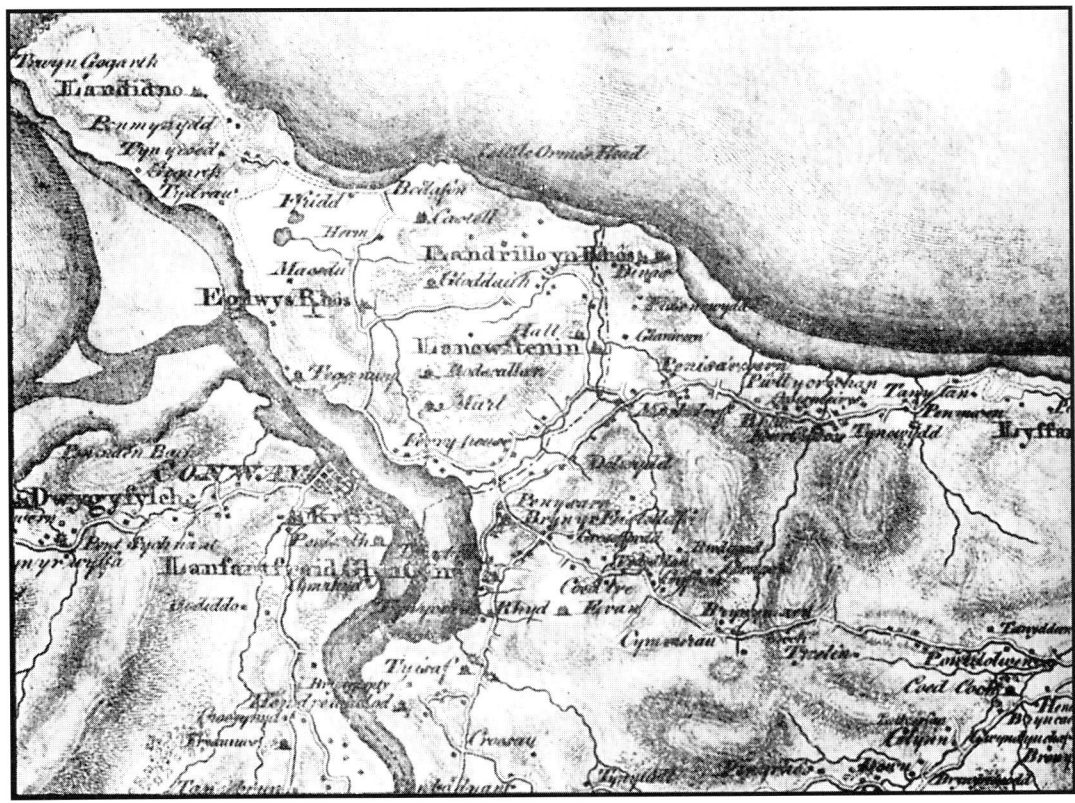

By permission Of the National Museum of Wales.

This portion of John Evans's wall-map of 1795 shows the road from Tanylan and Penmaen crossing Colwyn Stream and continuing past Tynewydd to "Groesyneirys". Mills are indicated on the Colwyn and Eirias streams. Pwyllycrochan and Rhiw are marked, but Four Crosses seems to be wrongly sited. After passing "Mochdref" the road passes Dolwydd to Penysarn (Glanconwy Corner) and thence to the Ferry House) now Llandudno Junction). The route followed appears to be that of the Old Highway.

ROMAN COINS IN STONE DRAIN

Excavations near Rhos Fynach brought to light several objects of archaeological value. A stone axe-head was found by a labourer in 1892. It was about 6.25 inches in length, and is now in the National Museum of Wales. In the same year a labourer found a stone chisel not far from the Rhos Abbey Hotel.[30] An illustration of a vase containing Roman coins found near Rhos-on-Sea in 1891 is published in the Llandudno, Colwyn Bay and District Field Club Proceedings, Vol. X page 70. Of particular interest was the discovery of Roman coins in the garden of Rhos Fynach when the site was being cleared in 1898, for the erection of an extension to the Rhos Abbey Hotel. The coins - six in number - were wrapped in a sheet of lead and were in an old stone drain. All were brasses of the reign of Constantine the Great (306-337 AD.). They were appropriated by the late William Horton, on whose property they were found.[31]

BRYN EURYN FORT

Of the 26 camps or hill-forts in Denbighshire, Colwyn Bay can claim one - that on Bryn Euryn. There are several in the Abergele district, such as Castell Cawr. Parc-y-meirch (at St. George) possessed formidable fortifications, but Pen-y-Corddyn Mawr at Llanddulas, and Bryn Euryn had weak defences[32]. Bryn Euryn, possibly so called from the sloes which still grow thickly in some parts, stands 427 feet high. It has precipitous rock faces towards the south and east, and a gentle slope to the west. On the north a small quarry cuts into the side, halfway up. It has lain disused for many years. The fortifications at the summit might be divided into two portions - a broad outer camp covering the entire top (which consists of two slight peaks with a hollow between), and (secondly) a small irregular circle, the highest point of which probably formed the last line of defence and is known as the citadel. It is only a matter of 36 paces across. The outer camp occupies about an acre of hilltop. From the citadel a line of rubble, which marks its rampart, can be clearly traced until it unites with the crags where no artificial protection was deemed necessary.

A track from the foot of the hill leads to the entrance, which is on the east side. Crossing this path there can be detected, in the turf, the remains of a strong wall linking with the citadel. In the hollow between the crests are two long mounds covered with thick grass. One seems to be broken across so as to make two sections, eight by four yards, and six by four yards. The second mound, which lies more to the east, is sixteen yards by five. Outside the rampart, about thirty paces to the west, is another mound with a shallow trench or moat around it. The mounds are described in *Archaeologia Cambrensis* of 1855, and remain virtually unchanged. *"To what date they should be assigned is a difficult question to answer,"* writes Chancellor Ellis Davies. *"That they are long barrows belonging to the Neolithic Age is not to be entertained."* No mention of the Bryn Euryn camp is made by Leland, Camden, Lhwyd or Pennant. Lewis in his *Topographical Dictionary of Wales* refers to *"a strongly fortified hill, called Bryn Euryn."*

The original name for the parish - Dinerth - may have been chosen because of this fort, some holding that it means "Din" (fort) "Arth" (a bear) from some semblance which the hill bore to a bear - a little difficult to recognize! The Rev. W. Hugh Rees, Vicar of Colwyn Bay comments (1950): "As the fort is described as a weak one, might 'Dinerth' not be the Welsh 'di-nerth' 'without strength?"

ANCIENT MONUMENT REPORT

The Royal Commission of the Ancient and Historic Monuments and Constructions of Wales and Monmouthshire, who inspected the place in July, 1912, made the following report:

"A camp of simple construction and weak defences, enclosing within its low stone wall an area of about 1.25 acres. The banks which are composed of limestone and earth are nowhere more than three feet in height though they have doubtless been much disintegrated and scattered by centuries of exposure; the ditch, too, is of quite a slight character, and has evidently not been deepened beyond what was required for the neighbouring bank. The area consists of the summits

of two hills and the slightly lower intervening ground but the southern side of the camp being craggy and steep is left without bank or ditch. At the north-east corner is an oval bank which cuts off a small area, but the dividing bank is too weak to have kept out an active and determined enemy. The original entrance was on the west, where the bank has been broken down. The camp has many points of similarity with that of Pen-y-Corddin, which is about ten miles to the southeast, though it is not so strong a position."

It will be noted that authorities differ on the position of the entrance. Particular attention should be paid to the unusual (and perplexing) structure which crowns Bryn Euryn in the plan prepared for Robert Davies in 1763. Here is depicted what appears to be a square, walled fort with a round tower at each corner. A possible explanation is that it represents an artist's imaginative intimation that the summit was once fortified.

THE COMING OF THE ROMANS

The first historical date which can be applied to this district is 61 A.D, when the victorious Roman general, Suetonius Paulinus, marched with some twelve thousand legionaries to conquer Mona, and put an end to druidism. It was a punitive expedition into unknown territory and any road used must have been a native trackway, perhaps widened by pioneers. The ravine between Bryn Euryn and the wooded slopes to the south, termed Nant Sempyr, is believed to have been named after Sempronius, the second-in-command who was killed at this time. It is alleged he met his death here; a likely place for an ambush, right in line with a march on Anglesey. The passage of the Conwy River would not have presented difficulties as Tacitus tells us Suetonius had with him flat-bottomed boats with which to cross the dangerous shallows of the Menai Strait. If a massacre occurred at Nant Sempyr it may have influenced the Romans to make their permanent road over higher ground - the route the Old Highway follows. Boadicea's revolt occured at this time and the Romans had to beat a hasty retreat. *"If,"* says Tacitus, *"Suetonius on the first intelligence had not hastened back by rapid marches, Britain had been lost."* Another passage in Tacitus is in accord with the legend of Nant Sempyr:

"A more active campaign has never been known, nor was Britain at any time so fiercely disputed. Our veteran forces were put to the sword, our colonies smoked on the ground; and the legions were intercepted on their march."

In 78 A.D. the Roman governor Agricola (who was probably with Suetonius during his attack on Anglesey) established a fort on the banks of the Conwy at Kanovium (still visible at modern Caerhun). It is surmised that the Roman road ran from St. Asaph to Tal-y-Cafn, en route for this fort, but there is no reason why there should not have been subsidiary roads. In addition to fields yielding corn in great plenty, Britain (according to Tacitus) contained mines of gold, silver and other metals, with which to reward the conqueror.

The Romans were attracted to this district by the surface metals, and probably mined copper on the Orme's Head and lead in the Conwy Valley. The Talar Goch lead mine (inland from Prestatyn) is believed to date from Roman times. Though the mere finding of coins is no conclusive proof of the presence of the people whose imprint they bear, the discovery of such hoards serves to confirm a belief already partly established. It is of interest, therefore, to enumerate the various discoveries of Roman coins, implements, or weapons in this vicinity. It will be noticed that they occur in an almost uninterrupted sequence. It is known there were Romans at Prestatyn, and traces of them have been found at Abergele. In 1842 silver coins were found in a ditch close to the road leading from Rhuddlan to Abergele. The Rev. W. Davies[33] terms Castell Cawr (behind Gwrych Castle, Abergele): *"one of the most complete Roman fortified camps in the kingdom,"* and refers to *"Some of the largest and most perfect Roman mines in Britain"* nearby. Here workmen discovered hammers and tools, also the golden hilt of a Roman sword. So far no trace of a Roman villa has been encountered in this area. The occupation was apparently military and commercial only.

ROMAN COINS DISCOVERED

This is a list of some finds made nearer home:

a. In a field of Pentregwyddel Farm - now destroyed by quarrying - half a mile north-east of Llysfaen Church. Roman coins (brasses) - Maximianus (A.D. 286-305) found in 1856.[34]
b. Pot of brass Roman coins with amber and glass beads in a field known as Pwll Morcyn, Llysfaen in 1693. "In an Urn in ye Highway together with some Amber beads, &c.," states Lhwyd. (The "Pwlh Morkyn" mentioned by Lhwyd is not now known).[35]
c. Roman coins in earthenware vessel a few score yards S. of the ruins of Llys Euryn. In 1902 by workmen.[36]
d. At Llandrillo-yn-Rhos, while quarrying near Llys Euryn in 1906, urn full of bronze coins (3rd brasses of Constantine the Great).[37]
e. Vessel, brick-red with grey slip, found in hedge base, Rhos-on-Sea, 1891, half-full of Roman coins.[38]
f. Coins of Constantine the Great wrapped in sheet of lead in old stone drain when site of Rhos Abbey Hotel was prepared, 1898.[39]
g. Silver coin of Hadrian (AD. 117-138) at Nant Sempyr. "Lately dug up in a field here," writes Rev. Robt. Williams in 1835.[40]
h. Red earthenware jar containing about 5,000 bronze coins at Penrhyn Bay, 1873.[41]
i. In 1907 opposite Shimdda Hir, Little Orme, 550 Roman coins. Nearly 97 per cent were British-struck money of Emperor Carausius.[42]

The progressive line of coin finds, like the strongholds mentioned, shows a continuity more than coincidental. In his MS "Rector's Book," the Rev. Owen Jones Humphreys, MA, Rector of Llanddulas, describes the discovery of the Pentregwyddel coins:

"A farmer seeking lost sheep picked up what appeared to him an old button, which upon examination proved to be a penny of the Roman Empire. Upon making further search, a large number of much smaller coins about the size of our fourpenny and threepenny silver pieces were picked up, some bearing traces of inscription, but many so corroded as to present no trace of any impression."[43]

This very summer (i.e.1950) a gardener, Evan Jones, 6, Woodbine Terrace, Penrhynside, digging in a garden at Rhos-on-Sea, turned up a small coin. It was found to be a silver denarius bearing the head of the Empress Sabina.

ROMAN ROADS

In his brochure on the Roman Roads in Denbighshire, O'Dwyer does not hesitate to assert that one ran from the ford at Rhuddlan to Abergele, thence to Nant Sempyr and the Creuddyn Peninsula. Much still remains to be done to acquire a comprehensive record of the Roman occupation of this area. Authorities consider the Imperial troops were withdrawn from North Wales to man Hadrian's Wall, but in all probability Roman influence lingered until the close of the fourth century.[44] Many of the coins found at the Little Orme were of the reign of Constantinus Maximus (AD. 306-337), which appears to carry Roman occupation of this area well into the fourth century. With the departure of the legions came the Dark Ages, during which the deserted Britons probably establishing themselves on hilltops and strong places, and strove to protect themselves against the raids of Saxons and pirates. This area would be then linked with Deganwy where, on the twin humps designed by nature for a fortified place, there arose a stronghold to which men could resort. *"There is no doubt,"* writes Edward Breeze, *"that prior to the conquest of Edward I, Creuddyn was an unannexed territory, with the Castle of Deganwy as its principal fortress."*

WELSH AND SAXONS

In the middle of the sixth century a definite figure emerges, Maelgwn Gwynedd, paramount ruler in Cambria, who, Warrington says *"usually resided at Diganwy."* Pennant asserts that Maelgwn Gwynedd had a palace on Bryn Euryn where the ruined house was *"formerly called Llys Maelgwn Gwynedd."*[45] Thanks to the monk Gildas and the bard Taliesin, something is known about Maelgwn, styled *"Draco Insularis."*

SAINT TRILLO

Of more particular interest to Colwyn Bay, however, was the advent of the local "saint" which occurred during Maelgwn's reign. Saint Trillo, who gave his name to the once extensive parish of Llandrillo, was one of the signatories of the grant that Maelgwn Gwynedd made to St. Kentigern, at the time the See of Bangor was endowed. The other signatories were Saint Deiniol (the first Bishop of Bangor), Saint Grwst (after whom Llanrwst is named), and Rhun, son of the King, who gave his name to Caer Rhun (Caerhun). Saint Trillo or Terillo was the son of Ithel Hael of Llydaw, and a brother of Saint Tegai and Saint Llechid. He is mentioned in an early pedigree as being of "Dineirth in Rhos."[46] Ithel and his children are supposed to have come to Britain from Armorica (the old name for Brittany) and Trillo is believed to have been educated on Bardsey Island to be a saint.

ST. TRILLO'S CELL

On the foreshore at Rhos-on-Sea is a diminutive chapel or cell of a type rare, if not unique, in this part of the world. It is built over a holy well, which, for centuries, supplied water for baptisms in all quarters of the extensive parish of Llandrillo. Considerable controversy has taken place over the age of this unusual structure but its origin remains obscured by the mists of time. It attracted many antiquarians and tourists in bygone days. They have examined it, criticised it, recorded their impressions - and left us little the wiser. Pennant, who saw it in the 1770s, describes it but ventures no hint at its age. His words are still applicable:

Capel Trillo, Llandrillo, Caernarvonshire. Reproduced from Arch. Camb. 1855.

"*Saw, close to the shore, the singular little building called St. Trillo's Chapel. It is oblong; has a window on each side, and at the end; a small door, and a vaulted roof paved with round stones instead of being slated. Within is a well. The whole building is surrounded with a stone wall.*"

The reference to the door is of interest. The late Miss Parry-Evans, of Rhos Fynach, told the writer that when she was a girl the building possessed an antique door of fine workmanship, but it was stolen. In the 1830s the Rev. Robert Williams remarked that the building was generally supposed to have been a chapel where prayers were offered for success in fishing. He was, however, inclined to agree *"it was built merely to preserve the well, which is the only one in the neighbourhood."*[47]

The building was becoming a ruin when it was described by the Rev. H. Longueville Jones, editor of *Archaeologia Cambrensis,* in 1855. The illustration which accompanies the article shows a hole in a peaked roof which is tufted with weeds. The disintegration continued and when the estate was purchased in the 1890s the structure was in a shocking state of dilapidation. The late William Horton altruistically undertook extensive renovations, to preserve this most interesting relic, but the repairs undoubtedly intensify the difficulties which confront the antiquarian.

The Rev. J. Longueville Jones wrote that the building was not more than eight feet high *"to the crown of the vault internally."* It was vaulted over in rough stones, *"nothing but boulders from the shore, wedged and mortared in so as to form the segment of a circle inside, though on the outside they rise into a low ridge, now much damaged and overgrown with weeds."* It will be noticed that this wedge roof has now disappeared. He mentions that *"the eastern loop has been repaired in the head with wood and brick internally."* His verdict is: *"the building, as it now stands, is not much earlier than the of the sixteenth century, though it may have replaced* one of older date standing on the same foundation." Halliwell, in 1860 noticed among the debris a portion of the upper part of a regularly carved stone column, possibly a fragment belonging to the ancient entrance to the chapel.

The next article in *Archaeologia Cambrensis* is in 1884, and by this time a third of the barrel roof had collapsed, and *"the external roof is covered with vegetation."* The sad story is continued in a Guide Book of about 1892, when an illustration speaks eloquently of the sorry state of the erstwhile holy well. *"It is very tiny, very dilapidated,"* says the writer, who thinks it might be mistaken for the ruins of a fisherman's hut. He understands the syndicate who have purchased the land intend to take prompt measures *"for the preservation of the ruin and for its restoration to decency before the autumn of 1892."*[48] That year the *"curious little oratory"* was visited by the Rev. Elias Owen, of Ruthin, who uplifted his voice (or pen) in protest:

"I was sorry to find that the vaulted roof had fallen in, that the well inside the chapel was covered with debris from the roof, and that the whole structure and its surroundings presented a ruinated and uncared for aspect. It is singular that the people of Colwyn Bay should be so indifferent to the preservation of this unique relic of former days."[49]

Archdeacon Thomas, in dealing with the history of the early church, wrote that occasionally a cell or oratory kept alive the remembrance of an early, if not the earliest, evangelist of the place, and quotes Trillo at Rhos. The cell was considered by Archdeacon Thomas to be especially interesting from being, so far as the diocese of St. Asaph was concerned, *"a unique illustration*

of those primitive Oratories which formed the type of the earliest British churches." The Archdeacon adds that it was not, indeed, identical with those primitive Oratories, but a later edition.

The Royal Commission who visited the place in 1912 were reserved in their judgement. They said it traditionally represented the well of the patron saint of the parish. According to earlier accounts, the vaulting was effected in the primitive manner of the earliest Christian oratories:

"*It is, however, doubtful if the chapel is not far more modern than it is assumed to be. The style of building does not differ from that of the covered way between the parish church of Clynnog and the adjoining chapel of Beuno, which is certainly of no great antiquity.*"[50]

The Commission would have to contend with the extensive alterations the cell had undergone in the 1890s, and Longueville Jones's observations made in 1855, when St. Trillo's was still in tolerable repair, presenting a closer and probably more accurate conception of the original structure. To place St. Trillo's Chapel with Dolwyddelen and Dolbadarn would bring it into line with Cistercian occupation of Rhos Fynach in the 12th or 13th centuries.

It is possible to detect a certain inconsistency in Longueville Jones's criticism. He uses the "*occurence of brick in one of the windows*" to determine its age, yet earlier he points out that the east window had been "*repaired in the head with wood and brick internally.*" It is manifestly unfair to regard repair work as relative to the origin of the structure.

Surely Capel Trillo's proximity to the weir is not without significance! The monks would be more likely to erect a sacred shrine than would people at the beginning of the sixteenth century. In view of the repute which the spring has had from time immemorial it would seem that the little chapel was either built to protect the holy well or else to mark the site of a wattle-and-daub structure which might have been used by the original saint.

Commendable in its restraint is the notice now displayed outside the tastefully renovated chapel which was reconsecrated by Dr. Havard, the Bishop of St. Asaph, in the presence of the Mayor and Corporation on St. Trillo's Day (16th June) 1935.

> ALL REVERENCE IS DUE TO THIS SACRED SPOT.
> THIS ANCIENT CHAPEL IS BUILT OVER THE
> HOLY WELL OF S. TRILLO, A CELTIC SAINT
> OF THE SIXTH CENTURY.
> PILGRIM TURN IN AND OFFER PRAYER.
> THE LORD BE WITH YOU.

Colwyn Bay Corporation secured the property, and the church authorities of Llandrillo-yn-Rhos were able to obtain control under a long lease. The chapel was tastefully restored under the supervision of the late Harold Hughes, of Bangor. It is used for occasional services, and there are periodic Celebrations of Holy Communion.

SAXON INVADERS

A few miles inland from Colwyn Bay lies a lonely land of heather and furze, where outcroppings of rain-scoured limestone break through the sparse grass. Here, on a bleak day when the clouds scud low against a grey sky one is conscious of a certain eeriness, as though the atmosphere of the dark ages still hovered about the wind-dwarfed hawthorns. Well might Lhwyd speak of beacons on the hilltops above Llanelian and Llysfaen. There would be many more ready to flare a warning when the glint of distant spears foretold the advance of the invader. Across these hilly moors marched the Saxons, pursuing their seemingly endless feud with the men of

Rhos or Gwynedd. There is no lack of proof that they came this way, though details after so many centuries are hard to come by. There may be more authentic history in some of the folk tales told in remote farmsteads than one realizes. Does Coed Coch, for instance, perpetuate some fierce contest? How else, if it were not with blood, could the wood be red? History books recall the great battle of Cymryd, on the banks of the Conwy, where the Welsh prince Anarawd revenged the death of his father Rhodri Mawr when he defeated the Saxons under Aethelstan of Mercia, King Alfred's son-in-law. That was in AD 881. A few years later there was the great clash between Offa and Caradoc, which has been perpetuated in the dirge, *Morfa Rhuddlan*. There is a link with a more romantic local colouring.

THE RING OF ALHSTAN

A strange tale of these Saxon days comes from Llysfaen; a story which fascinates by its mystery. Workmen engaged in cutting away part of a rock discovered two skeletons side by side, each mortared in the form of a human figure with the exception of the face, to all appearances like Egyptian mummies. A few days later they found a thick gold ring of peculiar octagonal design. The discovery date is not certain but it was probably about 1770, as a Dr. Pegge paid particular attention to the ring in 1771, and two years later read a paper on it to the Archaelogical

Society. The ring was of gold, enamelled, of good workmanship, and weighed over an ounce. It was composed alternately of discs and lozenges. The latter had emblems engraved on them, the discs bore the letters: A LH ST A.

Alhstan was the name of the fighting Bishop of Sherborne, and it is believed that when King Egbert invaded North Wales in 828 AD, Alhstan was the commander of his army. North Wales historian Miss Angharad Llwyd visited Llysfaen in 1823, to glean details from Mr Holland of Teyrdan, who was present at the discovery over forty years before. "Mr. Holland of Tyrdan," writes Miss Llwyd, "*saw them* (the two skeletons) *as found, lying upon a shelf of rock and until lately had in his possession a piece of mortar with the hair quite fresh.*" Miss Llwyd added that a few days after the discovery of the skeletons the workmen found a thick gold ring "*weighing five guineas and sold it for two to a Mr. Hughes, of Abergeleu, whose Daughter* married Mr. Humphrey's attorney at Chester and took the ring with her." The Alhstan ring ultimately found its way into the possession of the Editor of the *Chester Chronicle*, who wrote a description of it in the issue of 4 April, 1823, beginning: *"This precious relic of the ornamental taste and magnificence of the ninth century is now in our possession; and so singular a curiosity, we think worthy of particular notice."* After expatiating on the antiquity of rings, the writer continued:

"It was found between 50 and 60 years ago by a labourer, near to the surface of the ground, on a common at Llysfaen, in Caernarvonshire. It is of massy gold, weighing nearly an ounce and a quarter. The workmanship remarkably neat, and the enamelling distinct and perfect. The pattern is alternately a circle and a lozenge, and the other part wrought in a highly ornamental style. The circular compartments, four in number, bear the epigraph, on the first (all in Saxon characters) A, on the second LH, on the third ST, and on the fourth A, and the runic N (like an X) forming the word Althstan. The lozenges are occupied with different devices; on the first is a rude representation of a dragon, the cognizance of the kingdom of Wessex, under which Althstan, Bishop of Sherborne, often led the armies to battle."

Though there were three Bishops of London named Althstan, the ring is believed to have belonged to the seventh Bishop of Sherborne. Bishop Althstan of Sherborne occupied the episcopal chair from 817 to 867 and was "well known as an efficient member of the Church Militant." The account adds that soon after the discovery: *"another gold ring, of much greater weight, was picked up near the same place a situation close to the sea, but its manufacture was extremely coarse when compared with this."*

In order to account for the superiority of workmanship evident in the ring now under notice, at a time when the Saxons were so barbarous in their manners, the learned Doctor Pegge says Egbert the Great resided, in his younger days, not less than 12 years at the Court of Charlemagne, and it is not improbable that some artists in the enamelling way might have been brought by him into England. In Gough's edition of *Camden's Britannia* it states Dr. Pegge considered the ring *"belonged to a commander of that name in Egbert's army which invaded North Wales AD 818."*

THE HILL OF EDWIN

Another echo of strife between Saxon invaders and the dwellers in these parts comes down the ages. It concerns Edwin, the first Christian king of Northumbria. Early in the seventh century he embarked on a warlike expedition, invading North Wales, a land that had at one time accorded him hospitality. Somewhere on these uplands, between the rivers Conwy and Clwyd, he met a warband - the "teulu" - of one of the local chieftains, and was driven back after a struggle that raged over a considerable area. The chroniclers knew the scene of strife as "hill of Edwin." There is, apparently, no such hill now, but *"the Hill of Edwin,"* observes Sir John E. Lloyd, *"may be that known at present under the slightly altered form of Bryn yr Odin not far from Llanelian."* Local people, less romantic, say Bryn Rodin takes its name from a limekiln, for "odyn" signifies kiln. It might be worth noting that a neighbouring farm is called Moel y Rodwen, which certainly savours more of Edwin. The common near Bryn-y-Maen, known as Rhos Goch, may be associated with this fray.

DIVISION OF LAND

In "the time of the Princes" (to use the old euphonious phrase) this land belonged to various powerful chieftains. There are references to Llys Euryn being in the hands of a family descended from Gruffydd Goch "lord of Rhos and Rhufoniog." This must signify that Gruffydd would have been the hereditary chieftain. Politically the area was then part of the honour of Denbigh.

Marchudd ap Cynan, from whom Ednyfed Fychan traced his descent, was "lord of Abergeleu," while Ednyfed Fychan himself was styled "Baron of Brynfeingl in Denbigh Land." There is mention in Llewelyn the Great's Charter of Ednyfed's purchasing Rhos Fynach:

"from the heirs of Dineyrth (Dinerth) and their heirs, from Llwyth. Marchudd and their (sic) heirs, and from the nephews of Dueog and their heirs."

W.Bezant Lowe comments: *"Dueog or Duog, whose heirs are mentioned as being parties to the transaction, was obviously Dwywg ap Gwilym, who was the grandson of Rhys ap Edryd, a collateral branch of the same family, from whom is descended the present Lord Mostyn."* The point to establish is that all this territory apparently belonged to various noble families.

As time passes there is observed a gradual change from the days when the heads of the Welsh tribes divided the land among their progeny. First one finds a conglomeration of the territories of Welsh chieftains, marcher lords and Crown property. The Edwardian conquest took the lands from the local chieftains. Henry VIII put an end to marcher lordships. From 1536 the land assumed conditions approximating those of today.[51]

APPENDIX

From *Archaeologia Cambrensis*, 1855

CAPEL TRILLO

It is a very small edifice, being only eleven feet long by seven feet wide internally; it is built over a spring of water, which trickles out from the bank near the south-west corner of the building, is then confined in a small shallow well or bathing-place, and finally trickles out again under the eastern end, and so escapes through the shingle to the sea. The building is not more than eight feet high to the crown of the vault internally and is vaulted over in rough stones, most of them, like those of the walls, being nothing but boulders from the shore, wedged and mortared in so as to form the segment of a circle inside, though on the outside they rise into a low ridge, now much damaged and overgrown with weeds. It is lighted by three small loops, without any ashlar stonework or ornament of any kind. The doorway is broken through, but it appears to have been arched over – whether in a pointed or circular form it is impossible to conjecture. The eastern loop has been repaired in the head with wood and brick internally; and by its side, as well as in the southern wall, are two small square holes, probably intended to contain articles of devotion, or of use, for the frequenters of the holy well.

In the neighbourhood a great antiquity is assigned to this building, on account of its vaulted stone roof, but this proves little or nothing. The work resembles that of the stone vaults so common in Pembroke, and it is very probable that the building, as it now stands, is not much earlier than the commencement of the sixteenth century, though it may have replaced one of the older date standing on the same foundation. Stone vaulting is not common in North Wales . . . The vaulting of Capel Trillo is on the wedge plan, and resembles the work of Dolwyddelen and Dolbadarn, but there is no evidence to assign so early a date as the thirteenth century to it, though there is nothing against that date being admitted. The absence of ashlar stones, and of any kind of moulding, would have been an argument in favour of an early date, but the occurrence of brick in one of the windows, and of a wooden lintel, calls in the idea of a more recent erection too forcibly to be resisted. Buildings like this existed over many holy wells in Wales; though now, unfortunately, only traces of them are commonly met with. This particular well of St. Trillo has been in great repute throughout all Rhos from time immemorial. It holds the best water in the parish, and the fishermen come to fill their kegs at it whenever they put to sea.

THE GREAT SENESCHAL

C.W. Howarth, R.C.A.

The most consequential personage to whom this Borough can lay claim is Ednyfed Fychan, Seneschal to Llewelyn the Great to whom, for many years, he ranked second in importance. His broad acres stretched from Abergele to the Conwy. Criccieth was his, he had estates in South Wales, and several in Anglesey, which island most of his descendants appeared to favour. He traced his descent to Marchudd ap Cynan, lord of Abergeleu, who dwelt at Brynffanigl about the year AD 850. Fenton suggests Ednyfed was born at Penrhyn Creuddyn. Legends have been woven around his name, and tales of his prowess as a warrior, but it was as ambassador and statesman he earned his greatest renown. The best known story is that which tells of his slaying three captains of Ranulph, Earl of Chester, when North Wales was invaded in 1210. Pennant tells us that Ednyfed *"being general of the prince's host"* met the invaders and:

"killed three of their chief captains and commanders, and a great many of the common soldiers. The rest he put to flight, and triumphantly returned to his prince, who in recompense of his good service, gave him, among many gifts and honours, a new coat of arms, for the coat, which he and his ancestors had always given before, was the coat of Marchudd, being gules, a Saracen's head erased proper, wreathed or. The new coat was thus displayed, gules between three Englishmen's heads, a chevron ermin."

Marchudd's possessing a coat of arms charged with a Saracen's head seems pure fancy. Heraldry did not then exist and the worthy Marchudd would not have recognised a Saracen if he had seen one. Saracen might, of course, be a corruption of Saxon. But if Ednyfed, as is believed, went to the Holy Land, the device might well be his. However, the three Englishmen's heads (the famous "Pen Sais") appear on the escutcheons of many leading families. It is interesting to note that later shields, such as, for example, the escutcheon displayed at Mostyn Hall, bear the three heads in closed helmets. This was probably a diplomatic move on the part of one of Ednyfed's descendants - possibly Sir Tudor ap Grono, on whom Edward III conferred the honour of knighthood.

On account of the stories that have gathered about his name Ednyfed is in danger of becoming a legendary figure. The imagination is fired by his dramatic return from the Holy Land to find his wife about to wed. The theme is by no means original. Those who would learn more of it (in prose and verse) should consult the Rev W. Venables-William's book. Ednyfed was a very real figure. Sir John E. Lloyd, reviewing Llewelyn ap Iorwerth's most able ministers, observes:

"Chief among them was Ednyfed Fychan, who succeeded Gwyn ab Ednywain about 1215 as 'distain' or seneschal, and henceforth takes first place amongst the counsellors and envoys of Llewelyn. Tradition would have us believe that he first won fame as a warrior, but his true glory is the place he filled and the service he rendered until his death in 1246 as the prudent advisor

and skilful agent of two successive lords of Aberffraw. He first appears in connection with the Peace of Worcester in 1218 and next as a witness to the compact between Llewelyn and the Earl of Chester on the occasion of the marriage of John the Scot in 1222. From 1229 onwards he is constantly engaged in the business of the prince, and it cannot be doubted that the part he played in shaping the policy of Gwynedd was substantial. Of his private history little is certainly known; but the death of his wife Gwenllian, a daughter of the Lord Rhys, is recorded in 1236, and he would seem in the previous year to have made pilgrimage to the Holy Land. He had estates at Rhos Fynach (near Colwyn Bay), at Llansadwrn and Llanhystyd in South Wales, and, no doubt, also in Anglesey, where his descendants were mighty folk for many generations. Not the least of his claims to the respectful notice of the historian is that from him sprang, by direct male descent, the puissant house of Tudor."[52]

Ednyfed married twice.[53] His first wife was Gwenllian, daughter of the Lord Rhys ap Gruffydd of South Wales. By this marriage he had four children - Gruffydd of Tregarnedd, who fled to Ireland; Goronwy, who inherited Penmynydd, Trecastle and Ddraenog; Gwenllian and Angharad. His second wife was Eva, daughter of Llowarch ap Bran (according to some books, Tanglwst). The children by this second marriage were Sir Tudor of Plas y Nant and Llangynhafel; Llewelyn who had a moiety of Creuddyn, and Cynfrig, who had the other moiety; Howel who became Bishop of St. Asaph in 1235; Rhys of Garth Garmon near Llanrwst; and Iorwerth, a leper, who received Abermarlais, and was the ancestor of Sir Rhys ap Thomas of Dinevor.

Creuddyn, the district which concerns us, was thus divided equally between Llewelyn and Cynfryg. Who inherited Bryn Euryn is not known.

In the *Record of Carnarvon* of Edward III's reign, it is stated "Penruyn" (i.e. Penrhyn in Creuddyn) belonged to the descendants of Ednyfed Fychan. The heirs were – Eden ap Gron, Blethin ap Madoc, Eign ap Howell and Ken Brand. It says *"they suit at County and hundred courts, and they go with the Lord Prince to war at their own expense."* They were called upon for no further service or payment.

A record states that of all Ednyfed's manors the one in Creuddyn was his "chiefest" – possibly on account of its proximity to the demesne of the Prince who must have divided much of his time between his palaces at Trefriw and Aber. No doubt Llewelyn found the new abbey he had endowed at Aberconwy a convenient halfway house. It was there he closed his eyes in death. The construction of Llys Euryn will be dealt with elsewhere in detail. The name Fychan, anglicised to Vaughan, has spread far and wide. The times were troubled. Ednyfed's son, Bishop Howel, had to flee to England, and died in Oxford in 1247, because *"the Welsh Bishops,"* Browne Willis tells us: *"siding with their king against their countrymen, had their Bishoprics and Churches so spoiled and destroyed, that they were forced to beg their bread and live upon the Alms of others."*

Lewys Dwnn in his *Heraldic Visitation* gives Ednyfed's children as: (first marriage) - Grufydd, Gronwy, Gwenllian, Anghared; and (second marriage) - Sir Tudor, Llewelyn, Rhys, Ierworth, Howel. Men of such fighting stock naturally made their presence felt. They did not submit tamely to arrogance. The warrior spirit flares up in the pages of history. There is, for instance, Ednyfed's great grandson, Gronw ap Heilin (who held lands at Llysfaen and Eirias) rushing into the Madoc Rebellion and losing his lands because he "died against the peace;" there is Gruffydd Llwyd rebelling in Edward II's day; or Rhys and Gwilym Tudor capturing Conwy Castle in the Glyndŵr revolt. It was in 1409, that Llys Euryn is said to have been burnt. It was not the only place to go up in flames! One can imagine the smoke-blackened ruins standing forlorn until the excellence of the site commended itself to a kindred clan. So we find the house restored (or rebuilt) by Robin ap Griffith Goch of Graianllyn. But this was not until the days of the Wars of the Roses. There the story must be taken up again in its chronological place.

RHOS FYNACH BOUGHT

A charter dated May 1230 indicates when Ednyfed purchased the land of Rhos Fynach. It is a puzzling document and seems to conflict with the popular conception of Rhos Fynach's monastic origin. The original, now in the Panton Collection, has been copied in full by W. Bezant Lowe, and is included in *The Heart of Northern Wales*. The following extracts are taken from this charter:

"Know that Idneved Vachan, our Seneschal purchased with our assent from the heirs of Dineyrth and their heirs, from Llwyth Marchudd and their (sic) *heirs, and from the Nephews of Dueog and their heirs, in the presence of us, the aforesaid parties to the present (document) the land of Ros Veneych with all belongings and liberties in wood, in plain, in grazings, pastures, meadows, paths and waters and in all easements on sea and on land, to be held by himself and his heirs... Moreover, the said Idneved and his heirs, shall pay yearly to God and the Church of Dineyrth, two shillings towards lamps at Easter-tide."*

There follow details of boundaries in which reference is made to a *ditch "with all the water which flows down through the ditch itself as far as Aberdowyth, with all the appurtenances and its liberties, buildings, mills and fisheries, the said Idnevet and his heirs shall possess without challenge, so that no one else save Idnevet and his heirs, can fish or otherwise traffic in the same water."*

The writer feels it may have been for the purpose of building his "llys" on Bryn Euryn that Ednyfed made this purchase of land in Dinerth. According to the Royal Commissioners who inspected Llys Euryn and Rhos Fynach in 1912, this is the first mention of Rhos Fynach. They conclude that the place was bought

"doubtless to be transferred to the monks of Aberconwy, which monastery Llewelyn had founded some years previously."

It might be noted that the document refers to "the land of Ros Veneych" – not the building, yet the mere name Rhos Fynach – "the Marsh of the Monks"- suggests that already monks had some association with the place. Of course these "monks" might have been earlier than the Cistercians. Marsh is the popular translation, though "open country," or "moor" would be more accurate. The Royal Commission describes the existing edifice as *"a much modernised 18th century house."* The date 1717 is on one wing. It may be that the present dwelling was erected on the site of an older building. Some of the demolished stone structures, which stretched in front of the present house right to the edge of the sea, might have been of more ancient construction. Of these there is no record save an occasional photograph and an indication on the Ordnance Survey map of 1875. Further reference will be made to Rhos Fynach.

THE RUINS OF LLYS EURYN

Of all the ancient dwellings within the Borough that which most tantalises the imagination is Llys Euryn, which rears a forlorn chimney from its brambly site on a spur of Bryn Euryn, ten paces from a quarry's edge. Its desolation seems the greater by reason of the splendour it once knew. Just when the ruin acquired the name "Llys Euryn" is difficult to determine - old references term it "Bryn Euryn" (spelt variously), a designation now applied to the hill alone. Pennant, in

1773, terms it not actually as a ruin but "a large ruined house," and Robert Davies's map of 1763 depicts it with three gables. Pennant names it "Bryn Euryn" and adds it was *"formerly Llys Maelgwyn Gwynedd, who had a palace on this spot."* An excavation attempted by the writer at the southern corner of the great fire-place revealed a flooring of boulders about 30 inches lower than the present ground level, and part of a wall of dressed boulders underneath the limestone wall of the existing building. One might speculate as to whether this is a fragment of the Maelgwn "palace" to which Pennant alludes.

Pennant also says: *"About the twelfth century it was inhabited by the great Ednyfed Fychan."* It is known that Ednyfed purchased the adjoining land of Rhos Fynach in 1230, as a copy of Llewelyn ap Iorwerth's charter to him indicates. The arches of Ednyfed's private chapel are still to be seen in the north wall of Llandrillo Church. The problem to determine is whether the shell of Llys Euryn is in truth the remains of Ednyfed's "Llys," as Pennant believed. Should it be Ednyfed's home it ought to be accorded greater reverence, for Ednyfed was the ancestor of the Tudor monarchs.

As a building it is (at least so far as this vicinity is concerned) without parallel. Despite the irregularity of the courses there is a certain symmetry about the structure. The eastern wall was long ago removed (probably to fence farm fields) but the foundations now uncovered show the building to be practically square. The interior measurements are 64 ft by 66 ft, with outer walls of a yard width. The chimney and great fireplace, which are the most conspicuous features of the ruin, may be set aside as being of the least interest - they are obvious additions of a date far later than the outer walls.

R. J. Howard, B. Arch

Attention might be drawn to several unusual features. The remains contain no window; all light, apparently, emanating from arrow-loops of three inches exterior width. There were two storeys (with possibly an attic). There are no less than four (second-storey) guarderobes. The only entrance so far discovered is a small pointed doorway 6ft high and 2ft 6ins wide. No well has yet been found. On the south side is a wall fireplace. This must indicate either that the shell is not that of Ednyfed Fychan's Llys, or else that, contrary to popular belief, wall fireplaces were in use in private dwellings in the 13th century. Though it is generally accepted that central fireplaces were used in halls until Edward III's time, it should be remembered that there are a number of wall fireplaces in Conwy Castle (1283).

The Abbey of Aberconwy (to which Llewelyn gave a charter in 1198) probably resembled Valle Crucis. That Aberconwy Abbey possessed a high standard of architecture is exemplified by the lovely western door of Conwy Church. There is no reason why local craftsmen, having learned from the Cistercian masons, should not introduce innovations when erecting a neighbouring palace for their puissant master.

Once Henry VII was on the throne of England (helped there, incidentally, by Huw Conway of Bryn Euryn), he commanded a Royal Commission (of whom the bard Guttyn Owain was one) to inquire into his paternal descent. From the Welsh chronicles in the abbeys of Aberconwy and Strata Florida, the Commission established the first Tudor King's ancestry. It is set forth in Powell's *Wales* (1584). After referring to the King's grandfather, Owain Tudor, who married the widow of Henry V, the record states:

"This Owain was the son of Meredith, ap Tudor, ap Grono, ap Tudor, ap Grono, ap Ednyfed Fychan, Baron of Brynfeingle in Denbigh Land, Lord of Kriceth, Chief Justice and Chief of Council to Llewelyn ap Iorwerth Drwyndwn, Prince of Wales."

The next reference concerns Llys Euryn which is in the commote of Creuddyn:

"Ednyfed Fychan had in Wales divers goodly houses, royally adorned with turrets and garrets; some in Anglesey, some in Caernarvonshire, and some in Denbigh Land; but his chiefest manor-house was in the Commote of Crythin in Caernarvonshire, which was a royal palace now decay'd for want of reparation."

The last sentence is significant. The building appears to bear indications of several restorations. That it was made habitable is certain, for in Elizabeth's reign it was the home of a high sheriff. Next comes the reference to Ednyfed's chapel, which calls to mind the arches in the north wall of Llandrillo-yn-Rhos Church – which resemble the postern gate in the Llys Euryn ruins:

"He also built there a chapel in the worship of our Lady, and had licence of the Pope for evermore to sing divine service therein for his soul, and his ancestors' and progenitors' souls, always; and had authority to give his tithes and offerings to his chaplains."

What happened after Ednyfed's time is not known, though the presence of his great-grandson, Grono ap Heilyn, at Llysfaen in Edward I's reign indicates the family remained in the neighbourhood. The next reference is Lewis's statement that Owain Glyndŵr burned the llys in 1409. If this is so it would account for the place lying derelict until it was secured by the family of Conway, in the time of the Wars of the Roses. Some stones are still darkened by soot. Fragments of charcoal have been uncovered in the clay 30 inches below the present ground level and several limestones have been found to be discoloured as though by intense heat. Fragments of wall running N.E., at right-angles to the standing building, have recently been uncovered.

Llys Euryn's only Doorway by Norman Tucker

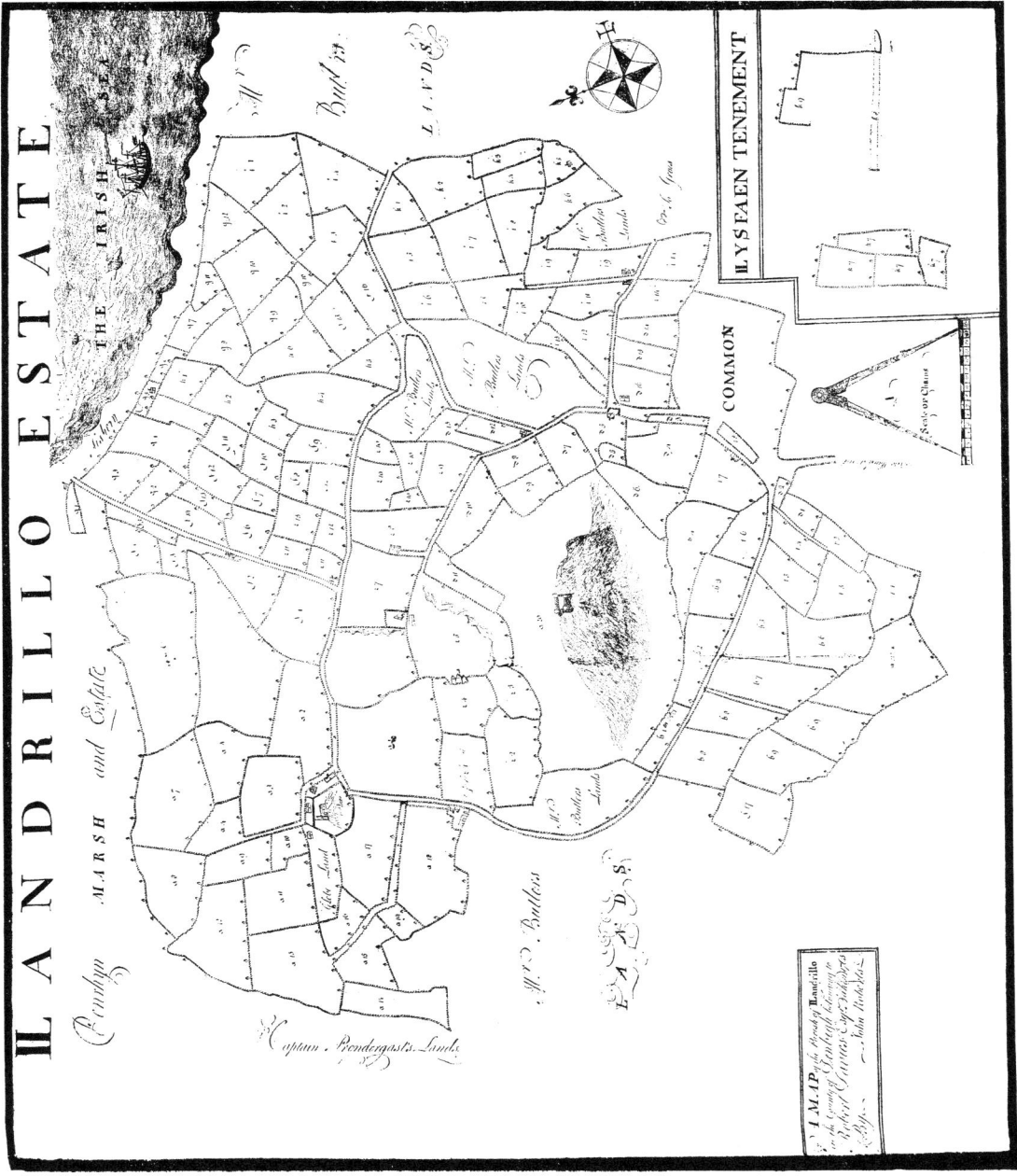

This map of 1763 shows Dinerth Road, Tan-y-Bryn Road and Rhos Road. Llandrillo Church (top left quarter) can be identified, together with the 1762 Vicarage and the original Ship Inn of 1736 (across the road from the present location). Bryn Euryn and Llys Euryn are clearly shown in the centre. Aberhod was on the shore, beneath the "S" in the title.

THE ENGLISH CONQUEST

An event which had a far-reaching effect in this district was the death, in 1237, of the last Earl of Chester, known as John the Scot. He was childless and his lands in North Wales, in addition to (or as part of) the earldom of Chester, escheated to the Crown. Henry III invested his warlike young son, Edward, with all the lands between Chester and Conwy "to appertain to the sword and dignity of Chester," of which Prince Edward was created the Earl. The gift was probably the primary cause of Edward I's tenacity when invading this area.

A book of this nature has no space for details of that protracted struggle. The interest, locally, is that from out of the armed knights who followed Edward I there emerges one figure with a stake in the borough – Sir Robert de Crevequer, a typical name for a Norman adventurer. He was the man to whom the King granted lands at "Penmayn and Lessemayn in the cantred of Ros,"[54] for the service of a knight's fee. In some way the transaction is linked with Prestatyn (or "Prestanton") and also with other lands in Maelor Saesneg (that little island of Flintshire which strayed into Salopian territory). Robert Banastre who served the Conqueror, obtained lands at Prestatyn, and was succeeded by another of that ilk, to whom is attributed the building of Prestatyn Castle - a low-lying fortress which Owain Gwynedd experienced no difficulty in dismantling.[55]

The Banastres lost their territory (probably when Llewelyn ap Griffith regained all North Wales) and retired to Lancashire. Then comes a claim in 1279 by our Robert de Crevequer for their lands at Prestatyn, to which he asserted his right. He was successful.[56] At the Inquisition held at "Prestanton" on Dec. 13th, 1279, Gronw ap Heilyn sat with the Justice of Chester and a jury of twenty-four.

It does not appear why Robert Banastre did not obtain restitution of the estate but it is evident Robert de Crevequer secured possession.[57] This Robert was a rough blade. During the insurrection led by Simon de Montfort he fought on the side of the Earl of Leicester, participated in the battle of Lewes, served at Rochester Castle, in the pillage of Winchester, and other affairs, and was proclaimed a rebel.[58] He must have ingratiated himself into royal favour, for the *Calendar of Patent Rolls* records several transactions of land purchase or exchange. In one instance it refers - the reason unrecorded – to *"pardon at the instance of Eleanor, the king's consort, to Robert de Creuequer, of all debts, arrears, penalties, usuries, and all other demands which may be exacted from him by reason of the Jewry, from the beginning of time to the present date, on account of any contract or other reason whatsoever."*[59]

Apparently Sir Robert made over to the King some of his lands in Kent in exchange for the new lands at Penmaen, Llysfaen and Prestatyn. It was in 1279 that he obtained the lands of "Penmeyn and Lessemeyn in the Cantred of Ros" in exchange for other lands in Kent, and, though we do not know of the date of his death, it is stated *"the said Robert died seised of those towns in fee."* He appears to have done a great deal of chopping and changing of land, for in 1283 he obtained a grant of the manors of Saham and Dytton in exchange for his lands in Maelor Saesneg. The grant was drawn up at Conwy.

The English Conquest

In December 1284, he received a "protection" for going "beyond the seas" with the King until the following Easter.[60] There are records of his acting in a judicial capacity as far afield as Bedford, but he evidently returned to the north, for he was given the custody for life of the castle of Bestan (Beeston), County Chester, and 100 shillings yearly for the custody of it. With this went a grant of £45 yearly of the issues of the king's mills and bridge of Chester "by the hands of the keepers or farmers thereof" in exchange for Robert's quit-claim of a moiety of the manor of Saham *"which moiety the king and queen formerly granted to him for life, in exchange for his quit-claim to them of his land in Maillorsaxeneyth."*

That he was turbulent while he dwelt in this region seems obvious, for in 1281 one of the complaints of the men of Rhos was that he vexed Gronw ap Heilyn, so that he could not go to Rhuddlan or Chester without a great guard of his kinsfolk.[61]

In the reign of Edward II there is a complaint by Robert, son of John de Crevequer, heir of Robert de Crevequer, deceased, that the Escheator had taken into the King's hands the towns (i.e. townships) of Penmeyn and Lessemeyn, held by the said King's grant (Edward I) to him and his heirs. At the Inquisition held at Caernarfon in the 10th year of the reign of Edward II, details of the grant as already stated were accepted, and Robert, son of John de Crevequer, his kinsman, aged 28, was acknowledged heir.[62]

One can imagine the confusion in time of invasion, when the country was overrun by troops, and men of war were covetous of fresh possessions. There is a record of a rebate being made to Reginald de Gray, justice of Chester, of 790 marks because the King, subsequent to his appointment to the castles of Flint and Chester and the cantrevs of Englefeld and Roos (Rhos) had granted to Henry de Lacy, earl of Lincoln *"the commote of Creudyn, and the land of Waynol in the cantred of Roos."*[63]

That was in October 1283, but in 1284 the King made a *"gift to the abbot and convent of Aberconeweye in frank almoin*[64] *of the town of Meynan in lieu of the site of their abbey and the grange of Creuddyn which they have surrendered to the Crown."* It would seem his Majesty had presented the grange of Creuddyn to the valiant Earl of Lincoln before the Crown had obtained it from the Abbot of Aberconwy! At all events it shows that Creuddyn was in the lordship of Denbigh in Edward I's time and remained part of it until (at least) the days of Queen Elizabeth. It must be stressed that in olden times Creuddyn - now restricted to the actual peninsula - embraced Llysfaen and Penmaen Rhos.

A final word respecting Robert de Crevequer is found in a *Notice of the Family of Robert Banastre, one of the Benefactors of Basingwerk Abbey.* "Pennant labours under the idea that Crevequer derived his claim by descent from the Banastres, but we can find no authority for this," says the writer, who adds:

"At a later period, Sir Henry Conway married Angharad, heiress to Sir Hugh Crevecoeuer, of Prestatyn, which continued in the possession of his family till the death of Sir John Conway, of Bodhrydden, Bart, in 1721, the last of the male line, when the estates were divided. One of the co-heiresses of Conway married Sir Thomas Longueville, Bart, and the estate of Prestatyn is now vested in his descendant, Thomas Longueville Jones, Esq., (who has taken the surname of Longueville)."

GRONW AP HEILYN

Only brief reference has been made to Gronw ap Heilyn's grievance against Robert de Crevequer. Gronw may not thus be passed cursorily for he was a power in this neighbourhood. It is not known where he had his abode, but the *Survey* mentions lands of his at Twnnan and Dolwen so it is possible he dwelt somewhere between Llysfaen and Abergele. In addition to acting as his prince's emissary and counsellor, he was Bailiff of the cantred of Rhos, and a king's Justice for

North Wales. He must have been an accomplished administrator of unimpeachable integrity thus to be trusted alike by Welsh prince and English monarch. It is customary to regard Gronw as the great-grandson of Ednyfed Fychan - Gronw ap Heilyn ap Tudur ab Ednyfed. The late Sir John E. Lloyd appears to accept him as such for, after alluding to two of Ednyfed's sons succeeding their father as "Steward of Wales," he adds: *"Of a younger generation was Gronw ap Heilyn of Rhos, prominent in the events of the disastrous close of the prince's career."* Professor Glyn Roberts, however, has recently put forward the disquieting suggestion that there may be two men of the same name. A case, he points out, was tried at Rhuddlan in 1278 with Gronw as one of the Justices. They heard a claim for land at Maenan[65] brought by Heilyn ap Tudur ab Ednyfed which, observes Professor Roberts, looks remarkably like Gronw sitting in judgement on his own father! Moreover, in the Survey, when reference is made to lands at Twnnan, Gronw's name is given as "Gron ap Heilyn ap Ken."

"The descendants of Ednyfed Fychan, Senechal of Llewelyn Fawr, probable chosen because he was a member of the largest tribal group in North Wales, were allowed to hold all their widely scattered patrimonies in Rhos and Rhufoniog free of rent." Gronw ap Heilyn, a descendant of Ednyfed, who again was seneschal of Llewelyn II, held the coastal townships of Llysfaen and Penmaen, and in every other township between Conwy and the Clwyd where he held land, his share was far greater than that of his fellow tribesmen"[66].

However, until these obscurities are clarified it might be advantageous to regard the Gronw ap Heilyn of our history as one entity. An enthralling story remains to be written about Gronw. He steps awhile into the full glare of the spotlight as warrior, statesman, and friend of royalty; then the light fades and darkness prevails. Yet some facts are preserved about the man with whom Robert de Crevequer clashed over his lands at Llysfaen. Gronw must have been proud of his high estate. The descendants of Ednyfed Fychan – constituting the largest tribal group in North Wales – were allowed to hold all their widely scattered patrimonies in Rhos and Rhufoniog free of rent, in return for which privilege they appear to have formed a *corps d'elite* whose task it was to protect the approaches to Snowdonia. Wherever Gronw held land, his share was greater than that of his fellow tribesmen. As one of the closest advisors of Llywelyn ap Gruffydd he acted in the negotiations leading to the Treaty of Aberconwy. He accompanied Llywelyn to London and participated in the Christmas festivities of 1277. A few weeks later he headed the prince's envoys who journeyed to Windsor to arrange the marriage with Eleanor de Montfort. By this time Gronw had attracted the notice of the King and, according to Professor Goronwy Edwards, *"was much employed by Edward in 1278."*[67]

An undated letter, written by Gronw between 1278 and 1281, shows he was engaged as a negotiator by Edward I. Gronw writes to the Vice-Chancellor, John de Kirkby, saying that when he was last with the King, in London, Edward ordered him, with other royal attorneys, to hold parley between Prince Llywelyn and Gruffydd ap Gwenwynwyn. The writer observes he does not know who would pay his expenses for he assumes he ought not to have them paid by either of the parties concerned. He asks the Vice-Chancellor, if he loves him, to learn the King's will, and also to send him his counsel by the messenger, so that the conference may not be delayed.[68]

Gronw was appointed to a commission of which Hopton was Chief Justice and as such must have taken the oath prescribed by Edward. He was also elected to a new commission to hear and determine pleas in the Marches. Several records exist of his sitting as a Justice. In December 1279 he, with others, took an inquisition concerning the manor of Prestatyn[69] which, it will be remembered, was claimed by Robert de Crevequer. Might this have been the cause of enmity? The King's confidence was enjoyed until the summer of 1281 when the Welsh Bailiffs were notified by the King that they were to be replaced.

Somewhere about this time occurred the persecution that reveals itself in the complaint (or "greefe") of the men of Rhos. Gronw, according to Angharad Llwyd, was "the most aggrieved of any of Llewelyn's subjects."

"It was he," writes James Conway Davies, *"who probably arrayed the long catalogue of complaints of the men of the cantred of Rhos, while his own list of personal grievances made a very imposing display."*

One of Gronw's complaints was that he was summoned to appear before a court at Caerwys, apparently at the order of Robert de Crevequer and one, Godfred de Marlieney. Gronw wrote to the Archbishop of Canterbury that he *"durst not go thither, but by the conduct of the Bishop of St. Asaph, for that Reginald Grey was there with his men in harness."*

Gronw must have maintained his position for he, with his grandfather, Sir Tudor ab Ednyfed, were the chief commissioners appointed by Llywelyn to settle the peace between him and Edward I in 1281. Though Gronw enjoyed the confidence of both Prince Llywelyn and the English King there could be no doubt where his real sympathies lay. *"In that fatal campaign of 1282, he was at the Prince's side giving both sage counsel and strong support,"* writes James Conway Davies. *"After Llywelyn's death he remained constant in his support of David and to the last acted as the last Prince's seneschal."*

A decade passed with Gronw, presumably dwelling in honourable retirement. Yet he must have been ill content. When the Madoc rebellion brought fire and sword to Denbigh and Caernarfon, Gronw was found among the insurgents. Was he slain in battle? Did his proud head fall beneath the axe? There is a curt reference in the *Survey* that his lands had escheated to the King because he *"died outside the law,"* or *"died against the peace and had forfeited his portion."*

Was this the time, then, when Llysfaen was broken from the lordship of Denbigh to be included in the royal county of Caernarfon? It would be interesting if the existence of this quaint "island" of Caernarvonshire in Denbighshire could be traced to the feud between Gronw ap Heilyn and the Norman adventurer who followed in Edward's train.

Edward Lhwyd mentions among the lesser houses at Llysfaen in 1698 "Tydbryn (?Tyddyn) Heilin" and "Plas Sion ap Gronw," so it would seem the honoured names lingered on for centuries.[70]

Referring to the inclusion of Penmaen and Llysfaen in the commote of Creuddyn in the fourteenth and later centuries, Edward A. Lewis wrote:

"They formed part of the principality lands, and in the time of Llewelyn were held by Grono ap Heilyn. Grono was apparently deprived of his rights by Robert de Crevequer. . . William de Monte Acuto (i.e. Montacute) was in possession of these vills in 1332. Before 1374 the vills were in the hands of the Black Prince, and from this point forward appear in the ordinary account of the commote of Creuddyn."[71]

NOTE

GORONWY AP HEILYN

It seems to me that there were two men of this name who were roughly contemporary. The confusion is worse confounded because they were both of the "Ednyfed Fychan" stock!

A. The first one appears to have the following pedigree:-

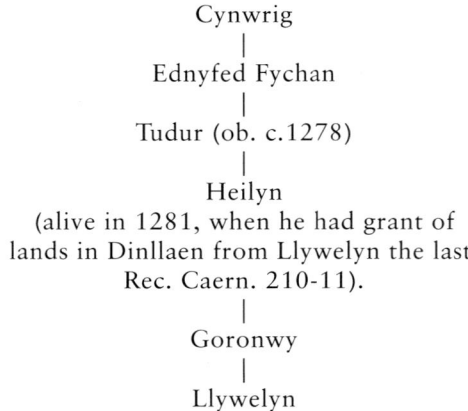

```
Cynwrig
   |
Ednyfed Fychan
   |
Tudur (ob. c.1278)
   |
Heilyn
(alive in 1281, when he had grant of
lands in Dinllaen from Llywelyn the last.
Rec. Caern. 210-11).
   |
Goronwy
   |
Llywelyn
```

B. The second would appear to have the following pedigree:-

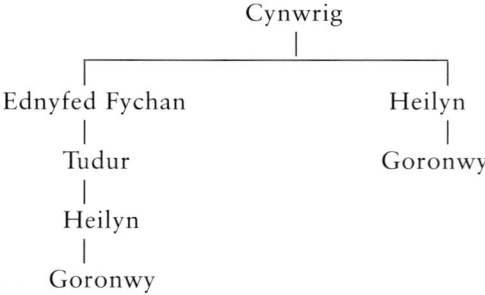

```
            Cynwrig
               |
     ┌─────────┴─────────┐
Ednyfed Fychan         Heilyn
     |                   |
   Tudur              Goronwy
     |
   Heilyn
     |
   Goronwy
```

This second Goronwy ap Heilyn is almost certainly the man who appears as an adviser of Llywelyn the Last in 1277 and 1278 (*Welsh Assize Roll*, pp. 9 & 39). After the Treaty of Aberconwy (1277) up to 1282 he seems to have served Llywelyn and Edward I.

When the final campaign came in 1282, he was on the side of Llywelyn and he it was who probably drew up the long catalogue of complaints of the men of Rhos and of his own grievances. After Llywelyn's death, he remained faithful to Dafydd. It is not clear what happened after 1284.

(The writer is indebted to Prof. Glyn Roberts, for help in preparing this note).

THE HONOUR OF DENBIGH

The "Lordship of Denbigh" or (as it was frequently termed) "Honour of Denbigh" was of greater extent than is generally realized and was distinct from the "Manor of Denbigh." The Honour of Denbigh stretched to the banks of the Conwy, and the Colwyn Bay area would naturally fall within it.

The presence of Llysfaen in Caernarvonshire when the obvious county boundary was the River Conwy has occasioned much speculation. It seems certain that when King Edward created his county of Caernarfon he wished to retain the approach at the mouth of the Conwy River and so he included the Creuddyn Peninsula in his royal county, and the Creuddyn in those days extended to Llysfaen. Similarly when he removed the monks from Aberconwy Abbey to Maenan he retained that portion of the east riverbank in his county.[72] What is now Denbighshire was originally marcher land divided among four powerful lords-marcher having their castles at Denbigh, Ruthin, Chirk and Holt. Such lords were puissant, and a monarch was careful neither to offend nor to permit them to acquire too much power.

The Lordship of Denbigh passed through a number of hands - Thomas, Earl of Lancaster; Hugh Despencer and Roger Mortimer of Wigmore. After Roger was hanged, the Lordship went to William de Montacute on 23 January 1331. In the next reign the Honour of Denbigh was back with the Mortimer family.

After this frequent changing it is comforting to find something tangible. In 1361 the Honour passed into the hands of the Black Prince, after the death of Roger Mortimer, and during the minority of his son.

Llysfaen was linked with the Prince of Wales's other lands, and so became cut off from the Lordship of Denbigh. *"This arrangement,"* says Professor A. H. Dodd, *"continued automatically when the county of Denbigh was made in 1536."*

The description in 1334 of Penmaen and Lassemayn as *'two vills added late to the Honour"* (of Denbigh), may have some bearing on this arrangement. As a result of Gronw ap Heilyn's death while he was in rebellion, these lands would have escheated to the Crown and were therefore already severed from the adjoining territory.

The Counties of Carnarvon and Denbigh (Llysfaen) Order, 1922, brought about the amalgamation, on 1 April 1923, of Llysfaen parish and the Urban District of Colwyn Bay. Llysfaen's prolonged inclusion in Caernarvonshire came to an end.

THE BLACK DEATH

The Black Death which had such far reaching effect on the lives of the villeins who survived its ravages struck this district a dire blow. Creuddyn is listed among the *vills* placed in the hands of the Crown *"through want of tenants."* Its dues were only partly rendered *"because the greater part of the tenants died from pestilence."* Only two *advocarii* were spared in the entire commote of Creuddyn. Evidently the plague spread right up the valley for it is recorded that before its outbreak there were 149 bond tenants in the Commote of Nant Conwy; after the pestilence there were but 47.[73]

Further confirmation of the Black Prince's possession of the Honour of Denbigh is to be found in The *Black Prince's Registers* of 1360 which record the commitment during pleasure to the Prince's yeoman, John de Delves, as constable of "Dynebegh" and also steward of the Lordship of Dynebegh, *"the said castle and lordship having come into the prince's hand by reason of the minority of Edmund, son and heir of Roger de Mortymer, earl of La Marche, who held of the prince in chief by knight's service, as of the principality of Wales."*

THE BLACK PRINCE'S REGISTER

This area was thus not unknown to the Black Prince. There is an unusual entry in his *Register*. On the 1 July 1359, it was recorded that "John Lloyt," chaplain, was appointed to the church of Lesevaen

"which is void and in the prince's presentation by reason of the temporalities of the bishopric of St. Asaph having lately been in his hand." Then follows a note that this presentation was repealed *"because John had deceived the prince and his council as to his name."*

On 10 July there were further letters of presentation to the church of Lisvaen, *"which is void and in the prince's collation by reason of the temporalities of the bishopric of St. Asaph having lately been in his hands during the voidance of the see."*

These letters were made out in favour of John ap Jevan ap Eign', chaplain. Was this, one wonders, the same John under his right name!

Then there is a reference to Llandrillo the same year, though the parish went by its original name of Dinerth. An order is made by the Prince in 1359 to deliver to John de Scolagh: *"three good oaks in the prince's park of Pecforton as a reward for his labours and costs in prosecuting his right to Dynnerth, to which he was presented by the prince."*[74] This record appears soon after rewards for service at "Poyters" (Poitiers), and may have some connection with the battle.

THE CAPTURE OF RICHARD II

For a brief moment Colwyn appears on the stage of British history. It is but a short interlude, but indubitably dramatic. The hollow to the east of Penmaen headland, near the entrance to the railway tunnel, was chosen for the ambush that was to cost King Richard II his life. The King had dallied in Ireland though he knew Bolingbroke was plotting his overthrow. When he finally arrived at Conwy Castle he had with him a small retinue; the army he expected to find awaiting him had dispersed. Bolingbroke was at Chester, and his chief supporter, Henry Percy, Earl of Northumberland vowed he would get Richard out of Conwy "by reason or by craft." By swearing on the holy relics on the altar of Conwy Castle's garrison chapel, he prevailed upon the King to follow him to Rhuddlan. Earl Percy rode ahead to the place where his men-at-arms were lurking behind Penmaen Head. In the King's retinue was a French nobleman named Creton who, in a metrical history, narrates what transpired. He leaves no doubt about the actual spot. Here is the narrative:

"The Earl rode on till he saw his men under the mountain, and then was he well pleased when he saw that they were careful with good order and prudence to guard the pass.. The King set out after him from Conwy, and on his road to Rhuddlan he passed a very broad and great water (the Conwy estuary) and then rode on four miles till he mounted the rock where the Earl was concealed at the descent. When he held them he was greatly astonished, saying 'I am betrayed; what can this be? Lord of Heaven help me!' Then were they known by their banners, which might be seen floating. 'I think,' said he, 'it is the Earl who hath drawn us upon his oath.' Then were all in bitter dread. I could wish myself then in France, for I saw them almost in despair; and by good right one ought not to be surprised that they were all in distress, for not a man of them could get away from that place to flee without being stopped or taken. But that I may be understood, I must tell you how that the King had come so near to them, that it was much nearer to return to the town than to descend the rock, which was washed by the main sea. We could not get away the other side owing to the rock; so, cost what it might, we were forced either to die or to pass into the midst of the Earl's people."

"He appeared armed in mail. Then did the King demean himself so sorrowfully, that it was a pity to behold. Often times did he say 'O true God, what mischief and trouble do I undergo! Now do I plainly see that this man is taking me to the Duke, who loves us not. O Virgin Mary!

Groes Fawr before the alterations. On the right is a fragment of the old smithy, demolished when the main road was widened

Sovereign Queen, have mercy upon me, for if thou deignest not to look upon me, I know I am lost.' Thus spoke the King, who on that spot had no power, for as it appeared to me, we were but twenty, or two-and-twenty. So every one descended the lofty rock to the great grief of the King. Then the Earl kneeled before the King and begged him not to be displeased, and offered him bread and wine, which the King durst not refuse."

"*They remounted and rode to Rhuddlan to dine sumptuously at the strong castle there."*[75]

WAS OWAIN GLYNDŴR THERE?

Some historians believe Owain Glyndŵr, and probably Gwilym ap Tudur, another Welsh squire about the King's person, were among those taken with Richard. If this were so it might account for Gwilym and his brother Rhys retaliating by capturing Conwy Castle in 1401 and burning the town.

Among those in the royal train were the Duke of Exeter - John de Holland - and his nephew the Duke of Surrey, a matter of interest to us as apparently they sprang from the same stock as the Hollands of Teyrdan. The Duke of Exeter was not at Penmaen Head, having ridden ahead to Chester to try to effect an agreement.

Percy, we are told, "*formed his men into two bodies under the rough and lofty cliffs of a rock (Penmaen Rhos); they were fresh and eager, persecuting traitors as they were, to take the King.*" The force was under the command of Sir Thomas Erpingham who, in his advanced age, gave the signal for the battle of Agincourt. Shakespeare mentions him in *Henry V*.

CROWN LAND

There seems reliable indication that this area – or much of it – from the time of the Edwardian conquest until the seventeenth century remained Crown Land. Even Queen Elizabeth's gift to her favourite, Robert Dudley, Earl of Leicester, of the lordship of Denbigh, was probably such that it escheated to the Crown at his death. Indeed, this seems certain, for in a legal case of 1610 it is stated that the petitioners were concerned with *"lease lands at Penmaen Llysfaen, co. Caernarvon, of which they and their ancestors have been time-out-of-mind tenants to the king."*

In Henry VII's day – 1506 - it was the same story, for there is reference to a "licence for the King's tenants of the lordship of Denbychlond (Denbigh land) alias Ros and Ryvoneok."[76]

A MILL AT RHIW

One of the most interesting facts which emerges is that there was a mill at Rhiw, and one finds it difficult to place it other than on the site of the ruined Groes Mill. It has been generally accepted that this mill was of Elizabethan origin, but it is doubtful whether anyone imagined the connection would stretch back to the days of Edward III.

The *Survey* states *"The entire village of Rue contains nine welau (households), one wele of freemen and eight servile."* It lists *"The Mill"* and states: *"The profits might be improved by 13s. 11d. a year as is shown in the various items. Robert ap Griffud holds the mill of the lord in this village and pays each year at the aforesaid feasts – 28s. 8d."*

Elsewhere it states: *"All these serfs together with those of Rue and Coleyne repair the earthwork of the mill of Rue and cart all the timber to the said mill when it is needed except the wood used for the axle and wheels of the mill but they do not cart mill-stones. This work is not valued because it does not happen regularly."*

The following extracts from Williams' *Ancient and Modern Denbigh* (p. 94) seems to confirm this:

J. R. Fearnside, Esq., of the Office of Land Revenue Record, in his Report of the 11th September, 1852 says: *"A small portion towards the Town (i.e. Denbigh) was erected during the period that the Castle was in the possession of the Earl of Leicester, to whom Queen Elizabeth sold it. It, however, remained but a few years Out of the Crown's possession for, on the death of the said Earl, she resumed possession in part liquidation of a debt due from him to the Crown."*

The *Survey* deals with the portions of this immediate district in the following order:–
TUENNAN.
The Village of LOYDCOYD with the hamlets of WHLEPTREUE and DYNERTH.
MOGHEDREUE.
The Village of RUE.
The Village of COLOYNE.
Village of PENMAEN.
Village of LASSEMAYN.

In each township the wele or family is set forth with the land held by them and details of service. As no one but a scholar would be interested in searching through the names it may suffice to select sundry extracts which assist in conjuring up a mental picture of those times. The expression "Wyrion Eden," which not infrequently occurs, may be translated freely as "the descendants of Ednyfed Fychan." The great chieftain had by his two marriages numerous children and it is easy to imagine how in the course of several generations numerous offspring were scattered about the broad acres over which he was once paramount chief. There is a particular reference to Gronw ap Heilin, Ednyfed's great grandson.

Below are given some extracts under the names of the Townships under which they appear in the *Survey*.

TUENNAN

Freeholders

"*The progeny of Ken' ap Ior (Kendric son of Iorwerth) ap Goug' (Gough), known as Wyrion Eden, who are Robert ap Griffud (it will be remembered that he had the mill at Rhiw) ap Hoel etc, hold two parts of the village of Tuennan; they pay no Tung or Treth, nor do they do any other service, except that of coming to the court of the Lord when they are summoned there, and that of following the Lord in the army, etc. And the third part of the same village, which did belong to Gron ap Heilin ap Ken' who died outside the law, has escheated to the Lord, together with all the other lands and tenements belonging to the same Gron, both in demesne land and in servile land, whether they were in his own hands on the day when he died or were by way of Tyrpride (tenantless land), or were held by some other tenure.*" The land was rented at 6d. an acre.

Later it adds that the whole village held 7 acres and 3 roods of land which belonged to Gron ap Heilin . . . "*and now all this land is in the hands of the Lord on account of the poverty of the village and the lack of tenants.*"

There was a mill at Dolwen in those days for it states: "*Robert ap Griffud and Gron' ap Heilin hold the mill of Dowen in the same place and they pay 20s on the aforesaid days.*"

THE VILLAGE OF LOYDCOYD WITH THE HAMLETS OF WHLEPTREUE AND DYNERTH

"*The village of Loydcoyd with the hamlets of Whleptreue and Dynerth were in the time of the princes (i.e. before the Edwardian conquest) in four welau (families) which paid as Tung in common each year 10s in Lloydcoyd, 5s in Whleptreue and nothing in Dynerth.*" One family paid "*for the food of the Prince at Christmas, 9d*" and another "*for the food of the Prince at Christmas, 13¾d.*"

From the number of families enumerated it would appear that Lloydcoed was the most thickly populated part of the area. Dealing with the Wele ap Idenerth ap Edred, it says:

"*And all the aforesaid free-holders pay each year in common for the food of the stallion and groom, the huntsman with the dogs, the Chief Page and young men at the feast of the Exaltation of the Holy Cross, 7s. 8d.*

The whole community of Loydcoyd and Whleptreue pay to the Lord yearly for the rent of the Lord's land which they hold here as pasture, and which portion contains in land, wood and waste, 194 acres, 3 roods, the sum of 46s. The whole village hold the right of cutting the turf of the Lord in the village and they pay each year on the aforesaid days 2d. Total 2s.

The community of the same hamlet give to the Lord yearly for pasturage on the waste land of the Lord in this place, which contains 8 acres, 3 roods, the sum of 3s 4d on the aforesaid days. And yet if it had been divided up, it would value 6s. 8d. per year. And so the increase would be 40d. per annum."

VILLAGE OF MOGHEDREUE

The village of Moghedreue contains three progenies of free-holders and one progeny which cannot be called really free or really servile. These four progenies hold two parts of the village of Moghedreue. The third part of the same village consists of servile holdings. First of the freeholders is "Madok Glotheyth ap Madoc" - which suggests that "Madoc Gloddaeth," whose name is associated with Gloddaeth Hall, held land in Mochdre. Having listed the serfs, the *Survey* adds:

"All these serfs together with all the serfs of Rue and Coleyne who are listed below, pay each year in common towards the food of the Prince's household 30.s; of this sum 15s is paid at Christmas and 5s at each of the other three aforesaid quarter days; and they pay for the food of the chief page and young men in fosterage $13^{1}/_{2}d$ at the feast of the Exaltation of the Holy Cross; and 2s 3d. for the food of the huntsman with the dogs at the same festival, and 3s for the food of a stallion and a groom at the same festival, and 7s 3d for the food of the servant and the greyhounds each year at the same festival ; and 16s 11d for the food of two warhorses and two grooms each year at the same festival. Everyone who has a house gives 1d. at Christmas instead of a hen, and $2^{1}/_{2}d$. at the feast of the Exaltation of the Holy Cross for the food of the Raglot's horse; and $^{1}/_{2}d$ towards the erection of houses at the same festival. And each of them pays $4^{1}/_{2}d$ instead of three days' work as a reaper in the autumn."

Then comes the reference already quoted to repairing the earthwork at the mill of Rue.

VILLAGE OF RUE

The entire village of Rue contains 9 Welau i.e. 1 Wele of freemen and 8 servile Wele. Under "Freeholders" is listed "Eign' Vaghan ap Eignon ap Tegwaret" which suggests he might be the ancestor of the Vaughans of Glyn.

Total number of hens at Christmas - 8 valued at 8d.

Total number of autumn works - 63 valued at 7s $10^{1}/_{2}d$. There are no payments for the food of the Prince in this village nor for the food of the Prince's household except what is paid in common with the serfs of Moghedreue.

The escheated land in the village of Rue ought to contain in land, woodland and waste if properly divided 272 acres and $^{1}/_{2}$ a rood.

"Ior ap Eignon holds 4 acres and pays each year at Pentecost and Michaelmas in equal portions 2s. All the serfs of the same village hold in common 114 acres $3^{1}/_{2}$ roods of land of which there are 43 acres and $^{1}/_{2}$ rood which are valued at 8d an acre and 71 acres and 3 roods valued at 6d an acre, and they pay each year at the aforesaid feasts.. 64s. $7^{1}/_{2}d$.

The whole village holds 42 acres 1 rood of escheated land and pays each year altogether at the aforesaid feast 13s. 4d. And yet each acre values 6d. a year. So the profits might be increased by 7s $9^{1}/_{2}d$. Four more holdings are held by the community as a whole. . .The whole village hold 70 acres of waste as pasturage and pay each year 3s. 4d. in common at the aforesaid feast. And yet each acre values about 1d. a year, some more, some less."

VILLAGE OF COLOYNE

The whole village of Coloyne contains three Weleu i.e. the Wele of Cradok ap Gethlok which is not entirely free nor entirely servile, and the Wele of Seisel ap Daniel, and the Wele of Ken' ap Daniel which consists of serfs. The community at Colwyn, like their neighbours, contributed (in their case 6d per year) to the food of the groom and the huntsmen, and so forth. "Total Tung" payments of Coloyne, on All Saints' Day, were 21d. Total number of hens due at Christmas - 3, valued at 3d.

There is a note that all the freemen and serfs of this commote or their tenants pay each year in common 13s 4d instead of building houses at the Feast of the Exaltation of the Holy Cross. Another ruling concerns the relief of freemen. "All the aforesaid serfs or their kindred, up to and including kindred of the third degree, pay as relief 2s. And beyond the third degree there is no hereditary succession but the land escheates to the lord." It adds that the land must be granted to the nearest relative who offers its full value rather than to an outsider. This applies to Welshmen and to Englishmen: an interesting observation as it suggests that the English were beginning to settle. In the lists of the various gwelau there is a preponderance of Welsh family names, though in Llysfaen and Penmaen, such names as John de Blacklorne, William le Hert, and Richard Banastr' indicates that Norman adventurers had established their claims. It is of particular interest to note that the villages of "Penman and Lesmaen" are listed as "new acquisitions of the lord William de Monte Acuto." (Montacute).

Penmaen was divided into four gwelau and all the tenants were serfs. Each gwele was in the lands of the heirs who paid 2s 6d as tung per year until they died. Under the heading "Customs of the same village," it states:

"Each of the aforesaid customary tenants who has two hens gives to the lord at Christmas one hen or 1d. But if they have only one cock or one hen and no more, they give nothing, so they say. And this customary due varies in amount in proportion to the number of hens the tenants have. And the custom is valued at 8d in ordinary years. Each of the aforesaid serfs who has a plough gives to the lord, instead of a ploughing service, 3d at Christmas, and if he has no plough or even a part share in a plough, he gives nothing. And this custom is estimated at 9d in ordinary years. And any one of them who makes a new hedge or repairs an old one gives to the lord, according to custom, 1d at the feast of the Apostles Philip and James. But he who neither makes nor repairs a hedge does nothing. This custom is valued at 6d in ordinary years. Everyone who holds land gives to the lord each year at the feast of the Exaltation of the Holy Cross 4_d instead of three autumn-works. The number of these works vary according to the number of serfs who hold land. There are now in this village 19 tenants, as is recorded above, and their autumn-works value 7s 1^1/$_2$d. a year."

VILLAGE OF LASSEMAYN

Llysfaen contained nine gavell and each whole gavell paid 13^1/$_2$d as Tung. There are references to "building work on the mill" but no mill is specified. The customs of the village were the same as those of Penmaen. "They estimate that in ordinary years 16 hens will be due at Christmas." Ploughing and harrowing services were estimated at 21d. "The customary payment of the customary tenants of the same village for wood for their fences is estimated at 6d. in ordinary years. The autumn-works for 39 tenants in this village now value 14s 7^1/$_2$d." The "Fixed rents" are listed.

"William de Wynton holds in fee the land which belonged to Bleth' ap Grono' in Penmaen which contains 4^1/$_2$ acres and half a rood of land and waste and he pays 6d each year on All Saints' Day."

In Llysfaen the heirs of Mad' ap Hona held 33 acres and 1^1/$_2$ roods of land and waste, and also 16 acres of "land which belongs to John de Blackelorne, and he gives each year on the aforesaid day one pair of gilded spurs which value 6d."

Griffuth ap Gro' ap Lewelin held six acres in fee and also gave one pair of gilded spurs. William le Hert held six acres in fee and paid 6d each All Saints' Day. The heirs of Richard Banastr(e) held in fee lands which belonged to Ph. ap Ithel ap Oweyn, etc.," 48 acres 1^1/$_2$ roods for which they paid 6d.

The heirs of Richard de Hoyland "hold by hereditary right half of one gavell which belonged to Eignon ap Ken' ap Rees, etc., "49 acres and 3½ roods and 10 perches in land and waste" and they give each year on All Saints' Day "two pairs of gloves or 2d."

"The Lord Ithel Person holds by hereditary right the lands which belonged to Tegwaret ap Yevan ap Rice and David his brother," 11 acres 3½ roods, for which he paid annually 6d. Ior' ap Ken, held one acre and paid 2d and there were four other tenants "by the same tenure." The total payments of free men were:

"on All Saints' Day, 5s 9½d., one pair of gilt spurs valued at 6d, and 2 pairs of gloves valued at 2d. On the Nativity of St. John the Baptist, one pair of gilt spurs valued at 6d."

After setting forth the rents of the villages, the summing up states:

Thus the sum total of the value of all the revenues of the villages of Penmaen and Lessemaen according to this survey is £10-0s-5½ d. and half-a-farthing a year. And it could be increased, as has been shown above, by 42s 5¾ d a year.

In conclusion the *Survey* says : "Total value of the castle and honour of Denbigh with the villages of Permaen and Lessemaen from all sources is £1,500- 7s-1¾d. a year. And it could be increased beyond this amount by £110- 9s-5½d."

It should be noted that even as far back as 1334 the villages of Penmaen and Llysfaen were regarded as an area separate from the remainder of the Honour of Denbigh. The *Survey of the Honour of Denbigh* was carried out in 1334 by command of Montacute, who is, presumably, "the Lord" from whom the tenants listed held their lands. The record suggests the existence of little communities where people dwelt in frail dwellings, which have long since disappeared.

(The writer is indebted to Dr. Una Rees, University College of North Wales, for a translation of the document.)

THE AGE OF THE TUDORS

The new type of administration which characterised the advent of the Tudor dynasty is reflected in law disputes which carried to the metropolis such homely names as Dinerth and Llysfaen. In the King's Court of Chancery, Sir Thomas Audley (Lord Chancellor from 1533 to 1538) heard a case brought by one Hugh ab David ab Vaughan. Though the complainant is described as *"parson of Blake Notley, county Essex,"* he was probably of the same strain as the Vaughans of Glyn. At any rate he had land in these parts for he complains that one Harry ap John ap David ap Howell, son and heir of John ap David ap Howell, *"late of Denerth in the county of Ughdulas in the dominion of Denbith,"* was *"seised of divers lands, tenements, meadows, feedings, pastures, woods and underwoods etc. in Denerth aforesaid,"* which he had sold to the complainant. The evidence and deeds of the transaction had got into the hands of one Thomas ap William ap John ap Robyn who, the complainant alleges, had craftily conveyed divers secret estates whereby he intended to disinherit Hugh. He had refused to give up the deeds though solicited "divers times."[77]

A LLYSFAEN SUIT

On the south side of Llysfaen Church, close to the path, is an imposing tombstone with a chain-pattern border. It records that Griffith Lloyd was buried the 15th day of August, 1599. He, too, was concerned in these land disputes. Under the year 1589 there is among the Exchequer Bills a complaint by "Hugh Lloyde ap Griffith Lloyd of the parish of Llissmayne, co. Carnarvon, gent." His claim was that Queen Elizabeth had *"demised to him lands and tenements in the township of Penmayne, Llismayne and Erias in the comote of Cruthyn."* The land had been granted for 21 years at a yearly rental of 58/7d.*(sic)*. The complainant adds – *"William, Bishop of St. Asaph, Robert and Fulk Holland of co. Denbigh, gents., have got the writings and evidences of the same in their custody."*

Some interest attaches to the answer of the two Hollands as they refer to the favourite Leicester's connection with this district. Robert says he believes:

"Robert, the late Earl of Leicester, was seized of the manor and lordship of Denbigh, co. Denbigh, whereof the lands mentioned lying in the township of Llisvaen and Penmaen were and are part, and the said Earl took the rents and profits thereof until his death."

The account continues:

"by his deed indented 17th. Elizabeth (1575) he granted Robert Holland all the escheated lands in Llisvaen and Penmaen reserving a certain rent, by force whereof Robert Holland entered the same and has taken the profits as it is lawful for him to do. He disclaims the lands in Erias, and Fulke disclaims all lands altogether."

The reply of the Bishop of St. Asaph records he had parcels of land at Llysfaen and among them one *"called Maes Mawr and another in a tenement called Place y pylous, and another parcel called Bronheuch, all containing 4 acres in Llismayne called wheat land."* The Bishop occupied the land for some years as tenant at will of Robert Holland. The residue he held of Edward Conway Esq. (the owner of Bryn Euryn), Hugh Conway, gent, and others.[78] *"Place y Pylous"* might refer to Peulwys. It is interesting to note this connection between a Bishop of St. Asaph and Llysfaen.

Mention is made of 20 acres that were William Holland's (possibly the eldest son of David Holland of Kinmel), and also of *"a messuage called Parke."*

Hugh Lloyd seems to have been either given to litigation or a much-wronged man. In 1588 he sues the Bishop of Bangor, Robert Holland, gent, and Ffoulk Holland, gent, of Denbigh, for detention of deeds.[79]

FREEHOLDERS

Hugh Lloyd is complainant in another suit in 1592, against numerous persons, most of them being inhabitants of the townships of Penmayne, Llisvain and Erias, and freeholders and occupiers of the said premises demised to the complainant. They had got his lease into their hands, he complained, and had broken all meres and bounds, and claimed the lands as their own, and had cut down the trees.[80]

"Meer" or *"mere"* is the old name for a boundary mark. The question of securing land seemed uppermost in the minds of the squires. The same Hugh Lloyd of Llysfaen appears in yet another lawsuit two years later, against the inhabitants and freeholders of the township of Penmayne, Llismayne and Erias, alleging the detention of letters patent. He accuses them of the *"destruction of meers between the Crown lands and their own freeholds,"* in the said township and the *"spoil of woods."* [81] This makes it plain that by this time, in addition to Crown lands there was also freehold. In 1610 he is referred to as Hugh Lloyd, *"late farmer of Llysfaen."* Lhwyd, in 1698, gives a John Lloyd as living at Ty Ucha; it might be the same family, as Hugh Lloyd's son was named John. These instances emphasise the scramble (one might almost say unscrupulous scramble) for land, which took place during the Tudor period. Henry VIII, particularly after the dissolution of the monasteries, raised money by the sale of Crown lands, and it is probable that portions of the demesne of the Abbey of Aberconwy (then at Maenan) changed hands at that date. *"Henry VIII,"* writes Dr. G. M. Trevelyan, *"sold great parts of the confiscated Abbey lands to Peers, courtiers, public servants and merchants, who at once resold much of it to smaller men."*

Two of the most influential of the squires in this portion of the lordship of Denbigh were the Salusburys of Lleweny (Denbigh), and the Wynns of Gwydir (Llanrwst), both of whom had acquired land in what is now the Borough of Colwyn Bay. A clash was inevitable. There followed one of those inter-family feuds so characteristic of that period.

SIR JOHN WYNN AT LLYSFAEN

Much has been written about the celebrated Sir John Wynn of Gwydir, Knight and Baronet, he whose spirit (according to tradition) is under Swallow Falls, there to be spouted upon and purged of the misdeeds done in the days of nature. He was considered avaricious, ambitious, and unscrupulous and his enemies watched for an opportunity to lay him low. It was at Llysfaen the incidents took place that were ultimately to bring about Sir John's disgrace. The *"farming"* of estates was then widely done. The expression is a legalized one and not, as might be supposed, modern slang.

Between the years 1603 and 1606 John Wynn *"one of the King's Gentlemen Pensioners,"* asserts he held by lease of £30 yearly from the King certain lands in Caernarvonshire, of which he and his ancestors had been tenants for 200 years at least. The King had been pleased to grant these lands in reversion to Dr. Atkins and others so that he *"never got anything for his services."* He begs that he may have a lease in reversion of some other lands. Not long after there comes a petition from persons in Penmayne and Llysfaen:

"Sir John Gwyn has of late got a lease of the premises and intends to put out the petitioners unless they will pay more rent than they have been accustomed to. Sir John is a knight of great means and countenance."[82]

Now the feud begins - the clash between the Salusburys of Lleweny and the Wynns of Gwydir! Sir Roger Mostyn, who married Sir John Wynn's daughter, writes complaining that cousin William Vaughan had been hardly used by Sir John Salusbury and his people:

"It is reported of this business in Llysvayne that Ellis Vaughan informed Wynn as to the King's land, and thereby wronged the poorer sort. Then came Sir John Salusbury who encroached on half the parish while Sir John Wynn did not oppose him."[83]

Nothing transpired and Sir John Wynn seems to have concentrated on commercial matters. The only exciting incident recorded in this locality is the murder of *"John Vaughan, clerk, serving the cure of Llanguestenen in the commote of Crethin, who was stabbed in the throat and elsewhere by one Williams and instantly killed."*[84]

By 1610 Llysfaen creeps back into the news. Sir John hopes to have a case heard in the Exchequer Chamber against John Lloyd, son of Hugh Lloyd, "late farmer of Llysfvaen."[85] The Bishop of St. Asaph was called upon to intervene in the "Llysvayne business" and appointed a meeting four or five times between Sir John and the King's tenants at Llysfaen. The Bishop had prevailed with Sir John to be content to suffer the tenants to hold the King's escheat lands at a reasonable rent. He regretted he was unable to effect an agreement between the parties.

In February 1614 the case by the tenants of Llysfaen had been heard in court and dismissed. Sir John's enemies, however, were resolved not to let the matter rest. The next move is an action by one Evan ap John Conway (tenant to Harry Salusbury of Lleweny) who charges Sir John Wynn and his men in the Court of the Marches with riotous and forcible entry upon Salusbury's lands in Penmaen and Llysfaen.

CHARGE OF OPPRESSION

It was alleged that oppressions were committed by Sir John Wynn under colour of his offices of Justice of the Peace, Deputy-Lieutenant, and Farmer of the King's Escheat Lands in Caernarvon. It was stated that: *"he put out whole families, some of them young children and naked, by three o'clock in the morning because they would not be his tenants."* For this Sir John was fined 1,000 marks and banished from the Council of the Marches.[86] Sir John was also deeply censured in a hearing taken in his absence, for issuing a warrant to the Constable of Llysfaen for the apprehension of Robert Owen (Owen ap Robert's son) who had since murdered a man at Llysfaen. Robert ap Owen would not be bound over to be of good behaviour for his son, and the constable, *"being a lame man could not take the young man to prison without a handlock."* Sir John was accused of maliciously proceeding against these people because he was engaged in the lawsuit concerning the lands they held from him. Sir John Wynn in his statement to the Court of the Marches said that after Sir John Salusbury's death he sued his son and heir, Henry Salusbury, and others who refused to appear. He therefore ordered his bailiff to enter two of the cottages *"occupied by two poor under-tenants of Henry Salusbury, who thereupon set on one of these cottagers named Conway, to proceed against him* (Sir John) *for forcible entry and riot."* In addition to the fine of 1,000 marks, Sir John Wynn was ordered to be put out of the Court of the Marches where he had served 13 years, deprived of the Deputy-Lieutenancy in which he had served 29 years, and dismissed from the Commission of the Peace in which he had served almost 30 years. This, briefly, outlines the part Llysfaen played in the downfall of the celebrated Sir John who, shortly after, petitioned the King to have the sentence pronounced against him reviewed. He did more: he bribed the judge with £350, and all was well!

VICAR CHORAL KILLED

What forgotten tragedy lies behind an entry among the list of Vicars Choral of St. Asaph Cathedral? Concise and cryptic it reads: *1617—Richard Evans, killed at Llandrillo.*[87]

THE PLAGUE

One would have thought the dark messenger would have passed by this sequestered spot. But Llandrillo was not immune from the plague. In 1605 Sir John Salusbury of Lleweny wrote to his brother-in-law, John Wynn of Gwydir, about relief for the infected parishes of Llandrillo and Llanddoged. Hugh ap Evan Lloyd was appointed High Constable to collect the money of the assessment to meet this emergency and he was to receive 12d out of every £1 for his travelling expenses. Llandrillo had eight houses infected, making 48 persons affected, *"besides the poor of the parish (which were many)."* Llansanffraid (then part of the parish of Llandrillo) had one house in which were six persons infected, *"and in one cabin there was one who died."*[88]

ELIZABETHAN DAYS

Whilst local squires endeavoured to extend their estates and to acquire fresh wealth and consequence, this area, small though it was, was not exempt from its national duties. After the defeat of the Great Armada, the war against Spain dragged on. The lordship of Denbigh was expected to furnish its quota of fighting men. There were orders for holding musters at places to which people could conveniently travel, for provisioning stores of powder and ammunition, and setting watches and beacons. Doubtless the beacons at Llanelian and Llysfaen which Lhwyd mentions were included in the national chain. At the close of 1595 Wales was required to send 1,006 *"armed and weaponed men"* to Ireland, whereof 46 were to be raised in Caernarvon county. By the following February the numbers were increased, and 50 men were also required from Denbighshire. The Bishop of Bangor commanded the clergy of the diocese to furnish *"seven light horses, 12 petronels, 6 musquets and 10 calivers."*[89]

In the list there appears the name of *"Sir John Roberts, parson of Rhiwe,"* who contributed one musket. The troops were to be better armed. *"Their bows must be changed for muskets, or other shot, and their brown bills for halberds."* The order adds *"the soldiers must wear a red livery, of kersey or Bridgewater cloth, indented with black."* Almost a *"Beefeater"* uniform!

CONSPIRACY

During the troublous times of the 1580s, when conspiracies were directed against the Virgin Queen, the coves and caves of Rhiwledyn (as the Little Orme was termed) provided an alluring haunt for Catholic missionaries - Welshmen, trained at Rheims and sent back to their native land to work among those of the "old faith." Robert Pugh of Penrhyn (Old Hall) was the prime mover in these parts, and he was outlawed by the President of Wales. The story has come to light of a secret printing press set up in a cave in the Orme. It was surrounded, but the twelve priests, believed to be in hiding, escaped. One of them was William Davies, born of good family in Groes yn Eirias. Robert Pugh's grandson, the bard Gwilym Pue, has written about *"Syr William"* as he terms him, and hails him as *"seren ei Wlad"* (The star of his land). T.P.Ellis describes him as being *"one of the most appealing of all the Welsh Martyrs."* William Davies, after being imprisoned in London, was released, but was again arrested at Holyhead, when he was trying to get several young Welshmen out of the country to train in Spain. He was imprisoned in Beaumaris, and after various experiences, during which he resisted all persuasions to escape, he was finally tried and hanged, drawn and quartered, on 27 July 1593, at Beaumaris Castle - the first to suffer there for the Catholic faith. His quarters were sent to decorate the castle gateways at Conwy, Beaumaris and Caernarvon.[90]

ELIZABETHAN SEADOG

There is another brief cameo of Elizabethan days. It depicts Captain Thomas Price, Plas Iolyn, son of the notorious Dr. Ellis Price (Dr. Coch). Captain Price, poet, soldier, seaman and explorer, was a friend of Captain Will Myddelton, and the two are believed to have been the first to smoke tobacco publicly in England, having captured a cargo in a Spanish ship off the Canary Islands. There are some strange tales of Captain Tom Price, who may have inherited some of his father's less admirable qualities, but if he erred he was forgiven, for in 1599 he was made High Sheriff of Denbighshire and was a Justice of the Peace. Perhaps it was in the latter connection that he and David Holland,[91] probably of Kinmel, were appointed treasurers to levy, collect and distribute money within the county of Denbigh towards the relief of maimed soldiers.[92] The two met *"at a place called y Groes yn Eirias (near the town of Conway)"* in execution of their duties. As there was *"no fit place to lodge, but only in Conway,"* they made for that ancient town. In Conwy was a certain *"Hugh Holland, gent."* acting in place of one of the town bailiffs, and he had for long born malice towards Captain Price and, *"since the general pardon, had attempted his life and overthrow."* The travellers, on reaching the ferry, found themselves confronted by this Hugh Holland, gent, and other evil disposed persons to the number of 15, who had assembled with swords, daggers, long staffs, picks, Welsh hooks and sundry other unlawful weapons. When Hugh Holland commanded his men to assault Captain Price, the watermen took the ferryboat to another place, but the riotous company followed Captain Price to his lodging and tried to break down the door *"until some well-disposed persons dissuaded them."* There the story ends, and one is left wondering whether *"Hugh Holland, gent."* was called to account for his misdemeanours.

This took place in 1601. Of particular interest to Colwyn Bay is the fact that David Holland and Captain Tom Price met at Groes yn Eirias. One wonders if Groes farm existed then - the water gristmill obviously did. There may have been an inn (and a cross) at Groes yn Eirias. W.Ogwen Williams (Caernarvonshire County Archivist), has recently brought to light a complaint made to the Justices of the Peace in 1609 by William ap Robert, ferryman of Conwy, who was troubled by one Hugh Vaughan, *"alehouse or innkeeper at the Cross in Eyrws."* The way in which the local squirearchy intermarried is indicated by the fact that Hugh Holland was the fifth son of Hugh Gwyn Holland of Conwy, who married Jane, daughter of Hugh Conway of Bryneuryn in 1543. Hugh Gwyn Holland died in 1584.

RHOS FYNACH

One of the most interesting buildings in the Borough is Rhos Fynach, though it is misleading to describe it as a monastery. The name Rhos Fynach undoubtedly goes back to monastic times - to the days when Llewelyn the Great founded a Cistercian Abbey at Aberconwy and gave broad lands, including the grange of Creuddyn, to the Abbot and monks. The weir at Rhos

Quiet gentility is the order of the day on the promenade at Rhos-on-Sea, here showing the entrance to the 1896 Rhos pier

Fynach may be traced to those far-off days, but the present building cannot be the original. It may, of course, stand on the site of the monastic dwelling, parts of which may be incorporated. At the end of the 19th century a number of stone-built structures lay between the present house and the sea. These included a fish-house (where fish taken in the weir were stored), a brew-house, bake-house, dairy and cheese-making place, and a laundry, in addition to other out-houses, but at the time of the building of the modern portion of the Rhos Abbey Hotel these were razed.[93] Close by the farm was a duck-pond. One would like to imagine it was the survivor of the monks' fishpond. The Royal Commission on Ancient Monuments, which inspected Rhos Fynach in 1912, dismissed it somewhat summarily as *"a much modernised 18th century house called 'Rhos Fynach'."* A plaque on the face of the western wing bears the imprint: P/RM/TP/1717. It indicates, in all probability, that Thomas Parry, ancestor of the late John Lewis Parry-Evans, was responsible for that erection. One is inclined to feel that portions of the structure are older, and may go back to the time when Robert Dudley, Earl of Leicester, bestowed Rhos Fynach on one of his followers for services rendered, it is said, against the Queen's enemies at sea. The name of this Elizabethan worthy was Morgan ab John ap David, and the Rev. Robert Williams, who alludes to him in his *History of Aberconwy*, adds "of Maesegwig." Lhwyd gives a "Maesygwyg" as a township in Betws-yn-Rhos. The late Mr. Parry-Evans claimed his family had an unbroken descent from Morgan ab John of Rhos Fynach, believing, undoubtedly, that the family had dwelt in that spot ever since Elizabethan days. His conviction was sufficient to impress a Government Commission of Inquiry.

Mr. Parry-Evans' grandfather found in an old chest a rapier of Elizabethan design, believed to belong to Morgan ab John, and with it the charter the Earl of Leicester gave to him. The Rev. Robert Williams, writing in the 1830s, would be more closely in touch with the situation than is possible for us to be today, and he tells us:

"An exclusive grant of all the fisheries along to Morgan ab John ab David of Maesegwig, an ancestor of the present proprietor, Thomas Parry, Esq., of Rhosvynach, by the great Earl of Leicester, who had the lordship of Denbigh. This indenture is dated the 30th of June, 17th of Elizabeth" (AD. 1575).

Leicester's peculiar agreement to allow Morgan ab John to have Rhos Fynach for sixpence *"and for divers other considerations him thereinto moving"* seems to suggest Morgan ab John was so placed that he might watch the Earl's interests. It would be interesting to learn more about so intriguing a character. In the year 1569 there is a *"Bill of Complaint"*[94] to the Queen from one *"Morgan ap John in the Countie of Caernarvon in North Wales, yeoman."* While there is no proof he was our Morgan ab John of Rhos Fynach the coincidence of name, date and county merit attention.

PIRATES OF YNYS ENLLI

Morgan ab John complains that the inhabitants of the county were troubled by reason of *"certayne pirats, arrivinge, commynge and resortinge to thos quarters and confines."* Some of the poor inhabitants, not knowing the malefactors to be pirates had, by favouring them, been indicted as accessories when they were ignorant of what piracy really was. The cause of the trouble was the Squire of Bodvel, *"one John Wyn ap Hughe, man of evill disposition, principall captayne, cheefe and onlie supporter, defender and maynteyner of all the pirates thither comynge fforth."*

This John Wyn ap Hugh owned Ynys Enlli (Bardsey Island) which he had stocked with *"beafes, stiers, wethers and others such lyke"* for victuals for the pirates. Morgan ab John suggests John Wyn ap Hugh should appear before the Star Chamber to answer these charges. Leicester was often in debt and was known to have had unscrupulous dealings. There may be more behind his grant to Morgan ab John than is now apparent.

The Conways of Bryn Euryn

The story of Llys Euryn is resumed in the reign of Henry VI, when Robin ap Griffith Goch of Graianllyn took possession, and turned the ruin into a palatial home. A bard's description is such that one can only conclude the building was very much larger than the existing shell. It gives colour to the supposition that the bushes and turf to the east conceal the remains of demolished walls, parts of which, in fact, have been uncovered. Even when allowance is made for the hyperbole of sycophant bards, the *llys* (it is even termed a "castle" and likened to Caerleon-on-Usk) must have been a building of more than ordinary consequence. Poems by Tudur Penllyn and Guttyn Owain depict its departed glories. Contemplating the verses with a historian's rather than a poet's eye, let us see what information can be extracted. Though Tudur Penllyn's poem is primarily a eulogy of Huw Conway, he begins by stating that Huw's father, Robin *"gave three hundred pounds for a single tower."* There never was a fortress higher than Robin's fortress. The princely hall was not its equal. Never was a castle built more finely. The poet exclaims that for the last year his only occupation has been contemplating the architecture of *"this white image,"* the wall of which was worth a thousand pounds. It was all made of freestone; a white mountain:

> *"Lengthwise beautiful it is, bold and free,*
> *Crosswise in four turrets,*
> *Helmets of lime, like clusters of white wax."*

He speaks of three fair storeys, and adds that in the hall *"which is at once both one and eight"* (whatever that means)[95] there were three painted hangings, presumably tapestries, for *"they have no thread that is not silk,"* and golden twigs are finely interwoven. There is *"lead on top of the hall"* which has eight lofts or chambers *"under the blue speckled ceiling."* That this is our building scarcely admits doubt for Penllyn describes Huw Conway as "the Lord of Rhos," and terms the llys *"the flower of Bryn Euryn."* [96]

Another poem attributed to Tudur Penllyn, but now believed to be the work of Guttyn Owain, claims the chicken delicacy of Huw Conway's court *"is a hundredfold better than that of earls."*[97] Where, now, are the "four turrets"? Where now the "three fair storeys"? Possibly the latter can be accounted for. The arrow-loops and guarderobes testify to a second floor, and a ledge in the southern gable indicates there was an attic. That immediately suggests the existing shell is Robin's "princely hall." Yet would he have built a place without windows? The writer is inclined to believe this building contains much that was originally the *llys* of Ednyfed, considerably restored. Possibly the building occupied by the Elizabethan High Sheriff has been demolished. Of the hundreds of fragments of pottery, which have come to light in the centre of the ruin, not one is earlier than the 17th century. The remains in the bushes may represent a separate building. Instead of solving a problem, excavations have merely produced additional perplexities!

When the Glan Conwy artist Hugh Hughes made a sketch of Llys Euryn for *The Beauties of Cambria,* published in 1823, he depicted the ruins as they are today except for a huge hole which gaped in the back of the fireplace. In 1857 the Editor of *Archaeologia Cambrensis* visited

The romantic ruins of Llys Euryn mark the site of Ednyfed Fychan's home – he was the ancestor of the present Royal family, via the Tudors. Until the site was cleared this year(2001), the old palace had lain more or less forgotten in a bed of brambles since the Llandrillo-yn-Rhos Bijou Opera Company used it as a natural backcloth for their 1929 production (below)

"Ednyfed Fychan", or "the legend of Llys Euryn", which was also shown at the Pier Pavilion

Found in Llys Euryn Ruins: brass shoe buckle, gun-flint, boar's tusk, part of candle-snuffer

what he terms "Llys Eurian." *"A fireplace surmounted by a tall chimney still exists,"* he wrote, *"and has lately been repaired - not, however, in the best archaeological taste."* He mentions a tradition that the perpetuation of *"a family in that district"* depended on how long the chimney stood.

Perhaps Whitehall Dod, owner of the Cayley Estate, had heard of this legend. Robert Roberts, Bryn Cryno, Llangystennin, aged 82 (in 1951), says that when he was a young man a contractor, Tom Williams, of Cae Cenna, told him Mr. Dod instructed him to build up the fireplace to prevent the chimney from collapsing. *"That was before my time,"* added Mr. Roberts, who did, however, recall seeing wallflowers and other garden blooms straggling amid the ruins. The chimney appears to have outlasted the family despite the attempt of mischievous youths who, in about 1920 tried to blow it down with gunpowder. A hole blasted through the back of the fireplace on this occasion was subsequently patched up by order of the local authority. Hughes asserts that Llys Euryn was Ednyfed Fychan's *"favourite residence."* He, too, describes it as *"a large ruined house,"* having, apparently, copied his facts from Pennant.

Traces of courts and rooms could still be made out when, in 1857, the Rev.H.Longueville Jones visited the site; and Richard Fenton, sometime in 1808, saw *"foundations that may be easily traced in all directions."*[98] *"I never saw a place so overrun with the sloe tree,"* comments Fenton, *"which, perhaps, gave name to it."* Fenton was as perplexed as we are to-day, and said the place was:

"of such architecture as puzzles one to decide on its age or use, for though by the chimneys in it it must have been a mansion, yet it appeared not to have any apertures that could be called windows, there appearing none but oblique eyelit holes."

The descendants of Ednyfed Fychan, seneschal of Llewelyn Fawr, probably chosen because he was a member of the largest tribal group in North Wales, were allowed to hold all their widely scattered patrimonies in Rhos and Rhufoniog free of rent. Gronw ap Heilyn, a descendant of Ednyfed, who again was seneschal of Llewelyn II, held the coastal townships of Llysfaen and Penmaen, and in every other township between the Conwy and the Clwyd where he held land, his share was far greater than that of his fellow tribesmen.[99]

Here is the opinion of the Royal Commission who visited the place in 1912:

"On the slope of Bryn Euryn, with a splendid prospect over sea and land, are the ruins of a considerable residence which is called on the Ordnance Sheet 'the palace of Ednyfed Fychan.'

The house had a frontage directly to the south of about 140 ft., and in places the walls are still standing to a height of 12 ft. It would seem that in the direction of dividing it into two or more dwellings, as a wall of which the lower courses are buried beneath debris is carried diagonally across the interior."

The report refers to the remains of *"a fine chimney opening which has been restored within the last century."* It adds the hall was probably open to the roof. The Commission give the frontage as l40ft (not 70ft) so evidently they considered the fragments in the bushes to be part of the original frontage. The work so far achieved seems to prove the 70ft square building was an entire entity. A photograph taken in about 1880 depicts the building as it is today, save that the walls were more heavily mantled with ivy, and the bushes had not developed. A stretch of land to the southward showed grass-covered mounds of what appeared to be foundations extending southwards towards the quarry.

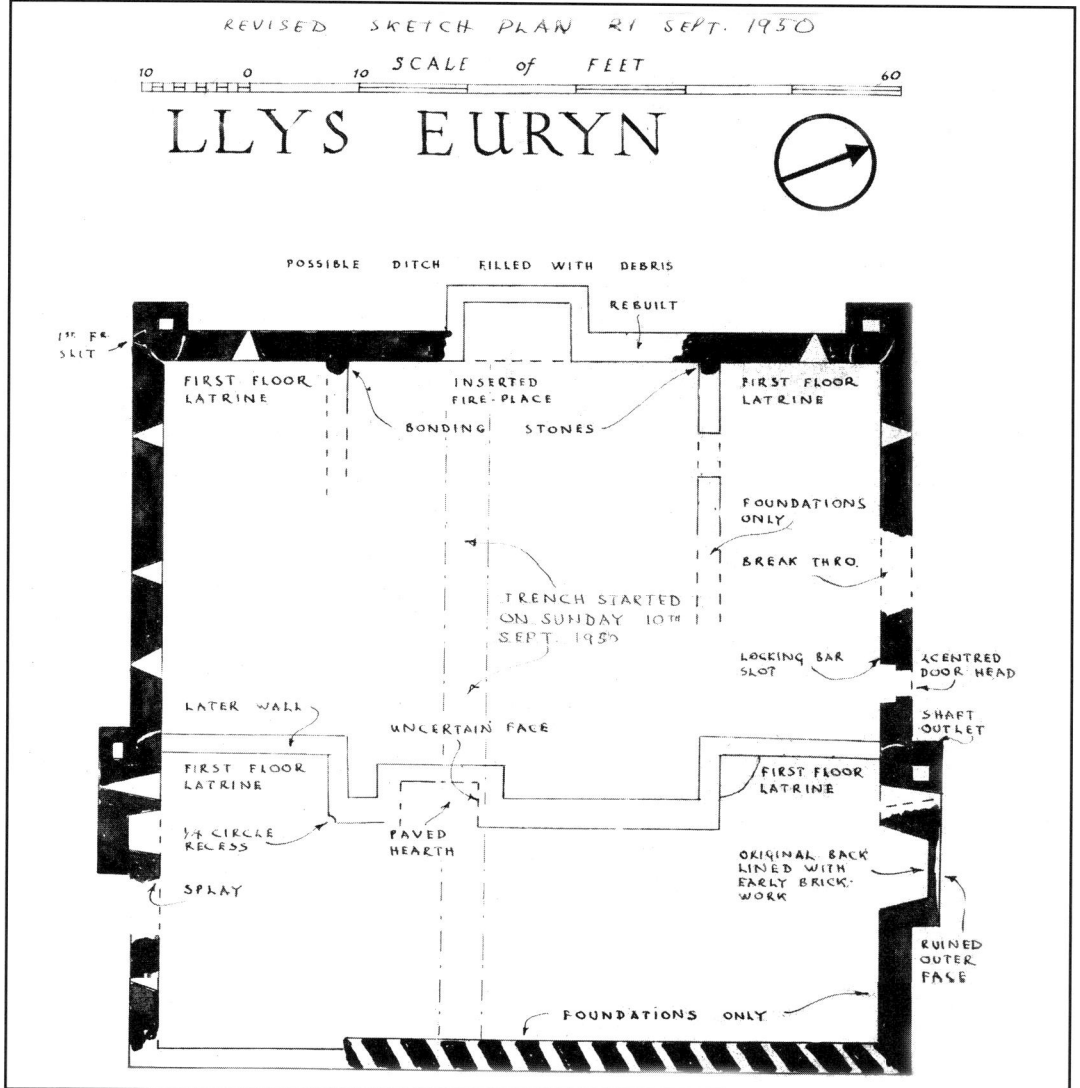

The 2ft wide fragment of a dividing wall to which the Commission refer is not bonded into the south wall. Its foundations, when uncovered, took an erratic course across to the north wall, assuming a 3ft width in places. A bay proved to be paved with heavy red sandstone slabs, with a kerb to match. These were set on red clay. It appears a fireplace had been introduced. The "back" was improvised and contained a medley of limestone, red and yellow sandstone and boulders. One wonders if this was the blocked-up entrance of the original doorway of a three-sided courtyard, the end of which was subsequently shut in by the insertion of the present great fireplace and chimney. At least four periods of roofing slate were indicated by the debris, which ranged from thick shale slabs to modern Bethesda slate.

THE FAMILY OF CONWAY

Reference must now be made to the family of Conway who resided here for two centuries. For the sake of clarity the name will be spelt Conway, though the rendering varies considerably. Tudur Penllyn chose Connway, Lewys Dwnn prefers Konwy, and other spellings include Conwey, Conowey and Conwy. The latter is used by the Bodrhyddan family to whom the Conways of Bryn Euryn were not related. To make matters more confusing, a Conway of Bryn Euryn married the heiress of Plas Nant, near Prestatyn, bringing that into the Conway family, while the Conwy family were but a few miles distant. It was Hugh, the elder, who, according to J. E. Griffith,[100] *"was the first to borrow from the river which bordered his territory the permanent family surname of Conwy."* He quotes the bard, Lewis Glyn Cothi:

> *"O'r afon a elwir Conwy*
> *Ei dir ael hyd ar wy."*

A less indefinite picture of the occupation of Llys Euryn follows its adoption by the Conway family. Ednyfed's *llys* may have lain derelict after Owain Glyndŵr's burning. At all events the excellence of the site attracted the attention of the eldest son of the local chieftain, Griffith Goch, who dwelt at Graianllyn, the old house up the valley to the south of Mochdre. Like Ednyfed Fychan, he traced his ancestry to Marchudd ap Cynan, lord of Abergeleu in the ninth century.

The period represents the last active phase of the old tribal system - days when the lord of a district was a law unto himself; when loyalty to blood ties was more potent than allegiance to constituted authority. Feuds between neighbours were an accepted part of every-day life. This area was densely wooded. The vast "Forest of Snowdon" embraced the counties of Caernarvon, Merioneth and Denbigh Land. Though we know nothing of Griffith Goch's mode of life it is safe to assume it resembled that of his rival, John ap Meredith, who is accorded so vivid a setting by Sir John Wynn, in his *History of the Gwydir Family*. Reading this record one catches a glimpse of those troublous times - a glimpse, as it were, through the haze of smoking thatches in the murky glare of torches.

One sees the struggling figures of armed men - some of them veterans of the French wars - raiding a homestead amid flights of arrows, or lurking in ambush, shaft on cord. Sir John describes his own great grandfather, Meredith ap Ieuan, going to the new church at Dolwyddelen, which he had built. Though he had twenty tall bowmen at his heels, he felt insecure, and despite watchers posted on the hilltops, he never returned the way he came lest he should walk into an ambuscade.

It is against a background such as this we must try to envisage Griffith Goch of Graianllyn and his sons. He does, for a brief moment, step on to the stage of Sir John's history. Griffith Goch was at strife with the powerful family of Thelwal, who dwelt in the Vale of Clwyd. The men of "Gruff' Goch," Sir John tells us:

"being more in number than the Thelwals, drove the Thelwals to take to the castle of Ruthyn for their defence, where theybesieged them untill the seidge was raysed by John ap Meredith, his

soones, and kindred to whome the Thelwals sent for ayde. In that exploite Robert the sonne of John ap Meredith was slayne with an arrow in a wood, within view of the castle of Ruthyn called Coed marchan in revenge whereof many of the other side were slayne, both at that time and afterwards."

Griffith Goch had three sons whose names have come down to us: Robin (the eldest), Hywel and Rhys. The latter is described as *"rector of Disserth,"* which was the old name for Llansanffraid Glan Conwy. They figure in a dramatic episode and though no date is given, the incidents suggest it took place in 1468. The men of Nant Conwy were ardent Lancastrians. Headed by Dafydd ap Jenkin (the "Welsh Robin Hood") and Ievan ap Robert, the warlike ancestor of Sir John Wynn of Gwydir, they burnt the suburbs of Denbigh which was a Yorkist town. In revenge Edward IV ordered Lord Herbert, who later became the Yorkist Earl of Pembroke, to lay waste the counties of Merioneth and Caernarvon, which he did so effectively that the whole of the Conwy Valley, according to Sir John, was reduced to "cold coals," and the marks of burning were on the ruins even in his day. Bearing that in mind, one may read the story set forth by the Rev. Robert Williams:

"During the civil wars between the houses of York and Lancaster, Conwy castle was the scene of much contention. It is recorded, that the friends of one party gained possession of it, while the influential family of Gryffyth Goch, and many equally powerful in the neighbourhood, were in arms for the other; it happened that his son Rhys, who had gone either out of curiosity, or more probably for the purpose of examining the strength of the place, was standing at Tal y sam on the opposite side of the river, when he was slain by an arrow discharged from the castle by Llewelyn of Nannau. As the distance is considerably more than half a mile, this is probably one of the longest shots on record. A few nights after, Robin ab Gryffyth Goch o'r Graianllyn, and his brother Hywel, with their followers, crossed the river to avenge the death of their brother Rhys; they took the castle by escalade, and beheaded the captain."[101]

This dramatic episode is of particular interest to us because it was Robin ap Griffith Goch who built (or restored) Llys Euryn. It was to be the home of his eldest son Hugh (Huw) who was the first to assume the name of Conway. He was known as Hugh "Hên" (the elder) to distinguish him from his grandson, another Hugh, who was buried in Llandrillo Church about 1540.

It will be recalled that Hugh Conway's sycophant bards sang that Robin, in building his fortress, had spent *"three hundred pounds for a single tower."* And now Robin, having avenged his brother Rhys, and seen his eldest son (by his second wife) Hugh, safely settled in a palatial home, fades from our picture.

Not so Hugh. He had married *"Gentle Elsbeth, golden plaited,"*[102] the daughter of Thomas Salusbury of Lleweni, near Denbigh. Her sister Catherine was the wife of Richard ap Howel, the lord of Mostyn, kinsman of Henry, Earl of Richmond, and one of his most puissant supporters. That memorable summer of 1485, when Henry landed at Milford Haven, resolved to put the issue to the sword with Richard III, Hugh Conway was one who was summoned to the Red Dragon banner of Wales. Clad in armour and followed by his retainers, he would have ridden forth from Llys Euryn, and doubtless joined his powerful kinsman of Mostyn, to follow the fortunes of Henry to the battlefield of Bosworth. He became one of the Privy Chamber of the King.[103] It may be that it was to this appointment the bard, Ifan Llwyd Brydydd, refers in his eulogy of Hugh Conway:

"Penaig y tir pan gant ti
Borthoriaeth arbyrth Hari
Ag at dref Lundain hefyd."

Which translates as: *"Chief of the land when thou receivest, The keeper's post on Henry's gates, Also in London town."*

Hugh Conway also received a grant in connection with mines.[104] A Hugh Conway was a trusted messenger between the royal exile in Brittany and his supporters in this country, but was it our Hugh Conway? There appear to have been two Hugh Conways serving Henry, for a knight of that name was Treasurer of Ireland in 1494.[105] There is no mention of any knighthood for Hugh of Bryn Euryn, but it may be assumed that as a loyal adherent of the successful claimant to the throne he was not unrewarded. There are other family links with Bosworth. Hugh Conway's daughter Elizabeth married Morgan Holland (of the Eglwysbach Hollands), who was Sergeant Porter to Henry VII. Lowry, the daughter of Robin's brother Hywel, was the wife of Sir Rhys Fawr of Hiraethog, who bore the Dragon standard at Bosworth, after Sir William Brandon was slain. Sir Rhys (more mutilated in death than ever he was by the swords of his enemies) reposes in effigy in the church at Ysbyty Ifan today, and at his side is Lowry Conway, Hugh Conway's cousin. Alas, there is not sufficient of her features left to show whether she was comely.

Though Henry's Royal Commission (circa 1485) described Llys Euryn as *"much decay'd for want of reparations,"* the building must have been adequately restored, for by Elizabeth's reign it was the home of a High Sheriff - an exalted office which signified more then than it does today. The chief discrepancy between the pedigrees prepared by Dwnn and Griffith seems to be that Dwnn places Harri as the eldest son of Reinallt, whereas Griffith puts Hugh Vychan (the younger) as the eldest son, and Harri of Plas Nant as the third. The Conways specialized in prolific families and it is not surprising that there is confusion. Griffith gives Reinallt's family as Hugh (Vychan), Edward, Harri Wynn, William, Evan, Thomas, David, Edmund, and Elin. Hugh Vychan married twice. By his first wife, Elen, daughter of Sir William Griffith of Penrhyn, he had Edward (the High Sheriff), Annes, Margaret, and Jane (who married Hugh Gwyn Holland of Aberconwy). By his second wife, Annes, daughter of Owen ap Meredith ap Llewelyn ap Hwlkin, he had Catherine (second wife of Th.Vaughan of Pant Glas), Elin, Jonet, Elizabeth, Jane and Ales.

Presumably it was this Hugh Conway who left instructions in his will of 1540 for his body to be *"covered with earth beneath the parish church of Llandrillo."* He left fifty shillings towards the building of a certain approach or porch at the door or entrance of the church, and the remainder of the £5 bequeathed, for the construction of a chancel. A portion of his will, in Latin, appears in *Archaeologia Cambrensis,* 1880. It was witnessed by his eldest son, Edward, who succeeded him, his wife, Elene, the curate D'no Jev'n ap Gruff, and also by his brother, David Lloyd Conway. (It will be noticed there is a David in the pedigree.) If one turns to the copy of the Presentment of 1572 (Record Office) which Mr. Porter gives in the appendix of his book, it shows that "David lloyd Conwey" held the farm called "fferme y Rhiw" with one barn, 150 acres of arable ground, 2 acres of meadow, 16 acres of wood, and 132 acres of waste, which lay between the Eirias Stream on the east and Mochdre on the west, and the lands of William Conway (also mentioned in the pedigree) and Edward Conway (the High Sheriff) on the west side. There is included *"one griste water myll"* and the watercourse thereto.

Here, surely, is the start of Colwyn Bay. One can picture David Lloyd Conway on Bryn Euryn, turning his eyes across the wooded slopes to the south east, and resolving to leave the family home which his nephew had inherited, and fend for himself. Along the old highway which led to the mill at Groes, he found an attractive site. The term Rhiw simply means slope - a most suitable appellation. The writer is inclined to think that the first farm of Rhiw, which David Lloyd Conway built himself, would have stood on the site later occupied by the house called Pwllycrochan. It is doubtful whether the Conways ever "owned" their extensive estates. These appear to have been "Crown lands" leased to the family, and so remained, in all probability, until they were purchased from the Crown by the Davies family of Llannerch. In David Lloyd Conway's day the entire district belonged to the Earl of Leicester, who owned the lordship of Denbigh, and David Lloyd Conway's agreement is with "my Lord" for twenty-one years, at an annual rental of 106 shillings and 8 pence. A David Lloyd Conway was one of the High Constables of Creuddyn in 1550.

Before dealing with Hugh Vychan's son Edward, who became High Sheriff, it might be well to refer briefly to another branch of the family who moved in the direction of Glan Conwy. They, too, could boast a High Sheriff. Hugh Conwy (of Bosworth fame) had a brother John who lived at Plas Ucha and married Nest, daughter of Griffith ap Howel Coetmor (of Gwydir). His sons were William and Owen of Trebwll, Glan Conwy. In 1564 John Thomas, the son of William, was made High Sheriff of Denbighshire, William, at that time dwelling at Y Tyddyn Du, Glan Conwy.[106]

John of Nant Ucha had a grandson who is probably the John Conwey concerned in an early Chancery case before Lord St. John, Keeper of the Great Seal, in the year 1547. This John Conwey stated that about three years before, he had by gift of King Henry VIII, *"a certain farm and land in Dynerth and Rew"* in the county of Denbigh, at a rental of £5 a year. He leased this to one Elis ap Richard, *"a man of great power and kindred,"* who paid rent *"until a quarter of a year last past."* He then refused to pay more and laid waste the land. John Conwey explained he could not be in North Wales to sue for his remedy as he was: *"my Lady Mary's servant, and daily attendant upon her grace here in London."*[107] My Lady Mary could be no other than Princess Mary, soon to be Queen Mary.

John Conway's name is soon after associated with a less regal court. In June 1552 there is an indictment at the Caernarvon Quarter Sessions which sets forth that his room was visited by a female burglar: *"Elsabethe vch Rulange of Rywe in Denbighshire, the wife of Robert ap Gruffithe, yeoman."* She was charged with:

"breaking and entering the house of John Conowey of the town(ship) of Eyrias in the County of Caernarvon, gentleman, and stealing a 'sheett', valued at 3s 4d from the bed of the said John."[108]

With Edward Conway, the family at Bryn Euryn appear to have attained their highest fame. He was well connected. His mother was the daughter of a knight and he married Anne, daughter of Sir John Puleston, High Sheriff in 1543. Edward was elected High Sheriff of Denbighshire in 1565, and of Caernarvonshire in 1576-7. He died in 1599. There are several mentions of his name in connection with lands. In 1579 it is recorded that the Earl of Leicester granted:

"Edward Conway and his heirs, one part of the Marsh called Morfa Dinerth, containing 34 acres of land lying in Dinerth Township between a stream dividing the Counties of Denbigh and Caernarvon."

As this marsh was *"overflowed"* by the sea at spring tides, Mr. Conway *"little minded it,"* and thus no rent was answerable to the Queen or to the Earl.[109] In a document of 1596 the name of Robert Conway, second son of Edward Conway, heads the list of those who volunteered as substitutes for service in the war in Ireland.[110] Sir John Wynn received a letter from Lord Chancellor Egerton's son in behalf of *"lyftenant Conwey"* who, in 1605, desired *"to be brought to trial at the next assize on the charge of killing Captain Owen."*[111] Might this be the *"Thomas Conawy, leften'nt"* who died in 1607 according to the *Bodysgallen Roll*? A duel, perhaps! Among the Catholic recusants in Llandrillo in 1592 there was a Hugh Conway of Rhiw, *"possibly identical with the Hugh Conwy whom the pedigrees describe as of the house of Bryneuryn."* [112]

Edward's heir was another Hugh Conway "of Llys Bryn Euryn." The *Bodysgallen Roll* records that *"Hughe Conway of Brynyryn, Esqr."* died on 28 May 1608. This Hugh Conway married Catherine, daughter of Thomas Bulkeley. He had one brother, Robert, and his sisters were: Elen, Catherine, Jane, Elizabeth, Margaret[113] and Ann, all of whom married. Elizabeth married William Hookes of Conwy - a name famous in that borough in Stuart times. Hugh's heir was Reinallt Conway and his other children were: Edward, John, Mary, Catherine, Ambrosia, Dorothy, Jane and Elizabeth. It is stated that the last of the family to occupy Bryn Euryn were *"the Ladies Conway."* Here are ladies in abundance to support the claim!

A record of Charles I mentions *"the Escheate lands of Dynnerth and Rhiwe in the tenure of John Conwey and Robert Conwey."*[114] John Conway of Rhiwe died in 1614, according to the *Roll*, and a Pyers Conway of Rhiwe died on 19 March 1623. Mention is made of Reinallt Conway's estate in the legal transactions connected with its acquisition by Robert Davies of Llannerch, so it is possible that the women were unable to keep up the property and were obliged to sell.

The purchaser of the Bryn Euryn estate appears to have been Robert Davies of Llannerch, whose father was Mutton Davies, and grandfather Robert Davies of Gwysaney, in Flintshire. One wonders whether there was some family connection between the families of Davies of Gwysaney and the Conways of Bryn Euryn. In the Gwysaney Papers, among the records of sales of land, is a transaction by:*"Robert ap Rynald ap Gruff, ap Res and Elizabeth, daughter of Reynold Conwey, wife of the said Robert."* The date is 1536. It will be noted that the Hugh Conway of Bryn Euryn, who died circa 1540, was the son of Reinallt Conway.

During the Civil War, one Robert Davies, High Sheriff for Flintshire, held Gwysaney Hall near Mold for King Charles until he surrendered it to Sir William Brereton on 12 April, 1645. He was a minor when his father died in 1636, and his guardians were Lieut-Colonel Thomas Davies (his uncle), Constable of Hawarden Castle, and Sir Peter Mutton, of Llannerch Park, near Trefnant, Chief Justice of North Wales. Sir Peter Mutton purchased Bryn Euryn from Rheinallt Conway on 18 March 1629/30.[115] Robert married Sir Peter Mutton's daughter, for whom Bryn Euryn may have been her dowry. Their heir, named Mutton Davies, inherited Llannerch. His eldest son, who was given the family name of Robert, married the sister of the first Viscount Lisburne. The nature of the transaction has not yet been discovered, but the family possessed land in this vicinity, for Robert's father, Mutton Davies, in his will of 14 Feb, 1684, leaves to his son Richard for life:*"that messuage called Ty given with the lands belonging thereunto in the parishes of Llandrillo and Llansanfraido."* This "Ty given" must be "Ty Gwyn" near Mochdre. If "Gwyn" was spelt "gwin" a copyist unfamiliar with the district might easily transcribe it "given." The land, it adds, was mortgaged to him by Nicholas Bettridge. Edward Lhwyd mentions a "Nic. Bertridge" as owning lands in Llanelian. The will also refers to household goods *"now in Plarissa in Llansandraid"* – doubtless Plas Isa.[116]

Reference has already been made to the lawsuit over Penrhyn Marsh, between Mr. Davies of Bryn Euryn and the Pughs of Penrhyn (Old Hall), which began in 1689. The writer has not yet been able to discover the outcome, but Mr. Davies undoubtedly experienced "the Law's delay." A letter[117] written in 1692 by a J. Calcott mentions:*"there is two other Surveys appertaining to Reynold Conway's estate, which I remember I wrote you word on. But nothing belonging to this Marsh of Morva Dynerth."* Another letter written by Mr. Davies' legal adviser, Edward Peirce, is obviously that of a man on intimate terms with his client. He tells Mr. Davies he must *"putt in a bill in ye High Court of Chancery."*

He meant the Chancery*"in the Excheq'r Chamber being more proper there for reliefe since you pay the King soe great a rent as £6 in Dinerth (as I am told) and it is presumed probable yt ye rent reserved upon yo'r graunt of E(arl):Leic(ester) being £2-16. is pte of ye £6. And then have you paid all y'r rent in yo'r wrong since yo'r Auncestory purchase, however This will have a just countenance in a court of Equity."*

He promised Mr. Davies he would hammer out such a rough piece of a Bill that a good workman with polishing would *"make it hold out a good suite & you be settled in yo'r possession for ever after."* He promised also an Injunction *"to prevent their breaking up of the Marsh & soweing it."* Mr. Peirce proceeds:*"I will send you a rough draught of a Bill in a few daies wch after you have p'used shall be sent to be polished in London by some curious honest Lawyer (if possible to meet such)."*

He confessed there was a little concern of his own in the matter *"wch must be setled before I can well shoote off all my shaftes"* He could not be *"soe exactly vigorous"* until it was settled. The matter was he owed Mr. Pugh's aunts £118, as he then confesses :

"I gott at St. Asaph Adm'stracon for one, John Williams, a Tennt of Mr. Holland, But by Tricking & ye P'rogative Court extorting a Jurisdiction to themselves that they ought Not to have assumed, & my nowe Lord Bp of Assaph would not minde it Mr. Pugh hath gott an

Administration. But yet ye Estate of his Aunts is to be shared & divided between both, onely Mr. Pugh hath but ye name if he bee just & honest. Now my Question (unlucky upon me) is whose debtor I shal be of the Two, if Mr. Pughs I must forthwth raise the money & pay him. If it happens that John Williams hath me his, then I have paid neere 30£ And I shall have time to looke about me, but paid they shal be (god willing) however."

After this pious resolve Mr. Peirce returns to the business of the lawsuit. *"As to ye sueing for our damage for ye stopping ye fresh water It cannot come to be tried till Spring Vacacon And I may begin at any time before ye 1st of January. This is the onely Iron I forebore to put in the fire at present till I heare ye successe how they divide the Estate of the Aunts & whose debtor I am."*

These two letters do not carry us much farther in finding out about the disposal of the estate, but they do throw a light on legal procedure of those far-off days.

In April 1625 Harry Conway of Nant died, and the *Calendar of Wynn Papers* (No.1391) contains a reference to the composition in the Court of Wards for Sir Roger Mostyn for the wardship of Henry Conwey of Nant's daughter. She married Sir Roger's son, Robert Mostyn. John Conway's son, Owen, who went to Trebull, Glan Conwy, had a son John, whose son assumed the name of Meredith Lloyd, and married Catherine, daughter of Hugh Conway (Vychan) of Bryn Euryn. Janssen in his map of 1646 marks "Brynyryn" so the house was then obviously of consequence. Pennant states that the "Ladies Conway" were the last occupiers of Llys Euryn, presumably in the reign of Charles II.

By 1687 "Mr. (?Robert) Conway" had conveyed the marsh of Dynerth to Robert Davies of Llannerch. A Robert Conway is mentioned in the Hearth Tax as dwelling in Rhiw about this date. In the north aisle of Llandrillo Church is a tombstone inscribed:*"Underneathe lyeth the body of Robert Conway of Pwllycrochan, Gent; was buried here by leave of Robert Davies, Esq., 1693."* [aged 75].

When a plan of the Bryn Euryn estate was made for Robert Davies in 1765 Llys Euryn is plainly indicated, and one assumes it was still occupied. In ten years, however, Pennant speaks of it as a large ruined house. The amount of crockery recently unearthed confirms the belief that it was occupied well into the 18th century. Much of the filling which banks the walls of Llys Euryn was probably tipped there by quarrymen early last century.

For further details of Catherine Conway, wife of Henry Vaughan, see the lecture by Dr. R. T. Jenkins, *Some Pages in the History of Pant Glas, Ysbyty Ifan*, Caernarvonshire Historical Society's Transactions, Vol. X.

The *Calendar of Wynn Papers* refers to a "Mistress Margaret Vaughan at the Glynne in Caernarvonshire" in 1658. Glyn is in Eirias, and Eirias was then in Caernarvonshire. The letter is from a lawyer in Shrewsbury - she came of a Shropshire family - and concerns £450 which the writer has *"in readiness to set forth for her daughter."* (2171).

There appears to have been a family connection between the Conways of Bryn Euryn and the Wynns of Gwydir, for Sir John Wynn, in his *History*, says: *"Rhys ap Howell ap Rys his sonne, cosen german to my great grandfather Meredith ap Jevan ap Robert"* married as his second wife *"Margaret, daughter of Hugh Conway, the elder."*

THE NEW ORDER

The close of the Elizabethan Age brings one phase of life in this district to an end. Times of strife presumably had ended. Castles were crumbling. Manor houses of the newly made landed gentry enlivened the countryside. Farms took on a more substantial appearance. Enough has been written to indicate that from the Edwardian invasion the place names with which we are familiar were in use: LHYS VAEN, EYROS, PENMAN, MOUGHTRIE, LHYDCOYT, LHAN ELIAN, COLOYNE, DYNNARTH (later LLANDRIGHLA). Every township is accounted for. These practically coincide with the boundaries of the Borough of Colwyn Bay as they exist today. The link with the distant past is forged, and now comes the time to depict the countryside slowly developing, as the more civilized life of its scattered manors and farms was made manifest.

PART TWO

THE RISE OF THE MODERN COMMUNITY

Colwyn Bay seen from the air in 1963 before the building of the A55 expressway. The ring of trees encircled the railway goods yard, now the Bay View Shopping Centre

THE DAWN OF MODERN TIMES

To form an idea of what Colwyn Bay looked like in the seventeenth century it would be desirable to choose a vantage point some distance inland, say, in the neighbourhood of Dolwen. There one beholds a vista of undulating countryside with groves in the hollows and tufts of furze on rocky slopes, meandering brooks, an isolated manor house, and here and there, amid the green, the white-washed walls of farmhouse or cottage. The highway must be little better than a rutted lane, narrow, possibly hedged in places, though hedges were not then as frequent as they are today. The cattle and sheep that grazed would be lean, for selective breeding was not yet contemplated. A beaten track would lead to the well without which no community could exist. The estates commenced by astute Tudor ancestors had acquired an appearance of permanency. Houses of consequence were being built - the comfortable, sometimes pretentious, homes of men who aspired to have graven on their tombstones those select appendages "Esq." or "Gent."

It was a simple and placid existence, self-supporting as far as possible. Rustics who plied a trade did so with an eye to making their contribution to the community, for their livelihood depended on inter-dependence. For sport there was the lucrative hunting of marauding foxes or polecats. Vestry-books of both Llandrillo and Llysfaen tell of many a half-crown expended as bounty for each fox slain. As late as the 19th century, pack animals were used, and a string of donkeys might have been seen bearing panniers filled with merchandise, or kegs containing drinking water, to the heights of Llysfaen or Penrhynside. Occasionally traffic would pass leisurely along the Old Highway, the ancient military road between the Edwardian boroughs of Rhuddlan and Conwy. Lhwyd has left us an informative list of the houses of importance round about Llysfaen and Llanelian. It is surprising how many of our more substantial farms were then the residences of the gentry. In the seventeenth century a number of Vaughans were still in the vicinity and one feels a certain confidence in assuming they were descendants of Ednyfed Vychan, whose name, long before this, was thus anglicized. There was a Vaughan at Plas Newydd, Llysfaen, in 1675.

On the whitewashed plaster of a discoloured wall of an outhouse at Glyn farm, is modelled a crude ring containind the initials IV and date 1620. The initials are doubtless those of John Vaughan, father, maybe, of the Henry Vaughan recorded on the lych-gate of Llandrillo Church in 1677. These Vaughans were connected with the Pant Glas Vaughans. Henry Vaughan may have been the son of Major Henry Vaughan, who was killed at Hopton Castle in 1644, and might also have been the Cavalier Captain Henry Vaughan, from Llandrillo. In Llandrillo churchyard there is a tombstone telling of the death in 1699 (in her 92nd year) of Margret Vaughan *"wife to Henry Vaughan of Glyn."* A coat of arms carries a rampant lion impaled with the wife's arms. The charge on the shield of the Vaughans of Llysfaen was a rampant lion. This can be faintly discerned in the centre of the tombstone of *"John Vaughan, gentleman,"* of Plas Newydd. Lhwyd mentions a William Vaughan at Plas Newydd in 1699.

If the local Vaughans were descended directly from Ednyfed Fychan, one would expect to find as their coat-of-arms the familiar "Pen Sais," or the later equivalent, three closed helmets. It is significant that the Vaughans of Glyn and the Vaughans of Llysfaen have on their tombstones a rampant lion. According to Pennant this was the badge of Marchweithian, Lord of Is-aled, founder of the eleventh tribe, who bore, in a shield *gules,* a lion rampant *argent,* armed *azure.* Pennant gives, as one of the descendants in the extinct or female line, the Vaughans of Llysfaen. Another of the line was the renowned Catherine of Berain, who claimed Tudor ancestry.

Glyn appears to be one of our oldest inhabited houses. Alderman D. O Williams, J.P., of Old Colwyn, considers that the 1620 portion was built on the site of a still older dwelling, and that the demesne included Ty Mawr and Peulwys. Near the top of Glyn's front door is a carved stone with a flat top. It is so weathered and coated with whitewash as to be well nigh unrecognizable, but it resembles the face of a man with a drooping moustache. So incongruous is it that one wonders whether it was removed from another situation. Nearby a small stone appears to have once recorded a date that might be 1667 or 1687.[118]

HEARTH TAX

A record of the Hearth Tax of this area indicates its rural character in the reign of Charles II. The list, in the Public Record Office, shows that in "Mouchtrey" township there were 20 hearths; "Dinarth" 25, "Riw" 13, "Lloydcoll" 17, "Killgwynn" 13. "Towynnan" was the largest with 39.

Of particular interest to us is the statement that in Dinerth township "Mr. Mutton Davies" paid tax on 12 hearths in three houses, while Robert Conway paid for two hearths in "Riw" township. This seems to indicate that Mutton Davies, of Llannerch, near St.Asaph (his mother's home) had by this time acquired Llys Euryn, and that Robert Conway had moved to Rhiw (or Pwllycrochan). Unfortunately no house names are given. In Dinerth township Harry Moston and Thomas Holland strike a familiar note, and Thomas Holland also pays for 4 hearths in Twnnan township, with one other in dispute. Evidently this refers to one of the Hollands of Teirdan.

The remainder of Rhiw township is as follows:

	hearthes
Rhiw township brought over	4
Pd. Richard Cadwalider	1
Pd. Jane John	1
Pd. Edward William	1
Ann William vacant	1
Pd. Harry William Pugh	1·
Pd. Robert Conway	2 (Pwllycrochan)
ditto another in dispute ...	1
Pd. William David	1
Total	13

From this one infers there were the following number of houses with hearths in the following townships: Mochdre, 14 houses; Rhiw, 12; Dinerth, 14; Cilgwyn, 10; Twnnan, 24; Llwydcoed, 15. Thus it will be noticed that, as in the *Survey* of Edward III's reign, the Twnnan and Llwydcoed area appears more populated than the Rhiw, Dinerth, Mochdre area.

Hearth Tax return for the townships of Mochdre, Dinerth and Rhiw, circa 1663

SCATTERED HAMLETS

Before the seventeenth century reached its close one catches a reflection of the district through Edward Lhwyd's eyes. Not only does he specify the houses of consequence, the commons and the wells, but he describes the hamlets. Betws, he tells us, was a village of nine houses, Llanddulas had five or six cottages, but Llysfaen had *"only two or three near the church,"* and at Llanelian there were *"but four or five houses near the church."* These must have included the inn, the White Lion, whose sign perpetuates the rampant lion of the Hollands of Teyrdan nearby - a place (Lhwyd points out with pardonable pride) worth £300 a year!

The houses of note in 1699, which Lhwyd lists, are:

Llysfaen: Ty Mawr, Pentregwyddel, Plas Newydd, Ty Ucha, Pen-e-Geuffus, Plas-yn-Llysfaen (also known as Plas yr Escob), IsaIlt and Peulwys (Tilehouse). And lesser houses: Plas Sion ap Gronw, Pwll Morkyn and Tydbryn Heilin.

Llanelian: Y Plas (belonging to Lord Willoughby), Teirdan, Pentre, Tan-y-Lan, Pentarad, Twnnan (Ucha, Ganol and Isa) Lhetty dy, Fernant, Glyn, Coed Coch ucha. (The Glyn referred to is near Coed Coch, not Eirias.)

The earliest statistics of population the writer has been able to discover are contained in a Rural Dean's report (now in the National Library of Wales) of about 1685, in which the names of all "housekeepers" in the parish of Llandrillo-yn-Rhos are set forth with *"ye number of all souls in ye family without names."* That is, the name of the head of the household is given, a figure denotes how many are in that household, and the ages of all under 18 years are set down. The total is 425. This is made up of the townships of Dinerth, 76 souls; Rhiw, 54; Kilgwun, 28; Bochdre, 99; Colwun, 20; Eirioes, 103, and Llwydcoed, 72. The actual word looks like "Llandcood," but the probability is that it is Llwydcoed. Llanelian numbers 318, and a comparison of the totals will indicate how scattered the population of "Colwyn Bay" was in those days. The Dinerth list is headed by "Mr." Henry Vaughan (of Dinerth), and the Rhiw list by "Mr." Robert Conway - evidently the Robert Conway of Pwllycrochan buried at Llandrillo in 1693. These are the only two who are distinguished by the prefix "Mr." The Eirias list accords first place to "Mrs. Vaughan, wid(ow)." She would have been the wife of Henry Vaughan of Glyn. Dinerth was taken by their eldest son, apparently (from the name in the church register) also called Henry. The Llwydcoed return contains the name of an "Ellin Conway, wid(ow)," possibly the Elin Conway of the Llys Euryn pedigree.

The names of popish recusants were: Mauris Wynne, Mary Wynn alias Woodcock, and Jane Pue alias Williams. Mauris Wynne was excommunicated. He was probably of Graianllyn. Note the first name in Mochdre hearth-tax return.

Eighteenth century parsonages were thatched. The churches had flagged floors over which rushes were spread, there were pews for the more opulent and benches for the poor, walls were whitewashed. Llanelian possessed no rectory, but houses were provided for the incumbents at Llandrillo and Llysfaen. The population of the three places was approximately the same. A visitation return of 1738 gives: Llanelian 75 families, and Llysfaen 63 families. A return for 1745 puts Llandrillo at 80 families. There were "no dissenters."

As a result of the "Forty-five" rebellion a watchful eye was kept for possible disloyalty and the Rural Dean's contemporary report contains such passages as: *"I never heard he was suspected for disaffection to his present Majesty,"* or *"he has a good character for hearty affection towards the present government."*

Despite his disgrace, Sir John Wynn clung tenaciously to his Llysfaen land, for his son, Sir Richard, the second baronet, mentions *"lands in the parish of Llusvaine"* in the will he drew up shortly before the outbreak of the Civil War.

THE CIVIL WAR

Though the clash between Charles and Parliament brought armed warriors to these parts, there is a discouraging dearth of information about their doings. A few miles away, across the Penrhyn Marsh, there was activity enough in the homes of the squires. One knows about Colonel Hugh Wynne, of Bodysgallen, Colonel Roger Mostyn and Archbishop John Williams, at Gloddaeth, Captain Robert Pugh, of Penrhyn (Old Hall), but of the Hollands of Teyrdan, the Conways of Bryn Euryn, and the Vaughans of Glyn - all men of fighting stock - there is so far no obvious record. Yet men of these parishes must have been included in the 250 levied for the King's forces, who assembled at Wrexham on the last day of February 1643/4.[119] Lord Byron surrendered Chester to the Parliament on 3 February 1645/6. The articles of surrender (in which Colonel Wynne of Bodysgallen participated) required that the defenders: *"shall have liberty to march to Conway, and five days are allowed them to march thither, with a convey of two hundred horse."*

Lord Byron's brother, Colonel Gilbert Byron, was at Rhuddlan as Governor, so it is safe to assume his lordship marched that way. The Royalists could not have reached Conwy save by the Old Highway. The imagination catches a glimpse of these ragged, emaciated, indomitable warriors stumbling along the road under our woods. Just before the surrender, men of North Wales, inspired by Archbishop Williams, made a resolute effort to relieve the loyal city. There was a rendezvous on Denbigh Green, where Sir William Vaughan was mustering loyalists from the Border castles. Mytton's Parliamentarians surprised and defeated them on 1 November 1645. Men from this district were in that battle. Professor A. H. Dodd has discovered among the Brogyntyn Collection, which Lord Harlech deposited in the National Library of Wales, a letter from Archbishop Williams to Sir John Owen, the Cavalier colonel who supplanted him as governor of Conwy. It is dated 28th October - a few days before the battle. Apparently it was hoped this district would contribute 240 men, but :

"of all the 200 foot and 40 horse agreed upon there was at the rendezvous in Croes yn irias scarce 40 men, and all those naked (i.e., unarmed) sent by Sr. Will. Williams from about Carnarvon. The fault clealye is this, that there were noe Captaynes appointed by the Commissioners, nor was it fitt or inst. any other shold name them - Volunteers from Sr. William Thomas and my selfe there marched over the Foryd (if non be returned backe) 100 and noe more. And these, by this direction hereinclosed, will be at Ruthinland this night. It may be well, the foote were so inconsiderable and so hardly gott together, that they were not fitt for you to covett the command of — But if you hadd beene pleased, to take command of the Horse, I doe believe we could (with addition of volunteers) have made you a Bodie of 80 horse or more, if they in the upper part of the Country would make any considerable advance."

The forty foot soldiers probably marched up Groes Road to Llanelian and Betws-yn-Rhos, on their way to Denbigh. Groes yn Eirias was a most convenient spot for the rendezvous.

EARLY ROADS

A memorandum of the proceedings of the Petty Sessions of 26 October 1616, mentions *"overseers of the poor."* The Sessions' business included the granting of certificates to alehouses and making arrangements for keeping the highways and bridges in "Llysvaen" and "Erioes" in repair. In "Llysvaen," runs the memorandum, *"there are no impotent old people, vagrants or bastard children."*[120]

The overseers for the work of repairing the highways were Robert Wynn, William Holland and Robert Coitmor. Lhwyd tells us there was no coal nearer than Llanasa, twelve miles away from Llysfaen, and people burnt gorse and wood unless they could fetch coal. Use was made of the local limestone. Apparently the lime it produced was spread on farm fields. The population increased slowly. There would not have been a thousand souls in the entire parish of Llandrillo-yn-Rhos. A more settled state is apparent towards the close of the century. Possibly the war had turned men's thoughts to less materialistic matters, for gifts to the Church are recorded in increasing numbers. The Justices of the Peace wielded more power than now. They, with the incumbents and churchwardens, would have been largely responsible for the management of local affairs. Each parish dealt with its poor as it thought fit, for (as Professor A. H. Dodd points out), it was possible for each parish to interpret the Elizabethan Act according to its own convenience. What made compulsory poor rates unnecessary was that population was still small enough for all men to be neighbours.[121]

Perusal of the records of Llandrillo, Llanelian and Llysfaen parishes brings to mind forgotten acts of benevolence. As far back as 1727 Elizabeth Edwards, of Ty Gwyn, Mochdre, left money for distribution among the poor and the education of four children. A silver chalice, weighing 21ozs, was given in 1608 by Thomas Edwards, Gent. Was he, one wonders, an ancestor of the altruistic lady of Ty Gwyn? Then there is the Charity of William Butler of Ty Mawr, Llysfaen, the gift of a sundial at Llandrillo in 1755 by Mary Jervis of Dinerth and other benefactions which will be traced in due course. Anyone who doubts the greatness of heart of these good folk should read the painted board which hangs on the wall of Llanelian Church.

APPENDIX
RURAL DEAN'S VISITATION

An account of the ecclesiastical state of the Deanery of Rhos in 1729, by the Rev. Thomas Wynne, now reposes in the National Library of Wales. Here are some of the comments following his visit to Llandrillo-yn-Rhos on August 20th:

"The Vicar preaches in his own Church every other Sunday. He often summon's ye Youth of his Parish to be catechized but none come's in Lent.

They want an English Bible in Folio, and a welsh comon prayer with cannons and articles.

They want a cover to ye Font.

The comunion table & carpet is much damaged & very indecent.

They want a poor's Box & a pulpit Cushion.

They have three Doors upon ye Church, two of them old and ruinous.

The Church Fabrick is in good Repair it is ye handsomest built Church in ye Deanery, but ye Pews within it are irregular, & ye common Benches mean and scandalous.

The west end of ye wall want's to be white-washed.

They have no silver plate but one Chalice and Cover.

They have a well-built steeple which would contain four or five Bells but there is only one in it & the wheel, frame and Clapper of it want mending.

The Vicar lives in his Glebe-house, & occupies his glebe land, which is worth about four pounds pr. ann. The Grass of ye Churchyard is valued at fourty shillings a year. The Glebe house consist's of six Bays & is in tolerable Repair, saving that it want's a little Thatching. The Barn, being four Bays, wants thatching & ten yards of ye side wall are ruinous & want Repair."

The report of the Rural Dean in 1749 (Rev. David Lloyd) stated:

"Mr. John Gwyn, a Southwales man, is Vicar. He has but a mean character for Learning and he is thought not to have lived over temperate - I never heard he was suspected of disaffection to his present Majesty - He never was at an university, but Serv'd for some years as Chaplain to a small Coaster in Queen Anne's Wars & was presented to this Living by the Lord Chancellor - which is worth near 80 lb. a year (i.e.£80).

The Chalice is large & marked near the Brim - I will receive the Cup of Salvation & call upon the name of the Lord - and below, Given to the Church of Llandriilo by Thomas Edwards, gentl. Prime die Marti, 1608.

The plate is of about 6 Inches Diameter & seems to be as Old as the Chalice. One large Pewter flagon and Plate.

The Service is all Welch.

The steeple is good and contains 4 bells.

Mr. Gwyn has a Glebe of about 4 lb. a year - he lives in the house wch, as well as the outhouses, is in good Tenantable repair - The fences and hedges are in unexceptionable order."

The Coaching Era

It would seem there was little development in this district until the first turnpike trust opened up the road from Abergele to what is now Llandudno junction, in the 1760's.[122] The turnpike encouraged travel, broadening the outlook of the inhabitants, and making progress not only possible but inevitable. Among the eighteenth-century wayfarers who paused at Penmaen Head, to look down upon the crescent sweep of our bay, would have been Dean Swift, Dr. Samuel Johnson, Thomas Pennant and the Rev. John Wesley. As this century advanced there was greater activity on the part of the incumbents and wardens. Overseers were appointed annually by the vestry to act (in a voluntary capacity) as collectors of the Poor Rate. As early as 1772 these vestry meetings were held at the *Four Crosses* Inn, which existed before a regular coaching service was in force. A George II halfpenny was found on the site of the *Four Crosses* Inn by Mrs. Jill Bardsley, whose house, Birchlands, now occupies the land. One wonders why Llandrillo parishioners chose to toil up the hill when The Ship was at their church gate. Known locally as "Y Llan," the aged hostelry is depicted in a painting. It was a small, squat, whitewashed structure with a wind-clipped hawthorn bowing over its low roof.[123] Built by Robert Davies in 1736 it remained until 1874, when it was demolished because Whitehall Dod had erected a more modern Ship, across the road.

CARE OF EARLY ROADS

Some official care of public roads was taken in James I's reign, for in 1616 the Petty Sessions levied £10 towards the repairing of the highways in the whole commote of Creuddyn, which would have included Eirias and Llysfaen. The age of many of the local roads must remain a matter of surmise. It is certain that those which lead to such places as Glyn and Teyrdan can have changed but little with the passing years. Roads to pre-Reformation churches must be old indeed. Groes Road bears every mark of antiquity. Possibly it took its name from a roadside cross. Ancient references to "Groes yn Eirias" indicate it was a well-known landmark. Though no trace remains of a cross, it is known that stocks stood on the spot, for the Vestry Books of Llandrillo mention £1 expended on "the New Stocks at Groes" in 1777.

There was some system of "posting" through this district early in the seventeenth century, for in 1623 a petition was made to the Justices by the Post Master of Beaumaris, who said he had been *"carrying the King's packet to Conwy"* for twenty years. One assumes the packet was forwarded to Chester by the Old Highway.

If further confirmation of a road through Colwyn Bay is needed it will be found in a letter which Sir Roger Mostyn wrote from Mostyn, to his father-in-law, Sir John Wynn at Gwydir, on 19 May 1624. Sir Roger refers to *"clearing the way under Llandulas towards Penmayn,"* and he begs his father-in-law *"to give Evan Jones charge to mend the way both above and under Penmayn, for a coach, lest the weather be foul, so that if they may not take one way they may be sure of the other."*[124] Not only does this prove there was at least one coach in North Wales in James I's day, but that roads existed above and under Penmaen Head, and both were sufficient to accommodate a coach. "Way" may be idiomatic, or it may indicate a track which did not merit the designation of road. There exists today a broad stony path from the cliff top down to the eastern hollow where the tunnel begins. This was the spot where (it is believed) Northumberland's men-at-arms lurked to ambush Richard II. The track has a primitive appearance and may well be the "way" up which three pairs of sturdy horses laboriously drew the Mostyn family coach. The steepness of the incline makes it understandable that the rock-face road would be preferable if weather was favourable.

There is no possibility of the Old Highway's having been constructed as part of a turnpike scheme. A map of 1720, in the possession of Arthur Clegg of Gwydir Castle, shows the road starting from the Conwy Ferry and passing through "Bochdre," where it crosses the Afon Ganol at the foot of the road which leads past "Grauanllin." It continues to "Groesyneiroes." From here it slants to the coast. Of particular interest is the naming of The Dingle. Though now known as the Eirias Stream it was, in 1720, the "Afonrhiw." The map records Llandrillo, Penrhyn, Glynn, Pwllycrochan (sic), Llysvaen and Penmaenrhoss.

The Caernarvonshire county boundary is traced from a spot near the foot of our present Rhos Road. The "island" of Caernarvonshire in Denbighshire included Eirias as well as Llysfaen. It starts from the east bank of the Eirias Stream and finishes at the Llanddulas stream.

Afon Ganol widens into something resembling a small lake just before it reaches the coast, and it finds its way to the sea through a short straight cut which might be artificial.

Before John Ogilby (who rejoiced in the appellation *"The King's Cosmographer"*) published his renowned road-book with its quaint strip maps in 1675, he must have passed near our border patiently recording the mileage measured by the assistants who trundled his "wheel dimensurator." But he did not come by way of the coast.

Preceding page: *An early painting of Llandrillo Church, showing the Ship Inn, demolished in 1874, and the old vicarage on the right. The Inn was built by Robert Davies in 1736: the vicarage by Rev. Isaac Charles in 1762*

The Coaching Era

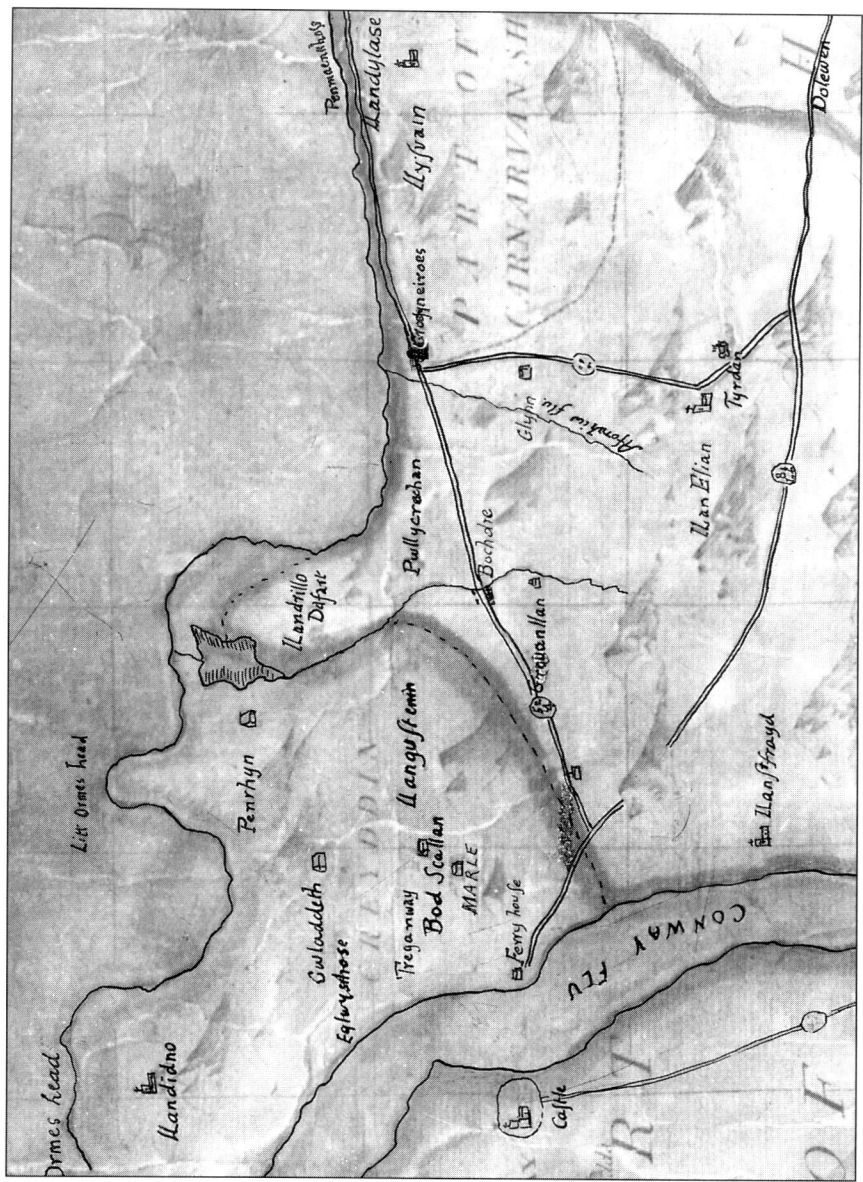

This map plainly shows the Old Highway running from the Conwy ferry house, through Mochdre and Groes-yn-Eirias to Penmaenrhos in 1720. The original belonged to Arthur Clegg of Gwydir Castle. Photographing a small section of a large wall-map. faded by over two centuries' exposure, presented difficulties and it has been necessary to outline the principal features for reproduction.

It will be noticed how the original county boundary joined the sea near the foot of Rhos Road, and how the Afon Ganol, after broadening into what appears to be a small lake, enters the sea by a straight cut. Local houses marked are Pwllycrochan, Glynn, Greuanllan, Groesynairoes and Tyrdan. Groes Road is marked, also the road from Dolwen to the ferry mentioned by Ogilby.

The favoured way from Chester was then by Denbigh, after which the route went through Henllan, Llannefydd, Betws-yn-Rhos, Dolwen and Groesffordd. The latter is now the insignificant crossroads south of the house Bryn Eisteddfod. A branch joined our "Old Highway" at Dolwyd. From Groesffordd, the route went by way of Sarn-y-Mynach to the Ferry opposite Conwy.

An old route that is apt to be forgotten is that which crosses the ford at Rhyd-y-Foel and ascends past Isallt to Llysfaen. From Llysfaen Common it descended in front of Ty Mawr into what is now Peulwys Lane and down to Colwyn. This, the only way from Llysfaen, is clearly shown in the Tithe Map of Llysfaen made in 1839. The lower portion is now built over but some hedgerows can still be traced. How few and bad the roads were when James I was King is indicated in another letter from Sir Roger Mostyn to Sir John Wynn. He asks if there is a possibility of a coach journeying from Gloddaeth to Gwydir for there is an old lady *"who can hardly ride."* His cousin tells him *"there is a way from Bochtrey* (Mochdre) *to come along the mountains, but the writer knows it not."*[125]

The inland route for coaches was not the only one. The Earl of Clarendon, journeying from Chester in 1685, spent the night of 28 December at St. Asaph. The next morning he wrote: *"We are now going to Conway which is fourteen miles from hence, and will take up five hours to go it."* A walking pace all the way! His coaches and baggage-waggon were ferried across the Conwy. Thomas Barker said the fashionable traveller of the 17th century *"had to have a guide to make his way from Chester over the mountains to Conway."* Apparently public coaches of a sort passed from Chester to Bangor in Commonwealth days. Dr. R.J. Heatherington, of Birmingham City Museum, is reported in *The Birmingham Post* of 12 January 1950, as saying:

"The first transport vehicle serving Birmingham was a coach which, in 1657, passed through on its way to Chester and Holyhead."

"It was not until 1776," writes Professor Dodd, *"that the enterprising landlord of the White Lion, Chester, turned dreams into sober realities by putting a flying post-chaise on the road to carry passengers daily (Sundays excepted) to Holyhead for the sum of two guineas each."*[126]

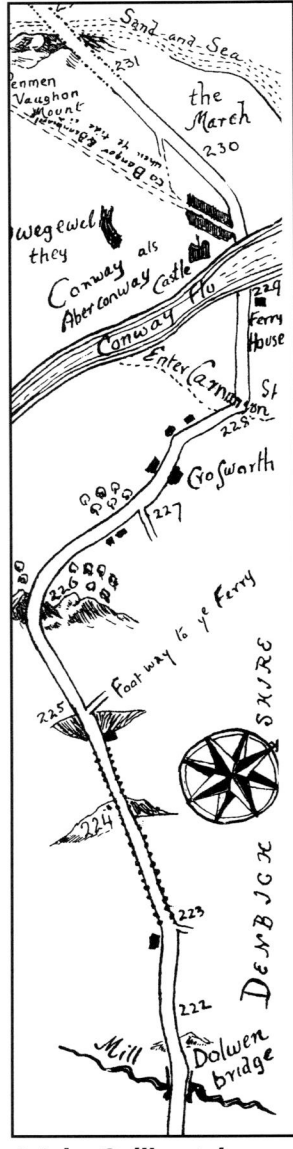

A John Ogilby strip map of 1675

THE TURNPIKE

At this period the district begins to assume a form which is recognizable. A series of trusts was created for extending the permanent highway from Chester to Holyhead, for "Chester Water" was silting and travellers sought a more convenient port for Dublin. Fragments of that early turnpike may still be seen.

The *Four Crosses* might be described as a "pre-turnpike" hostelry. Other inns sprang up with the influx of travellers. The inn at Rhuallt (east of St. Asaph) bears the date 1776, and this might well have appeared on many another hostel erected at the coming of the coaches.

Colwyn Fawr, the *Four Crosses* and the *Eagles* would have been welcome stopping places along this hilly route. The Old Highway was still in use at the beginning of the 19th century, patronized by all who wished to avoid paying toll. Alderman D.O.Williams, who was born at Rhiw, tells of his grandmother's describing the passing of the coaches along the Old Highway. The occurrence was impressed on her memory by the propensity of the guards to purloin any fowl that incautiously strayed into the roadway. There must have been much road making and road mending in the 1770's. One can picture the industry in the quarries, or the road-menders cracking stones at the roadside while the new traffic lines cut up the countryside.

Caernarvonshire Quarter Sessions in 1794 condemned the ancient Groes bridge as "ruinous and out of repair." The Caernarvonshire County Archivist holds a document containing the specifications for a new bridge to be completed by Christmas Day that year. It refers to the rebuilding of the Boundary Bridge between the Counties of Carnarvon and Denbigh on the Turnpike Road "called Pont croes yn Eirias." In the Record Office at Caernarvon is a plan of a new "foot road" from the Turnpike to Glan-y-Don, surveyed in October, 1797.

The records also contain a plan of a public footway "from a certain Dwelling house called Hafodunos over a field called Pant rhos Llwyd to the sea shore," which was closed in 1824 because "a new Public Carriage and Horse Road and Public Footway" had been made. This probably refers to Beach Road.

For perhaps seventy years coaches - stage coaches first, and then mail coaches - rutted our roads. Then the advent of the railway brought fresh diversion. Before turning to more domestic matters it might be well to say as much as one can about roads and road-users during these important eighty years. Before road-making was seriously undertaken in the second half of the eighteenth century, public wheeled vehicles would have been almost non-existent. Unless it was the Old Highway or Groes Road it is doubtful whether there was any road worthy of the name in these parts much before 1750. Merchandise was either water-borne or transported on the backs of pack-animals. One of the landmarks was Penmaen Head. So persistently is it mentioned by travellers that it is obvious its menace was extraordinary. Writing in 1798 the Rev. W. Bingley says *"the road winds round a huge limestone rock called Penmaen Rhos."*

Halliwell writes:

"Until within the last hundred years, the passage over this rock was one of the most troublesome on the north coast. Instead of there being, as at present, a good road at some distance behind the precipice, 'the traveller,' says Pennant, 'went along a narrow path cut on its front, like the road on Penmaenmawr, but infinitely more terrible and dangerous.' 'This path,' observes Windham in 1774, 'is so formidably narrow and unprotected, that few people dare trust themselves or their horses on it.' A similar account is given by Dr. Johnson who passed over it the same year :' To spare the horrors of Penmaen Rhos, between Conwy and St. Asaph, we sent the coach over the road cross the mountain with Mrs. Thrale, who had been tired with a walk some time before; and I, with Mr.Thrale and Miss, walked along the edge, where the path is very narrow and much encumbered by little loose stones, which had fallen down, as we thought, upon the way since we passed it before.' Cradock, who passed over Penmaen Rhos in the autumn of 1776, describes it as 'by far the worst part of the road between Holyhead and Chester: a nearer path was some time since cut along the side of the sea-cliff, but man and horse had lately been killed, and by order of the commissioners, it is now entirely broken up."[127]

In *Ancient and Modern Denbigh* (1856) Williams quotes *Pride and Luckmore's Travellers' Guide* of 1789 to show that the route through Dolwen was changed. Denbigh ceased to be a principal post town on the road between Dublin and London. The road moved nearer the sea and ran through Holywell, St. Asaph and Abergele. Williams says his mother, born in 1776, just recollected the Irish mails travelling by Denbigh and Dolwen. The first mail-coach to go through Abergele was on a fair day when there was a great flood - about 6 December 1785 or

86. Much of Pennant's fine coach-road - it appears pitifully narrow now - has been blasted away. The present Llysfaen Road going east past Penmaenrhos Schools merges into a grassy track, all that remains of the first coach-road! Alderman D.O. Williams considers that at first this road (on its western route) turned abruptly to rejoin the coast road. This would then traverse what is now Station Road, Old Colwyn, the meandering of which is suggestive of its remote origin. The Colwyn stream was crossed by a zigzag track so that the incline would be easier for the horses. A low structure beneath the present road bridge may be a link with an early bridge. One of the first undertakings was to do away with this deviation from Penmaen by making a new stretch of road past Rhuallt to the stream. This is now the Llysfaen Road. The coach route might be traced by a line of inns: The *Ship* and *Colwyn Fawr* at Colwyn, *Groes Bach*, the *Rising Sun*, the *Four Crosses*, the *Eagles* and the *Swan*. The *White Horse*, now prosaically renamed the *Mountain View*, is of later construction. The *Four Crosses* was sometimes known as Y Ffor, and the last vestry recorded there was in 1821. In 1808 the upper floor of the *Four Crosses* collapsed, according to "Old Price" who, when recording his reminiscences in 1874, refers to the incident:

"The cross-road (once on the Holyhead Mail Coach road!) close above Pwllycrochan boasted of an Inn of great notoriety very appropriately named The Four Crosses, and kept by a respectable old dame hight Dolly Evans. Here it was that militia and volunteer meetings and wakes were held; here rents were received and tithes were sold to the highest bidder; here, if I remember aright, justice business was transacted; and here it was, beyond all doubt, that, when a large party were 'at high tea' on the ground floor, the dancers upstairs plied the light fantastic toe' so heavily that the whole of the ceiling, unable to endure such perverse levity, yielding the preference to the legitimate force of gravity, came down bodily in a few huge slabs, and buried tea-makers and tea-drinkers."

Old Price mentions the shock he received in 1848 on finding *"nothing but the vestiges of this once renowned house of call."* He added *"the very pinfould had disappeared from its rocky nook."* But the pinfold was not demolished until about 1880, according to Mr. Porter who remembered it in his childhood.

THE FIRST TURNPIKE

In his survey of 1811 Telford wrote: *"Other dangerous hills on this road still require improvement, particularly Pen-man-Rhos, a little west of Abergele."* It is clear that the course of our present main road was in existence as a turnpike before Telford made this survey. The eleven miles from Abergele to Conwy Ferry was under the care of the Trustees of the Conwy Trust. Annual tolls amounted to £191. *"The several debts,"* runs the report, *"are secured by mortgage on the mail coach road, there being no other road."*[128]

The Old Highway was apparently by-passed for Telford describes a route which coincides with our main road, though there is a puzzling omission of any reference to the Eirias Dingle. One must conclude that the original bridge was such an accepted feature that it called for no comment. The Hyde Hall MS. clearly states that before the Telford Survey of 1811 there were "two bridges" at Groes-yn-Eirias. Here is the extract from Telford's report - with the writer's comments interpolated:

"After crossing the Conwy, the present road ascends a small hill (at Llandudno Junction) *at 1 in 19, passes to the south side of a tract of low marshy land, which separates the Orme's Head from the mainland* (Sarn-y-Mynach) *it then with a very quick bend* (at Glan Conwy corner), *turns parallel to this marsh, and continues with a succession of irregularities to ascend at 1 in 22, to a pass* (Nant Sempyr) *which separates another lesser point of land in Llandrillo; it afterwards goes in a tolerably regular manner for a short distance it then ascends at 1 in 20*

(The Dingle to Groes-yn-Eirias), *and immediately descends at 1 in 20 and 11, into a deep dingle* (Colwyn Stream) *where, after crossing the Colwin, only 28 feet above the level of the sea, it ascends at 1 in 7, 11 and 15, until it has reached the summit of Penmaen Rhos, at 360 feet above the level of the sea."*[129]

An accompanying map, dated 1811, marks "The Present Mail Road," and "The Improved Chester Shore Line." Colwyn is spelt "Colwin"; between Penmaen Rhos and "Landulas" is a place marked "Warn." The Afon Lwyd appears larger than the Eirias Stream. The report states it was permitted to charge 6d for the passage of each horse in draft, but actually only 4d was taken. There was double toll on Sundays. The map prepared for Robert Davies in 1763 shows there was no westward road through the Tanybryn "Common." To ride from Llandrillo to Llansanffraid it was necessary to ascend to the *Four Crosses*. Telford's map marks the tiny Wesleyan chapel near the gas works - then obviously a landmark in a lonely land. Mr. Porter considers it was between 1830 and 1840 that the main road at Old Colwyn was diverted from a spot below Rhuallt, so as to avoid the steep gradient to Penmaen Bach.[130] At this time the surface of the main road between Bethesda Chapel and the Llysfaen fork was raised and was known as "Cadwgan Cob."[131]

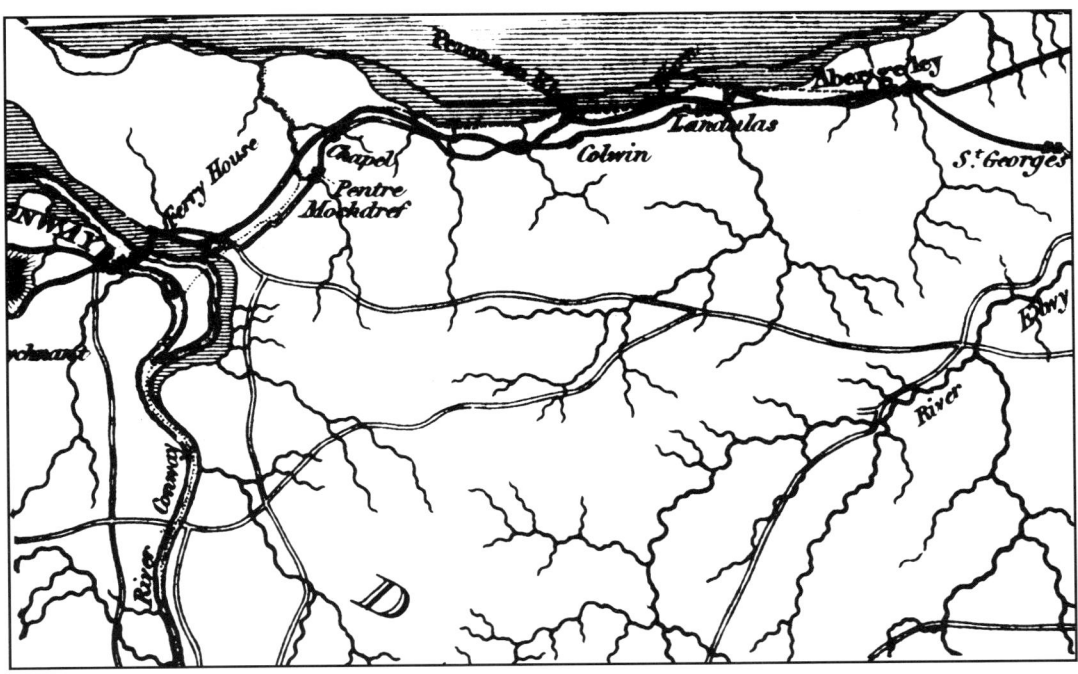

Courtesy of National Museum of Wales

This extract from Telford's report of 1811 shows the original turnpike contrasted with the proposed new coast road. The route surveyed by Ogilby in 1675 is seen well to the south

ROYAL MAIL

Once a regular service was established, the passing of coaches would have been a familiar sight. Frequently they travelled by night. One can imagine the sound of the horn and the jingle of harness as the lamps of the approaching coach glowed yellow through the darkness. In 1823 the proprietor of the Albion Hotel, Bangor, advertised in the *North Wales Gazette* of 23 October 1823:

"*Royal Mail to Chester, Liverpool and Manchester. Every evening at 7 o'clock through Conway, Abergele, St. Asaph, Holywell, and arrives at the Feathers Inn, Chester, the following morning at 4 o'clock.*"

On the 15 October 1832, Princess Victoria and her mother, the Duchess of Kent, who had been staying at Plas Newydd, the Marquess of Anglesey's seat, journeyed this way. It is said they paused at the Ship Inn, Old Colwyn, and local legend has it that the Princess drank a glass of milk at Maes Cadwgan farm. Does the name "Princess Road" refer to this? It might well be that the horses were rested here before the climb. It is known the Royal visitors were escorted into Abergele by a troop of the Denbighshire Hussars, commanded by Captain Heaton, and they stopped at the Bee Hotel to change horses.

LLYSFAEN TITHE MAP

The Llysfaen Tithe Map of 1839 shows unmistakably the original road from Llysfaen was that which passed before Ty Mawr. Three roads in an east to west direction are recorded - (a) the present main road; (b) Pennant's coach road past Pentregwyddel and Rhuallt, and (c) one which emerged from Llysfaen common, went north of Ty Mawr, down what is now Peulwys Lane and joined the turnpike opposite Maes Cadwgan Farm. Old residents speak of it as the "Roman Road" which may or may not have any significance.

A map of 1840 contains some information. It was published by Colonel Colby, and engraved in the Tower of London, at the Ordnance Survey Office. The railway is shown - apparently in course of construction, or added in a later edition. Off the coast is marked "Rhos Bay Pool" and "Abergele Road." Starting at our western border, a track from Penrhyn Isaf farm leads along the edge of the shore to Rhyd farm. The county boundary joins the sea between Rhos Fynach and Rhos Road. "Glan-y-Mor" indicates the old name for Rhos-on-Sea. The cottage "Ffordd" is marked and at the N.E. corner of Rhos and Llandudno roads is a cottage marked "Ty Fry." Then comes Bryn Euryn farm and the National Schools, and a "Dinas Isaf" (i.e. Dinerth Isaf) near where Whitehall Road joins Llandudno Road. "Bryn Dinarth" is shown, and a "Rhiw" is beneath the Four Crosses. "Cae Eithin" and "Pob lles" are in this vicinity, and near Penrhos footbridge is a cottage "Ty'n y Caeau." "RHIW" is printed in bold letters as if to denote a district. Other names are: Pen-y-Bryn, Pendorlan, Rhiw and Rhiw Ganol, Nant Uchaf, Nant Glyn, Glyn, Lletty yr Dryw, Pen Geulan, Glan y Don, Min y Don, St. Catherine's Church, Ty Newydd, Tuhwnt rafon, Parc, Dol ddu, Cae Eithin, Pentre-uchaf, Meifod, Cilgwyn, Tanllan, Ffynnon Elian, Cefn-Ffynnon, Fron Hurt. A road leads to "Groes yn Eirias." There is a "telegraph" at Llysfaen and another at Foryd.

THE COUNTRYSIDE

Pennant affords a brief picture of 1773: "*From Rhos Fynach the land recedes inwards, and forms a pretty bay. The country slopes to the water edge, and is varied with woods and cultivation.*"

There was a backwardness about agriculture. Even as late as 1810 the Rev. Walter Davies

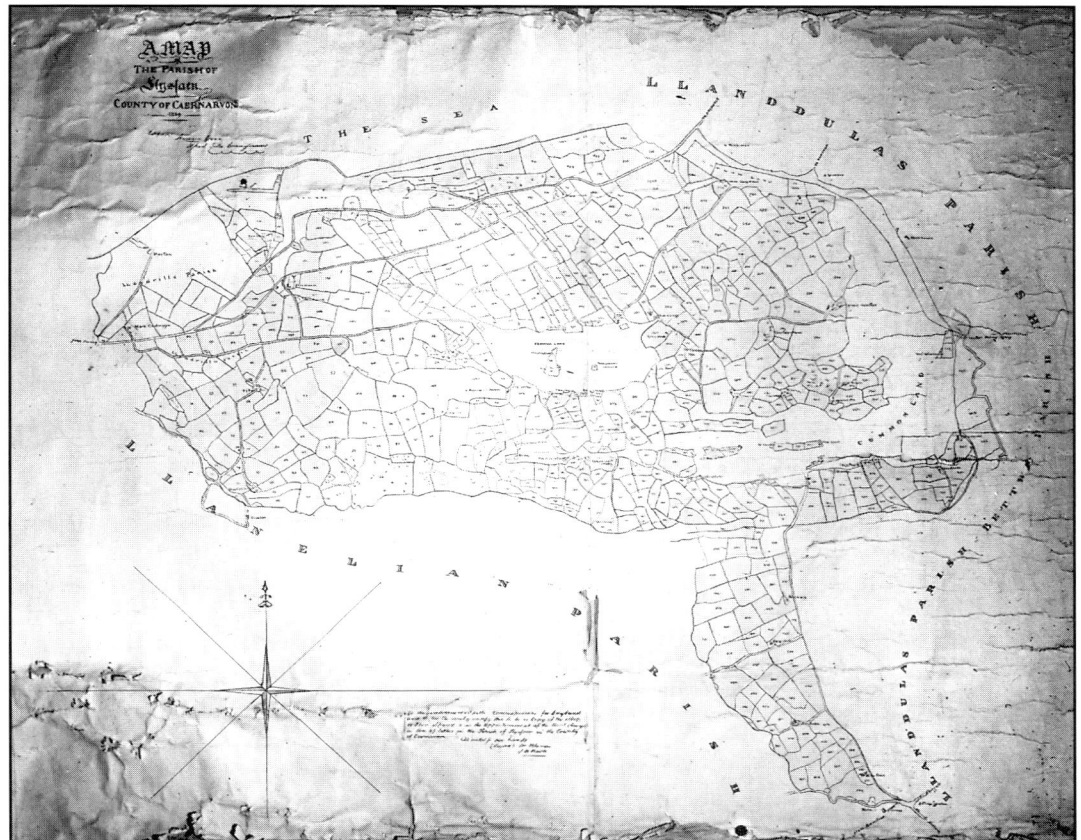

Llysfaen Tithe Map, 1839

(Rector of Minafon, Montgomery) spoke of the deficiency of manure. Cattle were high priced. Ox-teams were favoured, the oxen being shod for the work. There is a story of an ox-team carrying coal to Gloddaeth being trapped by the tide off Penmaen Rhos and the men in charge drowned. Referring to North Wales in general, Mr. Davies says: *"there were, comparatively but few miles of travellable road within the whole district. Coal for fuel, and lime for manure, could not be carried in quantities to any great distance."*[132]

With this as a background let us bring on to the stage some of the men who have left, in crabbed calligraphy, a record of their doings.

The Vestry Books

THE townships in Llandrillo-yn-Rhos parish were Dinerth, Rhiw, Mochdre, Llwydcoed, Cilgwyn, Colwyn and Eiras. The latter was an independent township, maintaining its own poor and making separate rates. It had its own overseers. The Borough Council holds, in its capacious safe, two long narrow, leather-backed tomes. They are the Vestry Books of the Parish of Llandrillo-yn-Rhos. One covers the years 1771 to 1803; the other 1804 to 1834. In the faded brown script of hands more familiar with spade than pen, there can be traced a homespun pattern of life in these parts, when George III was King. Llysfaen parish records go back to the Restoration, but generally speaking, they are not so rich in information. The Llandrillo books bear the stamp of the novice. A start has been made at either end and unorthodox flourishes suggest a few experimental strokes to limber the writer's stiff fingers. One facetious scribe even went so far as to essay a sketch of a man in a long coat, churchwarden in hand, and a tankard prominently displayed. Perhaps it is not surprising that the books contain sundry entries for ale consumed on the occasions of parochial deliberations. The wildness of the terrain is indicated by the payments made for wildcats and foxes killed. Between 1818 and 1833 no less than 68 foxes were accounted for.

Records of meetings are solemnly endorsed by the Vicar - sometimes by the curate - and churchwardens. At times there appears "X - his mark." More aspiring signatories have attempted shaky initials, such as "R.F." to which is added in an explanatory hand "the letters of Robert Foulkes." These good men and true wrestled with local finance, saw to the gathering of the tithe, administered the Poor Rate, aided the ailing, or apprenticed "parochial children" to be brought up, in the way they should go. One child, we learn, is sent to "The Poplas" to learn to be a weaver. Another goes to Mochdre to be instructed in "the art and mystery of shoemaking." Young Rachel is allotted to the household of the Parish Clerk where "the child must work as much as will be reasonably requir'd, and must not be indulg'd by any of the inhabitants to prevent her to be brought up in an industrious way."

Her employer, on the other hand, is bound *to behave himself in a fair and honest manner towards the said child.*" Most of the vestries were held at the *Four Crosses* (which at times lapses into "fore croses"), though occasionally the parishioners repair to the Parish Clerk's dwelling. Homely touches intrude. In 1772 five pounds of *"cannels at Cristmas Day"* cost 7d a pound. The same sum was paid for *"shingin on Cristmas Day."* Hugh Evans earned 10/6d for providing rushes and cleaning the "goled." Robert Thomas, smith, was paid 2/- *"for mending the ould spaide."* The tax (or Mize) throughout the parish in 1770-71 and 1772 was 4d per person. Two overseers were appointed annually. In collecting the poor tax these overseers apparently visited every person, township by township, meticulously accounting for every penny received. Their care gives us a record of the population. There were 761 inhabitants in Llandrillo Parish in 1772 - a fact of greater interest to us than the £12-13s-8d which was the "tottel" collected. Some names are baffling. For example, "tir Sur Walking" is incomprehensible, but that is what the writing resembles. It might be "tir Sir Watkin," i.e., Sir Watkin's land. All names are attempted, and the reader must sift the wheat from the chaff. When "risinson" indicates the *Rising Sun* Inn, it may be appreciated that the transcribing has not been without its obscurities. Many names are, however, recognizable and will help to indicate the age of well-known places. The improvement in style and penmanship is noticeable as the century nears its close. In the earliest records the parish is invariably "Llandrillo-in-Rhos"; not until 1797 does it become "Llandrillo-yn-Rhos." One wonders whether the sums paid to the wives of militiamen in 1778 had any connection with the participation of the Royal Welch Fusiliers in the American War of Independence. The writer is completely mystified by the entry under 3 February 1782, whereby a joiner is paid seven guineas for making a "horse" fourteen hands high! (For details see Appendix A.)

INHABITED HOUSES

A tabulated Population Return was compiled by the Overseers of the Poor in the Parish of Llandrillo-yn-Rhos following the Act of Parliament of 1821. In the Vestry Book this is set forth in detail. It lists houses occupied and unoccupied, those in course of construction, and gives the occupants occupations. The overseer for the east was John Foulkes; Ellis Williams submitted the return for the west.

Houses named in the list were:

East - Cae ithin, Poplas, Rhiw, Pwllycrochon, Cilcow, Ty n y caea, Pwllycrochon Ucha, Rhiw Bach, Scubor Ucha, Penybryn, Rhiw S.W., Rhiw R.W., Risin Sun, Penygroesffordd, Pengeylan, Ty-n-y-Maes, Rardd gam (?), Penybwlch, Gwern tyno, Kilgwyn bach, Kilgwyn mawr, Brynglyn, Nant glyn, Pendorlan, Tan pen man, Morfa bach, Cil llidiart, Bryn Gwynt, Colwyn, Ship, Rhyallt, Scybor Newydd, Colwyn T.H., Penbryn Colwyn, Colwyn Mill. Under the name of Colwyn are: Talybont, Groes Mill, Mifod, Tynuwydd (Ty Newydd), Glanygors, Moel rhodwen, Swch, Cymora, Brynmaen, Llwydcoed, Bryn, Tynffynon, Coed teg, Nant ucha.

West - Vicarage, Bryneuryn, Llan, Bryn defaid, Dinerth, Plasnewydd, Nant symper, Nant, Aberhod, Dinerth-isa, Ty'n rhiwl, Ty fry, Ffynnon dafydd, Hendu, Minffordd, Ffordd, Glanymor, Glanwern, Eagles, Tan'rallt isa, Tan'r allt ucha, Greanllyn, Bryncariwch, Hafoty Mynydd, Ty Gwyn, Mochdre, Swan, Bryn hyfryd (there are six dwellings under this name, and nine more under "Mochdre").

It will be noted that no White Horse Inn is mentioned. There are also: Llidiarty Pyllau, Llwyndu, Pontr'hwch, Mochdu Mill, Pen y binc, Pen'r allt, Castell, Penisa wern, Ganol y Waun, Pen y Waun, Pencarad, Penmynydd, Podlondeb, Bron'r haul, Pant y Gloch, pen y bryn, Llwyd Coed isa, Ty'n llwyn, Brynbadr, Corn gafr, Penllyn, Caeau, Coethuved (?), Frithmynydd, Tanyfron, Daunant, Nantycwm, Fourcrosses, Tal can Coul (?), Bronynant, Gwern y geufr.

In conformity with the Act of 1821 a return of all baptisms, burials and marriages in the Parish of Llandrillo-yn-Rhos was made by the Vicar, Rev. Thomas Alban.

	Baptisms	Burials	Marriages
1811	19	15	4
1812	21	15	9
1813	24	14	1
1814	17	12	5
1815	27	12	3
1816	13	16	9
1817	19	10	4
1818	15	18	11
1819	24	9	13
1820	26	6	6

The number of unregistered baptisms was 44. The record (with its addition a little erratic) is as follows:

At Colwyn Chapel	7 males, 5 females –	15
At Mochdre Chapel	17 males, 15 females –	32
		47

Funerals at Colwyn, five females.

There is also a copy of the return of the population of Llandrillo made by the overseers in accordance with the Act of 28 May 1821. Eirias township, being in Caernarvonshire, was treated separately. The combined returns (abbreviated) are: Inhabited houses 178; families 207; unoccupied houses 15; farm and agriculture 121; trade, manufacture and handicrafts 32; other occupation (indistinct, but apparently 33). Total - male 473; female 487; Total inhabitants 960.

SLOW GROWTH

Growth was slow. Lewis in 1833 remarks that the village of Llysfaen consisted of five houses and there were only three at Llandrillo. In lonely spots nonconformist chapels began to appear; humble places, served by lay workers. At Colwyn, in 1815, the Welsh Independents opened the first Ebenezer Chapel, which comprised only the north end, containing two windows, with a doorway between. At Mochdre, Calvinistic Methodists built a chapel, Nazareth, in 1832, though the cause had been in existence there from 1771. In the middle of the century Owen and Ellen Jones lent the kitchen of their cottage beside the turnpike for use as a Sunday School. It stood opposite the end of the present Belgrave Road. The Calvinistic Methodist records give the official date of the Sunday School as 1847, but add *"although it is evident that it existed some time before this."*[133]

A tombstone in Llandrillo churchyard records the death on 10 November 1882, of Daniel Davies, at the age of 76. He opened a tailor's shop in Mochdre in the 1820's and was for forty years a deacon of the C.M. Church. His grandson, D.Francis Davies, says his grandfather told him that in those early days, tailors used to visit farms periodically, carrying with them scissors, needles and sleeveboard. Farmers, having sheared their flocks, took the wool to a mill (possibly Trefriw), where it was made into homespun. The tailor remained several days at a farm until all necessary suits were made. The practice was termed *"whipping the cat."* In 1819 the National Schools were erected on Tan-y-Bryn Road.

The district still retained its rural character, but slowly it began to develop. There were several pounds or pinfolds for stray animals in the area. In addition to one in Beach Road, Colwyn, there was one below the Four Crosses, another at Nant, and another opposite Pant-y-gloch (Upper Colwyn Bay), where the Bartley family who owned the Nant smithy (Tanybryn bridge) had another smithy. An important event in 1821 was the marriage of (Sir) David Erskine (Bart.), to Miss Jane Silence Williams, heiress of Pwllycrochan.

It became fashionable for influential families in the vicinity to provide themselves with seaside homes to which they could resort in pleasant weather. At Old Colwyn, Coed Coch Cottage (later The Jungle) was erected by General Wynne of Coed Coch, in 1848, the year the railway opened, and the Wynnes of Garthewin had a substantial house built at the foot of Rhos Road. Perhaps such seaside houses suggested to some enterprising person the idea of attracting English visitors who were beginning to "explore" this remote coast.

By the 1840s matters were stirring, albeit sleepily, in this neighbourhood. In 1844 Colwyn became a parish of its own, breaking away from the huge parish of Llandrillo-yn-Rhos to which it was attached for centuries. It was formed from the townships of Eirias, Colwyn, Cilgwyn, with a portion of Llysfaen parish named Graig. Before this occurred the Church of St. Catherine had been built in 1837 as a chapel of ease to Llandrillo. Richard Butler Clough of Min-y-Don Hall (formerly Colwyn Farm), a member of the celebrated Denbigh family, was interested in its erection, and as his wife was named Catherine it is said the church was christened in her honour. Mr.Clough died in 1844.[134] The famous poet Arthur Hugh Clough (a relative of Richard) stayed at Min-y-Don, and so did his equally famous sister, Anne Jemima Clough, later Principal of Newnham College.

The Ecclesiastical Commissioners assigned to the new parish in 1844 a tithe rent-charge of £74, augmented in 1855 by £37-6s-5d for both of which they substituted, in 1872, a rent-charge of £395-17s-3d, out of the lapsed tithes of the Llandrillo sinecure rectory.[135] A glebe house was built in 1871 on land given by Oldham Whittaker of Min-y-Don Hall. The parish was re-arranged the following year.

Neighbouring farms at this time were: Groes Fawr yn Eirias, Glyn, Groes Bach, Eirias, Lletty'r Dryw, Ty Newydd (now occupied by The Rough), Tu Hwnt i'r Afon (Minafon), Maescadwgan, Pen-y-Bryn and Parciau. The date of Colwyn Mill is uncertain. There is a record in Llandrillo churchyard of a Hugh Williams, miller, Colwyn, who died in 1755. The six cottages known as Pen-y-Bryn and Bryngwynt are eighteenth century. In 1852 Frances Ridley Havergal, the hymn-writer, lived at Colwyn. In August she wrote:

"We came here on the 2nd. The change is doing us all good, and we think dear papa's eyes are a little better. Colwyn suits me much better than Llandudno, and I am as well as possible. We find pretty walks ad infinitum. The donkey-girl teaches me Welsh. I think I learn it very fast."[136]

VILLAGE CONSTABLES

Before the coming of the official Police force it was the custom of the Parish to elect certain parishioners to serve as voluntary constables, the men being given a special baton, or "staff," as an insignia of office - a badge which doubtless proved of practical value in time of strife. Francis Davies recollects that his grandfather served as a constable at Mochdre. *"When there were drunken frays on a Saturday night,"* observed Mr.Davies, *"his benign features did more to preserve the peace than the baton he bore."* W. Bezant Lowe mentions a Constable's staff which was left at Cilgwyn Mawr. It was marked with a crown and the letters: VR - CD.[137] Mr. Davies had the constable's staff that belonged to his grandfather; it was marked G.IV (George the Fourth), but has now disappeared. Similar batons are in the museum at Bangor.

COLWYN'S FIRST POLICEMAN

The late John W. Lloyd of the Marine Hotel told the writer he could remember Colwyn's first policeman. He wore a blue swallow-tail coat with brass buttons, blue trousers bearing a two-inch red stripe down each seam, a top-hat of patent leather with a leather brim and a piece of whalebone at each side.

APPENDIX A

VESTRY BOOKS 1771–1834

In recording the following the sums of money have been omitted as irrelevant.
"An Count how much is evry farm Tax all the Parish of Llandrillo at rate of four pence, pr. pn. 1772."

THE TOWNSHIP OF DINERTH

Number
- 35 Bryn Defaid
- 5   Cae'd ffynon
- 14 Dinerth
- 11 Glan-y-Mor
- 12 Dinerth Isa (corner of Whitehall Road)
- 9   ty Rhewl
- 14 Plas Newydd (Dinerth Road)
- 10 Bryn Eurian   Thos. Owens
- 6   Cwm Bach
- 8   Aber Hodni
- 9   Cae eithin
- 8   Nant   Jone Roberts
- 6   Nant   John Williams
- 3   ty usa   Thos. Williams
- 3   Rhallt

(Total collected £2-10-0d)

RHIW THOWSHIPD (sic).

Number
- 36 pwll y Grochon
- 15 Rhiw ganol William Avan
- 5   Rhiw gose i Pwll y Crochon JR.
- 3   Rhiw pen y groes fford D.D.
- 4   ry yn y fford T.P. (near foot of Grove Park, on Abergele Road)
- 6   ty yn y Caea WE. (beside Gilbertville, near the promenade)
- 6   Rhiw Owen Williams
- 1   Bryn Lwyn   Edwards Williams
- 2   Bryn Lwyn   Edwards Williams
- 4   Pen y Bryn David Edward
- 3   Rhiw   John Pritchard
- 4   gwern tyno
- 1   Poplas (Llanrwst old road)
- 5   Gwern y geifr
- 3   pen y dorlan (East Parade)
- 1   pen y geulan
- 9   Nant-y-glyn

(Total collected £1-15-4d)

MOCHDRE TOWNSHIP

Number
- 21 Glan y wern (said originally to have been called Rhyd y Wern)
- 21 Mr. Owen a Robert Rowlands tan y Railt
- 29 Mochdre   Thos. Hughes
- 12 Grianllyn
- 1 Thomas Hughes & Rhees Williams
- 21 tan y Railt   John Williams
- 3 gwerglod deunant
- 5 Mynyd
- 3 Bryn cariwch
- 18 ty gwyn
- 1 Jane Jones Mwen Bolwch
- 1 Litierd y Pyd   Thos. David
- 2 Jane Jones Waen boluh
- 3 Eagles & child   Thos. Hughes (The Eagles)
- 2 Mary Evans   Llanwedden
- 1 ty dy
- 1 pen waen
- 1 cae eithin
- <u>1</u> Nant Jane Roberts

(Total collected £2-8-8d)

LLWYD COED THOUNSIP

Number
- 12   Rhies Williams grainllin
- 2   gallt maelor
- 10   ty yn Lwyn   Hugh Williams
- 4   tan y fron
- 5   William Owen   frith wed
- 4   Bryn y maen
- 5   Pant y gloch
- 7   David Williams
- 4   Willm. Hughes   Llwyd coed
- 4   Willm. Williams   ty yn y caue
- 3   perth y Cw bach
- 2   Crycdo
- 1   Tyddun y berth
- 1   Cae matto
- 3   Corn gap
- 5   Coet teg
- 5   Cymere
- 2   Wm. Hughes (Dol y Grevan)
- 3   Thos. Piree (Ty n y Ffynon)
- 3   pen y Bryn
- 3   Will Evans (Mynydd Merki)
- <u>12</u>   Nant Evans Pirce

(Total collected £1-13-4d)

CILWYN

Number
- 19   Cilgwyn mawr
- 6   Ty yn coed
- 5   moel y rodwen
- 8   ty Newyd
- 8   Glyn bach
- 10   Meufod
- <u>6</u>   Cillwyn bach

(Total collected £1-0-0d)

COLWYN THOUNSHIP

Number
- 3   Thos. Williams (Colwyn)
- 9   pin bryn Colwyn
- 3   Ellin Evans tan Lan
- 4   Owen Morgan   Maegydwgan
- 7   Thos. Edwards   Colwyn
- 1   John fron goch
- <u>2</u>   yr erw fawr

(Total collected 9s 8d)

EIRIES THOUNSIP

Number
- 25   Ty Newydd
- 10   Rhos fonach[138]
- 47   Glyn
- 15   groes yn eiries
- 4   ty uche yn y groes
- 6   Colwyn Thos. Williams
- 7   tir Sur Walking
- 2   Pitter Williams Colwyn
- 3   Thos. Owens Hwyfa Parkie
- 5   Llittryr Driw
- 10   Glan y mor
- 8   Cefn
- 12   Rhyd[59]
- 3   Vron hyrt
- 2   Vedw
- 5   Parkie
- <u>3</u>   poors Land

(Total collected £2-15-8d.)

These make a total of 761 farm taxes collected, totalling £12/13/8d.

SUNDRY ENTRIES

One is reluctant to quit these old books while there is still information to be gleaned. We are told that Alis Owens received 9/6d *for "washing the surplice"* - probably throughout the year - and Will Davies "Taylor" received 2/6d for mending *"the olde Bier Cloth."* Tenpence was spent for a lock on the gate. In 1772 is the entry *"Pd. Elizabeth Hughes to buy an ass - 10/9d."* Evidently the church floor was strewn for in 1774 there is an expenditure of 9/-:*"for rushes in the Church."* Thomas Davies, for writing all the Parish Business, was paid a guinea, and 3/6d was awarded for killing a wood cat; 3/6d was also *"lost in a Guinea short of weight."* There is an entry: *"Ale for the singers, 10/-."*

Here are some more entries:

1774
4th April. the Minister, Church Wardens free holders and the inhabitants of the parish of Llandrillo in Rhoes agree'd with John Thomas for the sum of Seven pounds seven shillings for Teaching all the Parishioners that has a mind to Learn to Sing Psalms from this time to all Saints every Saturday eve and Sundays. - Evan Ellis, Vicar.

1777

Paid for the shroud of Hannah Pary	2s	7
6 lb. Candles at Cristmas Morning	4	0
New door for the pin fould	7	6
4 yards of Ribonds for the Singers	3	0
for the New Stocks at Groes	£1 0	0
for Fresh Rushes	10	0
for Washing the Church Linen & Mending them	10	0
for fastening the Bell	1	0
for the Glazier's eating	0	6

To Pay Owen Roberts of Bryn y Cariwch the Sum of one pound per year for instructing the singers Every Sunday Morning and Evening before Prayers as Long he Continues in the Parish of Llandrillo and Doeth his Duty.

1778
26 Ap. agreed for to Rise what Ever Money belongs to the Poor of Our Parish out of hand for to build houses for the poor as far as it will go and if the Money will be to short we will make it up from the Church Rate. - Evan Ellis. Vicar.

Paid in all to Elizabeth the wife of Owen Georg,e Malitia Man in the Denbighshire Malitia	£4	6	0
Pd. Grace Owen. the wife of Richd. Owen of Trefriw Malitia Man in the Carnarvon Shire Malitia	£3	1	6
for William Edwards Eating 15 days		6	0
for Hugh Owen his eating		1	4

1780

To Bassoon Chest	7	6

to pay any Person for fox killing in the aforesaid Parish two Shillings & Sixpence And One Shilling and three pence for a Puppy.

1782
Feb. 3. Also agreed at the same vestry above mentioned that Thomas Roberts Joinor for making a new horse Belonging to the said Parish and the said Thomas Roberts is to Receive in Paying for so doing the said horse the sum of seven pounds seven shillings and the whool of the said horse is to be Fourteen hands hoight. (?hearse).

1784
May the 31st. At a Vestry held and Lawfully called in the Parish Church of Llandrillo in Rhos. It was agreed and allowed by the Minister and the Inhabitants then present that Wm.Hughes of Llwydcoed in the said Parish afores'd a Liberty of erecting a new Pew or seat, and the broadth of the seat is to be three Foot and a Half and the place where she is to be build is on the South Isle of the afores'd Church Between the Pulpit and the Large Door.
Allowed by us as written our hands.- Richard Jackson, Curate.

May 31. Eliz'th Williams bryn is not to have any more per week be Pay for her house from the above date.
It is agreed at a vestry hold in the Parish Church of Llandrillo in rhos on the First of August 1784 by the Minister, Church Wardens and the Parishioners then present that from hence forward no person or persons not having a Legal Settlement in the sd Parish of Llandrillo shall Reside here any Farther and therefore we the Parishioners do authorize Wm Thomas and David Evans Overseers of the Poor of the afores'd Parish to remove each person or persons that have not Legal Settlement to their Proper Parish. - Richard Jackson, Curate. -

1785
Jan. 3rd. That Owen Robartes Has undertaken to Bild a House for the Nearse (? Hearse) as Hereafore mentioned for the sum of £6 (indistinct). NB. The outside to be 5 yds and the Brth in side to be 2 yd ½ and the Timber to be sollid Oach - rhe Dours mad of Dry Coack and two opening Properly Hung. Panted white with a Proper Bould & Loach.

1785
July 31. for erecting a new Hood for the Hoarse & also for teaching the Psalm Singers the sum of One Pound.

1787
April 29. A Vestry was held on Sunday Evening, at Hugh Hughes, Glanmor, Parish Clerk of Llandrillo in Rhos to settle the overseers for gathir tax six Pence in Pound.

1788
16th day of June. That David Thomas a Parochial child is to be Bound an Apprentice to Hugh Hughes of Mochdre to learn the art and mystery of shoemaking for the term of seven years and likewise he is to be Vituald by Robert Jones of Tygwyn for the term of two years of the above mention in consideration of Three Pounds and three shillings.

1790
Nov. 1st. Did allowd to Grace Thomas of Eirias two Barrels of Coals and a spinning wheel and so forth.Did Allowd to Agnes the wife of John Thomas 'Bryntirion' two Barrels of Coals.

1791
David Hughes Rhosfynach for maintaining from hence the clothing of Robert the son of Jane Thomas of Aberhod and to learn the art of Husbandry for five Pounds 10/- for the space of five years.

1793
June 8th. It was further allowed to John Williams overseer to discharge John Roberts Militiaman for the township of Dinerth in the County of Denbigh and to hire a man in the stade of him the

said John Williams is to hire a man with his own money and the Parish Liable to remit him the same sum. It was further'd agree to get a Law Book for the use of the Parish.

Nov. 30th. It was further order'd that Mr. Jno Oldfield of the Furnace (? near Bodnant) be appointed the Solicitor to act for and on Behalf of our Parish whom we Direct Parish Officers for the time being to consult upon every necessary Occasions and for his trouble in that respect we Engage to allow him an Annual Salary of One Guinea and also engage to pay him the Further sum of One Guinea for every Pauper or one Family that may be absolutely removed from our sd Parish by and under his the sd Jno Oldfield advice.

1797
June 24th. We the said Parishioners do agree that John Evans is to have NO more money For playing the Basoon.

1798
3 Jan. We the Parishioners do Order David Jones, Constable of the township of Dinirth to hire a Militia man for the Parish of Llandrillo & the sd David Jones Has Receiv'd Nine Pounds, twelve shillings of the Post money and also £18/11/0 of the Church mize & what Ever is wanted the parish To be able to sist him more, and David Jones is to be paid for his trouble.

1801
March 4th. Allowd William Thomas of Dinerth Issa One Pound One Shillings per year for playing the Basoon Beginning the 6 of Epiphany.

1818
Sinking Ground on South Side of Church £1.

1819
Ordered that three Prayer Books published by Gee and respectably bound be purchased for the Churchwardens and one for the use of the Clerk.

There is a notice under 9 April 1790, of the "Votalion of ye tithe" settled upon the Rector (i.e., the Bishop of St. Asaph), "and other materials both Mills, Tythes, Wears, Coals, Mines and other Minerals."

	TYTHES		REATED
18	10	0	Dinerth Corn
2	0	0	Dinerth Hay
8	10	0	Mochdre Corn
8	0	0	Llwydcoed Do.
4	0	0	Killgwyn Do.
10	0	0	Eirias Do.

APPENDIX B

CHURCH WARDENS' BOOK 1818-1882

Here are a few extracts:

1818
Jany. 5th. - It was unanimously resolved that this book be purchased & it was further resolved that all agreements relating to the Disbursements & offices of Church wardens of this Parish - the Church Rates & the Statements of the Church wardens when approved of in future annually regularly entered in this Book. & that it shall be safely kept locked up in the Chest in the Church. Ordered that the Church wardens do provide a carpet for the Altar & a Poor's Box. - Thos. Alban, Vicar; Thos. Ellis, Moses Roberts, Church Wardens.

1819
22nd Day of Oct.- That Casements be made for the Windows pursuant to the Intimation of the Lord Bishop of the Diocese. That the harness belonging to the Hearse be examined & if deemed irreparable that a new set be procured.

That the Church Wardens provide Benches or Seats & other accommodation for the use of the Children of Llandrillo Schools attending the Church.

That in consequence of the Church being kept remarkably neat & clean a Donation of two Guineas be presented to John Hughes by the Church Wardens for his extra care and Trouble.

1820
24th day of November - Ordered that a proper Tablet, under the Direction of the Vicar, be provided & set up in the Church commemorating the very liberal & benevolent Donations towards building the Schools.

1825
12th May - it was also ordered and agreed that a Church Rate of Nine Pence in the Pound be laid & levied for the Time of the current Year. It was also agreed that in future no more than two shillings and 6d. be paid for killing & destroying each Fox & one Shilling and 3d. for killing & destroying each Fox cub.

That all walks in the church yard be new gravelled properly to the satisfaction of the Vicar. That a new black cloth Pall be immediately purchased.

1826
8th May - It was also agreed and ordered that the hearse belonging to the Parish be not allowed upon any Terms or Condition whatever to be used for any Purpose except only for carrying or conveying dead Bodies to be buried in Llandrillo Church or Churchyard and that a good lock be put and always kept on the Hearse Shed.

1827
April 17th. - By paid for ale allowed and drank at Select Vestries last year being ignorant of the Magistrates' Directions for not paying for ale at the Vestries. £3-18-5$^{1}/_{2}$d.

1830
Steps to Dial	4s	0
Carriage on stones 2 Mason 1/3½d Day	8	9
Foxes killed and paid for From 1818 to 1833. 68 Foxes £10	7	0

1833
19th Day of September - It was agreed and ordered that an English 4to Bible and an English Prayer Book be immediately procured for the use of the Church.

1835
Thos. Foulkes, Groes. for candles Bellrope & mould candles	14	3
16 lbs. Bolt Iron for the Bell at sd. per lb	6	8
Journey to put the Bolt through the frame	3	0

NEW GATES FOR THE CHURCH (they are still there)

1836
30th Day of June - Stone Posts for the Church Yard Gate	£2	0	0
Cartage		15	0
Iron Gates 400 lbs at 3½d per lb		16	8
2 Men for three days' work in setting the gates		18	0
Boring Holes in the Posts		4	6
One Day's Team		7	0

1840
June 25th. - A Vestry was held in Llandrillo Public House and adjourned thence to the Vicarage House.

1843
May 18th. -Vestry held in Llandrillo Church and thence adjourned to the Ship Public House.

1847
2nd Day of June - Vestry held in Ship Tavern, Llandrillo.

SACRILEGIOUS ROBBERY

In 1827 the community was shocked to learn that the communion plate had been stolen from Llandrillo Church. A reward of £10 was offered for the detection of the thief. As a result one John Williams was arrested in Liverpool, tried, and sentenced to seven years' transportation to the colonies. The Church Wardens' Book of Llandrillo-yn-Rhos records the incident:

"Ordered also that the Premium of Ten Pounds agreed to be paid to the Person who should discover, or give such Information as might lead to the Discovery of the Person who sacrilegiously robbed this Church of the Communion Plate, be paid by the Church Wardens to John Rowland, Pawnbroker, Liverpool; who, it appears, detected Hugh Williams with Part of the Plate in his Possession, and for which the said Hugh Williams was tried, found guilty, and ordered to be transported for Seven Years.

"It appearing that Mr. John Miller, Police Officer, Liverpool, had been extremely active and industrious in conducting the Prosecution of the said John Williams, and in saving this Parish from all the attendant Law Expenses, which he promises shall be paid by the County of

Lancaster; this Vestry taking into Consideration his Services and kind Assistance, request his acceptance of Ten Pounds as a Mark of their approbation of his Conduct in this business which said Sum of Ten Pounds they order and direct the Church Wardens to pay him accordingly and the same shall be allowed in their account.

"It is agreed to accept from the Vicar, for the Communion Service, of two plated Cups and a Plate or Platen; upon each of which the words 'Llandrillo-yn. Rhos are inscribed.

Thos. Alban, Vicar
D. Erskine
Richd Butler Clough ⎤
John Jones   ⎬ — Church Wardens
Samuel Bartley   ⎦

John Poyser
David Jones

On the following page of the Church Wardens' Book the following entry occurs:
"Resolved that the thanks of this Vestry be given to the Reverend Thomas Alban, Vicar of the Parish, for his handsome present of the aforementioned Plate and Cups." It was signed by D.Erskine, Rich'd Butler Clough, John Poyser, and John Jones. (Sir David Erskine of Pwllycrochan and Richard Butler Clough of Minydon).

Other sidelights on the robbery are contained in the Books:

"1828
30 D(ay) of April – Pd, Robert Jones for printing 100 handbills (Sacrilege)		7	6d
Expenses of journey to Liverpool respecting Sacrilege	£2	8	0
Time and trouble 4 days	0	12	0
2 Journeys to Conwy on Do.	0	4	0
Paid Reward officers for discovering the person guilty of the Sacrilege £10	0	0"	

Another entry reads:
April 20th. – "It was also ordered that the Step of the Dial be properly repaired and that the Church be whitewashed.

Pd: Wm. Hughes steps to Dial	£4	0	0
Car: of stones to Do		7	6
Mason ½ day at Do		1	3"

APPENDIX C

AN OLD ACCOUNT BOOK

In Colwyn Bay Public Library is an ancient account-book in which is kept a statement of the fish caught in Bryneuryn weir during the eighteen-fifties. Many families living in the vicinity are listed among the customers, and there are entries of money paid for cartage to neighbouring towns. The book mentions two inns at Rhos which have disappeared - the "Kingfisher" (believed to be Moranedd) and the "Black Cat." This was one of three cottages at the rear of the Blue Bell Inn (now Cayley Arms) known as Cath Goch, Cath Wyn and Cath Ddu (Red Cat, White Cat, Black Cat). They have been renamed. The account book concerns "Bryneuryn Weir" in 1847 and is inscribed: *"Account of Expences paid and received on acct. of Bryneuryn Weir in the years* 1847, 1848, 1849 *and* 1850."

In 1847 the expenses for repairs, drawing, &c., of Bryneuryn Fish Weir were £82-17s-10½d.; the money received for fish sold was only £31-5s-0d. The next year the sums almost balanced. By 1849 "expences" were £51-5s 8½d, and receipts £89-13s-5½d. Men received one shilling per tide for collecting the fish. There were charges for fishing nets and twine. A horse and cart at 2/6d. per tide suggest some heavy catches.

SALMON 10d. PER POUND

Lady Erskine bought 8 lb. of salmon at 10d a pound. There were sales to *"strangers at Bodeuryn"* and *"strangers at Bryneuryn."* In 1850 there was a separate account for Mr. Allanson, Bryndinerth. Mr. Dod is also mentioned as being at Bryndinerth - doubtless the Whitehall Dod who was to purchase part of the Pwllycrochan Estate later, and give his name to Whitehall Road, as Mr. Allanson did to Allanson Road.

Customers included: Lewis Roberts, Lincoln; George Hughes, Bryndefaid; Anne Hughes, Colwyn; Robt. Hughes, Glanymor; Thomas Hughes, Clerk; John Roberts, Blue Bell; William Roberts, Penycha; John Foulkes, Bryneuryn; William Parry, the Rising Gull; William James, Schoolmaster; Thomas Owen, Ffordd; Captain Davey, Bodhyfryd; Thomas Roberts, Penmaen; Thomas Rogers, Rhos Quarry; Hugh Jones, Dinerthissa; John Jones, butcher; Mrs. Bell, Aberhod. In 1851 there were accounts for Owen Roberts, Poplas; Mr. Hesketh, Glandon; Mrs. Clough, Minydon; Hugh Jones, Cilcow; Edward Jones, King Fisher." In front of the old account book is pinned a receipt:

"Kingfisher, Nov. 24th/59.

	£	s.	d.
The Company of the Whear. To Jane Jones.			
To Ale & Porter 16 quarters and a pint at 8d.	0	11	0
March 17th, 1860. Settled. Mark Jane X Jones."			

Fish was despatched far afield for there were payments for journeys to Abergele and Chester. There is an entry of *"1/- for carry the casks from Liverpool."* Evidently these were landed on the quarry's "shipping stage" at the foot of Rhos Road.

THE COMING OF THE RAILWAY

The creation of Colwyn as a separate parish in 1844 coincided practically with the construction of the Chester and Holyhead Railway line. The effect on the life of the district was immediately apparent. The community began to develop with greater rapidity. The old Ship Inn and the Plough had been erected in the 1820's, and now the Red Lion and the Sun inns made their appearance at Colwyn. The task of constructing the railway embankment must have been colossal. The magnitude may be appreciated by contemplation of the viaducts over the Eirias Dingle and Colwyn Stream. Earth for the embankment was excavated from an area in front of Sea View Terrace, which was first called the gravel pit and later became known as "The Ballast Pit," (now the Bay View shopping centre). In Colwyn Bay's early days it formed an ideal, if unofficial, playground for children. Colwyn Bay was not then contemplated, and the first station was planned for a spot nearer Colwyn.

The present site was chosen in deference to Lady Erskine's wishes. The land was apparently sold to the company on the understanding that her carriage should be accorded precedence. At the start of the last century, when a horse-drawn bus carried visitors to the Pwllycrochan Hotel, this custom was still observed. "Colwyn" is marked in the Bradshaw timetable of 1849. According to the late Jos. H. Roberts, Deputy Town Clerk, the original station was nearer the tunnel than the present one.[139] Colwyn, as a village, had first claim. A site was acquired - the second small field east of Glanydon Crossing. Alderman D. O. Williams writes it is known locally as "Cae Sam." The station's official name was "Colwyn." It was stated that Lady Erskine imposed a condition that the Company should provide a 'halt' for her convenience. This was apparently first made at a spot west of Marine Road bridge. Later a "Colwyn Bay station" was built. It stood on part of the site of the present station.

One of the first pupils to arrive at Rydal Mount School in 1889 left a brief description of the original. *"This was a primitive affair of two platforms made out of railway sleepers, and indifferently lighted by oil lamps."*[140] There was no bridge at first; the only way from one platform to another was by a path of raised sleepers across the permanent way. Iron gates outside the station yard were locked as soon as the last train had gone at night. The first stationmaster was (so far as we can ascertain) Benjamin Jones. Old residents say that "Pwllycrochan Halt" was the name applied to the first stopping place, arranged for Lady Erskine. The first sod was cut and the first shot fired at the Conwy Tunnel on St. David's Day 1845. The line as far as Bangor was completed on 1 May 1848.

"This," writes Mr. Porter, *"represented a very creditable performance, for the line, passing through hilly North Wales, across valleys instead of along them, and involving the Conwy tubular bridge and about nine tunnels, presented an engineering task of some difficulty. For tunnel-boring the basaltiform greenstone of Penmaen Bach formed the toughest work, but our tunnel of Penmaen Rhos involved peculiar difficulties; the workmen found themselves breaking into the caves which penetrate the headland and much supplementary masonry was necessary."*

The work on Penmaen tunnel was probably completed about 1847. The half-yearly report

The coming of the railway

The old Colwyn Bay railway station with two platforms before it was widened to accommodate four tracks in 1906 and then reduced to two tracks in 1983

Hauled by two locomotives, the non-stop Holyhead-London express is about to use its side net to collect two Royal Mail satchels, seen suspended from the trackside frame on the right of the picture

View of old railway station, taken from Colwyn Bay Hotel. Note dingle near foot of Penrhyn Road, and the apparent importance of the roadway leading to the station from the hotel

of the Chester and Holyhead Railway Company, dated August 11th, 1847, states: *The work on the Bangor tunnel is more backward than any other between Chester and Bangor,"* from which it is inferred that the other tunnels were not completed at that date, but as the Penmaen tunnel was one of the shortest (1,629 ft long) it seems safe to assume it was finished about this year. Before the tunnel was completed coaches took passengers from the line terminus at the east side to a spot near the Donkey Path crossing, where Colwyn's first station stood. A Mr. George was stationmaster. The house named Pen-y-bryn, pulled down for road widening, was built to accommodate Irish labourers engaged on the tunnel construction. The lower part was used as drinking vaults. Pen-y-coed (later, Messrs. Raynes' Office) was built at the same time.

WATER TROUGHS

Colwyn Bay has an unusual claim to distinction in the railway world. It was at Mochdre that the first experiment was made whereby moving trains picked up water from troughs. The troughs were designed by John Ramsbottom, the Company's Engineer. They were installed at Mochdre-Pabo in 1860. The rectangular mounds, grass covered, which marked the reservoirs could still be traced until the making of the present A55 Expressway in 1985. The troughs were removed to Aber in 1871. A section of the original trough was on view at the Railway Exhibition at Conwy in 1948, when the centenary of the tubular bridges was celebrated by a pageant. During 1906 the railway from East Parade westward was widened to take a double set of rails. Owing to the difficulty of cutting through the headland at Penmaenrhos, the original line was not interfered with here or over the viaducts. The work of widening meant cutting into the East Parade, where previously a broad stretch of sward between the road and the railway's railings afforded an excellent playing ground for children. The transformation of the tiny station into the present spacious one was carried out with remarkably little interference with traffic. In April 1907 a newspaper records: *"The work has been carried on so expeditiously during the last few weeks that the builders now require the land on which the present cab rank is situated for the purpose of continuing the construction of platforms. This will be available for them in a few days, and in its place the new station front will be worked. To gain access to the present station a temporary bridge is being laid through the new premises, emerging on the down platform at the east end."*

The completion of the new station is dealt with almost cursorily in a local news paragraph early in July 1907:

"On Sunday the main line was diverted so as to bring into use the new down platform. Large gangs of men had been at work for two weeks previously carrying out as much of the work as was possible before the actual change was made. The railway presented a busy scene during the earlier hours of Sunday. The new island platform is ultimately intended for the down fast and slow lines, and another island platform is now to be built on the site of the old station for the up fast and slow lines. Until this is ready, however, the traffic will all be conducted over the roads on each side of the new down platform. The platform is about 600 feet long and is roofed over a length of about 400 feet."

The spacious waiting-rooms, bridges and offices are described, and the paragraph concludes: *"In view of the heavy traffic which is now to be expected it is fortunate that the narrow, inconvenient platforms of the old station have been superseded."* [141]

COLWYN IN 1860

A brief description of Colwyn as it was in 1860 is furnished by J.O. Halliwell:

"On the other side of Penmaen Rhos is the pretty bay and rural valley of Colwyn, one of the few spots where all the characteristics of the country are found up to the water-edge. Here are wooded glens, and numerous country walks. The small village, with its neat church, is at a short distance from the sea."

A picture of the land round about Colwyn in the 1860s is given by Alderman D.O. Williams in his notes. He mentions that a "hiring fair" was held at Groes-yn-Eirias, where men and women workers were hired for a year, a shilling "earnest" being paid to ratify the bargain. Here is his description of a walk from Groes to Colwyn:

"Proceeding along the narrow road, fenced on either side with high hedges, all that we can see are the green fields spreading into the distance. We come at length to Lletty'r Dryw. The house Ty Groes still remains, snug and isolated. Looking towards the sea, we catch a glimpse of Glanydon, the charming mansion of the Heskeths with its home farm, occupied by the then holder, Mr. Hilton, a nephew of Mr. Hesketh. As we come to the drive to Glanydon we see above on the right Ty Newydd farm. A narrow lane led up to the farm through a deep cutting from the junction of Llanelian Road and the turnpike road. Along Llanelian Road we come to Tu Hwnt i'r afon farm, the only habitation in this direction apart from Dolddu, and Parcia Farm on the slope to the right."

It is interesting to recall that the original road bore left between Dolddu and the Fairy Glen, crossing the stream by a ford to unite with Peulwys Lane. A possible clue to the date when the road was straightened may be the figures roughly scratched in mortar on the face of the stone bridge across the Meifod Stream. It gives 1813. Another date, almost illegible, appears to refer to the renovation of the bridge. A few yards further along is Pentre Isa', modernised now. The old building, demolished, was the boyhood home of the late Dr. T.Gwynn Jones, scholar,

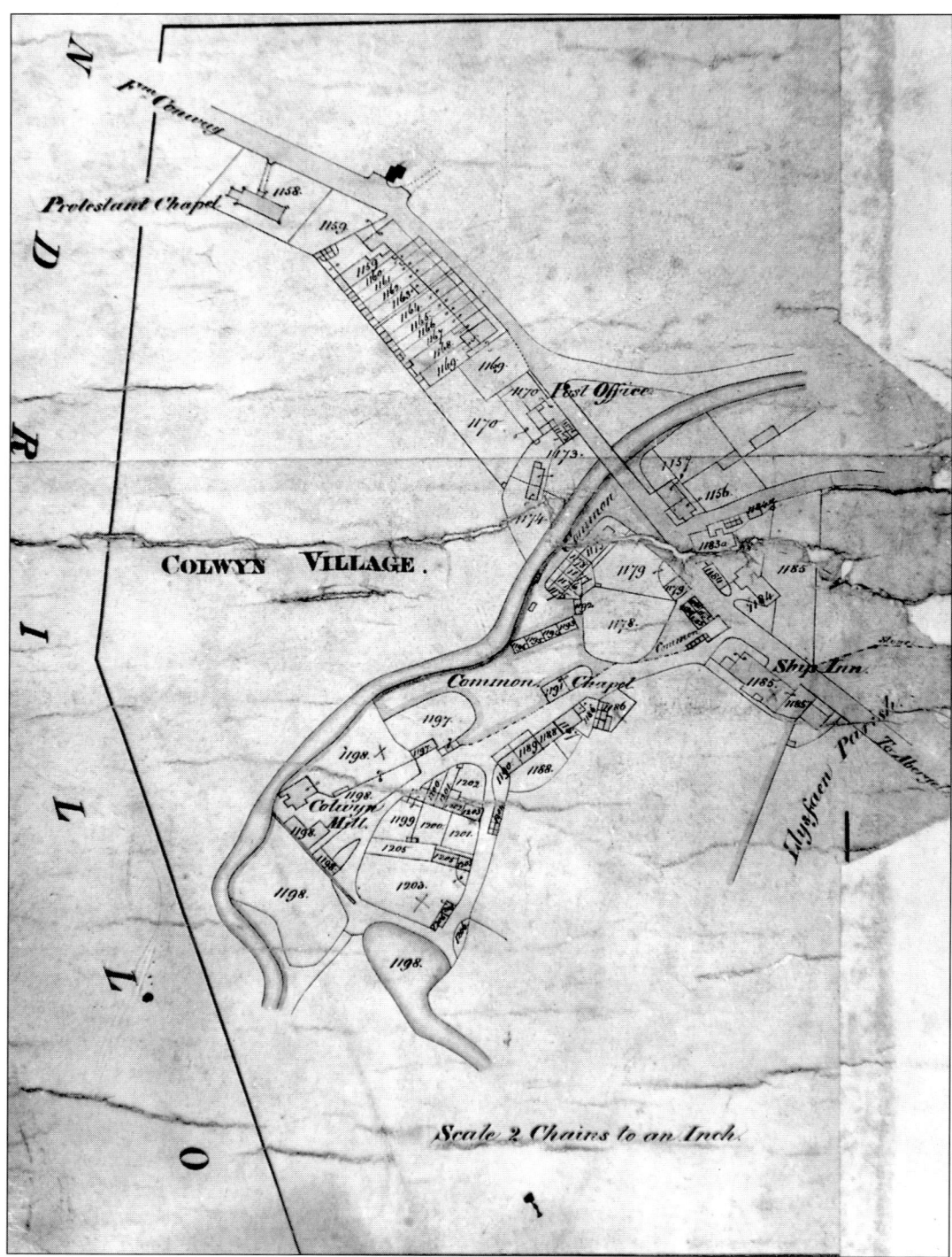

Old Colwyn as it appears in the tithe map of 1847. The "Protestant Chapel" is the Church of St. Catherine. The "Common" beside the Colwyn Stream is not to be associated with the "Chapel" nearby. This is the original Bethesda

The coming of the railway

Colwyn Stream near Llawr Pentre

author and poet. At the entrance are two gigantic yew trees. Their presence is hard to account for, unless one can associate them with the medieval practice of planting two yew trees before a monastic house where travellers might obtain shelter. But to return to Alderman Williams:

Looking towards the village of Colwyn," he writes, "we see on the left Ebenezer Chapel and burial grounds, a solitary building. On the north and east (the site of the present school-room) is a plantation of firs and larches, presumably intended to obscure the building. To the right is St Catherine's Church, the day school and school-house. The Vicar is the Rev. Evan Lewis who lives at Uchydon. A short distance on the left is the drive to Minydon and the lodge. The lodge is a single-storey building fronting the drive. It has a kitchen and two small bedrooms, with semi-circular iron railings at the gable-end. On the left of the cottage is a high door opening to the occupation road, which leads to the farm buildings. From the lodge down to Glanymor Road (Beach Road) is the boundary wall, and a plantation of trees. About halfway down is a small opening and a gate in the wall, with a path leading to the two cottages, Colwyn Fawr.

They stand back about forty yards from the road, opposite "yr artch" (the arch) - now the steps which lead up to Rose Place. Colwyn Fawr was built as a hostel and stood on the old track to the river. On the opposite side is Tai-newyddion and the Plough Inn. The lower cottages, owing to the cutting made when the bridge was built, stood high upon the bank, and about ten feet from the retaining wall, with a few stone steps leading to them. The cottages, ten in number, had the "artch" or entry between the fourth and fifth houses. The path leading through the entry took left across the field, and passing through the farmyard of Tu Hwnt i'r Afon Farm came out in Llanelian Road opposite the occupation road to Parciau Farm. Opposite Glanymor Road was the smithy occupied by William Williams who also kept The Post. The

The turnpike at Colwyn (looking east) flanked by the now demolished Plough Cottages

The coming of the railway

Maes Cadwgan farm, Old Colwyn (now demolished)

The yard and workshop of wheelwright Joseph Evans, beside the River Colwyn, at Llawr Pentre, Old Colwyn, photographed in the late 1880s

house was a double-fronted two-storey building presumably built at the same time as Tai-newyddion. It stood a few feet below the level of the road, with a few stone steps leading down to the door. Before proceeding over the bridge we go down Glanymor Road. Immediately on the right are Tanybryn Cottages (2).

On the opposite side is Tanybryn Bach, a dilapidated thatched roof bwthyn' (cottage) facing the main road. As we descend towards the river Tanybont Cottages (2) come into view on the other side. Between the cottages and the bridge is old Tanybont - evidently built after the bridge as its name implies. We come to Felin Eithin (Gorse Mill) opposite the old well: a two storey building the gable end to the road, and facing the sea, built by Mr Clough. In the river is a pit from which water is pumped up to Minydon. Just below is old Hafodunos, a neat three-roomed cottage, one-storey, with a small flower garden in front. Adjacent, and guarding the old entrance to Minafon, is Bantras Isaf, also a small two-roomed cottage. Projecting into the road is the boathouse with a loft above, facing the sea. Below the viaduct is a large coal-yard belonging to Minydon. (Later, two cottages - since demolished - were built on this site. On crossing the bridge we come to a shop, at one time Berthau Hall. The floor level is lower than the road, much the same as the smithy, suggesting that both were built before the surface of the road was raised. Running down alongside the bridge is a footpath to the river. In 1902, when the bridge was widened, the path was built over to provide a parapet. At the same time the present path under the bridge was made."

The notes state that beyond the Sun Inn and Red Lion was Sun Bach cottage, a pottery store, and lastly Bryn y Gwynt, three two-storey cottages, with slated roofs, on the bank some 15 yards from the road. In Llawr-pentre, four cottages faced the river on the site of Ty Mawr buildings. The doors were sawn in half and the top half was usually open in fine weather. Nearer the bridge was a larger one, where "Jones yr Offis," the coast guard lived. Opposite Sun Bach was Penffordd; two cottages fronting the road and two in the rear:

"A footpath led to Penybryn. Higher up, beyond the opening to Pengwern was the Ship Inn - old Ship Bach[142] - with large stables adjoining. Old residents said that in the coaching days it was customary to change horses at the Ship. We now come to Pendre - as the name implies, the 'last house in the road.' The old name for Station Road was Ffordd Bont Sych -Dry Bridge Road. At the back of the Red Lion is an old bwthyn - the Twlc - protruding into the road. On the left is Green Bank, the first house in the village to be called by an English name. Further on is Cil-llidiau, on the left another thatched cottage. The road narrows to the width of a cart. It has high hedges. We come to the cottage Coed Coch, built by General Wynne as a summer residence in the year the railway was opened. The old Morfa Inn stood on this site. We retrace our steps to Penybryn. On the right is Bethesda Chapel. On the way is the 'pinfold' where stray animals are kept. On the left, late Twnan Terrace, are venerable cottages - a row of six 'cegin a siamber' (kitchen and chamber) type.

Facing us as we proceed are Penygraig Cottages. Taking the left fork - at the gable-end of the terrace - we come to Siop Crydd belonging to Edwin Jones. Over the road is a shed in which he keeps a box mainly filled with sea-pebbles. At the rear is a pair of cottages facing the millpond, Penybryn. The occupier, William Williams, is credited with being the first man to introduce a 'carriage for hire' in the district. I well remember a threshing machine in the roadway nearby, with all the hustle and bustle of threshing corn. At the corner is the Gegin, an old limewashed, thatched bwthyn. The mill-pond is fed by a sluice from Llyn Dolddu. At times frozen over in winter the pond was the rendezvous of the village children. We see below the Felin, the village mill, and its cottage. Farmers from the country round about brought their corn for milling. To continue our tour in the direction of Penmaenrhos, we observe the roadway is wider, with hedges on both sides, but barely a house is to be seen. The shed belongs to a farm, Maes Cadwgan, one of the four biggest in the parish. The house and farm building stand

The coming of the railway

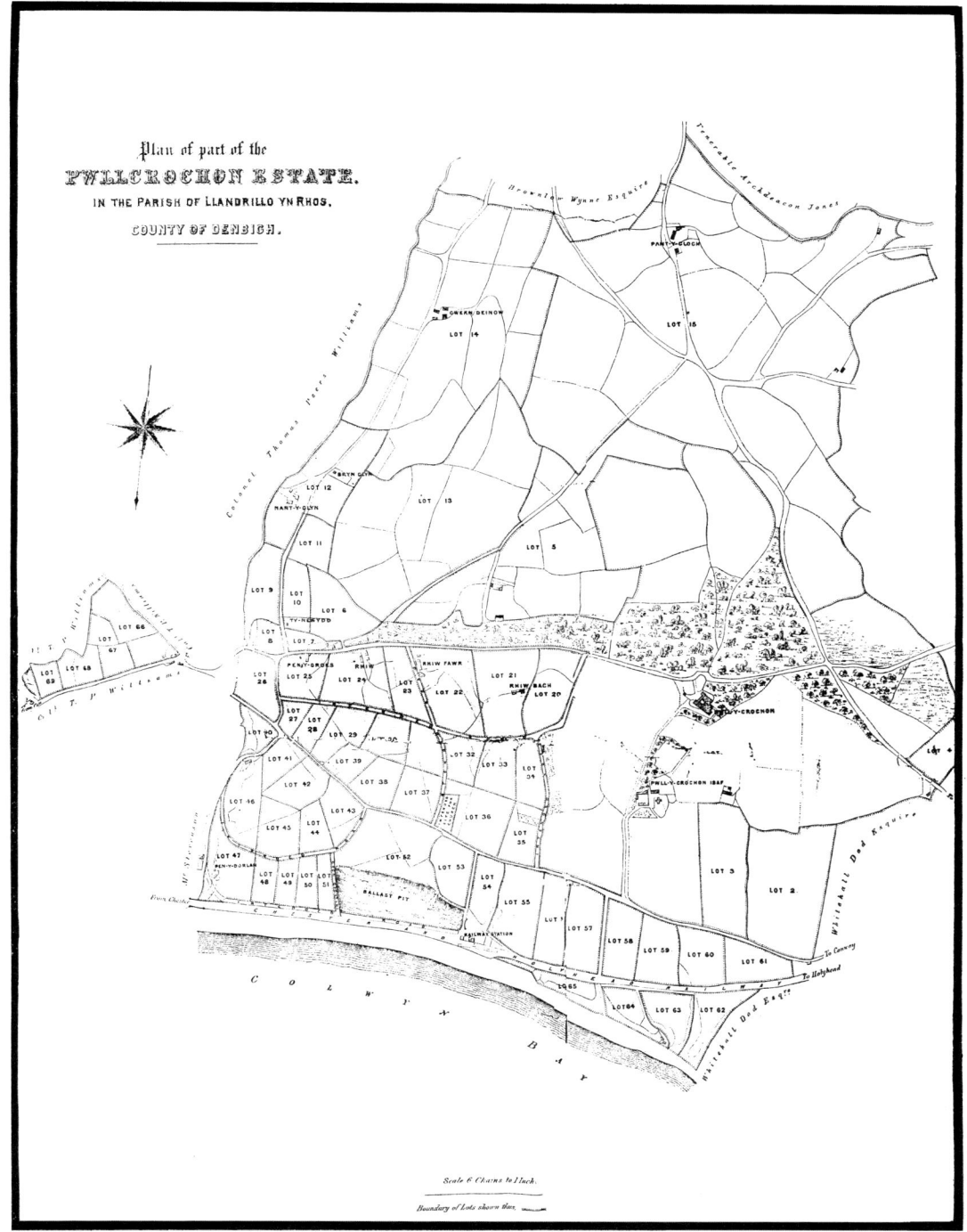

Map from the original sale catalogue of 1865 for the Pwllycrochan Estate

conspicuously among the green fields. It is a double-fronted building with a porch, facing the main road. Across the road from the gate another lane leads so Carmbwll (sandpit) the site of the bowling green, thence past Frongoch to Peulwys Farm. The most conspicuous object in the landscape is Rhuallt, probably built when the road was constructed in 1785."

At the end of his tour Alderman Williams comments: "By now the houses, with very few exceptions, have been demolished."

REMINISCENSES

A picture of the early days of Colwyn was furnished by John W. Lloyd, of the Marine Hotel, when the writer interviewed him in 1923. He recalled the day when Church Walks received its name. As a schoolboy he accompanied his master and another man across excavations made in the Plough garden, preparatory to forming a new road. A discussion ensued as to whether it should be called Church Street or Church Avenue. The schoolboy suggested Church Walks, and the master, taking chalk from his pocket, wrote the name on the top bar of an old gate. Mr. Lloyd also recalled how the Donkey Path came by its title. A footpath used to run across the corner of the field near the present path, crossing a stile and a brook on its way to Minydon. An idea was conceived of elaborating this path. A Mr. J.D.Jones raffled a black donkey which realised £60, and with the money a new path was constructed to the sea front.

The story of Victoria's stopping at the Ship was believed by Mr Lloyd, who said the "Queen" (then Princess) was supposed to have dined in the building. He was not old enough to recall coaching days, but his father and uncle had told him how the coaches came down the road from Llysfaen (Rhuallt) before the road past the Queen's Hotel[143] was constructed. The coaches, before the bridge was built, "had to cross higher up, coming out by the old Plough Hotel." Similar stories were told by Edwin Davies, Bryn Cethin, who could recall Colwyn in the 1860s. He remembered when the main road was a narrow turnpike with no dwelling save an occasional cottage or farm between Colwyn and Mochdre. The house known as Groes Bach was an inn. When Sir John Barlow's father bought the estate he had the licence abolished. The Foresters met in a room over the coach-house.

Colwyn people who travelled by train had to walk from Colwyn Bay station. It was a narrow, inconvenient lane, and passengers arriving late were glad of each other's company. People from Rhyl often alighted at the old Llysfaen station and walked to Colwyn from there. Mr. Davies said that in his young days there were (shops excepted) the following houses: Church Walks, 13; Green Hill, 3; Mount Pleasant, 11; Chapel Street, 3; Llaw'r Pentre, 23; Penybryn, 9. Water could only be obtained from a well in Beach Road, a spout opposite the Mill, and a well called Ffynnon Owen[144] near the entrance to Dolddu. Later water was brought from the Rhiw Reservoirs, the water being pumped from Groes Mill. Beach Road was chiefly used for the conveyance of coal brought by small vessels. It was used for burning lime at Llysfaen. Farmers joined to fill a small kiln. In his childhood the National School was where the Assembly Rooms now stand, and there was an infants' school on the site of the subsequent National School. When the British School (later the Council School) was erected the fee was a penny a week. Mr. Davies said that at one time a considerable iron ore industry existed at Penmaen, a fact which might account for the name of the Miners' Arms. Most of the product was sent to South Wales.[145]

THE BIRTH OF A RESORT

Now the time approaches for the momentous year 1865, which saw the sale of land responsible for the creation of the COLWYN BAY we know today. As our town emanated from the Pwllycrochan Estate something must be said about the old manor, and the family of Erskine. For details of Pwllycrochan one cannot do better than to draw freely upon George Porter's exceptional little book, *Colwyn Bay Before the Houses Came*, for the author was born at Pwllycrochan, and wrote from firsthand experience. This is augmented by records of the actual sale, kindly loaned by Mr. J.L.Porter, his nephew, who also lent an old scrap-book kept by his grandfather, John Porter JP, of Pwllycrochan, one of the founders of Colwyn Bay. In older records the name is spelt "Pwllycrochon" or "Pwll-y-Crochan." Its exact age is hard to trace. The oldest name of the land so far encountered is "Rew" (Rhiw).

DATE OF PWLLYCROCHAN

In Llandrillo Church is a tombstone inscribed: UNDERNEATH LYETH THE BODY OF ROBERT CONWAY OF PWLLYCROCHAN, GENT. WAS BURIED HERE BY THE LEAVE OF ROBERT DAVIES, ESQR. THE... NOVEMBER ANN. DOM. 1693. AETATIS SUAE 75.

Mr. Porter observed: *"I do not think that Pwllycrochan can have existed before this date."* A John Conway of Pwllycrochan was buried at Llandrillo in 1702. In the pedigree of the Hollands of Conwy there is reference to Jane Holland (1715-80) marrying Robert Williams of Pwllycrochan – who died in June 1760, aged 44. His raised tomb in the transept of Conwy Church records that he left four sons, Holland, Thomas, Robert and Hugh. His widow died in 1780, aged 65. Mr. Porter concludes that Robert Conway appeared to have adopted Hugh Williams of Rhydygwynt as his successor. Robert Williams was High Sheriff for Denbighshire in 1747, and the Jane Holland he married was heiress of the influential family which lived at Plas Isaf, Conwy. His son, Holland Williams, was squire until 1799. He died without issue and Pwllycrochan devolved on his younger brother, the Rev. Hugh Williams of Conwy (Vicar 1786-1791), who also held the Plas Isaf property. He died at Pwllycrochan in 1809.

BARONET BRIDEGROOM

In his will of 1808 he left the Plas Isaf and Pwllycrochan estates to his daughter, Jane Silence Williams, who, while touring on the Continent, met David Erskine of Cambo, Fifeshire. They were married in 1821, the bridegroom's receiving a baronetcy on his wedding day. Sir David was born in Sweden in 1792 and was a grandson of the ninth Earl of Kellie. Sir David and Lady Erskine chose to reside at Pwllycrochan. He was elected a burgess of Conwy in 1821, and alderman in 1822 and 1826. He was High Sheriff for Denbighshire in 1823

"OLD PRICE"

From about 1800 Pwllycrochan had been occupied by an eccentric clergyman, the Rev. James Price, MA, who rented it from his friend, Lady Erskine's father. It was here his son, John Price, was born in 1803. In his quaint book, *Old Price's Remains*, the latter has several references to the old house. Mr. Price (senior) undertook extensive alterations, so extensive, that *"whole rooms lay exposed to the open air and had to be guarded by dogs."* Old Price gives a picture of Pwllycrochan as it was when he was a little boy:

"I found him in the old dining room; I mean the original room where the rats' white feet used to show under the skirting-board, before he and his indulgent landlord (the Rev. Hugh Williams) had indulged each other with the deformation and reformation of that quaint red-brick mansion with steep slate roof, prominent garret windows and a high flight of stone steps few of the like now left in North Wales."

Pwllycrochan was destined to undergo several structural alterations in addition to those carried out by the Rev. James Price. When Sir David and Lady Erskine decided to make Pwllycrochan their home, the Prices removed to old Bodnant, where they dwelt for seven years. After this the Rev. James Price removed to Plas-yn-Llysfaen. He died at the age of 93 in 1850. "Old Price" died in Chester in 1887. One of Sir David's first acts was to wipe out the old red brick dwelling and to build an entirely new manor house, the nucleus of the existing building. Meadows were planted with trees and others introduced into the existing woods, which were laid out with walks and rustic bridges. The private drive through the parkland was later replaced by Pwllycrochan Avenue, which, however, does not follow the original private drive, which lay slightly to the west. A gardener's house and farm buildings adjoined Pwllycrochan. Behind were extensive buildings, coach-houses, stabling for a dozen horses, kennels, laundry, brewery and storehouses. The new baronet settled quickly into his new role and in 1823 was elected High Sheriff for Denbighshire. Sir David was a churchwarden, and his signature is in the minute book of the Llandrillo Vestry meeting held in August 1827.

FESTIVITIES AT CONWY

The *Chester Chronicle* of 24 January 1823, records:

"On Wednesday last Lady Erskine, Conway and Pwllycrochan, near Conway, attained the 21st year of her age; the morning between twelve and one, was ushered with a salute of 21 guns, and the bells rang a merry peal, to commemorate the hour her Ladyship was born. In the course of the day old Conway was enlivened by neighbouring and distant gentry, and the town was throng'd with their tenants, both from Carnarvon and Denbighshire. The whole of the day past with the greatest conviviality, cwrw da was abundantly flowing, and Bachus was not spared at Bodlondeb, the seat of her Ladyship's mother."

When the Menai Suspension Bridge was opened on 30 January 1826, by the crossing of the London and Holyhead mail coach, the vehicle was followed by a triumphal procession. After carriages containing officials there came *"the carriage of Sir D. Erskine, Bart, late proprietor of the ferry, drawn by four elegant greys, decorated with ribbons."* [146] It will be seen that Sir David took his part in the affairs of Llandrillo parish, and when he died in 1841, at the age of 48, he was greatly missed. An obituary notice records:

"He commenced a variety of most extensive improvements which afford employment to an immense number of workmen who are now bewailing his loss. He made his tenantry comfortable and happy, gave them additional accommodation, and at his own expense drained their farms."

Sir David was buried at Cambo, but the Dowager Lady Erskine continued to reside at Pwllycrochan. With her were the new baronet, Sir Thomas Erskine, and five other children, one of whom, Captain David Erskine, served through the Crimean War. Lady Erskine and Sir Thomas were active, and the triangle of younger trees in the Pwllycrochan Woods is doubtless due to their enthusiasm, as the tithe map of 1846 marks this site "Plantation, lately arable."[147] Lady Erskine (who died in 1886) was responsible for the erection of the crenellated dove-cote which stood near what is now Walshaw Avenue, but which was long ago pulled down. She took a kindly interest in the children of the neighbourhood. There is a record in 1850 of a gorsedd held at Pwllycrochan, at which the Dowager Lady Erskine was admitted to the degree of Ovate with the Bardic title of Ifores Gwynedd. Her daughter Mary became Mair Glan Conway.[148] When the National Eisteddfod was held in Conwy Castle in 1861 the Dowager Lady Erskine was president. As it was incumbent upon the new baronet to dwell for a portion of each year in his northern home, it was resolved to sell the Welsh estate.

COLWYN BAY'S FIRST HOUSE

Ivy House appears to have established beyond dispute its claim to be the first house in Colwyn Bay. It was built beside the turnpike by Thomas Hughes, who was born at Plas Eiddew, Llanrwst, and he bestowed an English variant of his boyhood home's name on the three-storey house he erected. At the start he was interested solely in farming, and his cows grazed on land now occupied by St. Paul's Church grounds. With an eye to trade, he experimented with a small grocer's shop, the door of which was at the south-west corner of the house. The village store grew in time into one of the town's flourishing grocery businesses. Ivy House was built in 1865, and the street which ran beside it took its name from the house. Cottages built at the lower end for workmen engaged on the Colwyn Bay Hotel were termed Ivy Cottages.

The first houses in Station Road were on the east side at the top, and were originally dwelling houses with small gardens in front - a more imposing type of the houses along Sea View Crescent. With the growth of the village they were, one by one, converted into shops. So far as can be ascertained the name "Colwyn Bay" was first applied to the Station in 1872.

Colwyn Bay's first house. Ivy House at the top of Ivy Street when it was the village grocer's shop. The porch was removed to Wern cottage, Mochdre

THE TOWN TO BE

In 1865 the Pwllycrochan Estate was offered for sale and land which had been farm fields cut by a turnpike road became the scene of such enterprise that within thirty years the new town was recognized as an Urban District. The rapid growth, the perspicacity of the pioneers, the pristine charm of the countryside, quickly attracted persons to the enterprising seaside resort. Imagination needs to be supplemented by pictures and maps to depict those early days when the main road, bordered by trees, resembled some little Welsh village, and even the wheeled bathing-vans and rowing-boats on the shingle had hardly become acclimatized. The dates on some of the town's older buildings still bear mute testimony to the faith and foresight of the founders. One of the first buildings was the Colwyn Bay Hotel,[149] another was the Coed Pella Hotel (now the British Legion Club), which stood well-nigh surrounded by fields, with the whitewashed farm of Rhiw Bach at no great distance. Glimpses of those early days remain - the dark and lonely streets, Rhos and Colwyn isolated and self-contained communities, a cluster of shops and houses near the railway station, a fragment of promenade, the massive Rhos fields which stretched, broken by a hawthorn hedge or two, all the way from Penrhos to Aberhod.

Until the Pwllycrochan Estate came on the market in 1865 it is doubtful whether Colwyn Bay was even contemplated. The date 1870 carved on the facade of Rhoslan (demolished in the 1980s) perpetuates the erection of the two stately villas which might be regarded as harbingers of the select resort. These, then known as Erskine Villa and Penrhos Lodge, arose at the top of what is now Marine Road, but which was then termed Sea Shore Road. They were in a direct line between the new Pwllycrochan Hotel and the proposed Colwyn Bay Hotel on the coast. If Ivy House was the first house in Colwyn Bay, the town came into being between 1865 and 1870. The main road, sometimes referred to as the London Road, was not then considered worthy of fficial recognition but was designated "the turnpike." It ran between hedgerows bordered by stately oaks, and must have resembled the remaining fragment which lies west of Eagles Farm at Mochdre.

View from Old Highway showing white-washed Rhiw Bach farm, near Coed Pella Road

THE GREAT SALE

During four days in September 1865, the Pwllycrochan and Bodlondeb estates, comprising about 3,000 acres of land, were offered for sale, at the Erskine Arms, Conwy. The auctioneer was William Dew. The following description is taken from the sale catalogue:

PWLLYCROCHAN ESTATE

This fine Property commands one of the grandest Marine Prospects in this most popular neighbourhood, with a splendid Sea Bathing Beach, 1¼ miles in length, forming a perfect Amphitheatre. The...

COMMODIOUS AND WELL-BUILT MANSION

With its extensive Preserves, Shrubberies, Pleasure Grounds, Walled Garden, and a portion of the Demesne, will be sold in one Lot, and the remaining portion fronting the sea will be sold in separate Lots to meet the great and increasing demand for MARINE RESIDENCES on this Coast.

THE FARMS

Which are well Tenanted and Cultivated, will be sold separately, as shown in the Particulars. This Property enjoys peculiar advantages over any in the Principality from its contiguity to the Beach, where Bathing can be had at all times of the Tide, its great facilities for House Drainage, its bountiful supply of Water, and particularly its...

CLOSE PROXIMITY TO THE RAILWAY

Which skirts its base, having a Station in the centre. It is intersected also by the Main and Turnpike Road leading from Conway to Chester - a combination of Resources which unquestionably will make this one of the most desirable and favourite Watering Places in the United Kingdom at no very distant date.

The mansion, the catalogue states, had been recently enlarged and beautified in the Tudor style of architecture. For background there was a flourishing plantation, 50 acres in extent. An Act had been obtained for the erection of a pier at Llandrillo, 400 yards in length, to which steamers could ply at all times of the tide.

Pwllycrochan demesne, mansion, farm buildings and gardens, with some adjoining land, were purchased by Mr. (later Sir) John Pender for £26,000. The accompanying plan marks, in addition to Pwllycrochan (spelt Pwllcrochon) the following buildings on the land now occupied by Colwyn Bay: Pwll-y-crochan Isaf, Poplas, Cil Cow, Pen-y-dorlan farm, Ty'n-y-Maes (Dinglewood), Ty'n-y-ffordd, Rhiw Bach, Rhiw Mawr, Rhiw, Pen-y-groes (ffordd), Rising Sun Inn, Groes Mill and a small railway station. The adjoining landowners are marked: To the west, Whitehall Dod Esquire; east of the Dingle, Mr. Stevenson; Groes and Nantyglyn, Colonel Thomas Peers Williams; Pant-y-Gloch vicinity, Brownlow Wynn, Esquire (east), Archdeacon Jones (west).

A PEACEFUL SCENE

A more picturesque description of the scene as it was several years later is given by George Porter, who recalled boyhood days spent at Pwllycrochan:

"Standing before the house I gazed on a tract of peaceful, sparsely inhabited, agricultural land sloping fairly steeply away for about a mile to the seashore close beside which ran the L&NW Railway line. About half-a-dozen houses at Rhos, the same number round the railway station, then called Colwyn, and the Colwyn Bay Hotel, represented the feeble beginnings of a town. Away across the large fields of Bryn Euryn farm stood the square tower of Llandrillo Church and the tall chimney of ruined Llys Euryn. As for the res - a few cottages and a farmhouse here and there peeped up almost hidden in the countrified expanse of fields, trees, streams and dingles. If in those days a visitor emerged from the hotel on a walk to the station he would at once find himself on a private drive fenced off by light wire railings from the spacious parks on either side. Looking over his right shoulder towards the woods, he would see the arbutus tree, now in the middle of the road, growing in the East Park. After passing through a gate he would see through a screen of trees Pwllycrochan Isaf farm, and from there on, the farm road and the drive, separated by a hedge, ran side by side to the turnpike road. After passing the final gate, he would find himself on the main road about fifty yards west of the present junction. He would then walk between hedges on a purely country road to the tollbar and down the lane to diminutive Colwyn Station, then partially encircled by a dingle. During the whole of his walk, with the exception of the tollbar he would not have passed a single building, and quite probably have not met a single soul. As likely as not he would have heard a covey of partridges whirring over his head."

The Ordnance Survey map of 1890 shows numerous oaks beside Conwy Road.

BUILDING PLOTS

Once the sale of the Pwllycrochan Estate had taken place little time was lost embarking on the project of creating a seaside resort. It spoke well for the courage of the founders that one of the first tasks was the erection of the Colwyn Bay Hotel and a stretch of promenade known then as The Parade. The new town hesitated timidly in the vicinity of the tiny railway station. An Ordnance Survey map of 1875 (the first) shows the cluster of houses and shops confined almost entirely within the triangle comprising the top eastern portion of Station Road to the corner now occupied by the Royal Hotel, and down Sea View Crescent to the bottom of Station Road, where a shop (still standing) was separated from those higher up the road by an open field. Nothing indicates the rural nature of the district in those days so much as the name of the house which stood on the site of the Royal Hotel. It was called Penmaen View. This was occupied by John Jones, father of Mrs. J.L.Hunt. He had the house demolished to build the hotel. John Porter, who turned Pwllycrochan into a hotel, the Rev. W.Venables Williams, Vicar of Llandrillo-yn-Rhos, and the Rev. Thomas Parry, were outstanding figures in the creation of Colwyn Bay. Ivy House, erected by Thomas Hughes, father of the late Councillor Hugh Hughes, at the top of Ivy Street, was the centre of village life. At the foot of Ivy Street, Rose Cottage, named from the white roses which grew over it, had fowls and pigs in its backyard. By 1872 Colwyn, as it was then termed, was described in the Press as *"a pretty and rising watering place, situated between Llanddulas and Llandudno Junction."*

MR. PENDER VISITS COLWYN BAY

John Pender, who had recently been returned a Member of Parliament for the Wick burgs, signified his intention of visiting the village that was growing on his newly acquired estate. He did so on 18 March 1872, and a public reception was accorded him. Arches of flowers and evergreens bearing *"Welcome"* spanned the roadway from the station to the Pwllycrochan Hotel, which building was gaily adorned with flags and banners, as were houses along the route. The day was kept as a public holiday. The train from Chester arrived at 11.10 a.m. to the strains of *See the Conquering Hero*. A large number of the inhabitants of the parish and workmen of the estate, all wearing favours, awaited the arrival at the station. Mr. Pender alighted in company with Mr. C.Ewing (Golden Grove, Hoole, Chester), and Mr. Douglas (Chester) architect, was received by the Rev. W.Venables Williams (Vicar of Llandrillo-yn-Rhos) and Mrs. Williams, the Rev. J. D. Jones (Vicar of Colwyn), and Mrs. Jones, Dr. Davies (Colwyn), Mr. J. Porter (Pwllycrochan Hotel), Mr. Parry and other influential residents in the parish, the large assemblage present giving him a most hearty reception. Mr. Pender entered a carriage, from which the crowd had unharnessed the horses, and was drawn through the village, amidst many signs of rejoicing, including salvoes of artillery.[150]

The original Royal Hotel, corner of Abergele Road and Seaview Road

The Vicar of Llandrillo presented Mr Pender with the following address of welcome:

"We, your friends and well-wishers in the parish of Llandrillo-yn-Rhos, beg to offer you our warmest congratulations on your being returned to the House of Commons, of which, we feel sure from your great mercantile experience, and the impetus which by your energy you have given to the extension of telegraphic communication throughout the world, you will prove yourself a valuable and useful member. We welcome you, too, amongst us with much pleasure as one of the principal landowners in the parish, and a large employer of labour in this rising neighbourhood which, under your auspices, we hope soon to see a favourite resort for visitors.

Hoping you may long be spared to enjoy your Parliamentary honours, and we may have more frequent opportunities of seeing you amongst us, we give you a hearty greeting.

(signed) Wm. Venables Williams, MA., Vicar, John Porter, John Thomas, Churchwardens, on behalf of the parishioners."

In course of his reply Mr. Pender mentioned that his mother-in-law (Mrs. Denison) resided at Bodlondeb, Conwy, which accounted for his interest in the Pwllycrochan sale. Mr. Pender said the estate which now belonged to him was being developed in a way which gave employment to a large number of the population, and would eventually bring into the neighbourhood a large influx of people who would encourage labour. He also trusted the locality would rise as a watering place, that with it the moral growth of the people inhabiting it would increase and that the population would be exemplary in their conduct and dealings. During the day Mr. Pender *"inspected the building operations that are at present going on for the beautifying of this charming watering place, which every year as it becomes better known is being more largely patronised by visitors,"* reported the *Caernarvon & Denbigh Herald*.

"So great indeed has been the increase of visitors that it was deemed necessary to build *another hotel in addition to the Pwll-y-crochon (which is so efficiently and courteously managed by Mr. and Mrs Porter), and Mr. Douglas of Chester furnished designs for the erection of a large and commodious building in every way suitable for this rising locality. The plans were approved, in a short time the work of building commenced, and now a really splendid hotel rears its massive form in view of every traveller by the railway. It is situated on the side of the line nearest the sea, and commands a splendid and uninterrupted view from all points of the compass. The building is nearly completed, and will in a short time be opened to those visitors - and their name is now legion - who visit Colwyn."*

In a list of Justices who had *"taken the Oaths during Her present Majesty's reign"* for the County of Denbigh, the name of John Pender, Esq., is given as qualifying on 5 January 1871. The Reverend William Venables Williams had been made a Justice of the Peace on 22 October 1868, and Sir Thomas Erskine, Bart., on 4 January 1856. Mr. Pender was made a Knight of the Order of St. Michael and St. George by Queen Victoria. He will be remembered for his work in connection with the Atlantic cables. He died at Foot's Cray in Kent, 1896.

About 1875 Sir John Pender decided to sell his land. A Manchester syndicate known as the Colwyn Bay and Pwllycrochan Estate Company was formed, and bought the bulk of the Pwllycrochan Estate. The auction was held by William Dew & Sons, at the new Colwyn Bay Hotel, on 12 October 1875. It was anticipated the sale would last three days, but it was completed in one. Five small lots were sold to the Railway Company and the Colwyn Bay Hotel. John Porter bought the freehold of the Pwllycrochan Hotel, and the Manchester syndicate purchased the remainder for £87,500. Among the syndicate the most active workers were Messrs. Haworth, Abraham Lloyd, Edmund Miles, Lawrence Booth, Dr. Read and Dr. Mould—all prominent Lancashire men. Mr. Lloyd subsequently became Lord Mayor of Manchester. Lawrence Booth (an architect) was a friend of Sir Henry Irving.[151]

In the 1890s when the town's west boundary ended at Marine Road. View from Bryn Euryn. Turnpike and Board School in foreground

NEW COLWYN

It will thus be seen that in a matter of ten years Colwyn had established a reputation as a seaside resort. At this time it was proposed to make a new road *"from the magnificent new hotel at New Colwyn to join the road from Llandudno, by the Little Ormeshead."* This would shorten the distance to Llandudno by 3½ to 4 miles. In May 1872 some parishioners met at the Pwllycrochan to present to the Vicar, the Rev. W. Venables Williams, a chiming timepiece and gold Albert chain and pendant *"in recognition of his indomitable perseverance in correcting the notorious abuses by the Conway Union."* Mr. Porter, who made the presentation, read the inscription:

"Presented to the Rev. W. Venables Williams, M.A., Vicar of Llandrillo-yn-Rhos, by a few friends, in recognition of his persevering and successful efforts to bring about a uniform and equitable system of rating in the Union of Conway."

NEW MISSION CHAPEL

In 1872 a new mission chapel was erected on part of the site of St. Paul's Church on land given by Sir Thomas Erskine, Bart. *"Last year,"* wrote the Vicar, *"in consequence of the fast increasing population at Rhos Bay, near the Colwyn station, it occurred to me that it was necessary to have a Sunday service there. Accordingly in the second week in June I commenced an afternoon service in a long open shed used for a sawing machine, kindly lent for the purpose by Mr. Abel Roberts. The service was well attended up to September."*

The first sod of the mission chapel was cut on 21 May 1872, and the building opened on 18 June at a cost of £170. A local newspaper comments:

"The new mission chapel which has been erected as if by magic at New Colwyn, was only commenced upon a month previous to its being opened. It is only a temporary building at present, and is forty-five feet long and twenty-six feet wide, built of bricks and timber, and is slated with red tiles. It is a very neat construction and is provided with all necessaries, including a bell. It is at present fitted up with chairs to accommodate about one hundred and seventy worshippers. . ."

The architectural portion of the work was executed by Mr. Douglas, the architect of the large new hotel close by, Mr. Beckett of Hartford, Cheshire, being the contractor. The ground upon which the chapel stands was liberally given by Sir Thomas Erskine, and is sufficient for a much larger building and burial grounds.

The village was obviously growing in popularity. A correspondent to the *Manchester Courier* of 15 July 1878, speaks of visiting Colwyn Bay *"sometimes called Rhos Bay."* He went on:

"Although the village or town of Colwyn Bay has attracted many visitors, I really wonder it is not more attracted. I was informed by a medical gentleman that, as a winter marine residence, Colwyn Bay cannot be surpassed. . . On the south is Llysfaen and Penmaen Rhos rocks; on the south-west the magnificent Bron-y-nant Woods, through which the old Roman Road passes, affording a pleasant, shaded walk. Here, conveniently situated, is the Pwllycrochan Hotel, once the charming residence of the late Lady Erskine, and amongst the attractions of the neighbourhood there are Bryn Eurin, Rhos Quarry Rocks, and the ruins of the Palace of Ednyfed Vauchan, secretary to Prince Llewelyn of Wales."

THE TOLL BARS

A source of annoyance in the early days was a toll-bar which stood at the top of Station Road, the collector's hut being on the corner of Abergele Road and Station Road. It proved an expense for vehicles going to the railway station, and an alternative route was devised by making a short road, which ran between the present Penrhyn and Station Roads. The move was spon-

The Birth of a Resort

Colwyn Bay as it was between 1875-1880 (Acknowledgement to H.M. Ordnance Survey)

sored by John Porter as agent to the Estate, and though a law suit resulted, Mr. Porter won his case. Drivers going down this short cut and coming up Sea View Terrace were able to go to Old Colwyn without paying toll, and a gate was accordingly placed at the top of what is now Greenfield Road to put a stop to the practice. One winter's night in 1871 some unknown persons tore down the gate and flung it and the posts into the sea, at a spot near the Colwyn Bay Hotel, then in course of construction. Ultimately it was cast up by the waves near Bangor.[152]

A correspondent in a contemporary newspaper wrote:

"The iniquitous, and we may say, ill-advised, action in erecting a tollbar immediately opposite a public refreshment room was not a thing to be borne quietly, and while we deprecate any illegal acts which were at first resorted to for its removal, the inhabitants of Colwyn were justified in testing the legality of such an obstruction. If trustees are empowered to erect two gates, as they have done at Colwyn, within three hundred and sixty yards of each other, and tax farmers who had passed upon a certain portion of the road without toll, we question the advisibiliry of it.... the extensive building operations which are going on at Colwyn opened several new roads to the station, and these were naturally used by parties in preference to paying toll. We also consider that a fair offer had been made by the owner of the estate as compensation for the total abolition of the impost."

Before long the tollgates were abolished. At a spot near the present corner of Greenfield Road - an appropriate name in those days! - there is marked on the Ordnance Survey Map of 1875 "COLWYN NEW T.P." One of the first builders, the Rev. Thomas Parry, started a brickworks at the west end. Here a special row of cottages for the men engaged was called the Brickfields, later known as Westwood Terrace. The pits from which the lay was excavated remained for many years. Filled with rain water they proved excellent lakes for boys' rafts. The glow of the fires at the brickworks on a dark night threw a lurid glow in the western sky, and to people in Colwyn Bay the district seemed (to quote an old resident) *"like another country."* When the town began to grow in the 1860s and 70s the houses along the "turnpike" had short gardens in front. As the district developed these were taken over by the local authority to permit road widening.

COLWYN BAY AND COLWYN IN 1875

An accurate picture of the district in 1875 is possible through the medium of the earliest Ordnance Survey map. Apart from the buildings along the Old Highway, already dealt with, the map records the Colwyn Bay Hotel with a road leading up to the turnpike at which are situated the two "Erskine Villas." There is no Pwllycrochan Avenue, the lane to Pwllycrochan starting about fifty yards further westward. At the West End were the brickworks. A Presbyterian Chapel and two other buildings - one the Station Hotel - are shown at the top corner of Station Road. There is no other building on the west side of Station Road. On the east side there is one building facing the station, then a gap until the upper shops are shown. Ivy House is named and there are two other houses between it and Sea View Road. The houses from the back lane down Sea View Crescent to Ivy Street are marked, and the cottages in the lower portion of Ivy Street. Several railway lines are shown in the Ballast Pit. Along the Abergele Road is one lone house marked "Emlyn." This was next to or part of the original Clock House, which was built in 1870. Other places were Pen-y-dorlan farm, Ty'n-maes and Pen-y-Maes, and some cottages near the mouth of the Dingle, the cottage Tyn-y-ffordd, and the Mission Room. The main road bridge over the Dingle is termed Pont-y-groes-yn-Eirias. A winding lane, bordered by trees and ending in a little dingle, marks the present Penrhyn Road.

Expansion and Development

At the time the hamlet of Colwyn Bay was first formed beside its railway station, its affairs were managed from Conwy by the Guardians of the Poor, as the parishes of Llandrillo-yn-Rhos and Eirias were included in the Conwy Rural District. The civic child was a healthy babe. By 1887 it was sufficiently developed to be considered a local government area of its own and was placed under the control of a Local Board.

This Local Board of twelve members was constituted on 25 April 1887, by Order of the Local Government Board (No. 21442). The following were the chairmen:

1887-1890	Rev. Thomas Parry JP
1890-1891	John Porter JP.
1891-1895	Rev W Venables Williams MA, J P.

One of the facts which strikes forcibly was the enterprise of the early builders. Consider the height and size of Bron Derw and Oaklands beside the Conwy Road! The date 1877 on the facade shows they must have stood among fields, yet they are still listed among the largest buildings of the town. So rapid was the growth that by 1891 there were 833 inhabited houses in Colwyn Bay, and a population of which had risen to 4,754. The first system of sewerage for the district was undertaken in 1877 during the days of the rural authority. The design was that of James Farrar, CE, of Bury (Lancs.). Three schemes were laid, one for Colwyn Bay, one for Colwyn and the other for Rhos. Each had a distinct and separate outfall discharging into the bay.

1887–1895

Between the time the Local Board was appointed in 1887 and the 1 January 1895, when Colwyn Bay and Colwyn became an Urban District, there was considerable building activity. The Local Board held their meetings in a building near the top of Ivy Street where the Electricity Power Sub-Station now stands. In addition to the Council Room the building housed the local Police Station and also a small, horse-drawn fire engine. For a long while a field, bordered by a hedge, stretched along the west side of Station Road between the Imperial Hotel (at the foot) and the Station Hotel (now the Central) at the top. A tall red brick building rose beside the lane which separated this field from the Imperial Hotel. The date 1892 can still be seen, and with it various designs which affirm that the structure served jointly the National Provincial Bank and the County administration. The Police Station was removed from Ivy Street and established in this building, entrance being obtained by a side door. Handcuffs are carved in the stone of one of the spandrels of the door facing Station Road. The first officer was Police Constable Harnaman, whose area extended from Rhos-on-Sea to Llysfaen.

From these humble beginnings the activities of the Police increased until their headquarters was removed in 1907 to the spacious County Buildings in Rhiw Road.[153] A handsome stone building was erected at the union of Abergele and Conwy Roads, effectively preventing the continuation of Station Road as far as Hillside Road as was, apparently, once contemplated. At

Looking down Station Road before the ornamental fountain was erected in 1895

Conway Road in the 1880s. On the extreme right is the first Presbyterian Church, pulled down before the Mews was built near the top of Station Road

Looking up Station Road from the old station yard. The Central Hotel at the top was then called the Station Hotel

first it served as a chemist's shop and incorporared in this was the Colwyn Bay Post Office, which was removed there from a shop on the east side of Station Road.

Water for the growing town was one of the most urgent problems and in 1891 the need was met by the creation of the Conway and Colwyn Bay Joint Water Supply Board. The year 1892 saw further developments. The Private Street Works Act was adopted. The main Abergele Road was widened from its turnpike dimensions. The approach to the beach and the "subway" were completed that year and formally opened by one of the prime movers, the Rev. W. Venables Williams.

Final arrangements for the creating of the Urban District were completed in 1894. Work was commenced on the sea front, where a section of promenade was to be made. Rhos-on-Sea was still remote. The only way a vehicle could go there was by Conwy Road, Tan-y-Bryn Road and Rhos Road, but there were plans to bring about its development.

NEW COLWYN

The name "New Colwyn" was changed - apparently at the suggestion of John Porter - to "Colwyn Bay." A writer to the *Christian World* in 1875 refers to *"the peaceful tranquillity of Colwyn Bay,"* and adds that the houses were but few, and mostly surrounded by gardens. During the early days when the new community was governed by the Guardians of the Poor of the Conway Union, Eirias found itself in a curious position, being in the middle of Llandrillo

Parish (of which it originally formed a part) and situated between Colwyn village and Colwyn Bay. There were stormy meetings of the Guardians, at which the Vicar of Llandrillo figured conspicuously. As the new town developed it was obvious that some fresh arrangements would have to be made. In 1887 the two parishes became a local government area under the control of a Local Board. For seven years the town continued to grow under these conditions. In 1894 the Urban District of Colwyn Bay and Colwyn was formed and formally came into existence the following January. During this period some important undertakings were dealt with, affecting the future prosperity of the district. One of the problems was the education of the children, and there were public meetings to decide whether Llandrillo and Eirias should have one School Board or two.

WATER SUPPLY

One of the first concerns of the local authority was to provide a water supply for the growing town. Details of this and the early gas undertaking were furnished by C.B.Farrington, who was the engineer in charge. In 1867 a small reservoir of a capacity of about 150,000 gallons was constructed at Rhiw, about 200 ft. above OD mains, and services were laid from time to time as required. During the next ten years some eighty houses were erected, and in 1875 the population was about 400. At this time the estate was acquired by the Colwyn Bay and Pwllycrochan Estate Company, and about 1877 as the development proceeded at a more rapid rate, the existing supply became inadequate. An additional reservoir, with a capacity of about 450,000 gallons, was constructed by Mr Farrington at Rhiw, alongside the old one, which was enlarged to a capacity of about 750,000 gallons. In 1878 the Colwyn Bay Water Works Company was formed, and Mr. Farrington was instructed to prepare the necessary plans for an application for Parliamentary powers to carry out new works.

The Act, obtained in the following year, authorized the construction of a pumping station at Groes Mill, 130 ft. above OD, and a large impounding reservoir above Pwllycrochan Woods, at an elevation of about 600 ft. above OD. Only the first-named of the above works was constructed, and water was raised from the Groes stream by steam pumps, through a 6-inch rising main, into the existing reservoirs at Rhiw. These arrangements sufficed for the supply to the district until 1886, when the works were purchased from the Company by the Conway Rural Sanitary Authority.

Up to this time the local affairs of Colwyn Bay had been administered by a Parochial Board appointed by the Conway Rural Sanitary Authority, but in 1887 Colwyn Bay was formed into a Local Board district embracing Old Colwyn, Rhos and other outlying portions. The plans of the district were prepared by Mr Farrington for the new urban authority. There was a total population at this time of about 3,800. A further supply of water being urgently needed, arrangements were made with the Llandudno Commissioners for them to provide it from their mains near Llandudno Junction, and Mr. Farrington was instructed to lay about four miles of 6-inch pipes to convey the water to Colwyn Bay.

The population, continuing to increase at a rapid rate, an augmented supply of water had again to be sought, and in 1890 it was decided to join with the Borough of Conwy and the Conwy Rural Sanitary Authority in procuring a supply which would meet the necessities of all three authorities. Plans were prepared by Mr Farrington for obtaining a supply from Lake Cowlyd, and the Conway and Colwyn Bay joint water supply district was constituted by virtue of the provisional Order of the Local Government Board dated 10 June, 1891, *"for the purpose of procuring a common supply of water for the constituent districts."* (The total cost of the works which were designed and carried out by Mr. Farrington, including purchase of lake and water shed, easements, etc., was £55,000.) Colwyn Bay was constituted a separate parish in 1893.

PROMENADE DEVELOPMENT

It is hard to imagine a strip of sandy sward stretching towards the shingle from the foot of the railway embankment, yet men are alive to-day (i.e. 1952) who recall football matches played between the boys of Old Colwyn and those of "New" Colwyn on the seaward side of the Dingle viaduct. Colwyn Bay's sea front grew piecemeal. The first and most imposing part was the "Old Prom" as it was termed, erected at the time of the building of the Colwyn Bay Hotel, circa 1872. Its distinctive appearance makes identification easy. Next came a strip at the entrance to what was later to be the Pier. This was extended towards the west, and then east of the Dingle. Between the western edge of the "New Prom" and the "Old Prom" the railway embankment was reinforced by gigantic wooden piles. The extension of the Promenade from Colwyn Bay to the Marine Path was formally opened on June 22nd, 1897. A drinking fountain[154] (over the Dingle Stream), donated by the Rev. Thomas Parry to commemorate this achievement, was erected on the promenade and formally presented in December of that year. A review of the promenade development is contained in a report submitted by the Urban District Surveyor, William Jones, in 1907:

"The author's experience under this head has been a very wide and extensive one, as he has been directly responsible for an expenditure on public works of this character to the extent of over £60,000. In 1890, the first year of his office, he was commissioned to carry out and construct approach roads and suitable access to the beach. These were completed in 1891 and now form the principal approach to the Promenades and to the Victoria Pier and Pavilion, the

The "Old Prom" in course of construction

The East Promenade in the 1890s before the Pier was commenced. Scene below railway station showing termination of the East Promenade

The bath-house on the cliffs between Penrhos and Aberhod. It was demolished when the Western Promenade was built

cost being £8,000. In 1895 he was directed to prepare plans, etc., for a promenade nearly a mile long on a part of the beach acquired from the Crown, and this extended from Colwyn Bay Railway Station for a distance of 1,423 yards. The work was carried out by contract under the entire supervision of the author. It was commenced in the early part of 1896 and completed towards the end of 1897. The total cost of this work was £15,000. In 1901 the author was further instructed to prepare plans for the construction of new promenades in both directions along the sea front, as it was thought that these improvements would not only prove of further attraction to the district, but they would also form a protection for the new intercepting sewer which the Council had now decided to construct along the foreshore in order to meet the growth of the district.

The first section extended from Rhos-on-Sea along the front of the Cayley Estate for a distance of 940 lineal yards, the owners of this estate making a contribution of £15,000 towards the cost, the estimate of which, with the cost of the land, was £24,835. Section No. 2 extended from the Colwyn Bay hotel to the railway station, a distance of 285 lineal yards, the estimated cost being £9,098: section No. 3 being in the east end to Old Colwyn, a length of 800 lineal yards, and the estimated cost was £9,091. These sections were approved by the Council, and an application made to the Local Government Board for sanction to raise the money to carry out the work, but owing to the cost of these, and the cost of the new intercepting sewer, and the sewage disposal works, which the Council had now taken in hand, together with the outstanding loans, exceeding their statutory borrowing powers, the application to the Local Government Board was dropped, and a Bill was promoted in Parliament for the carrying out of these Promenade works and the sewage and the sewage outfall works, at a total cost of £112,000, which received the Royal assent on 31st July, 1902."

THE GAS UNDERTAKING

The first attempt at street lighting was made in 1879, when a dozen lamp pillars with oil lamps were fixed by the Parochial Board. By 1883 the number had been increased to thirty. In October of that year, Mr. Farrington, Engineer to the Conwy and Colwyn Bay Joint Water Supply Board, was instructed by the promoters of the Colwyn Bay Gas Company to secure a suitable site, and prepare necessary plans, for an application to Parliament for a Provisional Order authorising the construction of gas works for Colwyn Bay and district. The present site was obtained, and in 1884 work was commenced. The original works were: a retort house, five retorts, one scrubber, two condensers, two purifiers 6ft by 6 ft, station meter and a gas-holder to contain 15,000 cubic feet. A 6-inch trunk main was laid to Colwyn Bay, a distance of about $1^1/_2$ miles, and this was continued by a 5-inch main to Old Colwyn, another $1^1/_2$ miles. A few two-inch branch lines were also laid. The total cost of the original works was about £5,000.

The total make of gas for the first year was 1,583,000 cubic feet. The price of gas was 6/- per 1,000 cubic feet. There were forty-one consumers. Forty-two public lamps were charged at 30/- per lamp. In 1896 an Act of Parliament was obtained authorizing the raising of additional capital. It included a clause enabling the Urban District Council to purchase the works within five years, by agreement or arbitration. The works by this time had been enlarged by the addition of thirty-seven retorts, two purifiers, 10ft x 6ft, gasholders of 60,000 cubic feet capacity, exhauster (with a capacity of 5,000 cubic feet per hour), and a Cornish boiler. The total length of main was about 6 miles; the total make of gas 20,000,000 cubic feet. Consumers had increased to about 3,800. Gas for lighting cost 4/2d. per 1,000 cubic feet. There were now 138 street lamps at 32/6d. per lamp. The progress since 1897 was described as "unexampled." By 1906 the gas make was 62,000,000 cubic feet, and 5,600 tons of coal were used, compared with 200 tons in 1885. The gas works were purchased by arbitration by the Council in 1901 for £65,000.

In pencilled minutes in the possession of the Gas Engineer and Manager there is a record of 13 November 1883: *"That Mr. T. B. Farrington be appointed the Surveyor and Engineer for this Company to prepare plans for the obtaining of a Provisional Order."* The first general meeting was held on 4 February 1884, and was attended by Dr. Thomas Shaw, Chairman of the directors, James Bromley, Price, Thomas, Allan, Halliday, John Porter, Dunning, Charles Frost, Leatherly, Thomas Carlyle and the Rev. W. Venables. Williams. Minutes of 1885 record a meeting of Gas Directors *"held in the board room, Ivy Street."*

The new company was known as "The Colwyn Bay and District Gas and Lighting Company Limited." By December 1885, the directors had removed their office to the Public Hall. Evidently it was chilly for it was *"resolved that this meeting adjourns to the Station Hotel,"* and it was further *"proposed by Mr. Porter, seconded by the Rev. W. V. Williams, that a gas stove be placed in the new office."* There is a reference to *"the gas at Colwyn Bay Station."* Great improvement followed the introduction of incandescent mantles and high power for most of the gas lamps. In 1907 there were 27 high-power lamps and 293 ordinary lamps fixed in the streets of the district, and 76 electric arc lamps. Of the latter, 67 were along the promenade. The public lighting cost to the Council in 1906 was £1,217. Of this £692 was for gas and £525 for electricity. For comparative purposes it might be pointed out that the make of gas for the year ending 31 March 1949, was 355,510,000 cubic feet. Consumers on 31 October 1949, were 7,844. Public lamps numbered 1,039. The price of gas for lighting and cooking was 5/6d per 1,000 cubic feet, on a sliding scale down to 4/10d per 1,000 cubic feet; industrial, 4/1d per 1,000 cubic feet; central heating 3/- per 1,000 cubic feet.

ELECTRICAL DEVELOPMENT

The Council's Electricity Works in Ivy Street have been there since the local authority first resolved to undertake electrical development.[155] It was in 1896 that the Council obtained a Provisional Order for the purpose of lighting the promenades and for private supply. In 1898 the Council erected on the east Promenade 24 arc lamps of the 12-Ampere, open type. The columns, 25ft high, were still in position in 1953.

"The current was supplied by a 25 B.H.P. engine," wrote the late A.R. Tudman, Urban District Council Electricity Engineer, *"driven by belt a 2-pole, 15 kW dynamo. The lamps are connected twelve in series. In the autumn of 1899 the Council put down a plant to supply current for private consumers, comprising a 60 kW steam dynamo, directly coupled, and a boiler capable of evaporating 4,000-lbs of water per hour; a battery of 252 accumulators, capable of giving 100 Amperes for one hour, or 25 Amperes for eight hours. The supply for private consumers commenced on 1 January 1900 [the first consumer being the Metropole Hotel.*[156]*]. This plant proved to be too small, and in 1901 the Council deemed it necessary to put down a larger plant, which consisted of a boiler capable of evaporating 9,500-lbs of water per hour, and a steam dynamo, 4-pole, direct-coupled, developing 120kW. In 1902 the Council put down a duplicate steam dynamo of 120 kW as the consumption was increasing very considerably. The spring of 1906 called for a further extension."*

HEAVY TRAFFIC!

Extract from the Surveyor's report in 1907:

"Motor car traffic in and through the district is greatly on the increase, and as many as 187 cars passed along the main road on August Bank Holiday last, of which strong complaints are made by the public generally and especially by the shopkeepers."

FIRST FIRE BRIGADE

Colwyn Bay was proud of its fire engine, purchased in 1893. It was the first "steamer" procured for a town in North Wales. The brigade also had a curricle fire escape, a hose-car and (runs an official report at the time) *"all modern appliances necessary for an up-to-date brigade."* The horse-drawn vehicle was kept in a building near the top of Ivy Street. The brigade's headquarters adjoined the electricity works (which have since absorbed it) and over the station a recreation room for the volunteer firemen was provided. A billiard table was installed. The bright brass helmets of the firemen and the burnished red and brass *"steamer"* with its sleek horses, were a feature of many a May Day procession.

First Fire-engine, with Chief Officer Thomas Roberts

TREE PLANTING

The pioneers showed vision, and one of their early resolves was to provide the new town with trees. *"It has been the wish of the Council,"* runs an early report, *"to plant trees in all streets where possible, so as to maintain the rural appearance desired for the place by both residents and visitors."* Attention might also be directed to the number of early buildings constructed of limestone, clearly indicating the activities of the local quarries.

View from the original Colwyn Bay Hotel showing foot of Mostyn Road and the Colwyn Bay Tennis Courts on Princes Drive

The Congo Institute students and staff – the founder, the Reverend William Hughes is wearing a top hat

CONGO INSTITUTE

In its early years Colwyn Bay attracted considerable attention by reason of an unusual venture on the part of a returned missionary, the Rev. W. Hughes, FRGS, a friend of Sir Henry M.Stanley, whom he met whilst a missionary in the Congo. On his return Mr. Hughes established in the house now used as a Clinic, in Nantyglyn Road, what was called the Congo House Training Institute - abbreviated locally to "The Congo." A broad field stretched before the house. With Mr. Hughes as founder and secretary, African children were first trained. There were at the start eleven - ten boys and one girl. They were taught trades and educated in Christianity. As the years passed, grown-up students occupied the Institute. It is said that Colwyn Bay was chosen for the experiment on account of its salubrious climate. *"The African children, walking in the streets of Colwyn Bay, have now become a feature of the place,"* observes John Heywood's Guide Book to Colwyn Bay (1892).

THE TITHE WAR

People still living can recall what is termed "The Tithe War," which broke out towards the close of the eighteen-eighties. These riots, and others in various parts of the Principality, assumed such proportions that a Government inquiry was held. The question of the payment of the tithe at that time excited bitter controversy. Forcible protests were made by some Nonconformists who could not see the justice of the tithe. Many prominent farmers were involved, and there were demonstrations of a serious nature. Conwy was one of the areas in which the Commissioners who conducted the inquiry met. The Rev. Venables Williams stated he had received an anonymous letter threatening to blow up the Vicarage with dynamite if he did not agree to the reduction. Rioters burnt down the mission church, on the site of the present St.Paul's. The date of the Mochdre disturbance was 16 June 1887.[157]

One resident told the writer that when a little girl she looked from the windows of Rose Cottage, at the foot of Ivy Street, to see red-coated soldiers and police march from the station yard at Colwyn Bay and take the road to Mochdre. Another recalls how, as a boy, he stood on his desk at the Board School to watch the militia go by. In the subsequent inquiry it was stated the troops disembarked at the spot later occupied by Mochdre railway station, and that as a result of this, a request was made for a station to be built at that convenient place. There was a level crossing there then. A Mochdre man, who was at the time a young farm-hand, told the writer his most vivid impression was that the troops *"tramped across growing corn."* According to the Chief Constable (Major Leadbeater) there were 76 police and 76 soldiers. They marched up Chapel Street towards the old mill, which seemed to be the rally point of the rioters. The incident was noted in a contemporary account.[158]:

"It appears that the police and soldiers came by rail to the point of the line nearest to the farm where distresses had been made. They were received in a manner which showed that there had been a concerted plan among many people to attend the sales. Three poles and flags were raised on neighbouring hills. Horns were sounded and a gun discharged on the other side of the line. Many meetings had been held in favour of the Farmers' Tithe Defence League. From this village (Mochdre) *many people immediately started to follow the police and military. The majority of them were respectable people who attended partly for curiosity and partly with a desire to enter their protest against the distresses but not with any lawless intent. The first farm to be visited is called Mynydd, in the occupation of Mr. Hugh Roberts. Close to this farm it was that a serious disturbance took place. There is a main lane out of which issues a narrow lane and that leads downwards towards a small brook. At a few yards distance from this brook the narrow lane leads up to Mynydd Farm, passing at first big fields with very high*

The Felin, Mochdre, where the victims of the Tithe War were carried for treatment

banks and hedges on top of them. The hedge on the left-hand bank was higher than the heads of the police in the lane.

The Chief Constable of Denbighshire halted the military and a part of the police at the brook and sent about twenty-six of the police and the bailiffs to the farmhouse. Mr. Roberts was at home and some time was spent in negotiations. The Chief Constable who at the time had remained with the military, after a while went up to the gate of the field and remained there until Mr. Roberts and others had come down with the police from the farmhouse. There were further negotiations near the gate, the police remaining drawn up in the lane, and while they were waiting a large number of people were constantly coming up from all parts, and standing in the field and in the lane above the police.

Here the number amounted to about 250, and there were nearly the same number on the other side of the brook. The cattle distrained upon were in the field at the gate of which negotiations were going on. No settlement was come to here, and the police were ordered to march down the hill. Immediately after they started, the people behind followed and overtook, and those in front began to press on the police, so that their rear files to avoid being driven forward too rapidly, so it is said, halted and turned round to the crowd and pushed them back with their open hands. There were then about fifty men in the field who, seeing the crowd in the lane pushed back by the police, thought there was a fight between their friends and the police, and began to throw stones and to use sticks.

The men in the lane, impelled by those behind them, came with a great rush against the police and some of them were, with the police, carried down the lane. Stones then came in greater numbers from the field. Sticks, and in one case a sling, were used against the police by the people who lined the right hand hedge. The police, when the rush came, drew and used their staves. Subsequently, the tithe was paid at this farm, and the Chief Constable proceeded to march his men to the next farm. As soon as they were got to the main lane and began to march down, stones were thrown from behind the hedge of the field to the left, whereupon it became necessary to clear the field. There was again resistance to police, and more blows were struck. Afterwards another farm was visited and the crowd followed. At this farm the Riot Act was read." The writer was told that this occurred at the Felin Gate.

Minutes of Evidence at the inquiry record the statement of Elias Owen, schoolmaster, of the "High School," Colwyn Bay:

"On the way from Mochdre to Graianllyn, beside which a brook flows part of the way, many an artist or photographer has paused to look down a side lane to the south-east, where stands a solitary white house with an attenuated pine tree at its side. It is too picturesque to be passed casually. The name Felin (Mill) still clings to it, and though it has been a dwelling place for several generations a huge millstone, now incorporated prosaically in a garden path, bespeaks the original occupation. This was the granary; the mill-house, now demolished, stood on the western side of the brook. A sequestered setting for strife, yet it was here, at this very spot, the "Tithe War" raged until the waters of the placid brook were ensanguined. "There was a big fight!" So said one who recollected. The wounded were carried into the front room of the old mill and there they lay until the broad slate slabs were red with blood. Close by in the garden lingers the old well–its water still as fresh and cool as when it was used to swill away the gore of the conflict. Mrs. David Lloyd, the wife of the householder, bandaged the wounds and gave succour. Many of the injured were her neighbours. Her little two-year old son was an unofficial spectator. Weeks afterwards, one of the wounded men appeared with a child's chair he had fashioned for the little lad. It was his way of showing his appreciation for Mrs. Lloyd's ministrations. The chair, ruined by worms, was burnt only a few weeks before the writer called at the Felin. It always went by the name of the Tithe War Chair.

On the other side of the line from Mochdre there is a rising watering-place in which many meetings have been held in favour of the Farmers' Tithe Defence League," runs the official report."From this village many people started to follow the police and military."[159]

One man who witnessed the scenes is living in 1950. He is Robert Roberts, Bryn Cryno, Llangystennin, aged 82 years. He had never seen so many people, men and women, gathered together, he said. They stood on the high places. He remembered flags flying from masts on the hill tops. In particular there was a flagstaff set up on "The Flagstaff" hill, and he thought this might have given the place its name. One man, Thomas Henry Jones, of Plas Newydd farm, an old cavalryman, appeared on a horse, but he was the only horseman he could call to mind. There was a lot of fighting *"until men's faces were red with blood."* He recalled one farmer named Owens, armed with a stick, attacking four constables and beating them down. There was no shooting. *"They were more like mad people, all of them,"* Mr. Roberts commented.

COLWYN BAY IN 1892

By 1892 - the year when the subway to the proposed promenade was opened - Colwyn Bay had assumed definite proportions. *"It can no longer be called a village,"* wrote a visiting writer. The subway - now taken for granted - was then an undertaking of major importance. Plans to make it and the approach roads, at a cost of £8,000 were put into operation in the winter of 1891-2. A dressed stone tablet, let into the wall at the approach to the Pier, records the opening by the Rev. W.Venables Williams. The inscription is almost obliterated. By that time the Public Hall – now (1951) the Repertory Theatre[160] - had been erected and was devoted to drama, music and other forms of recreative entertainment. The new St.John's Wesleyan Church was regarded as being the "most handsome by far" of the public buildings. Penrhos Ladies' College was housed on the promenade in the building known as Gilbertville.[161] Banking was initiated by Pugh Jones, of Conwy. Three banks were established: the National Provincial Bank of England on the west side of Station Road; the National Bank of Wales, and the North & South Wales Bank on the east side of Station Road. The hotels were: Pwllycrochan, opened by John Porter in June, 1866; the Colwyn Bay Hotel, the Imperial Hotel, the Royal Hotel, and temperance hotels -Moon's near the station, and Penrhyn and "a Home from Home" near Eirias Dingle. Churches were: St. Paul's, St. John's, English Congregational Church (Hudson Memorial), English Presbyterian, and Baptist. Welsh places of worship were the Independent Chapel in Abergele Road, Engedi and the Welsh Wesleyan in Greenfield Road. The last-named has for years been used as a garage. The Hydropathic Establishment, soon to be taken over to form the nucleus of Penrhos College, was also classed as a winter residence near the Promenade.[162]

The East Promenade in the 1890s before the pier was commenced

14
COLWYN BAY'S

THE start of the new parish of Colwyn Bay is concisely set out in the Minute Book of St. Paul's Church, which was still in use in the 1950s:

"The first service was held in a Carpenter's Shed, in Ivy Street, on Sunday afternoon, June 18th, 1871, when there was a Congregation of 70 people, and an offertory of £1-3s- 1½ d. On June 18th, 1872, the Mission Room was opened, and the sermon preached by the late Bishop Hughes. This building was very plain and small, cost only £170, and accommodation for 150 only. On June 23rd, 1880, the Iron Church was opened and the late Dean Edwards preached. 'This structure was burnt down on October 30th, 1886. It had been insured and the sum of £1,386- 1s-0d. was received from the Alliance Assurance Company in consequence of the fire. With that sum and other subscriptions and collections, the nave of St. Paul's was built at a cost of £4,794-5s-3d., which included the aisles and transepts, temporary chancel, organ chamber and architects' fees, etc. Messrs. Douglas and Fordham of Chester were the architects. The site was given by Lady Erskine. The nave of St. Paul's was consecrated by Bishop Hughes on July 13th, 1888. After the burning of the Iron Church, to the consecration of St. Paul's, the services were held in the Public Hall. On the 10th May, 1893, Colwyn Bay, which had up to this date been a portion of Llandrillo parish, was created into a separate ecclesiastical parish."

Extracts from the *London Gazette* of 19 May 1893 (pages 2914-5), and 4 August 1893 (page 4464) follow. They include minute details of the boundaries.

The Rev. Canon Hugh Roberts, B.A., was inducted Vicar of the new parish 17 June 1893. William Hawarth Cogwell and William Earp were church wardens. The sidesmen were John Marsden, J. M. Porter, Percy Hignett, D.Edwards, A.Grant, I.Welbourne, E.Allen, Dr.Lord. Clergy assisting Canon Roberts were, the Revs. John Jones, BA, R.Theophilus Jones, BA, J.H.Astley, MA, and I.G.Howarth (voluntary). The organist was Dr.W.M.V.Williams, and the choirmaster Westlake Morgan (organist, Bangor Cathedral).

The new tower was completed in July 1911. The tower clock was given by Mr.J.S.Littlewood. The land which forms the lawn before the Church was purchased by public subscription. Canon Roberts died 22 February 1916.

VICARS

1893–1916	Hugh Roberts, B.A. (Canon).
1916–1924	Lewis Pryce, M.A. (Canon, later Archdeacon).
1924–1927	T. J.Latimer-Jones, M.A.
1927–1939	Clement R. Thomson, M.A. (Canon. later Chancellor).
1939–1950	T. J. Davies, B.A. (Canon, later Prebendary).
1950–1974	William Hugh Rees, B.A. (Archdeacon)
1974–1999	Trevor Gwesyn Davies, BEd. (Canon)
1999–	John Thomas Evans (Canon)

The breaking away of Colwyn Bay as a separate parish, distinct from the mother parish of Llandrillo, was keenly felt by the Vicar of Llandrillo, the Rev. W. Venables Williams. His feelings are revealed in a circular letter, dated Colwyn Bay Vicarage, 25 May 1893:

"*My dear C.B. Parishioners - The final blow has at length fallen by the fact of the Queen's having signed an Order in Council assigning a District Chapelry to the Church of St.Paul, Colwyn Bay, which was published in last Friday night's Gazette. The time has therefore now arrived when I must reluctantly - most reluctantly - bid you 'adieu' and sever myself from a very loved portion of my labours in this parish, viz.: Colwyn Bay, the growth of which I have watched with ever-increasing interest, culminating (after the destruction by fire of the Iron Church in 1886) in the building of the handsome edifice of St. Paul's Church, consecrated on the 13th of July, 1888, by Bishop Hughes. I hope I may not be considered egotistical in saying that the Church would not have been erected up to the present moment but for my own untiring exertions, aided and supported by many kind and generous friends, by which means, I raised during the short period of three years, the no inconsiderable amount of £7,000 collected in small sums.*

I may now mention a fact, not previously made known, that when Mr.Douglas, the architect, gave his final certificate to Mr.Samuel Parry, one of the most honest and conscientious of contractors, for about £700, there was not a penny in the Bank to meet it, and, to save the credit of the Church, I had to deposit, with Mr. Parry, my own private securities for the amount. And now I am required to make way for someone who will reap the fruits of my labours. I have, I trust, kept well in the forefront of the Church progress in Colwyn Bay, having commenced in 1871, a Sunday afternoon service in a carpenter's shed, to which I shall ever look back with much pleasure. In 1872 I built the Mission Room, and in 1880, the Iron Church. I have the satisfaction of knowing that during my incumbency of 25 years the large sum of £20,000 has been raised and expended for Church purposes in this small Parish. I feel very keenly and bitterly the having to give up my ministrations at St. Paul's. I think the Division of the Parish need not have been so cruelly and relentlessly carried out (no reasons being assigned) during my lifetime. I intended on Whit-Sunday evening, bidding you all an affectionate 'Farewell,' but I did not trust myself to give utterance to my pent-up feelings - my heart was too full.

Thanking you one and all for innumerable kindnesses and very much forbearance with my own many shortcomings in the discharge of my duties, I pray that God's blessing may be with you all, and now I must say 'Finally, Brethren, Farewell'."

Correspondence concerning the formation of the new parish was printed by order of the House of Commons and may be consulted under the title of "*Copy of the correspondence relating to the creation of a New Benefice in the parish of Llandrillo-yn-Rhos (Colwyn Bay) 1893.*"

The Parish Church, Colwyn Bay

After the parish of Colwyn Bay was formed by an Order in Council, 15 May 1893, the Ecclesiastical Commissioners endowed the new parish with £120 a year. The nave of St. Paul's Church was consecrated on 13 July 1888, and the chancel on 7 April 1895. The tower was dedicated on 12 November 1911. The expenditure on the entire church amounted to £12,800. The foundation stone of the Church Room was laid by Miss Cogswell on 2 September 1895. On the same day Mrs Haworth laid the foundation stone of the Vicarage. The Church Room cost £1,200, and the Vicarage £2,210, apart from the land. St. Paul's comprises a chancel, with organ chamber on the north, vestries for choir and clergy on the south, with north and south transepts, large nave with narrow aisles under one roof, and an imposing north-west tower. The organ, which cost £1,200, was provided by subscription. The east window (of seven lights) has in its centre the Ascension. Other designs are St. Paul's Conversion, the four Evangelists, four Archangels, St. Peter and St. Paul. A light iron screen divides chancel from nave. This and the marble steps were the gift of Mr. W.H.Alty. The south rose window is the gift of Dinglewood School scholars. The octagonal pulpit, with pierced panels, was made by Edward Allen, JP, as his gift. The font and carved stalls were given by Miss Barlow. A window (St. Peter and St. Paul) in the south, is in memory of Richard Arhur Barlow, who died in America. One on the north is a memorial to "William Earp, Colwyn, sometime Churchwarden."

St. David's Church
The Rev. J. G. Haworth laid the foundation stone for St.David's Church on Whit Monday, 1902. On St. David's Day, 1903, the church was dedicated. It has a wagon roof and is floored with wooden blocks. The apse window was given by Mr. and Mrs. Hugh Hughes. The reredos, an expressive cast of the Lord's Supper, was given by Mr. R. B. Perkins. The choir seats are from Christ Church, Bala. The wrought iron screen is the work of a local blacksmith, David Jones. The lectern was given by the Hon. Mrs.Brodrick, Coed Coch, and the octagonal font by Miss Dean. The church cost £1,858.

St. Andrew's Church
The foundation stone for St.Andrews was laid by Mrs. Gamble on 2 November 1908. The site cost £750, and the first part of the nave £1,469.

BRYNYMAEN

A handsome church was erected at Brynymaen at the turn of the century, due to the munificence of Mrs. Eleanor Frost, Minydon, Old Colwyn, the daughter of Mr. and Mrs. William Jones, Rhwng-y-ddwyffordd. Mrs. Frost built both church and vicarage, and endowed the cure with a net income of £200 a year, vesting the patronage in the Bishop of the diocese. On 8 August 1895, Mrs. Frost laid the foundation stone of a mission room in which services were at first carried on. On 4 May 1897, she laid the foundation stone of the church, which was consecrated on 28 September 1899.

An Order in Council on 15 May 1900, formed "the consolidated Chapelry of Christ Church, Brynymaen." It comprised portions of the parishes of St. Paul's (Colwyn Bay), St. Catherine's (Old Colwyn), Llanelian and Llansanffraid Glan Conwy. In 1900 the population was about 320. The church is dedicated *"to the honour and glory of God and to the dear memory of Charles Frost."* Meredith Jones Hughes, FRHistS, (curate of Colwyn Bay, 1893-5, curate in charge of Colwyn, 1897-9), was appointed Perpetual Curate of Christ Church, Brynymaen, 30 July, 1900, serving until the end of 1908.

OLD COLWYN

St. Catherine's Church
The Church of St. Catherine was built in 1837 as a Chapel of Ease to Llandrillo, and remained so until a parish was assigned to it in 1844. The land on which the church was erected was given by John Lloyd Wynne, of Coed Coch, and the Rev. John Boulger. The Rev.Thomas Hughes,[163] priest-in-charge, has left an account of the stone laying which took place on 14 July 1837. It is now (1951) in possession of the Vicar, the Rev. H.I.Morgan, MA:

"On Wednesday the interesting ceremony of laying the first stone of a new church at Colwyn in the parish of Llandrillo-yn Rhos, near Conwy, took place before a large assembly of the inhabitants of that hamlet and the Clergy and gentry of the surrounding neighbourhood. At two o'clock a procession was formed from Minydon, the residence of Richard Butler Clough, Esq, where the Clergy had previously met, to the ground on which the church is to be erected, adjoining the hamlet of Colwyn and which had been generously given by John Lloyd Wynne, Esq., of Coed Coch, and the Rev. Mr. Boulger. Here they were met by children of the National School and the interesting ceremony commenced by their singing a hymn adapted for the occasion, after which Richard Butler Clough, Esq., who had been requested to lay the stone, addressed a large and attentive concourse of spectators. On the conclusion of the address a silver trowel was

handed to Mr. Clough, who, descending to the foundation, spread mortar and laid in it a fine new block of limestone, the foundation of the intended edifice. The Rev.Mr Parry, Vicar of Llandrillo, approached the spot and delivered both in English and Welsh appropriate prayers. The Church was consecrated by Dr Carey, Bishop of St Asaph, on 7 August 1838, and was dedicated to St. Catherine of Alexandria, and as a mark of honour to Mrs. Catherine Butler Clough, who showed so much interest in the erection of the church."

The east window, dedicated to Richard Butler Clough, was given by his widow. It illustrated the Agony, Crucifixion and Ascension. In 1892 a new east window, illustrating the Crucifixion, with St. Catherine on one side and St. Asaph on the other, was placed in memory of Elizabeth, wife of John Matthews Elliot, of Rose Hill, Newton Heath. The church has a western tower with stepped battlements and pinnacles, north porch, nave and chancel with south organ chamber and vestry. The clock in the church tower was installed in 1890 in memory of the Rev. J. D. Jones, Vicar, 1866-1887.

A glebe house was built in 1871 on a site given by Oldham Whitaker (Minydon) towards the cost of which £500, granted by Queen Anne's Bounty to augment the living, and two further grants of £200 each, were applied. The Vicar of Llandrillo is still the patron.[164]

St. John's Church
The foundation stone of St. John's Church was laid by Mrs. Eleanor Frost of Min-y-don, on 18 October 1899, and the church was consecrated 13 August 1903. It cost £12,300, exclusive of numerous gifts. A large chancel arch and a light screen of wrought iron divide chancel from nave. The fittings for the chancel were given by Mrs. Frost. The organ is a gift of Miss Cornelia Bagnell. A four-light window (The Good Shepherd) on the south side was erected to the memory of the Rev. D. Pryce Jones, Vicar 1888-1893, by his wife and children. Another window, St. Anne and St. Winifred, installed *"in memory of Anne Jones of Minafon, Old Colwyn, who died September 15th, 1894,"* was given by her husband. The tower, which is buttressed and battlemented, was added in 1912 at a cost of £2,300, of which £1,000 was given by Miss Howe and Mr. C.E.Howe.

The old National School, with the teacher's house, erected in 1848 near the Church of St.Catherine, was later used as a Sunday School and Church House. It was superseded in 1866 by a new one at a cost of £1,400 and enlarged in 1896 at a cost of £350.

ROMAN CATHOLIC

St. Joseph's Church
On 10 August 1898, the foundation stone of St. Joseph's Catholic Church was laid by Dr. Mostyn, then Bishop of Menevia. The church was completed in 1900 and blessed and opened on Whit Sunday, 3 June. In the town's early days Colwyn Bay formed part of the Llandudno Mission district, but in 1895 it was assigned a resident priest, who conducted a mission, services being held in a private house in Rhiw Road and in two local hotels. In 1898 the embryo church was placed in charge of the Oblates of Mary Immaculate. It was opened in 1900 by Dr. Mostyn, by then Archbishop of Cardiff. Five years after the opening of the church the Convent of the Sisters of Mercy was founded under Father Comerford. The foundation stone for the school was laid in December 1931 and the school was opened in January 1933. Golden Jubilee celebrations were observed in March 1950 when a visit was paid by the Bishop of Menevia, Dr. J.Petit.

NONCONFORMIST

Methodist (Wesleyan), Welsh
The following local churches form part of the Conwy Welsh Methodist Circuit : Horeb (Rhiw Road, Colwyn Bay), Bethesda, Old Colwyn, Seion (Bronynant), and Disgwylfa (Penmaenrhos). The first Wesleyan Chapel to be built in the area was at Bronynant in 1809, nine years after the

denomination started its mission in Wales. The chapel was renewed later and an adjoining schoolroom built recently. The first Colwyn Bay chapel was built in Greenfield Road in 1876, enlarged in 1888 and, after being used by the English Wesleyans pending the building of Nantyglyn Chapel, was sold. It is now (1951) a garage. The present chapel, schoolroom and two houses were built in Rhiw Road in 1900. Ministers at Horeb since 1894 were the Revs. John Kelly, T.C.Roberts, R. Jones Williams, F.E.Jones, Thomas Davies, F.E.Jones (second period), J.Wesley Hughes, Rhys Jones, D. Angel Richards, Owen Evans, R.J.Parry, Richard Jones, Lewis Edwards, G. J.Owen, E. Berwyn Roberts, J.Lloyd Hughes, Charles Jones. In September 1950, the Chaired Bard, Rev.Gwilym Tilsley, M.A., took charge. The first minister at Colwyn was stationed in 1913. The school-chapel at Penmaenrhos was built in 1901.

Old Colwyn
The first chapel was started at Pen-y-Bryn in 1832, to be enlarged in 1860. It still stands, though no longer a chapel, and the name "Bethesda House" affords a clue to its ancestry. The present chapel, on the main road, which retains the name of Bethesda, was opened in December 1886, when the preachers were the celebrated Rev. John Evans of Eglwysbach, and the Rev. Edward Humphreys. The other local chapel, Disgwylfa, at Penmaenrhos, was opened in November 1901. The preachers were the Rev. J.Jones-Humphreys, Rev. Philip Price and the Rev. E.E.Jones. Ministers stationed at Old Colwyn (post-probationer period) from 1913 are: W.P.Roberts (4 years), R Morton Roberts (3), W.O.Evans, R.Môn Hughes (3) - he was the father of Dr. Hubert Hughes (headmaster Abergele Grammar School) and R.E.Hughes (headmaster Pwllheli Grammar School) - W.O.Evans (3), T.G.Ellis (3), D.R.Rogers, MA. (5), W.P.Roberts (9), J.Gwyn Jones, M.A. (5), and R.G.Hughes.

Methodist (English)
The story of St. John's Church is unusual. When Colwyn Bay began, English Methodism in North Wales was in its infancy, and the Rev. Frederick Payne was officially termed "North Wales Coast Missionary." It was he who conceived the scheme, and on 11 August 1882, the stone-laying took place. The walls of the grounds, the artistic lych-gate and "Tranby" (the manse) were erected, and the foundations of the church laid, when funds gave out. For some years the site lay derelict, termed locally "Wesley's Folly." Then the great attempt was made. The first portion erected was the schoolroom. Here services were held until the church was completed. Mr. Payne then lived at Beech Holme. In the collecting-book which he issued, it is stated that the Church originally went by the name of "St. John's English Wesleyan Chapel, *Puncheon Memorial.*" The first subscription list started in 1880 with £739-9s-0d. The foundation stones were laid on 19 September 1887. The completed church was opened on 22 June 1888. The builder was Edward Foulkes, whose son, S.Colwyn Foulkes, FRIBA, designed the new Rydal Buildings.

The foundation stones of Nantyglyn were laid on September 19th, 1904, and the church, built by Messrs. John Tucker & Sons,[165] opened on 16 June 1905.

A cause was started in Old Colwyn. From 1904 services were held in the Welsh Wesleyan school-room. The stone-laying of an English chapel took place on 24 March 1908 and it was opened on 28 July 1909. It was extended in 1932 (opening, 24 August). The first services at Rhos-on-Sea were held in the Playhouse in 1916. After meeting in a recreation room near the Promenade, a permanent church was started on Rhos Road and dedicated in 1923.The schoolroom was opened 24 August 1932.

Presbyterian
Surrounding villages had Welsh Calvinistic Methodist chapels long before Colwyn Bay was talked about. Once Colwyn Bay came into being the cause was quick to establish itself. Its birth is traced to a cottage known as Ty'-n-y-Ffordd where, in the 1840s, there were informal

St John's Methodist Church before the oaks were felled, and the lych-gate moved back

meetings and a Sunday School. By the 1870s these were held in Ivy Street. Then came the decision to build a proper place of worship, and a handsome limestone structure arose beside Conwy Road, at a spot where the Cosy Cinema now stands.[166] It cost nearly £700. The chapel was opened in May 1873, and was used jointly by Welsh and English Presbyterians. The next move was to erect Engedi, which was opened in October 1879, built by a local builder, John Roberts, Fern Bank. An official Calvinistic Methodist record noted: *"November 19th, 1871.Report of Colwyn station school - average attendance* 29." In 1872 the report appears under the heading "Colwyn Bay." At first the school was held at Ivy House, the home of Thomas Hughes, one of the pioneers of Calvinistic Methodism in Colwyn Bay. Before it was properly started a room was obtained in the workshop[167] of Abel Roberts, builder, from Llandudno, who was erecting the Colwyn Bay Hotel and several other large buildings, and the school was removed to this room. Weeknight meetings were started by the workmen. In 1887, when Rev. John Edwards became minister of the English cause, there were only sixteen members. It was felt the site militated against the success of the cause, so the building was sold and a new place of worship built at the top of the Hawarden Road. In 1890 the present building was erected for £3,700 including the site, and was opened on 11 January 1891 by Principal Thomas Charles Edwards, DD, of Bala. With the building of Engedi the Welsh cause led a separate existence, though it was not until 1949 that the "English" Church was finally transferred from the Welsh Vale of Conwy Presbytery, which was responsible for its birth.

The Welsh Calvinistic cause in the Borough had chapels at: Mochdre (where the cause started in 1772), and the present chapel was built in 1833; Llanelian 1833; Moriah (Upper Colwyn Bay) 1818 and 1824; Hebron (Old Colwyn) 1861; Hermon (Colwyn Bay) 1908; Sion (Upper Colwyn Bay) 1895; Bethlehem, Lawson Road (1895); Rhiw Road (1901) (subsequently a Baptist Mission). Reference has already been made to Engedi in Woodland Road West, Colwyn Bay. There was also a small cause at Rhos-on-Sea.

Colwyn Bays Religious Institutions

The influence of the Calvinistic Methodists on this district stretches back to the close of the eighteenth century, when a few humble pioneers began services in surrounding hamlets. When it is known that the tiny chapels of Mochdre and Llanelian are regarded as the *"mother churches"* of Engedi and Hebron, it will be appreciated how centres of population have changed. Mochdre had a chapel as far back as 1780 and there is a record of an itinerant minister from South Wales preaching at Mochdre in 1772. Llanelian had a deacon in 1824, so evidently there was a cause there before the present chapel was built. Both Mochdre and Llanelian opened their chapels the same year. The "new" Nazareth chapel at Mochdre was opened 11-12 March 1833 and the "new" chapel at Llanelian on 22 May that year. As the chapel at Llanelian overlooks the site of the famous cursing well one is tempted to assume the spot was chosen with a view to counteracting the well's baneful influence. An old farm, Ty'n y Coed, is remembered as the place where a farm worker, Henry Rees, preached his first sermon. He became a celebrated Liverpool divine.

Reference has been made to meetings held in a thatched cottage known as Ty'n-y-ffordd, which flanked the turnpike almost opposite the present Belgrave Road. The cottage probably was one of the buildings attached to Rhiw Bella farm adjoining. It will be seen that the cause was firmly established when the sale of Pwllycrochan took place in 1865. About that time Ivy House was erected and religious meetings were started in the big kitchen (cegin fawr). These continued until, at the request of workmen engaged on the Colwyn Bay Hotel, public services were started in the Ivy Street workshop belonging to the builder, Abel Roberts. This was about 1870-71 and the Rev. Owen Jones (Meudwy Môn) of Llandudno preached the first sermon. He also lectured on ancient local topics. The Rev. John Williams of Rhyl assisted. One of the prime movers, however, was Abel Roberts' foreman, Thomas Parry, who undertook the organization. A native of Llangerniew, he married a Llandudno woman and settled in this district for the rest of his life. In those days it was not unusual for a man to be ordained and yet continue in his business. Mr. Parry was ordained in 1893 and established himself as a builder in Colwyn Bay. He also was one of the most active pioneers in municipal matters. Colwyn Bay's first church was a handsome stone structure built by the Welsh and English Presbyterians on the site next to the Central Hotel. This was in 1873 but before long the Welsh section considered they were strong enough to establish a cause of their own, and Engedi was erected in 1879 in Woodland Road West. The cause at Colwyn had started earlier. The first Hebron Chapel (now two private houses in Church Walks) was commenced in 1859 and dedicated on 6 March 1861. The present handsome building superseded it in 1904.

One of the pioneers of the cause in Colwyn Bay was Robert Roberts of Pwllycrochan Isa farm, the father of the Rev. John Roberts and the Rev. Robert Roberts, who later emigrated to America. As far back as 1847 a Thomas Daniel of Llandrillo, described as a man of more than average ability, started a school in a thatched cottage behind Aberhod, known as Aberhod Bach. The experiment was encouraged by neighbouring Calvinists. The Rev. Thomas Parry endeavoured to develop a cause at Rhos, and he built a small brick chapel on the Promenade just west of Rhos Road. It was found to be in the wrong situation and was disposed of so that Hermon could be built. It is now a cafe.[168] The Mochdre Chapel was re-built in 1883. Its first minister was a nailer named John Jones. Born in 1820 at the Mochdre blacksmith's shop, he began to preach at Mochdre in 1840, and after labouring for years in his native place was called to Caernarfon. Finally he went to Rhosllannerchrugog, where he died in 1886.

The first Welsh Presbyterian chapel at Colwyn was opened 6 March 1861; the present chapel was dedicated 17 January 1904. The first Welsh-English chapel at Colwyn Bay was dedicated in 1873. Engedi was built 1879. Bethlehem was dedicated 9 July 1897. Hermon was built in 1903 and dedicated 28 August 1904. Rhiw Road was dedicated 17 September 1902. Seion, Upper Colwyn Bay, was dedicated 18 December 1895. Nazareth, Mochdre, was built in 1832. The first chapel was erected in 1780. Llanelian opened for worship 22 May 1833.

Congregational

The birth of Congregationalism in Colwyn Bay resulted from a joint effort of Welsh and English pioneers. In 1874 a piece of land was secured for the building of a chapel which, however, was not undertaken until 1878. An iron structure, which seated 200, was dedicated on 22 and 23 July 1878. English and Welsh worshipped together for some years, under the Rev. W.B.Joseph, services being planned for different hours. Both sections were conscious of a disadvantage in this arrangement, and in 1882 the English formed a separate church, under the direction of the Rev. D.Burford Hooke, Rev. John Thomas, DD, and others. After formal separation both congregations continued to use the same building for several years. Then the English church paid the Welsh church out and took possession of the land on which the Union Church now stands. The first minister of the joint congregations, Rev. W.B Joseph, came from Ruabon in 1880 and was known as a scholar and poet. He left for Utica, USA, the year following. The Welsh church was established at Salem Chapel on Abergele Road. This was opened 28 and 29 September 1885, but was without a resident minister until 1894. At this date the Rev. John Evans, of Bala-Bangor College, received a call and was ordained minister that year, continuing in charge of Salem until 1899, when he left for Pembrokeshire. In 1903 the Rev. H.R.Williams of Widnes came to Salem, which had been re-built and improved that year. He was inducted at the meeting which solemnized the opening of the new chapel on 20 September 1903. After a long ministry he died on 13 May 1942, at Bod Enynt, Colwyn Bay. The next minister, Rev. E.Pryce Jones, M.A., after being educated at Bala-Bangor College and St. Catherine's College, Oxford, came to Salem as his first pastorate in 1937. After ten years ministry he accepted a call to the joint pastorate of Llwyncelyn and Mydroilyn, Cardiganshire. In 1949 the Rev. Hugh Owen, B.A., who was trained at the University College of North Wales, Bangor, came from Hirwaun, South Wales, as minister.

Welsh Congregational

Among the Nonconformist pioneers were the Welsh Congregationalists in Colwyn, where a cause was started in Bryn-y-Gwynt cottage by the Rev. Thomas Jones, Moelfre (near Abergele), as far back as 1804. The first sermon was preached by the Rev. Azariah Shadrack on 28 May that year. Services were held regularly at Bryn-y-Gwynt for eleven years. On 4 May 1815 the first place of worship built in Colwyn was opened. Later the building, enlarged, became the home of Colwyn Welsh Congregationalists. For the benefit of visitors services in English were held during the summer months.

Colwyn Bay (English) Congregational Church

In 1882 the English section formed an English Congregational Church - with a membership of eleven. The names of the founder members were: Mr. and Mrs. Atkinson, John Jones, JP, CC, Thomas Goodman, Mr. and Mrs. Evan Richards, Mr. and Mrs. Edwin Greenfield, William Roberts, Mr. and Mrs. William Williams (Oakfield). The Rev. Thomas Lloyd was ordained the first minister on 22 January 22 1884, and commenced with thirteen church members. He remained for forty years. On 25 May 1885 the foundation stones of a permanent church were laid. It was erected as a memorial to R. S. Hudson, for many years chairman of the Union, who was interested in Colwyn Bay, and dedicated on 21 September the same year. The cost was £2,450, and by 1893 the debt was cleared. In 1901 the building was extended to accommodate 650 persons at a cost of £4,700. The Lecture Hall was added. A cause was started in Colwyn Bay when, in May 1898, services were held in the Welsh Congregational Schoolroom. An English Congregational Church at Colwyn was opened on 12 April 1925.

Rhos-on-Sea Congregational Church

The old Welsh CM Chapel on the seafront, after being turned into tearooms was rented. From March 1907 to 1910 evening services were held in *"the chapel-cafe."* Thomas Roberts, who was church secretary until the year of his death, 1941, was the prime mover. In 1909 an appeal was issued for money, as it was intended to extend the church. William Horton gave a site of 2,000 square yards at the corner of Colwyn Avenue and Penrhyn Avenue. A beginning was made in September 1909, and a branch church was created with four deacons and 44 members in December 1910. On Good Friday the new building was opened by Lady Roberts. The Rev. T. Greenhough, MA, preached. An organ was purchased in 1912. In November 1912 a call was sent to the church's first pastor, Rev. W. T. Tutton. In July 1913 a transept was added, and in 1919 it was decided to purchase land at the corner of Abbey Road for the erection of a more imposing church. A legacy left by Florence Crellin, in 1924, was conditional on a new church being commenced within ten years and completed within twelve. The foundation stone was laid on 25 September 1929, and the building was opened for worship by Gerald Ford on 3 December 1930. The debt was paid off by 1934.

English Baptist

The English Baptist cause in the Colwyn Bay district had its origin during 1884, when a few English-speaking people approached the deacons of the Welsh Baptist Chapel (a small building accommodating about 50 people, then situated in Church Walks, Old Colwyn), with a request for the use of their premises for the holding of English services, to which a ready consent was given. Welsh services were held at 9.45 a.m. and 6.0 p.m., and English services at 11.0 a.m. and 7.30 p.m. In 1888 Welsh Baptists opened Tabernacl Chapel in Colwyn Bay. English worshippers followed them from Old Colwyn.

In April 1891 the English worshippers began to raise funds for their own premises, and in 1893 they purchased a site on Abergele Road, near Erw Wen Road, and a temporary corrugated iron church was erected. The Rev. H. T. Cousins commenced his ministry on 3 September 1893. In 1909 he was succeeded by the Rev. David Griffiths, a blind preacher who, during his seven years ministry, attracted much attention. In 1913 the site was sold (it is now occupied by Stermat's shop), and premises in Princes Drive (Hawarden Road) corner, were opened on 18 December 1913 by Simon Williams, JP. From February to December 1913 services were held in the Cosy Cinema, owing to the Abergele Road chapel having to be vacated. This building is now erected in Lawson Road as a schoolroom to Bethlehem Chapel. In 1926 a new baptistry was installed, and in 1933, vestries, a kitchen and other additions were undertaken. These were opened on 21 June 1933, by Sir William Barton, JP; in May 1938, a pipe organ was installed. The jubilee was celebrated on 19 May 1940, the special preacher being the Rev. J. Williams Hughes, MA, BD, Bangor. The church united with the Congregational Church in March 1946, to be known as the Union Church.

Welsh Baptist

Tabernacl Chapel, Abergele Road, Colwyn Bay, was opened in 1888. The first minister was the Rev. William Hughes, a returned missionary from the Congo.

The Salvation Army

Local headquarters were opened at 22, Park Road, by Lieutenant Rolls (Lieut-Colonel by 1953), in November 1909.

Society of Friends

A place of worship was opened in Erskine Road in 1898.

EDUCATION

LLANDRILLO-YN-RHOS NATIONAL SCHOOLS

IN 1819 parishioners provided a school, at a cost of nearly £400, beside Tan-y-bryn Road at a spot later occupied by the Tan-y-bryn Hotel.[169] After a chequered career, at the close of which it was converted into two cottages, the school was finally demolished, its usefulness having been ended by the creation of the Board School in 1876. A glimpse of the school is provided in the official record of a visitation by Government inspectors in 1847:

"This parish is partly in the county of Carnarvon. It contains 1,176 inhabitants, consisting of farmers, miners, and a few farm labourers. It is stated that they are very poor and that many are unable to pay even the 1d per month, which is required in the following school.

"National School: A school for boys and girls, taught by a master only, in a school built for the purpose. Number of scholars, 124; number employed as monitors, 8. Subjects taught—reading, writing, arithmetic and grammar, the Scriptures and the Church Catechism. Fees 1d per month (for repairs).

"I visited this school on the 4th of March, and found 39 boys and 29 girls present ; of these, 17 had attended the school more than two years, 11 more than three years, and 4 more than four years; 28 were above 10 years of age. There were 17 who could read with ease; 40 copies were shown, but only one was well written. There were 4 scholars who could with difficulty answer a few plain questions in mental arithmetic and English grammar; no one could work a plain sum in the Rule of Three. Out of a large class who were reading the Scripture, I found only 9 who could answer simple questions ; and only two possessed a competent knowledge of the subject. One said, that 'Moses was the "servant" of the wilderness'; another said, that 'Christ came to condemn the world,' and in answer to the question, 'Who wrote the Gospel according to St. John?' one said Matthew; another Mark; a third, Luke, and a fourth, (as if purposely passing over the very gospel we were reading) said, 'The Arts.' As only four understood English, my questions were explained in Welsh. The majority of the pupils knew exceedingly little of any subject, and the information of the rest was desultory and uncertain.

"The master has kept school for more than 20 years, but was never trained. He appeared exceedingly anxious to keep the school in order, and to prevent blunders. But he conveyed his directions in a harsh manner; and I observed a birch rod, though it was not used while I stayed. He speaks English with a Welsh idiom and pronunciation; he conducts his school upon the old-fashioned system of private adventure schools. In teaching arithmetic, he allows the children to count on their fingers.

"The girls are taught needlework three times a week by the master's wife. The building is in very bad repair; there was a hole through the roof; the school furniture is in a very indifferent condition. The out-buildings are not sufficient, or in proper repair; there was a deficiency of all school apparatus, and no maps at all. The fees charged for repairs are spent to buy coals."[170]

Another inquiry was held by the Charity Commissioners, on 12 February 1889, in the Local Board Room at Colwyn Bay.

"Rhos Fields" from Bryn Euryn. In the centre will be seen Llannerch Road bridge with the Board school behind. Penmaenrhos headland was then virtually intact

RELIGIOUS EDUCATION

Efforts to train the young began early, amid humble surroundings, and the various religious denominations founded Sunday Schools at a time when day schools were conspicuous by their absence. The pioneers in this district appear to have been at Llysfaen, where the Church of England began a Sunday School in 1787. Mochdre was next, when the Calvinistic Methodists started a school in 1795, to be followed by one at Meifod in 1804. The Wesleyans began schools at Bronynant in 1812 and at Colwyn in 1832. Immediately St. Catherine's Church was built a school was started in connection with the church, in 1837. The National Schools at Llandrillo, inaugurated in 1819, has been dealt with under secular schools; there are references to religious teaching in connection with these. A private "chapel" school is recorded as having been started at Colwyn in 1845. It was apparently conducted by the Independent minister—previously a carpenter. His salary was £26.[171]

FIRST SCHOOL

Colwyn Bay's first school appears to have been one started by the Welsh Independent minister, in a small building (now destroyed) which stood near the rear of the present English Congregational (Union) Church.

AN ISOLATED SPOT!

When the old Board School was built in 1876, alongside the road to Conwy, it stood alone, and the broad fields at its back were used for football and cricket. The remarkable growth of Colwyn Bay is emphasised by a comment in *John Heywood's Illustrated Guide to Colwyn Bay* in 1892. "These schools," says the writer, "are built *well, and have a good appearance, but one rather marvels at finding them in such an apparently out of the way spot. We suppose there were good reasons.*"

PENRHOS AND RYDAL

Penrhos College and Rydal School have been accepted as part of Colwyn Bay's life for so many years that it is difficult to visualize their first appearance in Colwyn Bay, or to appreciate the courage, enterprise and perspicacity of those responsible for their creation in a place which was little more than a seaside village.

Penrhos College

When Penrhos came into existence education along such lines for girls was practically unknown, and the founders may be regarded as true educational pioneers. It was not until 1872 that the Girls' Public Day Schools' Company (later Trust) was established in England. Penrhos College was started in 1880, or about ten years after the first houses appeared in Colwyn Bay. The term "college" was no affectation; it was the term by which girls' boarding schools were known in those days. It was one of several schools under the auspices of the Wesleyan Methodist Church. The Colwyn Bay Hotel had not long been completed, and with it the "Old Promenade," then known as "The Parade." The only adjoining buildings on the front were those leased by Penrhos — known as "*Gilbertville.*"[172] The tiny cottage alongside was used as the school sanatorium. The "Bath-house" stood half way down the embankment between Penrhos and Aberhod. This old building was being undermined by the sea at the time the construction of the promenade, which hastened its demolition. Penrhos, according to the late Miss Rosa Hovey, B.A., Principal of the College from 1894 to 1928:

"*owes more than one can say to the Rev. F. Payne, a Wesleyan minister living in North Wales, and notable for his old-world courtesy, as for his great ability and foresight.*"

Station Road, Marine Road (which was then known as Penrhos Road) and Pwllycrochan Avenue, had made their appearance, and there were a few shops at the top eastern side of Station Road, when Penrhos College took this important step. These shops, says Miss Hovey, were rented at £25 a year or, with a house, £50 a year. Small dwellings and apartment houses in the village sold for £150. Land was 2/6d a yard.[173] Miss Wenn and Miss Martin came from a small girls' boarding school in Norfolk to be the first Principal and the first Matron of the new Penrhos, which was opened on 23 September 1880, by the Rev. Dr. Morley Puncheon, president of the Methodist Conference. Mr. R.Haworth, JP, Manchester, was chairman, and the Rev. F.Payne, honorary secretary. The number of pupils rose to 33 in the second term, and there were 60 by the end of the first year.

There was no English Church, and, as Prince's Drive did not exist, Penrhos girls used to go by a path over the fields to the little Welsh Methodist Chapel at the east end of the village (Greenfield Road). On dark winter evenings, a lantern was carried by the leading girls, another by the mistress at the back, and sometimes a third by a girl in the middle of the file.

Miss Pope succeeded Miss Wenn and was principal for 13½ years. In 1895 the School Governors decided to purchase, from the Pwllycrochan Estate Company, the Hydropathic Establishment, with its contents, as the nucleus for a larger school.

Education

Hydropathic Establishment, built in 1882 and still clearly recognisable as the nucleus of Penrhos College, which acquired the building in 1895. The school was founded in 1880 in a collection of houses on the promenade. It merged with Rydal school in 1995 and the old Hydro, and adjacent buildings, are scheduled for demolition during 2001 to make way for houses

Miss Rosa Hovey was headmistress of Penrhos from 1894 to 1928

No finer position could have been found in the whole country; more important still, there was open land down to the promenade, and right away to Rhos, and thus the great future development of the school became possible.

In 1898 the school house was built, with the gymnasium, classrooms, bedrooms and six music-rooms. First extensions to the Dining Hall followed in 1900; the Library wing, Mistresses' Rooms, more music-rooms and classrooms and bedrooms in 1907; the separate Botany House two years later. The Preparatory School House (later the Domestic Science House) was begun in 1910, the foundation stone being laid by David Lloyd George (who had earlier spoken at the National Eisteddfod in Colwyn Bay). It was during his speech at Penrhos that the then Chancellor made his first public pronouncement which led to the provision of pensions for teachers. The second addition to the dining-hall was in 1913-14. In 1919-20 three large classrooms were added in a separate building. Other buildings were bought, bringing the total ground area up to 33 acres. In 1920 a private house off Oak Drive was purchased for a separate Junior School. The Great Hall was completed in 1925. Science rooms and Recreation room were opened in 1928. Miss Wainwright, succeeded Miss Hovey in 1928.[174]

Rydal School
The School now known as Rydal, but which was originally Rydal Mount, was founded in 1885, under the headmastership of Mr. T.G.Osborn, MA. Though scholars were few at the start, its sponsors had vision. The small school, encouraged by the Rev. F.Payne, was at first housed in the north-west corner of the block where the Common Room and the Head Master's study are now placed. Though it opened with only fifteen scholars, its growth was so rapid that a spacious addition along Lansdowne Road was added – as a date on the facade implies – in 1890. In five years the number of pupils had increased to one hundred.

"*Rydal School: 1885-1935*" is a handsome volume with which the Rydal Press celebrated their school's Jubilee. At the Speech Day of 1905 Mr.Osborn said he did not aim, and never had aimed, at the ordinary idea of an English public school. He wished to make that domesticity which was incompatible with life in a large public school a feature of school life at Rydal Mount, and he wanted his school to be conducted upon lines leading to the highest possible education, combined with high religious culture. It is of interest to note that Edenfield, on the opposite side of Lansdowne Road, was, at the start, one of the Rydal houses. An Old Rydalian writes that in 1889 "*school matches were at first played on a meadow in Abergele (sic) Road, where the Presbyterian Church now stands, and later, on a field known as Board School Field, close to the junction of Conwy and Llandudno roads.*" In 1896 another Old Boy wrote:

"*Colwyn Bay was a village and when some epidemic placed it out of bounds, the one shop which Rhos possessed did a good trade in such biscuits as it could command. The tunnel beyond Old Colwyn was known as 'the prison gate,' and when we passed through it after holidays we were in our own little world, in a sense which it must be difficult to understand at the present day.*"

On the death of Mr. Osborn the school headship was assumed by his son, Mr. G.F.A. Osborn, BSc. Then came the Rev. A.J.Costain, MA, as headmaster in 1915. In a short time the attendance was raised from 45 to 220, and the school, now known as Rydal attained public school status. School House was bought about this time. About 1922 association football was changed to rugby. Land was purchased in Walshaw Avenue, trucks and lines bought, and for many months masters and boys laboured to level what came to be known as New Field. In 1951 New Field was further extended to the King's Road boundary. On the first night of the school year, 1928, the old army huts which served as laboratories were burnt down. In their place arose "the handsomest building in Colwyn Bay" with classrooms, laboratories, engineering shop, library and observatory.

Junior School came into being in September 1931. At first it was at Ingleside, then Glan

Education

Rydal School with the original Rydal Mount building on the left

Aber was added, and finally the school removed to Walshaw. During the 1939-45 war the main school was transferred to Oakwood Park in the Sychnant Pass, Conwy.[175] On the return of the main school to its original home the juniors were moved to Oakwood Park. In 1951 the Pwllycrochan Hotel was purchased for use as the junior school.

NATIONAL SCHOOL SYSTEM

No account of the educational growth of the district would be complete without reference to the National School system which brought education, from its humblest to its highest form, within reach of all children, the richest and poorest alike. For the administration of this scheme locally the County Education Committee is, of course, responsible. For children under eleven the main consideration has been improvement of amenities, especially school buildings. Few of the local elementary schools can boast any great age. The town therefore has been fortunate enough to acquire, in a relatively short time, several well-built schools, notably the Council Schools at Penmaenrhos (1914), Rhos-on-Sea (1927) and Old Colwyn, infant and junior (1931). At Mochdre a "sunshine" school was built for infants in 1939, and has proved deservedly popular.

For the older schools much remains to be done when kindlier world conditions obtain. Children in their teens presented a more complicated problem in the early days of the 20th century. The problem was to provide education for children of admitted promise but poor financial circumstances. There was no school within the bounds of the present borough to fit them for a professional or university career. To get such facilities they had to travel to Llandudno or Abergele.

An attempt was made to solve the problem by building a Higher Grade School on Dingle

Hill — a building opened on 12 January 1903. The date was, apparently, recorded on a terracotta plaque now covered with plaster for some reason unknown to the writer. The school did not satisfy the demand for long, perhaps because there was insufficient scope, and children continued to attend neighbouring County Schools. On the conclusion of the 1914-18 war the problem again asserted itself but was quickly settled. It was resolved that a municipal Secondary School should be established under the Act of 1902, on the premises of the Higher Grade School. The new school was opened in 1920, with Mr. W.P. Dodd, MA, MC, as its headmaster. Numbers rose rapidly, and by 1923 semi-permanent accommodation was added to cater for another 150 children. Laboratories and subject rooms were still too small, and in 1932 the original block of permanent buildings was more than doubled. This was providential, for when war broke out in 1939 a Liverpool Girls' School (Blackburne House) was evacuated and allotted part of the premises. After their departure an even larger influx of evacuees and Civil Servants' children crowded the school to its fullest capacity. The peak number enrolled was 476. Even that total is only 20 more than the present roll (1951), and further extensions are indicated.

Grammar School provision was not the only problem. There remained the pupils unfit academically for such a form of education, or with inclinations of a more practical type. A Central School was the first solution. Its aim was to train children of eleven years and over for careers in industry, commerce and technical employment. A dignified building was opened in December 1930 on East Parade, under Ernest Roberts, BSc. It grew rapidly and played its part in accommodating the great influx of the war years.

The Education Act of 1944 ushered in bolder conceptions and called for improved facilities for practical work. In all areas the Central School was superseded by the Secondary Modern School. In Colwyn Bay the change was accentuated by the provision of an annexe containing workshop and craft rooms, admirably equipped. This was opened in 1949 The number on the Modern School rolls exceeds 500. (The school has just adopted the name Pendorlan.)[176] Thus nearly a thousand pupils in the borough receive post-primary education of various types. One wonders if the pioneers of education last century ever dreamed of such expansion.

SCHOOLS OF THE BOROUGH

The dates of the formation of local schools are here tabulated:–
Old Colwyn Junior Non-Provided School, built 1868. Two classrooms and main porch added later.
Llysfaen Junior N.P. School, built 1871. Central heating installed in 1928.
Colwyn Bay Junior Mixed Council School (Conwy Road), built 1876. Two classrooms added in 1906.
Llwydgoed Council School (Brynymaen), built 1880.
Colwyn Bay Infants' Council School (Douglas Road), built 1895. Structural alterations 1908.
Colwyn Bay Secondary Grammar School. Nucleus of present buildings built in 1903 for a Higher Grade School. In 1919 it was decided to replace this with a Secondary School administered under the Act of 1902. As a Secondary School it was opened in 1920.
Penmaenrhos Junior Council School, built 1914.
Old Colwyn Junior Mixed School, built 1931.
Llandrillo-yn-Rhos Mixed Council School, opened October 17th, 1927.
Old Colwyn Infants' Council School, built 1931.
Colwyn Bay Secondary Modern School, built 1930. Annexe opened 1949.
Mochdre Infants' School, built 1939.
Comprehensive secondary education introduced 1967.

From Urban District to Municipal Borough

1894

THE URBAN DISTRICT COUNCIL

THE year 1894 proved to be a memorable one. Under the provisions of the Local Government Act of 1894 the local government district became an Urban District. The Groes Bridge was re-built and widened, and in April 1895 Rhos Pier was opened. Until that year an ordinary lamp stood at the top of Station Road. This was replaced by an ornamental drinking fountain given by John Porter, J.P., and was officially presented on 17 January 1895; the first occasion of its kind in the new Urban District.[177] A Local Government Board Order of 5 March 1896 vested the Council with the power of appointing overseers; there was also an Order conferring upon the Council the power to appoint and revoke appointments of assistant overseers, and other powers of a parish council, and the powers of a vestry under the Poor Rate Assessment and Collection Act of 1869. The Colwyn Bay and Colwyn Urban District Council Act was passed in 1897.

EARLY POST OFFICES

The first postal address was "near Conway." The postman's round stretched from Mochdre to Llysfaen. *"I am told,"* wrote the late Jos. H. Roberts, whose association with the local authority went back to its early days, *that the first post office* (really a sub-post office to Conwy) *was a little shop kept by Mr. Frank Madren.*

This shop (long since taken away) was situated near the offices of Messrs. F A.Dew, auctioneer, on Conway Road. The date would be in the 1870's. The next sub-postmaster was Mr.W.H.Roberts, whose shop was in the lower part of Station Road. This Mr. Roberts built a shop on the site of the present N.P. Bank,[178] and here the postal business was conducted for several years. A post office with whole-time Post Master (Mr. Isaac Jones) and staff was opened in Queen Buildings, Station Road.

Colwyn Bay was one of the first places to acquire telephones. In the early days of the National Telephone Company, situated at 8 Station Road, the number of lines was 200. The number of subscribers to the population was regarded as high. The office was removed to the top of Station Road, where it remained until the service was taken over by the Government.

COACHING DAYS

No review of the Colwyn Bay of 1900 would be complete without reference to the four-in-hand coaches which bore visitors to the beauty spots of the district. On the site of the Cosy Cinema[179] stood a Mews belonging to Edwin Jones, and subsequently acquired by J. Fred

Francis. Opposite, at "The Little Iron Shop," was the "Tally-Ho" Mews of Francis Davies. Tours included trips to Betws-y-Coed, St. Asaph, Penmaenmawr, Bodnant and what was termed "The Loop." The *"well appointed new patent coach"* known as the DUKE OF YORK[180] left to the clatter of hoofs, the jingle of harness, and the tooting of the long copper horn by the red-coated guard, for a day's excursion to Betws-y-Coed, where luncheon was awaiting the passengers at the Waterloo Hotel. Here the horses were changed, and the coach rolled on past Capel Curig and down the Nant Ffrancon Pass. At Bethesda tea was provided and the horses again changed. Returning by Aber the coach reached Colwyn Bay about 6.45 pm. *"Fares for the entire route, 10/- each; box seats, 2s extra."* [181] Edwin Jones, who resembled King Edward VII in appearance, had a remarkable collection of whips, many of which came from celebrated personages. For many years the Little Iron Shop, defying convention, remained incongruously in the heart of the town on Burton's Corner. Poultry, fruit and vegetables were sold from a small corrugated structure which went back to the 1860's when it was erected as an outpost of the Pwllycrochan Hotel to refresh early visitors. Later it was turned into a shop and long remained a quaint link with the past.

OUTDOOR ACTIVITIES

Before the Boer War the spacious Bryn Euryn fields provided admirable camping facilities for the Rifle Volunteers from many parts of the country. The red-coated soldiers were a source of endless interest as they marched up Station Road, and their sham fights round about Bryn Euryn were regarded as fascinating free entertainment.

Horseracing and pony racing took place in the huge field at the back of the Board School through which Victoria Park was later cut. In 1887 the whole town went to the Flagstaff for a picnic, in honour of Queen Victoria's jubilee. In the days when the town was in course of construction there was a great deal of haulage to be done. Extensive stables occupied land at the top of Penrhyn Road. The Pendorlan Fields were a favourite sports ground in the early years, and it was here the first football matches were played. The solitary cottage on Greenfield Road is still in existence, differing in appearance from the adjoining houses.

VICTORIA PIER PAVILION

A progressive step in the development of Colwyn Bay was the building of the pier and pavilion. This was the work of a private company. The preliminary task of creating an approach had already been undertaken by the Council. The Victoria Pier and Pavilion was named in honour of the Queen.

Since the construction by the local authority of about a mile of promenade, at a cost of about £15,000, the young resort had shown marked progress. The first pile in connection with the pier was driven on 1 June 1899. The architects and engineers were Messrs. Magnalls & Littlewood, Manchester. The contractors for the whole of the works were the Widnes Foundry Company, and the pavilion was constructed by Messrs. William Brown & Son, Salford. The ticket offices at the entrances were *"designed in the Moorish sty*le." They are all that remain of the original buildings.[182]

The width of the pier was 40ft, and the first section 316ft in length. It was arranged that later a second section, extending the pier to 1,050ft would be added, and the original intention was to have a landing stage. The pavilion, situated 50 yards from the entrance, was capable of seating 2,500 people. There was a cafe-lounge and refreshment room. Shops were provided on either side of the main entrance. The pier and pavilion were lit by electricity, and the building was ventilated by a 48-inch electric fan, fixed in the dome.

From Urban District to Municipal Borough

Colwyn Bay's first Pier Pavilion

Securing the services of M. Jules Riviére as Musical Director was regarded as a great achievement on the part of the Directors of the Company, for though advanced in years, the veteran musician was still vigorous. The Deputy Conductor, M. Henri Verbrugghen, was acknowledged to be one of the finest living violinists. Three thousand invitations were issued for the opening ceremony. At 7 o'clock in the evening a great crowd assembled at the entrance gates. Mr. Littlewood, of Messrs. Magnalls & Littlewood, presented a gold key to the Chairman of the Pier and Pavilion Committee. On one side of the key was an illuminated view of the pier and pavilion; on the other the following inscription:

"*Presented to W. F. Mason, Esq., by the architects, on the occasion of the opening of the Victoria Pier and Pavilion, Colwyn Bay, June 1st, 1900. J. & W. H. Littlewood, Architects and Engineers.*"

The chairman of the Urban District Council, George Bevan, JP, expressed the Council's "*great appreciation of the enterprise and progressive public spirit which had animated the Directors of the Company.*"

VISIT OF MADAME PATTI

The following day Madame Adelina Patti sang in the Pavilion. She was given a civic reception at the station, which was red-carpeted for the occasion. The chairman of the Council presented her with an illuminated album, bound in sage-green, containing 14 photographic views of local scenery. It bore the following inscription:

"*Presented on behalf of the town and members of the District Council of Colwyn Bay and Colwyn, by George Bevan, Esq, JP, to Madame Adelina Patti (Baroness Cederstrom) as a memento of her visit to Colwyn Bay, North Wales, on the occasion of the opening concert of the new Victoria Pier — June 2nd, 1900.*"

The drive from the station to the Pavilion was decorated for the occasion and was afterwards called Victoria Drive. Hitherto it had been known as the Marine Drive. Hung prominently across the road was a streamer of blue with white lettering WELCOME TO THE QUEEN OF SONG. Madame Patti was accompanied by her husband, the Baron Cederstrom, and when the crowd found they were unable to glimpse the prima donna there were shouts of "*Pull down the hood.*" This was done, and the carriage advanced at a slow pace through the crowded street. Prolonged cheering greeted the singer's appearance on the Pavilion platform. She sang the *Jewel Song* from Gounod's *Faust*, followed by further songs in Italian. Madame Patti finally sang the song associated with her name *Home Sweet Home*.

In the evening a welcome was given to M. Jules Riviére. The programme opened with *God Save the Queen* and *God Bless the Prince of Wales*. The Victoria Pavilion was destroyed by fire in 1922. A new pavilion was built and this was burnt down in 1933. The present pavilion was designed on fireproof lines.

BOER WAR VOLUNTEERS

Following military reverses in South Africa a call was made for volunteers, and a number of Colwyn Bay men responded. The local men were entertained to a farewell dinner, presided over by the Chairman of the Council, George Bevan, and on the last day of January 1900, they left by train for Wrexham, *en route* for the front. The men who went were: Sergeant Alfred G.Allen, Cyclist T.Jackson, Private R H Jones and Bugler R.Hughes, with the reservists Sergeant McCormick, Private Harley and Private J.Williams. So many persons assembled to see them off that the Railway Company officials were forced to close the station gates. About a hundred people overcame this handicap by purchasing tickets to Old Colwyn, thus securing admittance to Colwyn Bay's tiny railway platform.

From Urban District to Municipal Borough

The return in May 1901 of three of Colwyn Bay's Volunteers was an event of colourful importance. Two World Wars have brought about wholly different conceptions. Only those who were there at the time can appreciate the intense stir of this formal homecoming. One of the writer's earliest recollections is the sight of the procession descending the hill from the Public Hall (which was then used as the local Armoury). Following the leading files of soldiers of the old 2nd Volunteer Battalion, RWF, in their familiar red tunics, came three men in khaki - alone. *"Soldiers of the Queen!"* Never before had a local boy actually *seen* khaki. Scarlet seemed drab in comparison with this novel uniform, which smacked of the dust of the veldt. The occasion was such that a quotation from the *Welsh Coast Pioneer* of 17 May 1901, reporting the train's arrival, might be considered appropriate:

"The first to step out was Sgt. Allen, who was quickly surrounded by the officers and his particular chums. His poor arms were kept going in a way which reminded spectators of a windmill. Bugler Hughes broke through the crowds from one direction and encountered his sister, and in the presence of the sympathetic spectators, brother and sister enfolded each other in a loving embrace. The next to be overwhelmed by heartfelt handshakes and eager and anxious questioning was Private Jackson. The three heroes looked bronzed, very fit and well, and in the best of spirits. Then the gates were opened, and amid cheers, they rushed into the arms of their comrades, who were waiting expectantly without. After the distinguished visitors had held a short 'levee,' the word of command was given and a procession was formed, headed by the band, with the 'gentlemen in khaki' in the centre. The band struck up a lively quickstep, and followed by an excited throng, proceeded via Station Road and Conway Road, to the quarters of the Regiment."

Later they marched to the Imperial Hotel for a civic dinner. Sgt. Alfred Allen, Cyclist Fred Jackson, and Bugler R. Hughes were the guests of honour, and with them their comrade Private R.H.Jones, who had been invalided home earlier. All responded to the toast in their honour. Bugler Hughes said he had come through 23 engagements without a scratch.

A PLACID AGE

At the turn of the century Colwyn Bay possessed a quiet dignity which has departed like the age it represented. Many of the wealthy people dwelling in the large houses in the outskirts were the possessors of a brougham, or "carriage and pair." These glistening vehicles, sleek horses and fawn-coated, cockaded coachmen, were a familiar sight in the streets.

Keeping abreast of the times, Colwyn Bay introduced *"animated pictures"* or a *"Warograph."* Of a summer's night these were flashed jerkily on to an open-air screen - erected either on the grass embankment of the Promenade, east of the Dingle, or amid the oak trees of the little glade at the bottom of Penrhyn Road. It was an age of black-faced minstrels, of visiting German bands, and an itinerant string quartet which discoursed melodious music on the soft summer air. There were sand-castle competitions, horse-drawn bathing vans, donkey and pony rides across the sands, or, in winter evenings, Gilchrist lectures in the Victoria Pier Pavilion, or an occasional visit of Poole's Myriorama, which staged colourful reproductions of the Russo-Japanese war. It was a placid age when the town's excitement, to judge by newspaper reports, was restricted to a weekly inebriate or a runaway horse.

PUBLIC LIBRARY

The Libraries Act of 1892 was adopted and came into operation on 1 May 1901, though it was not until 1904 that it was possible to complete the Public Library. The beneficence of Andrew Carnegie, who contributed £3,785 towards the cost, inspired a committee of townspeople to

Colwyn Bay Public Library (above) and the scene (below) when it was opened on 24 April 1905

carry through the negotiations that resulted in the erection of the present building, in Woodland Road West. The public subscribed £1,250, and the Library was opened on 24 April 1905. The total cost of land, building and furnishing was £5,436. After the opening the building was handed to the Urban District Council. The first Librarian was Mr Thornsby, who was soon followed by Mr. O.Jones Roberts, member of an old local family. He was succeeded in May 1932 by Ifor Davies.[183]

RAPID GROWTH

By 1901 the town had a population of 8,689, and was growing rapidly. Buildings, many of them of a substantial character, were rising. Fresh roads were cut through the broad fields. Conway Road still boasted a large number of stately oaks to line its route. The Roman Catholic Church was opened and might be regarded as marking the western end of the town, though a few houses straggled past Ellesmere Road, which was then partially completed. Prince's Drive ceased at its lower end. Westward were fields through which flowed a brook lined by trees and bushes. It passed under the railway on its way to Penrhos grounds. A footpath ran across the meadows west of Penrhos as far as Aberhod, where it merged into a farm lane. The cliffs fell abruptly to the shingle, and halfway down (near the site of the old Cayley Embankment bandstand) was a substantial dwelling, known as the Bath-house. It was to these Rhos fields that children of the Sunday Schools marched, headed by banners, to celebrate the coronation

Ellesmere Road as it appeared in 1901

Combermere Lodge, Rhos Promenade, corner of Cayley Arms on right of picture

Rhos-on-Sea where the promenade now stretches. The house on the left is Moranedd, in the centre is the Blue Bell (Cayley Arms), and on the right the wall of Combermere Lodge

of Edward VII. The following table shows the rapidity with which houses were erected 1901, 133; 1902, 163; 1903, 75; 1904, 103; 1905, 105; 1906, 127. The Colwyn Bay and Colwyn Urban District Act of 1902 authorized the construction of a new promenade and sewage works. It was in 1902 that Colwyn Bridge was improved and widened. In 1904 the bridge over the railway, leading to Llannerch Road, was widened and improved. This was necessary owing to the doubling of the railway tracks; Tan-y-bryn Bridge was also widened, an undertaking which resulted in the demolition of the picturesque Nant Smithy. Bron-y-Nant cemetery was completed at a cost of £2,000. In 1903 the Council had acquired $2^1/_2$ acres of land from the Cayley Estate for an Isolation Hospital, which was opened two years later.

NEW COUNCIL OFFICES

Increasing responsibility made it necessary for the local authority to seek larger premises, and in 1903 the Council purchased for £4,500 two large semi-detached houses at the corner of Conway Road and Coed Pella Road, known as Glan Aber and Rhianfa. They stood on about an acre of land. These were converted into Council Offices and a large room added for a Council Chamber. The formal opening took place on 15 July 1904.[184] A portrait of the late Rev. W.Venables Williams, by J.K.Makin, purchased by public subscription, was presented to the town. The number of County Councillors was increased from one to four on 30 December 1904, and in the same year the Electoral Divisions were enlarged from one to four.

In many respects the year 1905 was a memorable one. The work of extending the promenade was completed, and Colwyn Bay found itself with a dignified seafront curving with uninterrupted grace for over two-and-a-half miles. Many residents took pride in walking from end to end, and on a summer Sunday morning it was fashionable to indulge in a "church parade." On 21 June the illuminating of the Rhos section of the Promenade by arc lights was completed. Another important improvement was the purchase of the beautiful Pwllycrochan Woods, for £7,500, from the Estate Company, on 31 October 1905. The woods are still one of the town's greatest attractions, and cover 39 acres.

The town's growth was reflected by changes in administration. The urban district was divided into four wards. The number of councillors was increased from twelve to twenty. By an Order of the County Council, of 5 May 1905, a triennial election of councillors was instituted.

Among the outstanding events of 1906 was the formal opening of the Fairy Glen, Old Colwyn (previously called The Nant), on 1 August, and the inaugurating of the Upper Colwyn Bay Water Supply Works on 9 October. A drinking fountain was erected on the Promenade at Rhos-on-Sea, as a tribute to the late Vicar, the Rev. W.Venables Williams.

In 1907 Colwyn Bay was selected for the conference of Municipal and County Engineers, who met here on 31 May. In order to supply interesting facts to the delegates there was a delving into records which is of considerable assistance to us to-day. In 1891 there were 833 houses, a population of 4,754, and a rateable value of £24,751. In 1907 the figures were 2.311 houses, 12,000 people, and £79,767 rateable value. The estimated visiting population was 15,000. The new sewerage works were formally opened on 14 June 1907.

THE LIGHT RAILWAY

An important event in the development of the area was the completion, in 1907, of the first portion of the Llandudno and Colwyn Bay Light Railway. At a time when people were dependent on horsedrawn vehicles or the railway for transportation, this innovation proved acceptable. Tram-sheds were built in a district named Klondyke, on account of its isolation, at the foot of Rhos Road. The first portion of the railway stretched from West Shore, Llandudno, to the tram-sheds. It began to operate on 19 October 1907, when the first cars started simultaneously from both ends of the track. There was no semblance of a ceremonial, to quote a contemporary account, but the ringing of bells and cheers from curious spectators heralded the event.

Early in November a Board of Trade inquiry was held to determine whether this novel service should be extended to Old Colwyn. There was opposition to the scheme, on account of the narrowness of the main road which, one witness asserted, was only 17ft 6ins. wide at the junction of Llanelian Road. Up to this time there had existed a building between the Cayley Arms and the sea known as Combermere Lodge. It was enclosed from curious sightseers by a high stone wall. One stipulation was that Combermere Lodge should be demolished and its grounds used for promenade widening.

At this time there was a sporadic service of horse-drawn "brakes" from Colwyn Bay to Old Colwyn. Progress was leisurely and not infrequently the driver lingered until there were sufficient passengers to make the trip a financial undertaking. By 1910 the tram track had been extended to the top of Station Road; on 26 March 1915 it ran to the Queen's Hotel,[185] Old Colwyn. At this time the limed walls of the Plough Terrace cottages jutted into the narrow road, and it is surprising that vehicles could pass a tram at this spot. By 1930 the increase of traffic necessitated the closing of this portion of the service.

It was in 1908 that the new Territorial Army Act came into force, and in the spring of that year Colwyn Bay said farewell to its old Volunteers, to be replaced by "G" Company, 5th Battalion, Royal Welch Fusiliers. There is a record of the new company, headed by the Colwyn Silver Band, marching to Old Colwyn, under the command of Captain T.H.Morgan, to participate in a public meeting at which ministers of religion spoke in support of the new movement, for the threat of war with Germany was becoming more pronounced. The same year the Boy Scout movement was launched, and in May a troop was formed in Colwyn Bay. It met in the YMCA, Abergele Road, the secretary, Samuel Johnston, acting as the first scoutmaster. The Premier of South Australia, Rt.Hon.Thomas Price, visited Colwyn Bay. Denbighshire Education Committee held its first meeting in Colwyn Bay.

The following year, 1909, saw the proclamation ceremony of the National Eisteddfod, at the Flagstaff, in September. The National Eisteddfod was held in Colwyn Bay from 13-17 September 1910. The pavilion was pitched on Dinglewood field. A feature was the visit of the new Chancellor of the Exchequer, the Rt.Hon. David Lloyd George, who was the object of the attention of some militant suffragettes. By an Order of the Privy Council, dated 2 August 1910, a County Court was allocated to Colwyn Bay.

AN AIR PIONEER

The year 1910 was notable for another memorable event. On 10 August people along the main road stopped and stared into the sky for their ears were greeted by a peculiar throbbing sound, the like of which they had never heard before. Over the rooftops came a huge kite-like affair, which seemed to be held together by innumerable wires, and perched precariously in the midst, with feet hanging over space was a human being. Colwyn Bay residents knew that they must he looking at one of those new flying machines to which the papers devoted so much space.

The strange object came lower and lower. People ran or leaped on to bicycles to follow its course. The plane – an Antoinette[186] – came down on the Rhos Golf Links, and out stepped the actor-aviator Robert Loraine, attempting the first flight to Ireland. So far as we are aware this was the first aeroplane to land in Wales.

Electric lighting was extended to Old Colwyn in 1911. The coronation of King George V and Queen Mary was observed on 22 June 1911; and on 15 July the new drill-hall in Prince's Drive was opened by Major General Cowans. The Notification of Births Act (1907) was adopted

Actor and aviation pioneer Robert Loraine is seen taking off from Rhos-on-Sea golf course in August 1910 in his Farman biplane. Using the pseudonym Jones to confuse his rivals, he had taken off from Blackpool air show to establish two records: the longest oversea flight of 63 miles, and the first aircraft to land in Wales

and brought into operation on 18 September 1911. A Provisional Order was confirmed on 18 August for the Promenade and Sewerage schemes, whereby the works were authorized and additional borrowing powers granted.

In 1912 an Order of the County Council increased the members of the Council from 20 to 24. The policy reverted to the annual retirement of councillors. On 6 September the town was visited by the Library Association.

The next important municipal undertaking was the acquisition, on 28 January 1914, of the Cayley Promenade Embankment. War having been declared on 4 August, troops were quartered in Colwyn Bay on 30 December. The Colwyn public gardens (now known as the Wynn Gardens) were acquired by a gift from Lt-Col. (later Sir) R.W.Williams Wynn, DSO (Lord Lieutenant). A lease of the railway embankment for 99 years was secured from the London and North Western Railway Company on 24 June 1916.

Colwyn Bay's first lady councillor, Miss E.M.Hovey, was elected to the Urban District Council on 7 April 1919. Peace was celebrated on 18 July, and the demobilized men were entertained on 11 November 1919. A tank was presented to the town on 12 January 1920 and was placed on the lawn outside the Council Offices, providing small boys with their first unbreakable toy.

In 1920 a painting by Augustus John, RA., of Lord Colwyn, PC, was presented to the town by public subscription. "Workmen's dwellings," were completed at Rhos-on-Sea on 30 November. Eirias Park, comprising 47 acres, was acquired in April 1921. In May 1921, the Llandudno-Colwyn Bay through road was opened for traffic.

The first Chairman of the local Board (1887) and Urban District Council (1895), the Rev.Thomas Parry, had his portrait painted by Leonard Hughes, RCA, by public subscription, and this was presented to the town in August 1921.

From now onward the local authority devoted much of its energy to the problem of again widening the main road, which was insufficient to cope with the ever-increasing motor traffic. The way to Llandudno having been the first consideration, the next was the widening of the hill at Groes, which was made more gradual. This was completed in August 1922. The work, which proceeded in stages, necessitated setting back garden walls and felling a number of stately oaks. Possibly the most spectacular achievement was taking down and setting back the artistic lych-gate at St. John's Methodist Church. This was done so adroitly that a person unfamiliar with the circumstances would never dream it was not in its original position.

Colwyn Bay was interested in the official opening of the new Cowlyd Dam, by Sir John Snell, Chief Electricity Commissioner, on 20 September 1922. The town's war memorial, an infantryman in the battle dress of the 1914-18 war, paid for by public subscription, was placed in front of the Council Offices and formally unveiled on 11 November 1922 by Lord Colwyn. It is the work of T. Cassidy.[187]

Lord Colwyn inaugurated a new electricity transformer station in Ivy Street in November 1923.

On 1 April 1923 Llysfaen parish was amalgamated with the Urban District by virtue of the Counties of Carnarvon and Denbigh (Llysfaen) Order of 1922.

Following the disastrous fire at Colwyn Bay Pier Pavilion, the Victoria Pier undertaking was purchased in 1923 under the Colwyn Bay (Victoria) Pier Order. The Pier structure was restored and a new pavilion was formally opened in July 1923. At this time the corner of the main road at Brompton Avenue presented a dangerous, narrow right-angle bend, owing to the existence of a large house with a high garden wall. It was known as Wayside, and to allow road improvements this was purchased in May 1923. The house was subsequently demolished, the corner widened and a small park formed. Old residents still refer to this spot as Wayside Corner. On the other side of the main road the property known as Monaville was purchased in June, so that the land at the rear could be used for a Council depot. Eirias Park playing fields were opened in September 1923. Colwyn Bay was represented when the North Wales and South Cheshire Joint Electricity Authority was established on 23 October 1923. On 2 November consent was given to the conversion of the electricity supply from direct to alternating current.

The Prince of Wales paid a visit to the town on 2 November, 1923, and was officially received at a platform erected on the Cayley Embankment slope. His Royal Highness inspected the local ex-servicemen, Scouts, Guides and other voluntary bodies who participated in the parade.

On 11 November 1923 the Old Colwyn War Memorial was unveiled outside St. Catherine's Church.

In July 1924 the Tan Lan Estate was acquired. A ten years' lease was obtained on Bryn Euryn in November, and on the last day of the year Min-y-Don Park was purchased.

A portrait of the late John Porter, JP, was presented to the town on 25 March 1925. On the same date there was a formal opening of the new sewerage works at Mochdre. The annual conference of the Union of Post Office Officials was held in the town. The donor of Wynn Gardens at Old Colwyn, Lt-Col (Sir) R.W. Williams Wynn, performed the opening ceremony. Colwyn Bay and West Denbighshire Hospital, which was a development of the Cottage Hospital started in 1899, was opened on 17 October 1925. The electricity supply was extended to Penrhyn Bay on 16 December 1925.

From 1 April 1926 the local authority's title was changed from the Colwyn Bay and Colwyn Urban District to the Urban District of Colwyn Bay. The first lady to be Chairman of the local authority, Miss E. M. Hovey, J.P., opened the new Post Office, Princes Drive, on 7 August 1926.[188] Tanycoed, Old Colwyn, was purchased in 1926, to add to Minydon Park.

The Colwyn Bay Urban District Council Act of 1926 empowered the Council to run an omnibus service. The Act also authorized the consolidation of all parishes in the district into one parish,[189] named the Parish of Llandrillo-yn-Rhos, and to consolidate the rates of the district.

The picturesque Nant Smithy at Tan-y-Bryn Bridge before the railway track was doubled

Flying-boats of the RAF visited the Bay on 12 September 1927. In March 1928 the Eagles Farm at Mochdre, with an area of 29 acres, was procured. That May, NALGO held its annual conference in the town.

Minydon Recreation Ground was opened in July, and in August Plastirion was acquired as a Maternity and Child Welfare Centre. Electric lighting of Llysfaen was inaugurated on 28 December. The electricity supply was extended to Llangystennin in 1929, and to Glan Conwy in 1930.

Rydal public gardens[190] were laid out in 1930, the land having been purchased in December 1929. The further widening of Groes Bridge was completed in 1930. The same year saw the conference of the Urban District Councils' Association, in June. In 1930 a lease of ground in Penrhyn Avenue, Rhos-on-Sea, was secured from the late William Horton. On 5 July the rock gardens and model yacht lake at Eirias Park were opened.

In 1931 Rhos Recreation Ground was acquired. A portrait of George Bevan, JP, painted by Raeburn Dobson, R.A, waspresented to the town, by public subscription. The abattoir at Mochdre was opened in 1932.

The Council secured possession of the hill of Bryn Euryn, the ruins of Llys Euryn, and the Bron-y-Nant Wood in 1932. A Maternity and Child Welfare Clinic was opened at Llysfaen. The Incorporation Inquiry was held on 26 April 1933. That was the year when the second Pier Pavilion was destroyed by fire, on 16 May, and the Bijou Pavilion, at the pierhead on 28 July.

The Denbighshire Review Order came into effect on 1 April 1934, whereby the alteration and extension of the proposed borough boundary came into effect. The official opening of the new Pier Pavilion took place on 8 May 1934. The Urdd National Eisteddfod was held in the town in 1934.

September 20th, 1934 was the date of the presentation of the Charter of Incorporation.[191]

PART THREE

ANCIENT PARISHES AND VILLAGES

Llandrillo-yn-Rhos or Rhos-on Sea

RHOS-ON-SEA has known a variety of names: Dinarth, Llandrillo-yn-Rhos, Glanydon, Rhos Trillo, and finally its present designation, bestowed upon it, presumably, by the late William Horton, JP, when he purchased the 250-acre estate of the late Mr.Bostock of Liverpool. It was Mr. Bostock who built Rhos Pier, which was opened in April, 1895.

Initial development occurred in the sixties when the first portion of the Rhos Abbey Hotel, and the adjoining houses, were constructed. Old Price speaks of *"a very large grass plot which has long since been, for want of a sea-wall, swept away by the waves."* Old Price loved the rural charms of the neighbourhood. First, he deplores the precipitous rock at the back of Bryn Euryn farmhouse being blown to fragments and shipped off to Liverpool; next, he complains that the neat fields were turned into a prim arrangement of large fields, which *"look like a piece of Norfolk"* grafted upon Llandrillo. But it is this terrace which provokes his most vehement outburst:

"Along this expanse of turf at Rhos one has thought fit to erect a set of lodging-houses and a hotel, in which the spirit and letter of ugliness are carried out but too faithfully by an architect who, if his own handiwork be not the death of him, will surely live to see them pulled down as a nuisance."

Bryn Euryn quarry was apparently developed in the 1840s. At all events there was a legal dispute between Mr. J.L. Parry-Evans, of Rhos Fynach, and the Quarry Company in 1856. A plan prepared in connection with this has been preserved, and shows a railway line from the quarry running some yards west of Rhos Road to the shore, where it terminates in a shipping stage. What is more interesting is that it marks an area at the base of the shipping stage as the site of *"The Old Rhos Quay."* This confirms the story that Rhos was once a port. Workmen digging near the promenade in the 1890s came across what appeared to be huge lock gates. It was Mr. Horton's intention to preserve these, but the wood was so rotten that it crumbled.

It is said there was a ship-building yard on the ground now occupied by the Rhos County Garage.[192] A branch of the Afon Ganol, along which the county boundary was traced, entered the sea opposite the end of Penrhyn Avenue. If this stream had once been a deep creek, it might explain Old Price's cryptic reference to ships "under" Llandrillo Church.

The stone-built houses in Rhos Road, which bear the date 1857, probably mark the approximate period of the establishment of the quarry. But Rhos Road - which, until it was widened in the 20th century, was a narrow hedge-fringed lane - is far older than this. It is clearly indicated in the map prepared for Robert Davies in 1763. Thus it existed before the turnpike (now our main road) and one wonders why this straight road to the shore was constructed at a time when few persons were interested in road making. It might have linked Llys Euryn - the squire's home - with the quay. The 1763 map marks Aberhod, standing well back from the shore, and the Rising Gull near the foot of Rhos Road. This was a thatched cottage, like a lodge, at the entrance of the lane to Rhos Fynach. It achieved some notoriety because part was in Denbighshire and part in Caernarvonshire. Since those days the county boundary has been moved farther west. How the cottage came by its euphonious name is a

Rhos-on-Sea from Bryn Euryn quarry – about 1900 AD

Rhos promenade showing the first Rhos Abbey Hotel - the last building on the right of the terrace. The pier gateway on the extreme right still survives

Foot of Rhos Road before widening

mystery; the writer has come across no reference to it as an ale-house. The cottages higher up the road, known as Ffordd, are still with us. There was also a small dwelling, Ty Fry, on the north-east corner of the crossing of the present Rhos and Llandudno roads, but this has disappeared. Bryn Euryn farm is shown.

Unfortunately the plan, while marking the Penrhyn Marsh, does not include Rhos Fynach, Rhyd Farm or St. Trillo's Cell, but all three must have been there at the time. At any rate, a witness at the inquiry into the Rhos Fynach weir's age testified to having been born at Rhyd farm in 1792. The buildings mentioned (with, of course, the old vicarage, built 1762) might be taken as constituting the whole of Rhos-on-Sea less than two centuries ago. Rhyd farm, demolished about 75 years ago, was the first clubhouse of the Rhos-on-Sea Golf Club. According to David Roberts, Cynlas, Old Colwyn, Mr. Bostock practically re-built Rhyd farm in the nineties. At the same time he ordered the erection of the original sea wall nearby. Mr. Roberts, who was engaged on this work, says there was so great a scarcity of lime that they made their own kiln, which can still be seen. The workmen took their meals in the ruined shell of St. Trillo's Chapel. The late Miss Parry-Evans told the writer that at one time there were many vipers at Rhos, and several vessel-loads of Irish soil were brought across and spread over the land in the hope that *"snakes would not live on Irish soil."* Mr. Parry-Evans kept an aquarium, for he secured many rare marine creatures in the weir. Dealers visiting him walked along the shore. Miss Parry-Evans said that when her father fractured his leg he was taken by coasting vessel from Rhos to Mostyn, and there transferred to a Liverpool-bound ship.

Rhos as a sea port is difficult to comprehend, but a writer who visited the place in 1857 observes:*"It is a locality particularly well adapted for a small secure port, sheltered from all winds, except the north-east, and where, even now, a trade of some value is carried on in limestone and timber."*[193]

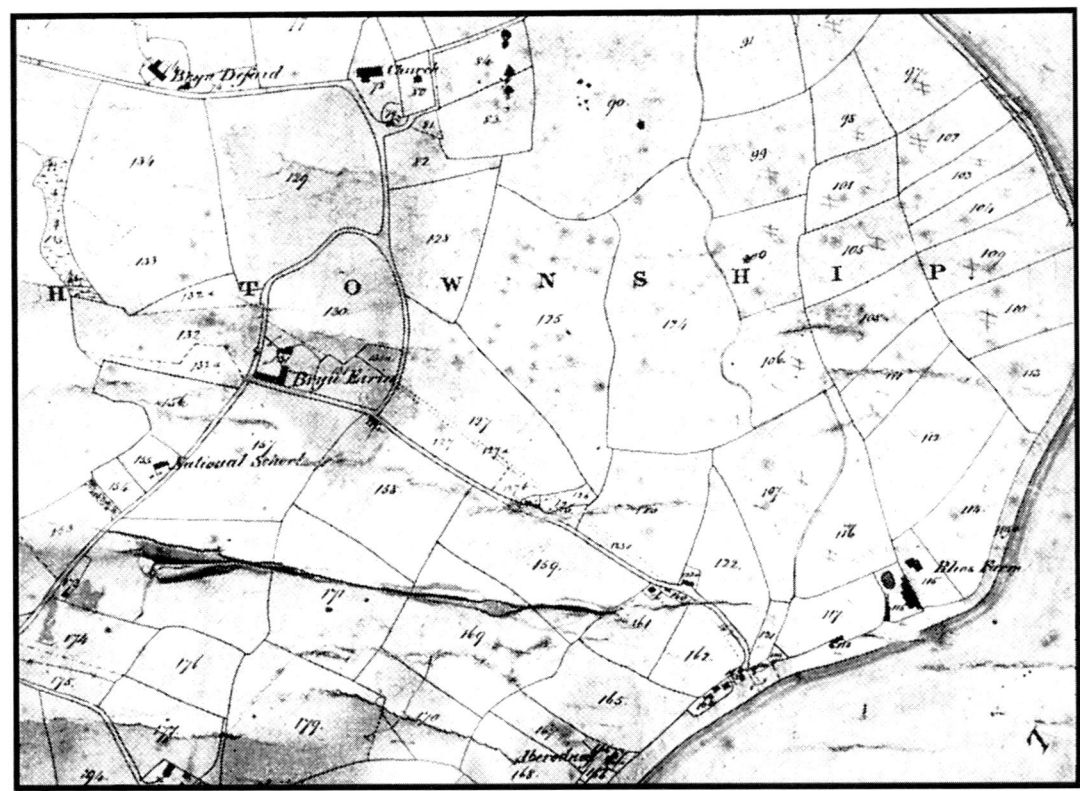

Courtesy National Library of Wales

This section of the tithe map of 1848 shows how undeveloped Llandrillo-yn-Rhos was then. The cottages at the foot of Rhos Road are for the most part recognisable. "Rhos Farm" is Rhos Fynach. Aberhod is indicated, also Tanybryn Road (with National School) and Dinerth Road near Llandrillo Church. The dark patch is a tear in the map

RHOS IN THE FORTIES

In his Topographical Dictionary of 1845 Lewis says the parish of Llandrillo contains 1,176 inhabitants and is situated *"on the great Holyhead road."*

The area is computed to be 1,890 acres, of which 610 are arable, 1,200 pasture and 60 wood. The "gentlemen's seats" include Pwllycrochan, Minydon, Glanydon and Bryndinerth. The village of Llandrillo is composed of two houses only, of which one is the vicarage. The townships in that part of the parish in Denbighshire are united for the maintenance of their poor while that of Eirias, which forms the Caernarvonshire portion of it, supports its poor separately. There are two weirs by the shore where an immense quantity of fish of various kinds is taken during favourable seasons.

Lewis describes the church as *"a large handsome structure,"* and says it *"contains some elegant specimens of ancient stained glass."* He mentions Llys Euryn, which he terms *"Llys Bryn Euryn,"* a large building *"erected by Ednyfed Fychan as a residence for himself and his descendants."* According to Lewis the family of Conway were resident there *"so late as the reign of Charles II."*

The *Parliamentary Gazeteer* of 1844 describes Llandrillo-yn-Rhos as a parish partly in the hundred of Isdulas in the county of Denbigh, and partly in the hundred of Creuddyn, union of

Conway, county of Caernarvon, the parish including the township of Eirias. The charities of Llandrillo-yn-Rhos in 1837 were £14 10s. 0d. The poor rates the following year amounted to £741. There were 181 houses. The population in 1801 was given as 769, and in 1831 as 1,133. The account adds *"Excellent wheat is grown here."*

The pronounced discrepancy between the number of houses listed in the *Gazeteer* and the figures given by Lewis might be accounted for by the *Gazeteer's* including *all* dwellings in the entire *parish,* while Lewis refers only to houses of consequence in the "village."

A plan showing Llandrillo Pier was contemplated as far back as November 1864, is in Caernarfon County Records Office (Piers, No.12). The parcel includes Colonel Colby's map of 1840 (re-engraved), which marks the cluster of cottages at the foot of Rhos Road.

LLANDRILLO-YN-RHOS CHURCH

Now that houses have been built on the adjacent broad meadows, and main road traffic rushes along what was once a sequestered country lane, it is difficult to visualize the venerable church of Llandrillo-yn-Rhos as it stood, centuries ago, when its whitewashed walls rendered it a valuable landmark for mariners sailing to the port of Liverpool.[194] An illustration drawn in 1856 immediately after the church's restoration gives it a singularly isolated appearance with one solitary upright tombstone visible in the now crowded churchyard.

Llandrillo-yn-Rhos is regarded as the mother church of the district, though the earliest name was Dinerth (spelt in various ways). It first occurs in the sixth century: Dinerth Goch Rufoniog. This is unusual because "Rhos" was the term applied to the coastal strip, whereas Rufoniog was the corresponding area inland. Egbert, King of the West Saxons, in AD 819, seized the lordship of Rhos-Rufoniog. The Saxon ring found at Llysfaen may be a relic of this invasion. There is a record of Gruffydd ap Cynan, founder of the first of the royal tribes, giving ten shillings to the church of Dinerth Goch Rufoniog. Archdeacon Thomas laments that the scribe of the Norwich Taxatio of 1254 has corrupted the name into *"Eiuenth."* The Lincoln Taxatio (1291) calls it *"Eccl'ia de Dynerth."*

The Valor of 1535 calls the parish *"Rectoria de Dev'gh."* This appears to have been the last occasion on which the name Dinerth was used. Henceforth the church becomes Llandrillo, perpetuating the name of the patron saint, St. Trillo, whose festival is on 15 June. Trillo was the son of Ithel Hael of Llydaw, and brother to the saints Tegai and Llechid, who established their missions in the vicinity of Bangor. In earlier pedigrees Trillo is said to be of "Dineirth in Rhos." The family probably came to North Wales from Armorica (Brittany) with their kinsman Cadvan. Trillo is believed to have been educated on Ynys Enlli (Bardsey Island). St. Trillo's Chapel on the foreshore bears his name and may mark the site of his original cell or church. Sir J.E.Lloyd says "Llandrillo or Dineirth" was *"an important church in 1137."*

The early parish of Dinerth or Llandrillo was particularly extensive, embracing considerable portions of the present parishes of Llansanffraid Glan Conwy, Llanelian, Llysfaen, Llanrhos, Colwyn, and a portion of the low-lying Morfa Rhianedd, now covered by the sea.[195] There are indications that the present building is not the earliest. The font is considered to be Norman, and the Rhos Fynach charter of 1230 has a clause requiring Ednyfed and his heirs to pay yearly *"to God and the Church of Dineyrth two shillings towards lamps at Easter-tide."*

Even more convincing are the two built-up archways in the north wall. Their provocative silence tantalizes the imagination. The consensus of opinion is that they are all that remains of Ednyfed's chapel – possibly the *"Church of Dineyrth"* referred to. The earliest part of the church is the north aisle, and these pointed arches, and the closed doorway in the north wall, are of the 13th century. Only part of the north aisle was built first; the join can be seen behind the organ. The extension was added much later.

Llandrillo Church in the ninteenth century

According to H. Hughes in his *The Beauties of Cambria* (1823), the two arches communicated with *"Ednyfed's family seat, under which was his cemetery, where he was afterwards buried."* Hughes adds: *"The cemetery, falling into ruins, the tombstone over Ednyfed's grave was removed to the south aisle near the altar, where it now lies."* He considered the tombstone *"a rare treat"* for the antiquarian, but he does not give his authority for stating that Ednyfed had been buried at Llandrillo.

In 1936 when it was decided to cut an opening in the centre of the western blocked-up arch, masons were pleasurably surprised to find that beneath the plaster an old pointed door already existed. It seems to be of a date later than the pillars and does not contribute to the solution of their mysterious origin.

The tradition that the original church, founded by St. Trillo in the sixth century, was overwhelmed by the sea *"on the submergence of Morfa Rhianedd,"* and that Ednyfed's chapel was substituted for the lost church, is discredited by Archdeacon Thomas:

"This can hardly have been the case, inasmuch as more than a hundred years before his time Prince Griffith ap Cynan had bequeathed, in 1070, ten shillings each to the churches of Meifod, Llanarmon and Dinerth. It is much more likely that Ednyfed built his chapel on to the existing church, and the square pillar between them indicates that the wall was broken through for the purpose."

Attention should be paid to the hard red sandstone of which these pillars are made. The next step, says Archdeacon Thomas, was to lengthen the church eastwards. When the Ladies Conway, whom he describes as *"the last occupants of Llys Euryn,"* built the south aisle in the beginning of the sixteenth century, the chapel was taken down and the materials used up in the work.

There is a fallacy here. It seems certain that the Conway family was responsible for the building of the south nave, the porch and the tower, but the "Ladies Conway," the last occupants of Llys Euryn, apparently lived not at the beginning of the sixteenth but towards the close of the seventeenth century.

That the enlarging of the church was undertaken fairly early in the sixteenth century seems obvious, for the will of Hugh Conway mentions the building of a chancel and porch. This must refer to an earlier porch. The present one is of considerably later construction. The commencement of the will, in Latin, is given in *Arch. Camb.* (IV, XI, 217). Dated 1540, it read:

"My body is to be buried or covered with earth beneath the parish church of Llandrillo. Also I leave five pounds stirling to the aforesaid church, to be disposed of in this manner, namely, fifty shillings of the same towards the building of a certain approach, or a porch at the door, or entrance of the same church; also the other aforesaid part of five pounds for the construction of a chancel to the aforesaid church."

A cupola, or bell-cote, was on the west of the church originally, but this was removed when the tower was rebuilt by the Conway family in 1552. The erection of the tower thus seems to have followed quickly after the building of the chancel. Beside the path under the east window is the tombstone of Margeret Conway, who was buried in October, 1654.

The church tower possesses distinctive features. Apart from Llanbeblig,[196] no old church tower in Wales resembles it. At the southwest angle, at the top of the staircase, there rises a square turret known locally as *"the Rector's chair."* Antiquarians who inspected it in 1848 regarded it as a *"beacon turret,"* and considering the turbulent times in which it was erected, when corsairs were visitors to these coasts, it was, in all probability, intended to serve as a lookout and signalling post. This *"curious western tower"* was constructed after the plan of Irish towers, with double-stepped battlements. The staircase is lighted by several narrow slits. There is no exterior door, but the stair is entered from the vestry by a small pointed door.

The church was re-opened on 3 September 1857, after considerable restoration under the care of Mr. Kennedy of Bangor. This was probably the time when the old east window, with its interesting glass, was dispersed. The Rev. W. Venables Williams secured two fragments, which he had built into the window of the vestry. The prevailing hue is amber, and one piece depicts part of a bearded face, but is not sufficiently clear to warrant reproduction. Several travellers have left references to this window. The Llandudno artist, H. Hughes, visited the church while preparing pictures for his *Beauties of Cambria* in 1823, and commented:

"The remains of a beautiful painted window, wherein are the arms of Ednyfed, and twelve figures in different Habiliments, almost entire, would be a rare treat for the Antiquary"

Richard Fenton, in 1808 observes that the window had in two places *"Ednyved Vychan's old Coat, a chevron between three helmets,"* and comments: *"so it is clear that it was added before he had acquired his new coat, viz., three Saxon's head."* [197] The reverse is the case. It was when one of Ednyfed's descendants - Sir Tudor Vychan - was knighted that he tactfully enclosed the *"Englishmen's heads"* in helmets, so the coat-of-arms Fenton saw proves the window was not there in Ednyfed's day.

Lewis, in his *Topographical Dictionary* (1835) says:

"The east window is in the later style of English architecture and contains some elegant specimens of ancient stained glass; in one compartment is a fine head of Marchudd, founder of one of the fifteen noble tribes of North Wales, above which are the arms of Ednyfed Fychan.... in the others are figures in flowing drapery, representing the tribes of Wales."

One can only lament that this choice glass was lost, for it might have thrown light on the family which dwelt at Llys Euryn in the days when the "llys" lay across the fields within sight of the church, and Bryn Euryn was encircled by a country trackway which has now become Tan-y-bryn Road and Dinerth Road.

The existing east windows were a thank-offering, in 1873, by Edward Brooks of Pabo, on his recovery from a long illness. The Vicar, Canon Jenkyn Jones, points out (1952) that a rood screen, probably not more than five foot high, stretched the width of the church, in line with the first pillar, at one time. No trace is now visible. Canon Jones says there have been six occasions when the church has been extended. At one time there were oak pews.

In 1850 Sir Stephen Glynne wrote:

"At the east end of the southern aisle (now used as the chancel) is a large window of five lights, containing some good fragments of stained glass, amongst which appear armorial bearings of Welsh tribes."

He adds that at the east end of the northern aisle is "*a smaller and inferior one of three lights*" with a transom. This has now been refashioned to a Gothic design. The description of the interior of the church shortly before its restoration should prove of interest in Sir Stephen Glynne's words, written on 19 September 1850:

"*The whole is late, except, perhaps, the arches built in the north wall, which are low and plain to all appearance, and the capitals of the pillars square; but the arrangement of the piers themselves is not easily distinguished. There are no windows at all on the north side; on the south are ordinary third Pointed, of three lights. . . . The arcade consists of four Tudor arches with the usual mouldings, and springing from octagonal piers. At the points of the spring of the arches are angels bearing shields. The roof of the south aisle is an open Welsh one. At the angles of the square spares are rude quasi foliations. There are collars and brackets. Over the sacrarium the roof is boarded with ribs. The north aisle is rather narrower, its roof plain and open. . . . There is a recess in the north wall, near the east, which may have been a door; a square recess in the east wall of the north aisle; and a piscina south of the altar, which has a flat arch. . . . There is a rude, large porch, and a Tudor priest's door in the south aisle of the chancel.*"

The Rev. H.Longueville Jones, in *Arch. Camb.* 1857, comments that the north aisle roof was of a plan rarely found in churches of that period. If the three angels with shields are scrutinized it will be noticed that the pink sandstone of the arches has been chipped to admit them, suggesting they were added after the church was enlarged. Whence came they? From the ruined abbey of Aberconwy? From an earlier church? Their material and design differ considerably from the surrounding architecture.

THE FONT

"*The font is a curious and early one,*" writes Sir Stephen, "*the bowl, octagonal, with convex sides, having a nail-head cornice round the top, and mouldings at the angles. The base, a sort of octagonal block.*" Antiquarians who inspected it in 1848 classed it as Norman,[198] and a writer stated in 1857:

"*The font is an octagonal basin of rather unusual design, standing on a base more recent than itself; and it would seem to belong to an edifice earlier than that which now exists.*"

In the church porch an ancient tombstone bearing the name *Ednyfed* has been built into the wall. It has aroused considerable speculation. A note in the Llysfaen Church register (1661-1760) says the Ednyfed tombstone was originally "*before the Communion Table in the Alley of Llandrillo in Rhose church.*" Some person commenced to copy the inscription into the register, but left it incomplete, and it is finished in another hand. The second writer has added: "*Tho' more the pitty, no Date.*" The much-discussed tombstone reads:

✢ HIC IACET DNS: EDNEVED: QVODAM VICARIVS
DEDYNEYRT: Cz ANIME PROPICIETVR: DEVS: AMEN.

In the list of pre-Reformation clergy occurs the name:"*1407 Ednyvet ap Bleddyn.*"[199] One suspects the tombstone is his.

Noting some of the tombstones in the church, Archdeacon Thomas referred to that of Robert Conway, in the northern aisle, adding: "*It would appear that another Conwy was buried alongside, for part of a tombstone records (M)ARTHA CON(WAY) (16)75. The remainder is concealed beneath a pew.*"

Another stone records:

"*Here Lyeth the Body of Mary Wynn, sister of Maurice Wynn of Greanllyn who died the 17th day of December aged 22 Ano Domni 1698. R+P.*"

The bell bears the date 1752, and was cast by Ralph Ashton of Wigan. It is marked with the names of

"Edward Hughes and William Evans, Churchwardens, and John Gwyn, Vicar."

"*The churchyard has very uneven ground,*" comments Sir Stephen Glynne, nevertheless with its wind-bowed yew trees and elevated position, it possesses a dignity denied to many."*The Church stands in an elevated spot overlooking a tract of marsh not far from the sea. It is rather more imposing in appearance than the generality of Welsh churches.*"

The churchyard has altered its appearance since Sir Stephen visited it one and a half centuries ago. It has been necessary to extend the churchyard on two occasions.

The lych-gate, one of the oldest in the district, was restored in 1907.[200] It is inscribed with the names of: HENRY VAVGHAN and OWEN WILLIAMS, WARDENS, and dated ANO: DOMINI 1677, with the additional letters M.R.

Henry Vaughan was probably the son of John Vaughan of Glyn, a descendant of Ednyfed Vychan. A pedestal tomb south-east of the church records the death of Henry Vaughan's widow, "*Margret Vaughan,*" who died in 1699. The tombstone bears the Vaughan lion (similar to one in Llysfaen churchyard), impaled with the arms of her own family - Bonam Norton of Straton, Co. Salop. The stone was formerly inside the church. The church registers record the death, in 1708, of "*Anne, ye Wife of Henry Vaughan of Dinerth.*"

The sundial is a conspicuous adornment of the churchyard. The dial itself was "*The gift of Mary Jarvis of Dinerth, 1755.*" Under the edge is "*Th. Ow(en), 1756,*" and on the base of an older column, 1712. The Church Wardens' Book records steps being provided for the sundial in 1830. Examination of the names of tombstones will indicate that persons were brought from a distance to be buried at Llandrillo.

The Church plate comprises two silver cups, the gift of the Rev. Evan Ellis, and a paten, to which reference is made elsewhere in the account of the "sacrilegious robbery." A terrier of 1774 mentions a silver chalice of 1608, but this has gone without trace. There is also a massive pewter flagon, mentioned in a Rural Dean's report of 1749 as *Phiol y Ddiod Offrwn*, formerly used at funerals. In 1901 a new paten, chalice, flagon and credence paten were presented by Mrs. Dean, of Hafod Euryn.

Llandrillo Church registers begin in 1693. The first Latin entry is on 14 November 1714, and Latin entries continue until 1733. A note states: "*The Register of the Township of Llandrillo in the county of Denbigh, bought by Edward Daniel and Richard Rowland, Wardens.*" A catalogue of books is included. These represented legacies of 100 books to the parish in 1714/15 and seventeen in 1739. One of the entries in 1817 is "*Hair-Powder taxed.*" Other items of interest include: 1831, buried Mary Roberts, Rising Gull. 1835, burial of Thomas Jones, Rising Sun. 1845, a dead Body of a Man cast on Shore near Cil Co, by authority of the Coroner's Warrant '*that he was found drowned.*' Cil Co, sometimes spelt "Kill Cow," was a cottage which stood near the shore, at the mouth of the Penrhos dingle.

A Consistory Court record of 1721 states:[201]

"*i. The Vicar of Llandrillo has a right to the moyety of the tithes both small and great within the township in the Parish of Llysfaen.*

ii. The Vicar of Llandrillo is to preach or cause to be preached four sermons every year in the said Parish Church of Llysfaen on such Sundays as the present Vicar of Liandrillo shall think most convenient, and that the said Vicar do preach the said four sermons for the year 1721 before the 25th day of March next ending.

iii. That the Rev. Thos. Lloyd, Vicar of Liandrillo, be allowed to be paid by the Rev. Roger Jones, Rector of Llysfaen, 40s. for the year last past ending the 25th day of March, 1721, in lieu and instead of the said part of the moiety of the tithes in the township of Penmaen in the Parish of Llysfaen in consideration that no sermons have been preached by the said Thos. Lloyd at Llysfaen within the said two years."

In Williams's *Aberconwy* it states:
"The Rectory is a sinecure held since 1759, by the Bishops of St. Asaph in commendam, and the vicarage is in the gift of the Bishop; the Rector and Vicar have also a share of the tithes of Llanelian, Llansantffraid and Llysvaen."

THE VICARAGE

There have been several vicarages. The present one, built in 1903 at a cost of £2,100, is on a one-acre site given by Sir Everard Cayley, Bart. There are five acres of glebe. A Terrier of 1636 states:
"They say that there is a mansion house [202] and other out-houses, containing tenne bayes, two gardens and one p'cell of arrable land thereunto adjoyning (2½ acres) lying near the churchyard belonging to the said Vicarage."

This was replaced the following century, a new vicarage being erected in 1762. In the churchyard is a tombstone bearing the following inscription:
"To the memory of Isaac Charles, Clerk, late Vicar of this Parish, buried July ye 9, 1763. He was a worthy Clergyman and General Benefactor to this Church in building in 1762 a Decent House for the Vicarage thereof which he lived to finish but not to enjoy."

Further reference occurs in a Terrier of 1791:
"The Mansion was built about 30 years ago and ye present Vicar (Rev. Evan Ellis) in ye year 1777 took down that part of ye old building wh. was left standing when ye new House was erected and has rebuilt on a larger scale with different materials. The present Building consists of a Passage wh. communicates with ye Kitchen on ye right hand, and on ye left are a Scullery, Cellar, Store-room, Pantry, and over all is a large Room six yards by five. This Building is mostly built of Bricks and covered with slates and ye whole is cieled."[203]

The old Llandrillo Vicarage showing the bay windows added by the late Rev. W. Venables Williams

The building, erected by the Rev. Isaac Charles, had three storeys, each of two rooms. Part of the older building may have been incorporated. *"The Vicarage was enlarged by me in 1869,"* wrote the Rev. W. Venables Williams:

"by the addition of the present Dining Room and Bedroom above, and the building of bow windows to all the rooms in the front of the Vicarage ; also an underground water tank, containing about 3,500 gallons of rain water, since superseded by the introduction of town's water supply in 1893.[204] *The Church and Vicarage were first lighted with gas in 1887."*

DIVISION

After the formation of Llansanffraid, Llanrhos, Llanelian and Llysfaen parishes, Llandrillo-yn-Rhos still retained 4,800 acres. This comprised the townships of Llwydcoed, Mochdre, Dinerth, Rhiw, Cilgwyn and Colwyn (in Denbighshire) and Eirias in Caernarvonshire. In 1844 the townships of Colwyn, Eirias and part of Cilgwyn were taken to form Colwyn parish. A fresh division occurred in 1893 when Colwyn Bay parish was formed. Archdeacon Thomas found the area reduced to 1,481 acres, with a population of 2,190. Only the townships of Dinerth and Mochdre were retained.

In 1901 land in Elwy Road was given by Sir Everard Cayley, and a church-room was built on it with stones provided by William Horton, of Bryn Dinerth. A gale ripped the roof off. The building was completed in 1903 at a cost of £1,480. It was extended in 1909. In order to cope with the demands of a rapidly increasing population the handsome Church of St. George was built on St. George's Road.

The apportionment of rent charge in lieu of tithes, in the Parish of Llandrillo-yn-Rhos, was awarded on 13 October 1846. The Assistant Tithe Commissioner, Aneurin Owen, having held a meeting in the parish for the benefit of landowners and tithe-owners, submitted his award and schedules, a copy of which is in the possession of the Vicar of Llandrillo-yn-Rhos.

It was found that the estimated quantity in statute measure of all the lands in the parish amounted to 5,426 acres. This comprised 3,000 acres arable; 2,120 acres meadow and pasture; 300 acres common land; with three acres of rectorial glebe land and three acres of vicarial glebe land. The customary payments were: one penny for each milch cow, in lieu of tithes of milk and calves; two pence for each brood mare in lieu of tithes of foals. The Clerk of the parish was entitled to certain dues called Bell Corn, i.e. eight measures of wheat from the tithe in each township in the following proportions: three from Dynerth, one each from Mochdre, Eirias and Llwyd goed, and half each from Cilgwyn and Colwyn.

All the unmerged tithes of Corn and grain (except as above excepted), and of hay, except the Tithes of hay or payments in lieu of such Tithes, which arise or accrue upon the same or upon or in respect of those lands which are specified in the first schedule hereunto annexed, as subject to payment of such Tithes to the Vicar, and also three fourth parts of the Tithe of Wool, Lambs, Pigs, geese, Hemp, Flax, Eggs, and customary payments in lieu of Tithes arising and accruing within the Townships of Dynerth, Mochdre, Cilgwyn and Eirias, and all the Tithes except as above excepted and prescriptive and customary payments in lieu of Tithes arising and accruing within the Township of Llwydgoed belong to the Bishop of Saint Asaph as appropriate Rector of the said Parish.

The other Tithes belonged to the Vicar. The commutation was valued as follows: To the Vicar, £310; to the Bishop, £640, and to the Parish Clerk, £4; a total of £954. Wheat sold at 7s $1/4$d per bushel, barley 3s $11 1/2$d, and oats 2s 9d.

The schedules show there was some Crown land in the parish, and there was a charge on the newly formed Chester and Holyhead railway. Every owner and occupier of the land is set forth with the names of the premises and (in almost every instance) the names of the fields.

At Mochdre there was the Swan Inn and Eagles Farm, but there is no mention of the White Horse Inn (Mountain View). Lord Mostyn was recorded as the owner of Graianllyn, and Glyn had as owner Thomas Peers Williams. The house, smithy and garden occupied by Samuel Bartley were given as "Pt. of Plas Newydd." Glan-y-Wern had a field called "Gadlas felin eithen" (gorse mill) - all trace of which seems to have vanished. The mill at "Felin Mochdre" is mentioned, also a smithy at Mochdre. Whitehall Dod is the owner of most of the land in Dynerth township. Among the fields occupied by the Rev. Thomas Parry (Vicar of Llandrillo), is a pasture termed "Cae Elizabeth Conway" - obviously a link with the Llys Euryn family. "Tram road" presumably referred to the railway from Bryn Euryn quarry to Rhos landing-stage. Bryn Euryn farm includes a field known as Maes y gaer (fortress meadow). The house on Rhos Promenade known as Aberhod is termed "Aberhodney." It was owned by Whitehall Dod and occupied by William Williams. The house occupied by Whitehall Dod is not named, but is termed "Hall and pleasure ground &c." Would it be Bryn Dinarth? Poplars is given as a farm, and Rhos Fynach termed "Rhos Farm." The landowner was Mrs. M. Parry Evans, and the occupier Thos. Parry. The farm "Ty gwyn rhyd" (Rhyd Farm) has a pasture called "Ynys" (island), and another "Bryn rhyd" (ford hill). Groes yn Eirias had a public house and garden. Ty Newydd farm had a field named "Rough," from which, doubtless, "The Rough" acquired its name.

Colwyn has the inns: Plough (in Eirias Township), Sun, Ship and Red Lion (Colwyn Township).

RHOS FYNACH WEIR

More recent reference to Morgan ab John of Rhos Fynach is contained in the report of a Government Commission inquiring into Fisheries. An Act of Parliament of 1861 had decreed that all sea weirs should be demolished unless they could substantiate a claim to have existed before the Magna Carta. John L. Parry-Evans claimed exemption on that ground for his weir at Rhos Fynach. A Court of Inquiry sat at Conwy in January 1867 to ascertain whether the "fixed engine" (as the weir was legally termed) complied with the clause. The Commissioners were James Paterson (Chairman), Captain T.A.B.Spratt, CB, RN, and Major Henry Scott. A similar claim had been made by Whitehall Dod, who owned what was later termed the Cayley Estate. He was unsuccessful, and the outline of his demolished weir can now be traced at low tide off the Cayley Embankment.

The Chairman asked: *"Is there a manor there?"* and was answered: *"No, not a manor, but a monastery."*

Chairman: *"This fishing weir then is on the sea coast adjoining lands formerly belonging to the monastery?"*

Mr. Griffith (for Mr. Parry-Evans): *"Yes, and is called Rhos Fynach, that is, the fishery (sic) of the monks."*

Mr. Griffith submitted a deed of bargain and sale, and other documents listing fines levied by John Parry, apothecary, a former owner of Rhos Fynach Estate. (John Parry's sister, Elizabeth Parry, had a daughter Ann, who married Thomas Evans.)

Mr. Parry-Evans claimed *"an ancient right or mode of fishing as lawfully exercised at the time of the passing of the Act of 1861."*

The Chairman: *"That is, that we may reasonably presume a grant did exist at the time of Magna Carta. No person probably can produce a grant so old as anterior to Magna Carta, but he may produce evidence which may lead us to believe that such a grant did exist at some time, but that it has been lost."*

Mr. Griffith then gave in the document of Elizabeth's reign, which was in Latin, saying: *"I have got a translation. It is from Elizabeth, between the Earl of Leicester, Master of the Horse of Queen Elizabeth to Morgan ap John ap David."*

The Chairman: *"What is the date of it?"*

Llandrillo-yn-Rhos or Rhos-on-Sea

Mr. Griffith: *"It would be the 1st June, 1575:"Witnesseth that the aforesaid Earl for and in consideration of the sum of 6d. and for divers other considerations him thereinto moving, grants so many acres of land etc, and goes on: together with all and singular fishing waters pools of water, &c., to the same appertaining."*

He said there were two weirs originally, but one had not been in use for a great number of years.

A terrier of July 10th, 1774, was also produced. It read: *"Also there is a tithe of fish due from Rhos Fynach weirs according to ancient custom, three parts in four of which belong to the Rector of Llandrillo and the remaining fourth belong to the Vicar."*

The Chairman: *"What fell to the owner then?"*

Mr. Griffith: *"You will see that it means 'three parts in four' of the tithe belongs to the Rector, and the remaining fourth of the tithe to the Vicar. That is, the tithe."*

The Chairman: *"I thought it was all the fish. I thought it was too much!"*

A lease was submitted, dated 10 February 1804, to Thomas Ellis, of Rhos Fynach, *"and all weirs, fisheries, fishing places for 21 years at an annual rent of £88."*

One of the witnesses was John Jones, aged 75, who said he was born at Rhyd, which adjoined the farm of Rhos Fynach. The weir was the same shape as when he played in it as a child.

Mr. Parry-Evans said he caught more salmon recently than formerly, but only in July and August. In October and November they took herrings, cod, bass, flat fish, sprats and all kind of fish not eatable, such as dog-fish and shark, and sometimes sturgeon and porpoises.

Much evidence was given as to whether salmon could have free passage during close season, and on the morning of 10 January

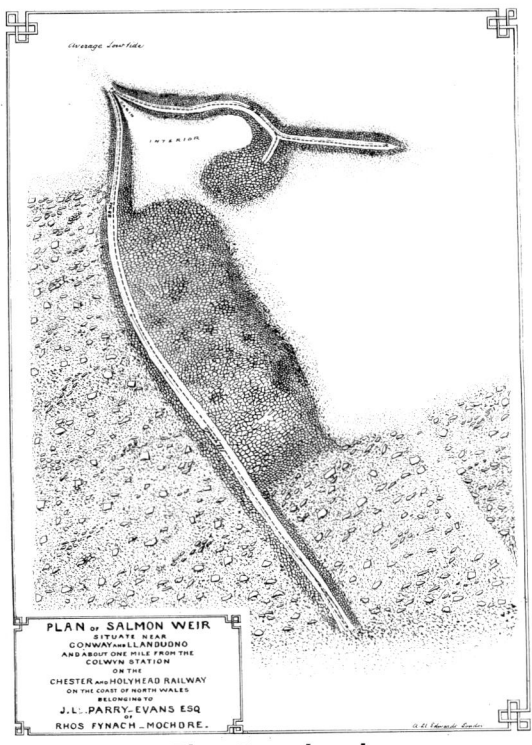

Rhos Fynach weir

the Commissioners inspected the weir. When delivering judgment the Chairman said:

"In this case Mr. Parry-Evans claims a fishing weir or fixed engine, consisting of poles and brushwood on a foundation of stone, for catching salmon situated on the sea coast in Llandrillo Bay. Inasmuch as the public have at common law the right of fishing in the sea and all parts of the sea coast no individual can establish his right to maintain a weir on the sea coast, unless he can show either a grant from the Crown prior to Magna Charta or can produce evidence from which such a grant may reasonably be presumed.

In the present case in order to show the legality of this weir the claimant has given in evidence certain documents of title, the first of which consists of a grant made by Queen Elizabeth to Morgan ab John ap David, of certain tenements in Rhos Fynach, the property of a dissolved Abbey, together with, inter alia, all pools, waters, fishing weir and watercourses.

We think the above evidence is sufficient to enable us reasonably to presume that this weir now claimed did exist before and has continued since the passing of Magna Carta and therefore that it is a privileged fixed engine."

Ancient farm buildings in front of Rhos Fynach long since demolished

A clause was added that a four-foot gap was to be made to permit a free passage of salmon. Subject to this being complied with a licence would be issued. The weir remained in use until the 1914 war, when it was allowed to fall into disrepair and has gradually been washed away.

In 1865 an eight-foot shark was caught in the weir, and exhibited in Llandudno market place before being sent to be stuffed. The year before that a sturgeon weighing over 200 lb. was taken. The greatest catch of herrings was 35,000 in one day. This was on the night of 2 November 1850.[205]

For the quarter ending 30 September 1907, the record catch of mackerel on the west coast was at Rhos Fynach weir. Ten tons were taken at one tide, but realized only £20. The writer remembers carrying some of these mackerel home on a walking-stick.

No account of the Rhos Fynach Weir would be complete without reference to Jack, the dog which attained such fame as a catcher of salmon that it was presented with a solid silver collar, subscribed for by its admirers:

"This collar was presented to 'Jack,' the celebrated dog fisher, by public subscription, as a recognition of his skill as a salmon fisher, October, 1868."

The dog arrived aboard a Prussian schooner which dropped anchor off Rhos, because the crew were short of potatoes. Jack was about eight months old at the time, and the manner in which he swam around the ship attracted the notice of Mr. Parry-Evans, who gave a bag of potatoes in exchange for him. He was called an "otter-terrier." The Rev. W. Houghton, in *Sea Side Walks of a Naturalist*, has left behind a naive account of a visit with his children to the weir, to watch Jack at work:

"How immensely rapid is the motion of a frightened salmon. 'Quick as an arrow' is hardly a figure of speech. Bravo! Jack, bravo! He has caught the salmon firmly by the head. Good dog. And then, at the close of day: *The old dog, no doubt, thinks he has done a good day's work, and walks quietly behind his master home; and we are all of the same opinion as the old dog, and leave Rhos-Fynach Weir Fishery with impressions that will perhaps never be effaced.*"

Jack died as a result of wounds sustained after killing a small shark. At the time of writing (1952) a somewhat dusty Jack, with his paw on a dustier salmon, reposes in a glass case in the house of Mr. Parry-Evans' daughter. The silver collar was also shown to the writer.

LLYSFAEN

As Llysfaen is mentioned by name in the time of Henry III it suggests a "Llys maen" (stone hall) existed before the Edwardian conquest, and that it was sufficiently rare to have a township named after it. In an age when most dwellings - according to Geraldus Cambrensis - were of a temporary wooden nature, this must have indicated a structure of more than ordinary consequence. Who held his court here in ancient days ? Archdeacon Thomas says it was "not clear" whether the man was the ruler of an ecclesiastical court (Plas yr Esgob) or a civil chieftain (ddol y Fran). There follows a perplexing statement:

"*The greater portion, representing probably the original foundation, is enclosed by a considerable dyke, which ran from shore to shore, and is still plain on the east side, and is traceable by the remains of a stone wall and significant place names most of the way.*"[206]

It will be noted that Lhwyd gives "Plas yr Esgob" as an alternative for "Plas-yn-Llysfaen." The old residents have their own theory about the origin of the name. Beside the road which leads past Isallt to Rhyd-y-Foel is a gigantic pillar of stone, which has detached itself from the cliff face, and rises from a grassy glacis like a rugged tower. Legend has it that this was named the "stone hall," and that the wise men met near it to conduct their deliberations. An ancient stanza places the foundation of Llysfaen's church in the eighth century. Though it mentions the local saint it does not assist in tracing the origin of the name of Llysfaen.

Eglwys wen Gynfran	The white church of Cynfryn
A fildiwyd yn gadarn	So solidly builded,
Saith can a dau saith	Seven centuries and two sevens
Oith oed Crist pan wneud hon.	Was the age of Christ when this was made.

The ambiguity of the third line leaves the date at 714 or 777. An ancient church took its title from its founder, and Llysfaen Church was originally called Llangynfryn.[207] Cynfryn, according to *The Lives of the British Saints*, was the reputed son of Brychan, King of Brycheiniog, master of Brecknock, and came of a family which "*produced an incredible number of saints.*" Cynfryn was a brother of Cynbryd the martyr, whose church is nearby at Llanddulas. Cynbryd, according to old records, was slain by the unbelieving Saxons at Bwlch Cynbryd, though where that pass might be is a mystery. At all events, the incident supports the claim that Llysfaen's first church was destroyed by the Saxons. It must have been built of wattle and wood, so the reference to the white church of Cynfryn being strongly or solidly built in the eighth century would imply that the reconstructed place of worship was of limestone. In his book, *The Church of the Cymry*, the Rev. William Hughes places Cynfryn and Cynbryd in the fifth century, which would make it possible for them to have been the sons of Brychan. The building of the church in 777 could not apply to the original.

St. Cynfryn's patronal day is placed, by some authorities as 12 November, but Browne Willis gives it as 11 November, and Lhwyd says Cynfryn's "wake" was on the "eleventh day of Winter."

The festival does not occur in any Welsh calendar. The somewhat exposed position of the church (which has a magnificent prospect of coast and ocean) is explained by the proximity of St. Cynfryn's well, 200 yards to the north. In distant days a well had both symbolical and practical significance. Lhwyd tells us the people "offered" at this well to prevent disease among their cattle, and prayed for the blessing of God and Holy Cynfryn on their beasts. St. Cynfryn, like St. Bridget at Llansanffraid Glan Conwy, appears to have been benevolent to horned cattle. This fondness for cattle may be suggested by the lolling tongue portrayed in the carved face which reposes over the door of the church. It is reputed to be a (not-too-flattering) likeness of the saint. Archdeacon Thomas considers the lowest courses of masonry may be of the same date as the huge, irregular stones which frame the doorway.

These resemble stones at Abergele and Llanefydd churches, and may be of the date mentioned in the stanza when the church was "strongly built." Their bevelled edge must have been added considerably later. The church is of the twin-aisled type, common in North Wales. Its appearance internally and externally was materially altered during the restoration undertaken in 1870. It was at this time that the south porch and the western bell-cote were added. The church was reopened on St. Luke's Day, 8 October 1870, the work having cost £1,950. Much of the 14th century roof, with its wooden pegs, was kept intact. Archdeacon Thomas tells us the old walls were retained and those portions which were of native limestone were re-wrought, and pierced with windows in the early English style. A buttress was added. Fortunately for the antiquarian, Sir Stephen Glynne visited the church on 17 July 1851 and left his impressions:

"Much resembles Llanelian, but is somewhat inferior to it. The site similar but more dreary, the form the same in almost every particular. The arcade here is of four arches only, but just like that of Llanelian. There seem to have been no original windows on the north, but some modern ones inserted. On the south they are debased, without foils and very flat. The two eastern ones, also flattened, of three lights, without foils, but some remnants of ancient stained glass. The roofs are open and Welsh, of rude character. There is no distinction of chancel, except in the slight contraction of the north wall, approaching eastward. The church is pewed, and has a west gallery. The font is very small, of octagonal form, and doubtful age. The exterior is partly white-washed."[208]

The beauty of the rood screen is accounted for by the fact that it was modelled on a pattern obtained from fragments of the original. In front of the choir stalls portions of the old screen may still be seen, pierced by primitive designs. The east window, depicting the Nativity, Crucifixion and Resurrection, is a memorial to the Rev. Edward Oldfield (of Fferm, Betws-yn-Rhos), rector for thirty-three years. The next window is the gift of the Rev. Ellis Price, added in memory of his grandmother and brother. It represents the Annunciation, Christ blessing children, and the two sisters at Bethany. The organ is by Hill & Son, London. The reredos of Caen stone was added during the 1870 restoration. It possesses a cross of white marble in the central compartment and floreated circles filled with variegated marbles. The pulpit and font are of Bath stone.

Llysfaen originally formed part of the huge parish of Dinerth. It is difficult to state when it became a separate parish. In the Norwich Taxation of 1254 mention is made of *"Ecc's de Llesvaen."* In the Lincoln taxation of 1291 reference is made to *"Rectoria di Lisnaen."* The Valor of

Sketch by R. J. Howard, B.Arch.

Plough Terrace as it stood beside the turnpike at Colwyn. The view faces west with the wall of Min-y-don grounds on the right

Henry VIII (1535) gives its clear value as £12, on which £1-4s-11½d was payable to the King, as tenths. Lhwyd states the parish was composed of the five townships of Isallt, Is-y-ffordd, Pant, Penmaen and Rhwng-y-ddwyffordd. He speaks of a beacon which probably occupied the site of the semaphore station. He lets us know that in 1699 there were *"only two or three houses near the church,"* and that in the parish there were buried fifteen families who lived at Bryn Ffanigl. The church was situated on a rock, but *"when burying they get golden sand 4 yards deep."* One inhabitant, Martha Bach, was aged 102 - *"so she says,"* adds Lhwyd.

Sources of revenue have proved complicated. All the tithes of Bryn Rodyn, which is in Llanelian parish, were payable to Llysfaen rector. An old terrier states that half the township of Penmaen tithed to the Rector of Llandrillo, and out of the remaining moiety the Vicar of Llandrillo received a third, but had to pay twenty shillings for four sermons. The record adds:

"And the tithes of one day's math (mowing) *in Gweirglodd Isallt doth belong to the township of Twynnan* (in Llanelian parish) *or the sum of one shilling in lieu of the same; whereof sixpence belongs to the Rector of Llanelian; and two-pence to the Vicar of Llandrillo."*

The commutation returns give £232-16s-2d to the Rector; £41-14s-9½d to the Bishop of St. Asaph (as Rector of Llandrillo) and £1-10s-0d. to the Parish Clerk. The tithes of Bryn Rodyn, which were £17-17s-9d, also belonged to the Rector of Llysfaen.[209]

In 1810 the Rev. John Hughes came from Eglwysbach (where he had been vicar since 1785), and two years later built himself "a good house." It was enlarged in 1848 when the Rev. Edward Oldfield was incumbent. His initials and crest are to be seen over the Rectory entrance.

There were 18 acres of glebe. The rectory of 1812 was not the first. Another building is described in a *True and Perfect Terrier of all and singular, the Edifices and Lands appertaining unto the Rectory of Llysfaen,* prepared on 29 May 1749:

"IMPRIMIS. One messuage built with stone and mortar containing five Bays of Building, three Rooms and a Sellar below stairs floored with Clay and morta,r and three rooms and a closet above stairs, neither of them wainscoted or hanged but plain plastered walls. Thatched with straw all in good repair.

"One Stable two Beast Houses and a Store-house containing four Bays of Building, thatched with Straw and clay floor One Brew-house of two Bays, thatched with Straw with clay floor. One Barn of two Bays thatched with Straw the Threshing floor boarded, the rest of the floor Stone and clay A Rickyard A Garden."

There follows a description of various fields, given with meticulous detail. Neighbouring landowners are Sir Watkin Williams Wynn, Hugh Holland, gent., Sr. Thomas Prendergast (probably of Marl Hall), Robert Williams of Pen-y-Coed. Reference is made to a terrier of 1636 in which the name of Edward Peirce, of Ty Mawr, gent., appears. The Rectory possessed "A right of Commoning in all the Commons of Llysfaen which are extensive." (Lhwyd lists the commons by name.) It states:"The Clerk has a strike of Barley for every Township in the parish of the Rector's tithe, and is appointed by the Rector."[210]

The Rev. T. Llechid Jones (former Rector) wrote about the old Rectory:

"This is not, in my opinion, at all incorporated into the present house. It strikes me that one would have to see the main divisions of the roof in order to decide the number of "bays" in a house. My opinion is that the old Rectory described was a longish oblong building, situate partly where the present dining-room is and extending to the south (for they would hardly have a new cellar made in a new house if there was one in the old) having one end forming one room and the other divided into two rooms."

Mr. Llechid Jones considers there was no break in the continuity of incumbents during the Commonwealth. He discovered in the Public Record Office's *Liber Institutionum* under "Llysvayn" in the Deanery of "Rosse" the entry: "Thos. Vaughan, instituted 19 June, 1646."

By whom was Vaughan instituted we cannot say. The power of the Bishops was over in 1646,[211] and yet they could and did institute men to livings, in spite of that, sometimes. We find from the records of the Sheriff of Carnarvon for 1652 the entry "*Llysfaen—Thos. Vaughan, Clk., now incumbent there.*"[212]

THE SUN-DIAL

The sun-dial is undated, but records the latitude 53-30. According to the Vestry Book it was presented by William Butler, Ty Mawr, in 1731. It is inscribed:

	Translation:
Mae'r Haul ac Amser ar eu hynt,	Both Sun and Time, their speeding round
Yn myned rhagddynt beunydd;	Each daily are renewing;
Gwna, ddyn, dy orchwyl heb ymdroi,	Do, man, without delay, thy task
Mae rhain yn rhoi i ti rybydd	To thee are these a warning
Ni byddi yn hir rhodio'r llawr	Thou shalt not long the earth a-walk
Dy oes fel awr a Dderfydd.	Thy life is as the hour wrought

CHURCH POSSESSIONS

"These belong to the Church" concludes the old terrier quoted: "an old Pewter flagon that holds about a Quart and a very old pewter plate, a Silver Chalice with a lid that holds about a pint and a half marked 'Llysfaen Cup, 1712.' One burying or Biere Cloth, a green Cloth for the Communion Table. Do for the Pulpit with an embroidered Cushion, 2 Surplices, 2 Table

The early bridge at Llannerch Road known as the Board School Bridge Before widening two carts could not pass. Photograph taken about 1900

Cloths, 2 Napkins." There follows a catalogue of sacred books. The list ends: *"In the Churchyard five Ash Trees of about twelve shillings value. One yew tree of no great value."* The terrier is signed by: *Thomas Lloyd, Rector; Morris David, Luke (LW) Wynne's mark, wardens.*

There is an added note: *"A Salver mark'd S.B. given for the use of the parish 30th July, 1749 in the presence of ..."* The cup, with its footed cover, and the footed paten, bear the Britannia stamp.

TOMBSTONES

The wall of the south porch contains two memorial stones, inserted for preservation. A note among Mr. Llechid Jones' manuscripts throws some light on them.

"The mural stones in the church porch were embedded in the wall in 1939 on the occasion of the oak panelling of the nave of the church, having been removed from inside the church where they stood plastered to the wall of the south aisle, under the West windows. Previously they had been discovered resting against the East wall of the churchyard, approximately 20 yards on the North side of the main entrance gates. John Roberts (mason) fixed them up in the church approx. in 1916.

(1) *Within a yard of this stone lieth buried ye body of old Mr. William Owen of Pentre Gwyddel: who was interr'd ye 24th of ianw. Underneath this stone lieth ye body of Elizbeth Owens alias wynne his granddaughter in law who was interred ye 4th day of X. 1679. Within a yard & a half of this stone lieth ye body of John Owen of Pentre Gwyddel her son & heir who was interr'd 26th of Feb. 1702. Underneath this stone was buried ye body of Alice Holland alias Owens his heires who was interred ye 6th day of X. 1717.sic transit Gloria Mundi.*

(2) HERE LYETH THE BODY OF ELIZABETH CONWAY ALS VAVGHAN WHO WAS BVRIED THE XXIst OF AVGST 1671.HERE LYETH THE BODY OF Mr. THOMAS VAVGHAN RECTOR OF LLYSVAIN WHO WAS BVRIED THE XXth OF FEBRUARY, 1673."

Would this be the Elizabeth Conway whose field is mentioned in the Llandrillo tithe schedule? In the graveyard are a number of aged stones, some so weathered as to be illegible. Close beside the path to the south of the church is a large slab surrounded by a chiselled chain pattern. A crack near the base renders the last date indistinct. It reads: *"Here lieth the Bodie of Grifith Lloyd who was buried the 15th day of August, anno di'ii 1599."Here lieth also the Bodie of Grifith Lloyd his grandchild who was buried the first day of November Anno di . . 1646"*

Another stone records:*"Anno Do. 1642. Underneath lieth . . . body of Foulk Lloyd of Denbigh, Gent, who was interred. November. Aged 63. Underneath lies inter ... the Remains of the . . . Anne Lloyd Young daughter of Edward Lloyd of Pentre Ll. who died the . . . April, 1782. Aged 65."*

Lhwyd in 1699 mentions *a "Pierce Lloyd, Gent."* dwelling at Pentre, in Llanelian parish, and also puts him as owner of "Plas yn is-allt" (Isallt) in Llysfaen. Would the Foulk Lloyd of Denbigh, Gent, be Ffoulk Lloyd of Foxhall?

Another stone bears in its centre a shield which appears to display a rampant lion. (Pennant gives this as the device of the Vaughans of Llysfaen and Pant Glas.) (Vol. III, p. 442)."*Here lieth the body of John Vaughan Gentleman who died the last day of December Anno Domini 1675. Aetatisove Swae 38."*

The tomb of the donor of the Butler Charity carried on its west panel a gruesome carving of a skull and cross-bones, surmounted by an hour-glass. A metal tablet preserves the inscription: *"William Butler Esqr. of Ty Mawr of this Parish. Died March 6th 1742. Aged 63 years. In the same Vault lieth Sarah Butler, Spr. sister of Wm. Butler, Esq., who dyed June 6th, 1762, aged 92 years."*

CHURCH REGISTERS

A long, narrow, leather-bound book (restored at the National Library of Wales) contains the church registers for 1661—1760. The record opens in the calligraphy of the Rev.Thomas Vaughan, who dwelt at Peulwys during the Commonwealth. Indication of the size of the community is found in the record of burials for 1666 - there were six.

"A Dial and Dial Post set up in Llysfaen Church Yard at the charge of William Butler Esqr. of Ty Mawr for the use of the Parish afores'd. Ano. 1731." There is a 1734 catalogue of books left by John Peirce of Ty Mawr *"to ye use of ye minister of Llysvaen his successours."*

In March 1740 six elms were planted, one on each side of the gate and two on the south side of the stile leading to Llanddulas. Three lime trees were planted in the glebe. Damage by foxes and polecats was such that the bounty for killing them was increased. Here is a vestry minute:

"1709: Whereas the severall Freeholders & Inhabitants of the Parish of Llysvaen in the County of Carnarvon being so assembled att a Vestry in the parish Church of Llysvaen aforesaid on the sixth Day of January 1708/9 did then think fitt to order and direct that for the future there shall be allowed to any Company of Huntsmen for the killing of a ffox within the said parish, the summe of two shillings & six pence and for the killing of a Cubb or young ffox one shilling and for the killing of a Pole Catt one shilling and six pence."

The records went on to say the parish had found *"great damages and Inconveniences"* from this order, as the Company of Huntsmen had been discouraged because the sum was *"too small and inconsiderable."* The result was *"a great increase of ffoxes Cubbs and Pole Catts"* which had proved destructive to all manner of poultry and a great number of lambs *"which has occasioned great losses and prejudice to several Inhabitants of the said Parish."* Therefore, the account went on,*"We whose names are hereunder written"* assembled on May 20th, 1716 *"upon full and mature consideration of the matter thought fitt to revoke, annul, & sett aside the Order herein mentioned."*

Instead, for the better encouragement of Huntsmen there would be allowed:
"for the killing of every ffox that is hunted the sum of five shillings and for every ffox that is shot or taken in a Trapp or Engine, two shillings and six pence, for the destroying of every Cubb or young ffox two shillings and six pence, and for killing every Pole Catt one shilling and six pence."

Signatures include the names of Hugh Holland, Peirce Wynn, Thomas Peirce, Wm. Peirce and Robert Peirce. Another page records :

"That an assessment of six pence in ye pound shall be laid & collected for ye defraying of ye expences of ye said parish for ye year 1723 wth all convenient speed.

That ye present Cch wardens provide a Plumber to view ye Lead sheet upon ye Church, & agree with ye sd Plumber for making up the Defects of ye Roof sufficiently."

December 1716 contains the announcement of :

"an assessment of three pence in the pound laid upon all land's (landlords) *Gen'm* (gentlemen) *and heredit's* (hereditaments) *for repairing of the Church of Llysvaen & defraying the ordinary and general expences."*

A small memorandum book, undated and unsigned, among the Church records contains some items of interest:

"It is related that up to the 19th Century burials were never by coffins, but by a corpse plank, 'ystallen corph,' the winding sheet being linen, but with wool it became taxable."

"The churchyard on the south of the Dial sloped steeply to the South from near the pedestal, and consisted of Ty'nllan garden. Carting of soil from Raynes Quarries, in order to raise the level to its present state was continued for several days. In those days Ty'nllan consisted of two thatched roofed houses, one being the public house, Y Llan. One proprietor, Tom Foulkes, was about the only one able to read. Hence large crowds assembled at the public in order to hear the news. Tom Foulkes, it is stated, was fond of relating news he thought his audience ought (to) know whilst he was making a pretence of reading the newspaper.

"Trees planted by John Jones by the Hearse House opp. roadway. Through this gap the soil was carted. The slope started by the Yew Bushes. The site of the old School was also by the yew nearly opposite the present Church porch. Soil was carted by Rd. Morris, Ty Mawr, Isaac Hughes, Penycefn. Approx. 1910.

"'Monfa' is built upon the old 'Fault,' where they used to intern stray donkeys. There were large numbers of Donkeys in Llysfaen in early part of 19th Century. 'Strings' of donkeys used to carry coals & merchandise up to Llysfaen at 1d & 2d per cwt. The donkeys used to follow each other so as to form an Indian file of about 20-30."

There is a note that "pwll cadarn" meant "stronghold." The book probably belonged to the late Llechid Jones. The writer was told by a well-known resident that an old blacksmith informed him he had frequently shod the cattle of the speaker's grandfather, for driving to Barnet fair. A considerable amount of lime seems to have been burnt in Llysfaen. In the eighteenth century terrier there are references to "Cae Calch" and "Cae Rodin"— Lime Field and Kiln Field.

LLYSFAEN TELEGRAPH STATION

On the highest point of the common, probably on the site of a beacon, stands the semaphore station, now converted into a private dwelling. The whitewashed brick wall, facing seawards, bears a broad slate slab on which is cut: *"LLYSFAEN TELEGRAPH Built in 1841 by the TRUSTEES of the Liverpool Docks."*

The Llysfaen tithe map of 1839 indicates a *"telegraph station"* here. Lewis states a *"signal staff telegraph"* was erected in 1827. The semaphores had six arms and a code was used.

The *"Alehouse Recognizance Book"* in the County Records Office, at Caernarfon, indicates there were six alehouses in Llysfaen in 1626, and that two years later three were *"suppressed"* by the Justices as *"unnecessary and unfit to sell ale, beer and victuals."*

The Hearth Tax roll for 1662, in the County archives, lists 30 houses in Llysfaen of sufficient importance to pay Hearth Tax. There were three dwellings containing three hearths, three with two hearths, and the remaining 24 with one hearth. Though the houses are not named, the first three might be identified. The first name is "Thomas Vaughan, Clerk," and his house is probably The Rectory (or perhaps "Peulwys"); "Edward Pierce" would dwell at "Ty Mawr," and "John Vaughan" at "Plas Newydd." The next three houses (two hearths) were inhabited by William Bowen, John Lloyd and Margaret Lloyd, widow.

It is only in recent years that Llysfaen has developed perceptibly. Lhwyd, in 1699, found only *"two or three houses by the church,"* and Lewis in 1833 says the village consists *"of five houses only,"* and puts the population of the township at 585. Halliwell, in 1860, describes *"a village of some dozen scattered houses and a church."* He found *"fine and extensive prospects"* from the telegraph station. There were numerous commons and Lhwyd lists eight: Yr Alhtwen, Penmaen Rhos, Marian-is-alht, Marian y Lhan, Marian Kanol, Marian Galchog, and also "Marion a galwant vyvyndhe y Kerrig Kalch," and "Marian Gwgan enw Kae." He also mentions seven wells by name, including Ffynnon Owen, which may be that at Doldduu, beside Colwyn's Fairy Glen. In 1826 a great number of silver coins, in excellent preservation, were found. These were struck in the reigns of Stephen, Henry I, John, Edward I and Edward III.[213]

On 1 November 1898 a formal application was presented to the Caernarvonshire County Council, by the parish council, asking that Llysfaen might become an urban district. One reason for the change was the inadequacy of the water supply. In 1898 the population was estimated to be 2,110. There were 481 houses, eight chapels and three schoolrooms. The population in 1911 was 1,686, the acreage 1,879.

New schools were opened on Whit-Monday, 1871, at a cost of £1,700. The benefactors were those who subscribed for the restoration of the church with the addition of grants from the Woods and Forests, the National Society and the Education Department.

ANCIENT HOUSES

Houses listed by Lhwyd in 1699 as Y TAI KYVRIVOL (i.e. "responsible" or "important houses") included: Y Ty mawr yn Lhysvaen, Y Pentre Gwydhyl, Plas newydh, Ty Ycha, Pen y Geyffos, Y Plas (als Plas y Escob), Y Plas yn is-alht, Plas yn y Peilws (Tilehouse).

An Account of the Ecclesiastical State August 21st, by Rural Dean Thomas Wynne, 1729, tells us:

"Mr. Owen Williams AB is Rector. He was removed here three years ago from Llanrwst School, where he had been Head Master about fourteen years. He catechises but in Lent & has but few that come to him.

"The Rector has but a third part of ye Tithes of a Township called Penmaen; the Rector of Llandrillo has nine pounds ten shillings out of it; and ye Vicar of Llandrillo three pounds.

"I presumed to mention these odd divisions of ye Tithes of Llansanffraid, Llandrillo, Llanelian

& Llysfaen, because they were thought to be so irregular, that Bp.Lloyd, as I have been informed, projected a Subscription in order to procure an Act of Parliamt to regulate the Tithes of these four Parishes.

"Mr. Williams the Rector confessed that he was married sometime in March was (sic) twelve month to his Servant Maid, by Virtue of a Licence, but not in Church, within canonical hours, as I was credibly informed."

REGISTER. They have one Register Book, from 1660, to this present year. A copy of it is sent once a year to yr Lordship's court.

CHARITY. There are severall small sums bequeathed to the poor of this Parish, which amount to forty pounds, the Interest whereof is duly payd & distributed.

CHURCH & CHURCHYARD. There is an indecent vacancy at ye south end of the Comunion Table. Mr. Lloyd of Pentre a Parishioner petitioned for a Quorum Interest to erect a Pew there, but was denyed it, being opposed by the late Mr.Lloyd of Gwrych, who had no House in this Parish. It were to be wished for decency's sake that some body should be persuaded to erect a Bench or Sitting Place in this Vacancy.

> They have but one lock upon ye Church Chest.
> They want an English Bible in Folio.
> Their Welsh Bible is Old & Imperfect.
> They want a cover to ye Font.
> The ten Commandments are almost obliterated and the King's arms defaced.
> They want a door to ye reading seat.
> Their pewter Flagon & Plate are old, dirty & Scandalous, & should be changed.
> They have a poor's Box but not set up.
> The walls of ye Church are in good Repair.
> The west End of ye inside wants washing.
> The east window wants mending.
> The fence of ye Churchyard is ruinous & indecent.
> The north door of ye Church is mean & scandalous.
> Their hand-bell is cracked.
> The Parish Clerk is illiterate and not licenced.
> They want a Beir-cloth, but Mr. Butler promise's to make a present of one to ye Parish.
> They have no table of Charity, no Book for ye Wardens account nor Vestry Book.

GLEBE. There is a parsonage House, where ye Rector lives: It consists of five Bays of building; it wants no repair but Thatching. There are five Bays of Stalls and Cow-houses, which want Thatching very much. There are two Bays of a shed down, which ye Rector promise's to rebuild. His glebe land is computed to be eight pounds pr. annum.

TERRIER. In an old Terrier dated 1636, May 19, there are severall Quilets of Glebe land mentioned, the Rector can give no manner of account of. A new Terrier is promised.

SCHOOL. They have no Charity-School. The Rector petitioned your Lo'ship for leave to keep a School in his Parish, which he did for a little while, but has already dropt it.

CURATE. None.

After visiting neighbouring Llanddulas the Rural Dean added a footnote to his Llysfaen report:

N.B. - The Rector of this Parish did confess to me that He marryed Mr. Williams Rector of Llysfaen to his Servant-maid sometime in March was twelvemonth. He marryed them by virtue of a licence granted by Mr. Babington. & within canonical hours, but did it in a House. He is very sorry for so doing & says, that what made him do it, was Mr. Williams's being loath to marry his Servant; Because also Mr. Williams told him, that he suspected his intended Wife was a-breeding. This young Clergyman otherwise bears a fair Character; and I did not hear that he ever was before or after guilty of such Practice."

Twenty years later the report of the Rural Dean (the Rev.David Lloyd) noted:

"A Rectory of 60 or 70 lb a year. Mr. Thomas Lloyd the present Rector is, as I am credibly informed, of an exceptional life & conversation, diligent in his charge and of undoubted affection to his present Majesty. This church also is of two Isles. The Roof is in good repair. There is a crack in the East end of both Isles, but as the Wardens averr'd not dangerous. The Arch of the South window next the Altar seems very bad, and all the windows want some Panes of Glass. The Church within is lightsome and well beautified, and both Isles handsomely flagged with Free Stone. The chancel part of the North Isle has only an earthen floor and very uneven. The Altar is good and covered with a moth-eaten Green cloth. The Rails are loose. The Linen cloths for the Table and Elements are clean & whole, and the Surplice is in the like condition. The pulpit is comodiously placed close to a large Window in the South Isle and about it there is a tolerable good Green cloth with a silk fringe. The font is good enough but has lid. Here is wanted a Table of Charity. The Welch Comon Prayer Book is old and ragged. The Bible is fresh and whole, save that two leaves in the first Book of Kings are loose. Here is a New Folio English Comon Prayer Book, The Gift of the late Mr. Butler of Ty Mawr in this Parish.

"There are some other Books belonging to this Church ..... The Silver Chalice contains about a pint and is marked "Llysfaen Cup 1712." The Patin being of the same mettal & plain is of 6 Inches Diameter. An old fashioned Pewter flagon.

"The Church-yard Wall wants repairing on the East and South-East sides, but on the West and South-West it is very bad & in some parts for several yards together even with the ground. There is a very unhappy dispute which has long subsisted between the Rector and his Parishioners about the Repairs of these parts; which I endeavoured to accomodate, but in vain. I have found both Parties so positive and stiff, that I fear, nothing but the Law can bend them, unless your Lordship will interpose.

"The Glebe land is worth nine pounds a year & the fences are in good condition. The House and outhouses, all covered with a straw Thatch, are far out of order, but the parson, I find, has provided materials for repairing them this Sumer. All the Furniture & Utensils of the Church, not specified here are good & decent. The Service is always in the British tongue. I can hear of no Irregularities."

Lych Gate at Llandrillo

MOCHDRE

"Moghedreue" is mentioned in the *Survey* of 1334 but the township's existence must go back to days before the Edwardian conquest. The village occupies a desirable site beside a stream, at a spot where the main coastal route is joined by a track from the hinterland - the road which runs past Graianllyn, a manor mentioned in the days of the Wars of the Roses.

The spelling of Mochdre varies. "Bochdre" is the name used in the census of all "housekeepers" in Llandrillo parish taken in 1685. The township then contained 99 souls. The hearth-tax of about this date shows 14 houses taxable. On several eighteenth century maps Mochdre appears as "Bochdre," which also occurs a number of times on tombstones in Llandrillo parish churchyard. The registers spell it "Boughetre" in 1695, and "Boughtre" in 1701. The present spelling appears in 1753. In Charles I's reign a legal document gives it "Moughtrie." In Llandrillo churchyard the following inscriptions may be deciphered on worn tomb-stones: *"Here was buried Owen Williams of Boughtre, 1st day of March, 1694, aged 48; Mary Owen of Boughtre, 1703; Mrs. Mary Owen of Mochtre in this Parish, 1737."*

The map of 1720 shows the Old Highway passing through "Bochdre" from Conwy Ferry, on its way to Groes-yn-Eirias. Graianllyn is marked on the map. Mochdre assumed importance in the coaching era. Early parish registers mention two inns - the Eagles and the Swan. When a tithe map was prepared in 1848 the Swan was the only inn remaining. By that time the Eagles was turned into a Post Office. The site now occupied by the Mountain View Hotel was then marked "common." This inn was first named the White Horse. The Eagles appears to have been the inn

Swan Inn, Mochdre

of greatest consequence, named possibly from the coat-of-arms of Owain Gwynedd. The Calvinistic Methodists had a cause in Mochdre as far back as 1772 and their chapel, Nazareth, was opened in 1833.

There were village stocks *in situ* as late as 1880. Old residents believe boats used to come to Mochdre, possibly from the stream which ran into the Conwy before the railway embankment to Llanrwst was constructed in the 1860s. For many years a ship's figurehead - said to have been salvaged from the ill-fated *Ocean Monarch*, burnt in Abergele Bay on 24 August 1848 - was fixed to the wall of the Mountain View.

On 26 March 1928 the Council acquired 39 acres of land belonging to the Eagles Farm estate,

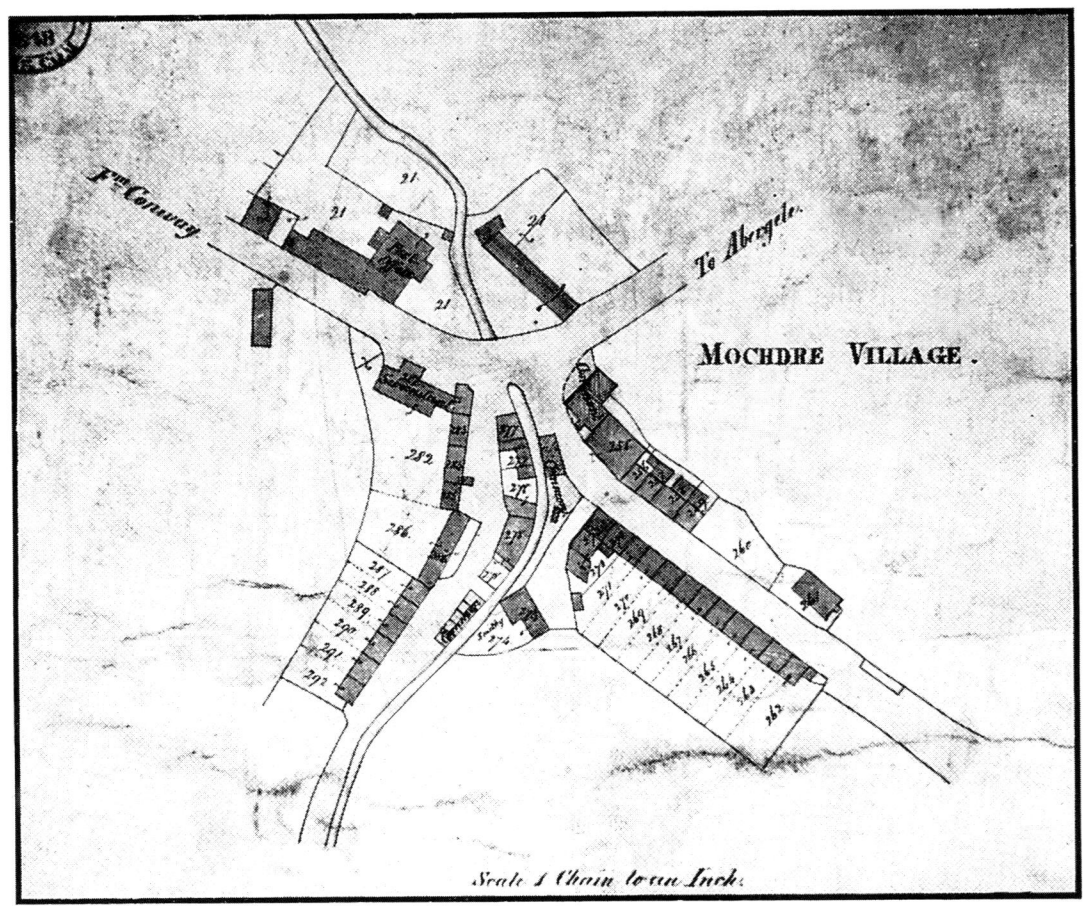

Courtesy National Library of wales

The Llandrillo-yn-Rhos tithe map of 1848 shows the development of Mochdre. The Old Highway is shown bottom right, descending Tanyrallt, to join the Conwy-Abergele turnpike road. The Eagles is marked "Post Office," the Swan is named, but the site of the Mountain View is shown as "Common." Afon Ganol runs through the centre.

Llanelian

No spot in the district recaptures the atmosphere of the past so adequately as Llanelian. The tiny crossroads hamlet still lingers, with the ancient inn at the gates of the old church which stands on its high mound, like an ecclesiastical fort protecting the safety of the dwellers round about. It is 530 feet above sea level. Strictly speaking, the village of Llanelian is just beyond the actual boundary of the 1934 Borough, but some of the houses in the parish are incorporated in Colwyn Bay, to which Llanelian's destiny is linked. That is sufficient justification for inclusion in this work. Comment has been made elsewhere on Lhwyd's reference to the few houses which were near the church in 1699. The hamlet, of course, took its name from the church, which was founded in about 540 AD. The wattle and daub structure of those far-off days would have been succeeded by a stone building. The oldest part of the church, the north chapel, is said to go back to the ninth century. That is the part where the organ is now situated. The belfry portion was added and then the south nave. The church now has two equal naves with five bays. Some filled-in doorways, obviously very ancient, invite speculation.

The well-worn carved head over the entrance is believed to represent St. Elian. Though the church dedicated to St. Elian or St. Hilary has been tastefully renovated, the interior still retains links with the distant past. The lower portion of the old rood screen has been restored to its original position after being discovered in an outhouse. The curved wood ceiling of the sanctuary was once richly adorned with painted monograms and devices, but coats of whitewash have almost obliterated them. Pictures preserved include the Visit of the Magi, St. Ann teaching the Blessed Virgin, and the Crucifixion. The north nave also has a vaulted canopy of timber. At one time there was an altar in each nave. Paintings from the old rood screen, discovered in a loft in 1874, have been framed and placed against the north wall. The first three represent the Judgment of Souls, the next three The Passion, and the last three the Legend of St. Hubert. A panel near the organ is worth examination. It is beautifully carved with a "P" surrounded by foliage, and underneath "R.M." with a rose and 1722. It is said that only two silver chalices in the Principality go back to pre-Reformation times. One of these is at Llanelian and dates to about 1460. Long ago the church was whitewashed externally and was straw thatched. A sundial was erected in 1722, and there is mention of parish stocks in 1731.

According to one old record a school was held in the church in 1600. Thirty children were educated in 1751 by the Rev. Lewis Lloyd, who lived at Meifod. It is thought the small low building opposite the White Lion inn would have been the schoolroom. One gravestone bears the date 1587. Marks of swords and spears are to be found on tombstones. There is a twelfth century stone font near the door, but it is not in use. The bell bears the date 1799 with the names of Edward Williams and Richard Williams. The church was once a sanctuary for refugees. There is mention of Elian's Chest (cyff Elian) in old records, but the poor-box referred to has disappeared. The Elian "wakes" were once held on three Friday evenings during August, but in 1804 they were confined to one and finally abandoned.[214] In recent years children of the village revived this old custom. According to Archdeacon Thomas the parish was originally known by the name of the township – Bodlenyn, but was superseded some time after 1291 by the name of its founder St.Elian. The parish comprises the four townships of Bodlenyn, Teyrdan, Twnan and Llaethfaen. The *Taxatio* of 1254 gives the parish as *"Ecc'a de Bechwylenyn,"* and in 1291 as *"Eccl'ia de Bodwelennyn"*, taxatur £4 2s Id. In the *Valor* of 1535 it appears as *"Rectoria de Llan Elion."*[215]

A Terrier of 1730 shows how the tithes of the parish were intermingled with those of Llysfaen and Llandrillo. As the ornamental gates of wrought-iron (designed by Harold Hughes) are in memory of Alexander Borthwick, of Plas Llewelyn, some extracts might appropriately be taken from a booklet which Mr. Borthwick published privately in 1922. He commences by recalling that in 1579, and for seven successive generations, the squires of Llanelian and owners of almost all the land in the parish, were the Hollands of Teyrdan. This widespread family established at Berw, Pennant, Kinmel, Hendrefawr and Denbigh, were all descended from a common ancestor, Sir Thomas Holland, who lived in the reign of Edward I.

"The late lamented Lieutenant Edward Wynne, the gallant young squire of Coed Coch, who fell in one of the battlefields of the Great War, face to face with the foe, was a direct lineal descendant of this ancient and venerated family," writes Mr. Borthwick.

The raised tomb of the first of the Hollands of Teyrdan, Humphrey Holland, who died in 1612, is a conspicuous feature of the churchyard. During the latter part of the 17th century the rector was the Rev. John Griffiths, and in the next hundred years five clergymen occupied the living. The earliest record of a vestry in the parish is in 1685. For more than one hundred years afterwards vestries were:

"commonly convened on Sundays, in the chancel of the church, thence by adjournment to the ale house. For instance, it is recorded that the vestry meeting held on Sunday, 8 October 1752, by adjournment to the house of 'Morris Davydd, Inn Keeper at Llanelian,' was 'for the purpose of going over the parish accounts'."

Of ten ratepayers attending, only two could sign their names.

In 1701 the Rev. Sampson Roberts, successor to Mr.Griffiths, was presented with a new surplice out of the parish rates. It cost £1-18s-6d., *"and the making thereof 5/-."* Ale for the Singers of Psalms occurs not infrequently in the accounts. On 11 October 1727:

"it was ordered, consented and agreed by the wardens and parishioners then assembled, that the sum of 2/6d. shall be paid and allowed out of the church tax, for ale, at every vestry hereafter to be summoned and called to transact the business of the parish."

Each parishioner was compelled (in rotation) to undertake, free of charge, the office of Overseer *"and bear his own expenses and charges attending the same, during his continuance therein."* John Pritchard, tenant of Tan y Dderwen, was the first appointed when the order was made in 1751. An outbreak to protest against the payment of church tax broke out in June 1762. The delinquents were dealt with by the Church wardens. Mention is made of one, Thomas Humphreys, and it is recorded *"that he shall be prosecuted at the next visitation of the Chancellor of St. Asaph for obstinately refusing to pay his church rates."*

BATHING PLACE

In 1765 the Rev. David Price, the Church wardens and parishioners *"ordered, consented and agreed that a bathing place be forthwith made, near Llanelian Well, upon the land of John Holland, Esq."* The sum of 4/6d. was spent to advertise the attractions of the bathing place in a Chester newspaper. The man who wrote it received one shilling. There is a record of a parishioner who went to Denbigh on parish business: 6d for hiring a horse, 3d for hay for the horse, and 10d for meat and drink for the messenger.

In 1800 the parishioners resolved *"to have the Rector of the parish live and reside in the* parish as it is in other parishes in our neighbourhood." There was an impost of 1/- in the £ to keep and maintain the Militiamen sent from the parish - an echo of the Napoleonic wars.

In 1826 the Wardens' accounts contained: Mending the Bass Violin, 2s; Repairing the Ten Commandments, 5s. The Rev. Thomas Alban, under whose auspices the present rectory was built, came into possession of the living in 1832, when a census revealed 326 males and 273 females.

When Sir Stephen Glynne visited Llanelian Church on 17 April, 1851, he wrote:

"The church is in a very elevated situation, commanding a grand view including a fine extent of sea. It is of a common Welsh type, two aisles or bodies, equal in length and height and breadth, with single bell gable at the west end of the southern, and a plain south porch. The chancel is undistinguished except for the boarded, panelled ceiling over the east end of the south aisle which forms the sacrarium. The roofs of the remainder of the church are open, of a kind almost universal in North Wales; but there is a panelled cornice to part of that at the east end of the north aisle. There is an internal arcade of five very coarse Pointed arches with rude square piers, having no caps. The prevailing style is rude three-pointed. At the east end of the south aisle is a three-light window of poor character, which seems to have once had a Pointed arch; on the north a square-headed one trefoliated, of three lights. In the west gallery appear some remnants of the panelling of the rood loft. The font is an ordinary octagonal bowl, on a similar stem. There are a few plain old bench ends, but the church is generally pewed. The outer walls partly whitewashed."

A footnote in Arch. Camb. 1884, p.100, states the church was restored in 1859. The east windows were filled with memorial glass, that in the chancel to John Lloyd Wynne, of Coed Coch and Teyrdan (died 1862), and the other to his wife, Mary, daughter and heiress of John Holland of Teyrdan (died 1844).

THE REGISTERS

The first Register (1589 to 1722) written on sheepskin, is almost unreadable. The entries, in Latin, are in a cramped hand, the writing brown with age. Some English entries later appear. The Rev. William Evans was Rector during the Civil War and was apparently undisturbed, for his writing continues each year (although there are not many entries) until 1649. It ceases with the establishment of the Commonwealth. His successor signs himself Johanne Wynne. In 1652 there is an entry concerning "Griffith de Colwyn" - an earlier reference to the name Colwyn than that of Edward Lhwyd's. There are two legible entries concerning the Hollands:.

"John Holland ...ealdest sonne of Thomas Holland" appears in 1655; and *"Humphrey Holland the . . . sonne of Thomas Holland was Baptised the fourteenth day of Aprill 1658."*

In 1663 the register is signed by "Johannes Conway" as one of the Churchwardens. There is a baptism in 1665 of Thomas, fillius Thomas Holland, armiger.[216] One of the last entries, in 1716, records : *"Anne the daughter of Thomas Holland Esq. & Margaret his wife was Xnd ye 2nd Day of May."* There is reference to a Catherine Salusbury of Tan y Dderwen - evidently a relative of the Elln "Sliesbury" of Tan y Dderwen who bequeathed six pounds to the poor, according to the board setting forth the list of benefactors in 1735. The second register starts in 1722 and ends in January 1795. The Vestry Book of 1877 records a Vestry held at the White Lion, when the Poor Rate was fixed at 1s 2d in the £. On St. Thomas's Day £5-7s-2d was distributed.

LLANELIAN BENEFACTORS

On a painted board dated 1735, which hangs on the south wall of Llanelian Church, is *"A list of all the Benefactors of the Poor of this Parish with the severall Summs bequeathed by their Respective Wills.*
Lowry Jones of Tan y Ddewen fawr, Five Pounds
Edwd. Dafydd of Vigin, yeoman, Five Pounds
Elln Sliesbury of Tan-y-Dderwyn, aforesd, wid; 6 Pounds
Edwd. Hughes of Bettws Gent, ten Pounds secur'd on a certain field in Twnnan called Orsedd Gelyn
John Humphreys of tan y Llan. yeomn: Ten Pounds
Willm. Hughes of Llaethfan yeom: Four Pounds
Elizth. Edwards, late of Vigin: Widow, Forty Pounds
Mary Foulks: of Gwyn Dy in the Parish of Bettws, Spinster 50££
Foulk Lewis, late of Cwmere, Yeom: five Pounds
Willm. Pierce of Myvod in the Parish of Llandrillo; Yeom: three Pounds
Marian Jones: of St. Asaph, widow: two Pounds
Thomas Evans of Tyn y Wal for churchyard: One Pound per annum
William Hughes of Tyn Newydd for Church Yard: One Pound per anm."

Inside the covers of one of the registers is written: *"The names of ye Rectors of Llan Elian from ye year 1590 to ye year 1727,"* to which several later names are added.

THE CURSING WELL

No reference to Llanelian would be complete without reference to its far-famed Cursing Well. Though it has now been obliterated there was a time when it was known far and wide. Pennant writes of it:

"The well of St. Aelian, a parish not far from Llandrillo, in Caernarvonshire, has been in great repute for the cures of all diseases, by means of the intercession of the saint ; who was first invoked by earnest prayers in the neighbouring church. He was also applied to on less worthy occasions, and made the instrument of discovering thieves, and of recovering stolen goods. Some repair to him to imprecate their neighbours, and to request the saint to afflict with sudden death, or with some great misfortune, any persons who may have offended them. The belief in this is still strong; for three years have not elapsed since I was threatened by a fellow (who imagined I had injured him) with the vengeance of St. Aelean, and a journey to his well to curse me with effect."

A further contribution is made by J. R. Halliwell, FRS. who came this way in 1860:

"We were trudging along not to see Colwyn," he writes, *"but to have a peep at the celebrated cursing well of Llanelian, a village higher up on the hills. Here is a plain church. In a corner of the churchyard is a fragment of an ancient cross. There are about a dozen houses in the immediate vicinity of the church, a few others being sparsely scattered about the parish. The views from this spot are good. 'Fynnon Elian, the cursing well, is situated in some field about half-a-mile from the church, near the left-hand road which leads to Colwyn. It derives indeed, its only interest from its being one of the places where obtained the barbarous custom of invoking the presiding saint to injure an enemy, who was at the same time cursed with a supposed peculiar effect."*

The well was circular in shape, covered with a stone arch and sods and enclosed by a strong square wall seven feet high.[217] Its singularity as the 'Cursing Well' bespeaks its pre-Christian character, and the long survival of its dread influence, the stubborness of the conflict between Christianity and Paganism. One tradition is that hermit passing through (? Elian the Pilgrim) fell ill at this spot and praying for a drink of water, a copious spring burst forth at his side, and he drank and got well. Whereupon he prayed that the spring might be the medium to grant to all who asked in faith anything that they might wish.

"Of the good fruits we have no record, unless we may recognize them in the large offerings of the Valor of 1535, 'in oblaacionibus & aliis decimis ac emolumentid iiij,' and in the enrichments and ornaments of the church. But of the evil fruits the whole country was long and painfully conscious in the terror and misery that attached to it. But even this must have had some compensation in that it deterred scores, whom nothing else would deter, from running the risk of such fearful consequence."

A footnote adds: "The ceremony (of cursing) is performed by the applicant standing upon a certain spot near the well, whilst the owner of it reads a few passages of the sacred scriptures, and then taking a small quantity of water, gives it to the former to drink and throws the residue over his head; which is repeated three times, the party continuing to mutter his imprecations in whatever terms his vengeance may dictate. At that time (1832) it was visited by hundreds of persons for that villainous purpose. I have myself known a well-to-do farmer in a former parish who lost £180 rather than ask for it back again, for fear of being put into the well, and I have met with a person in England pining away to death under the belief that she had been so cursed.There is reason to believe that this wretched superstition is not yet obsolete.[218]

"An intelligent Welsh writer in 1846 informs us that this is the most dreadful of all wells, and the one in whose miraculous powers the peasants of the present day most fully believe. Persons who hear any malice against others, and wish to injure them, frequently resort to the minister of the well, who for a sum of money undertakes to offer them in it. The penalty consists either in personal pain or loss of property, as the offerer pleases. Various ceremonies are gone through on the occasion; amongst others the name of the devoted is registered in a book—a pin in his name, and a pebble with his initials inscribed thereon are thrown into the well. When the curse is to be removed, the ceremonies are to a certain extent reversed, such as the erasing of the name from the book, taking up the pebble, with several other practices of a superstitious character."

The well was abolished by the influence of the clergy, prominent amongst whom was the Rev. Robert Phillips, Vicar of Betws. The last custodian, according to the report of the Ancient Monuments Commission of 1914, died in 1858. The ceremonies had ceased some years before. Baring-Gould and Fisher give January, 1829 as the date when the well was filled in.

OLD HOUSES

Llan Farm, near the Church, is a good example of old wattle-and-daub construction. Sometimes it is known as Hen Siop (Old Shop). It was once the home of Jabez Jones, sexton, who died December 1915, aged 84. Another character was John Parry, landlord of the White Lion, a noted bard, who died at the age of 54 years in 1820. A nearby farm, Ysgubor Newydd (New Barn), when demolished in 1910, revealed a carved piece of wood marked: E.T.N. 1269.

Edward Llwyd, in 1699, stated that the chief houses in Llanelian parish were: Y Plas, Teirdan, Pentre, Tan y Lan, Pentarad, Twnnan Ucha, Lhetty du, Fernant, Glyn, Coed Coch Ucha. As set forth in *Parochialia* they read, in the primitive Welsh of the period:

"LHAN EILIAN
1. Y Plas a b. i'r Arg. Willoughby (i.e.belongs to Lord Willoughby).
2. Teirdan Tho: Holland Esq. 300££ yn y blwydhyn. (i.e. £300 per annum).

3.   *Y Pentre. Pierce Lloyd Gent.*
4.   *Tan y Lhan. Richd Parry yeom' in right of his wife Mary Bertridge, Daughter to Mr. Nic:Bertridge.*
5.   *Pentarad. Mrs. Griffiths Widow.*
6.   *Twnnan ycha ag a chanol i Louri Jones Etivodhes, &c.* (Upper, Lower and Middle, belong to Lowri Jones, Heiress).
7   *Lhetty du*
8.   *Fernant a berthyn i Mr. Piers o'r Ty mawr ym hlwy Lhysvaen.* (i.e. belongs to Mr. Pierce of Ty Mawr in the parish of Llysfaen).
9.   *Y Glyn Edw : Price. 20 ££ per annum.* (i.e. £20 per annum).
10.   *Y Koed Koch ycha. John Wyn Gent.*[219] (i.e. Coed Coch Upper)."

Then follows the note: *By mwdwl eithin Ao.1666 ar ben Mynydh Lhan Elian et alibi Teste-Foulks Vicario de Lhan-drihlo.* (i.e. There was a beacon A.D. 1666 on top of Llanelian Mountain).

THE TERRIER OF 1749

"*An exact Terrier of all such Glebe, reserved Rents, Tythes &c. as do belong to the Rectory of Llan-elian together wth an account of all Books and utensils at this time belonging to the sd Parochial church exhibited the fifteenth day of August 1749 at the Primary visitation of the Right reverend Father in God, Robert, by divine Permission, Ld. Bishop of St. Asaph, at Denbigh.*

    IMPRIMIS - *There is one parcel of Glebe Lands belonging to the sd Rectory containing about two accres in the Township of Bodlennin adjoining upon a Parcel of the Lands of Edward Lloyd Gent, called Cae Llwyd on the East end thereof, South upon the Lands of Teyrdan called Gwaredydd. The west end thereof partly upon the lands called Gwaredydd, and partly upon a parcel of Lands called Caeae'r Mudan and on the North Side partly on the High way leading from Llan-elian to Llys-faen and partly upon a parcel of the Lands of John Parry of Rhos fyhach, Gent: Deceased, and at the upper end of this Parcel of Glebe Lands Mr. Holland of Teyrdan has a road or Passage into the sd Parcell called Gwaredydd wch he had through the Permission of the late Rector of this Parish, and for which he pays one shilling yearly.*

    Also there belongeth to the sd Rectory on yearly Rent of thirteen shillings and four pence payable out of the Lands of Teyrdan for church Lands lying intermixed with that Estate, but the Mears and Bounds are not now known.

    All the Tythes of the Township of Bodlennin and of the Hamlett of Teyrdan do belong unto the said Rectory and also the third part of all the Tyth Corn and Hay of all the rest of the Township of Twnnan (excepting the Tyth of Bryn yr odyn whereof nothing belongs to the sd Rectory) and all the Small Tythes, viz: Wool Lamb Geese Piggs Flax & Hemp &c. of the said Township of Twnnan, excepting the small Tythes of Pendarad and Bryn yr odyn before excepted, do likewise belong to the said Rectory—

    And also the moyety or one half of all the Tyth corn and Hay, and two third parts of all the Small Tythes of the Township of Llaethfan do likewise rightfully belong to the sd Rectory of Llan:elian.

    Moreover all the Easter Duties of the whole Parish belong to the said Rectory.

    All the Tythes of the Parish aforesd are paid in kind, and the Rector is not liable either to the repairing any part of the church or fencing of the church yard, but the whole lyeth upon the Parishioners of the said Parish.

    Here is no House nor any building belonging to the sd Rectory.

    As to the Books and Utensills &c. of the sd church, There do belong to it at present two large Bibles, in Folio, the welsh one of the best Translation and edition, and the English of an old Print, also two Common Prayer Books in Folio, of best Translation & edition, one in Welsh & the other in English, and also one welsh Common Prayer book in Quarto for the use of our Parish Clerk.

Two surplices, a Communion Table Cloth, a carpett for the Communion Table, only a Cushion for the Pulpit, an old fashion'd Silver Challice, containing about a pint, a new Pewter Flagon, containing about two Quarts, a new Pewter Dish & Platter."

RURAL DEAN'S REPORT 1729

An account of the Ecclesiastical State of the Deanery of Rhos, 13 September 1729, by Thomas Wynne, Rural Dean:

LLANELIAN. visited Aug. 21, 1729. Mr. William Williams, AB, is Rector of this Parish. He has been here about two years. The tithes of this Parish are divided between severall persons viz.:

INCUMBENT TITHE & DUTY. Your lordship has about ten pounds pr. ann. The Rector of Llandrillo eighteen pounds pr. ann. The Vicar of Llandrillo four pound pr. annum. The Rector of Llysfaen three pounds ten shillings pr. ann. The Rector of ye Parish ye Rest, who will be more particular in ye new Terrier. He catechi's in Lent, but complains that his Parishioners do not send their youth to be catecized.

REGISTERS. They have two Register Books, ye first from 1590 to 1722, the other from that year to this present time. A coppy of ye Register is sent once a year to Court.

CHARITYS. They have severall Charitys which are regularly pay'd, but having no Table, we cannot set down the Particulars.

CHURCH & CHURCHYARD. The Comunion Table want's to be better fixed. A Napkin to cover ye Elements is wanting. The Pulpit Cloth doth not half cover ye Pulpit. The parish ladder is indecently hung over ye Pulpit. They have a poor's Box into which the popishly affected offer frequently to St. Hilary the Saint of this Church. The Minister & Churchwardens distribute ye money twice a year to ye poor. Their Roof Loft is very ruinous & should be either removed or repaired.

The Church walls & Roof are strong & in good Repair, But the inside of ye Church is void of Ornament, & wants white washing and painting. The Church floor wants paving. The Church yard fence on ye West end want's repair.

Their Chalice is old and too small for ye Congregation, & therefore should be changed. Their Pewter Flaggon & Plate are kept dirty.

They want the Proclamation & the Acts of Parliamt necessary to be read in Churches.

The Parish Clerk is not licenced.

GLEBE &c. There is no Parsonage House, nor Glebe Land, except one field valued at twenty shillings a year. Mr. Holland of Teyrdan pay's thirteen shillings & four pence as prescription for some Church Lands among his own Lands, but ye Meares of ye Church Land are not known.

TERRIER. They have no Terrier, but promise to provide a new one against next Lady Day.

SCHOOL. They have no Charity School: But there is a little reading School, the Master of it is not licenced.

CURATE. None.

RURAL DEAN'S REPORT OF 1749

Twenty years later the Rev. David Lloyd, Rural Dean (and Rector of Gwytherin) visited Llanelian. His report is revealing of the attitudes of the day, and the Church of England's concern about loyalty to King George II:

"A Rectory, valued at 60 lb a year. Mr. William Williams Rector - non Resident, lives in his own Paternal house call'd Pabo, in the Parish of Llangwstenin. He has no great character for sobriety, is well esteemed for Learning and always well affected to his present Majesty. Mr. David Lloyd the Curate was licenced by Bishop Maddox in 1738. He bears a good character for sobriety, industry and care of his Parish and for hearty affection to the present Government. The Church, as to Fabrick & windows, is in very good repair. The flaggs are good, neat and even. The font is very neat & well covered. The Pulpit and Reading Seat are firm & good. The Pulpit cloth & cushion are of Good blewish broad cloth. One new Surplice & an old and much worn. The Linen to cover the Table is full of holes and darnings. That for the Elements is fine & New. Here is a curious old chalice with our Saviour upon the Cross well carved upon the side of it. An Old Pewter flagon & Plate. The Welsh Comon Prayer Book is new, but one leaf in the Litany is loose. The Bible is Imperfect in the End. Here is a New English Bible & another of the old English letter and imperfect in the beginning. The Register is of Vellum and the names regularly inserted but the Pages are not subscribed. The Altar is loose in the Joints and cover'd with a handsome neat Carpet, but the white Linen cloth is bad. Here is a fine Table of Charities. No Table of Prohibited Degrees. The Curate shew'd me at last an old Welch Homily Book, Imperfect in the beginning and end. Here is no Glebe house but one small field of 30s value. The service is allways in Welch. The Church consists of two handsomes Isles."

CONCLUSION

With incorporation as a municipal borough, in 1934, Colwyn Bay entered upon a new phase of life. A story was started which some other writer must tell.

This book has set out to place on record facts which might otherwise be forgotten. Tradition is not to be despised. The civic oak is symbolical. Sturdy roots are needed to withstand the storms of time. Old families die out; records are lost; trees are felled; pleasant meadows are cut into building lots. Already pastoral Colwyn Bay becomes a dim memory. Yet some of the old links remain - the cross-roads at Llanelian hamlet; the lych-gate at Llandrillo; the wayside pump in Tanybryn Road; Bryn Euryn's ruins; the Old Highway; the sylvan paths of Pwllycrochan Woods; the tranquillity of Nant-y-glyn Valley.

May these be preserved for all time. Colwyn Bay has no mean heritage. As we benefit from the labours of our forefathers who fashioned Colwyn Bay, let us see to it that we preserve a trace of the leisurely, restful past for those who follow after.

BOOK 2

COLWYN BAY
A 21ST CENTURY OVERVIEW

by Ivor Wynne Jones

The following pages are an updated and expanded version of the book *Colwyn Bay, a brief history*, by Ivor Wynne Jones, written in 1959 and first published in 1995.

Harry Reynolds 'Nigger Minstrels' – white performers with blackened faces – would not be allowed to present their entertainment today

A 21ST CENTURY OVERVIEW

FROM HAMLET TO BOROUGH

Colwyn Bay now forms part of Conwy County Borough, an administrative area created in 1996 by spanning the medieval political and diocesan boundary with neighbouring Llandudno and Conwy. The borough of Colwyn Bay had earlier merged in 1974 with eastern and southern local authorities to form Colwyn Borough, which was subsumed in the 1996 reorganisation of local government. The town's growth within a century from an obscure Victorian hamlet to a borough with the biggest rateable value in North Wales by 1960, presents an interesting sociological study. Midway through the 19th century most of the present town was a private park of green fields and natural forest, yet by the time Queen Victoria died it had been transformed into a leading seaside resort.

British hill-dwellers had a camp here, Suetonius Paulinus and later Julius Agricola passed this way with their Roman legions; a Breton monk built himself a chapel on our seashore; and Llywelyn the Great's chief administrator built a mansion here. Edward I specifically included the headland at the eastern end of Colwyn Bay in the county of Caernarfon, when consolidating the English conquest in 1284, and Richard II was ambushed here a century later. Yet during his famous tour of Wales Thomas Pennant found nothing more than *"a pretty bay"* in 1778. *"The country slopes to the water edge, and is varied with woods and cultivation,"* was all Pennant had to add about the land between Penmaen Head and Rhos-on-sea.[1]

When Edmund Hyde Hall compiled his *Description of Caernarvonshire* in 1811 he duly recorded the Caernarfon outposts of Colwyn (now Old Colwyn) and Groes-yn-Eirias (the cross-roads at the entrance to what is now Eirias Park), which together made up the Township of Eirias - aspiring even then to becoming a bathing resort. He added:

"The two little hamlets, already mentioned as lying at the two extremities of the Township, are clusters of a few houses; and at Groes a sort of bathing place for the season may strike the traveller as a snatch at improvement ... Little addition seems to have been made to the population of this district since the Government returns published in 1800 [sic] for I could only increase the number of 35 houses, inhabited by 40 families, by two new ones.[2]"

The phenomenal growth of the resort began in 1865 when Lady [Jane Silence] Erskine's Pwllycrochan Estate was offered for sale, by her son Sir Thomas. That was the era when Lancashire industrialists were retiring with fortunes amassed during the Industrial Revolution, and it had become the vogue to acquire a seaside residence in North Wales. In his brochure for the sale of the estate, auctioneer William Dew wrote:

"This fine property commands one of the finest marine prospects in this most popular neighbourhood, with a splendid sea bathing beach $1^1/_2$ miles in length forming a perfect amphitheatre (sic).[3] *The mansion will be sold in one lot and the remaining portion fronting the sea will be sold in separate lots to meet the great and increasing demand for marine residences on this coast."*

A Brief History

The auctioneer correctly forecast that what was to become known as Colwyn Bay possessed a combination of resources *"which unquestionably will make this one of the most desirable and favoured watering places in the United Kingdom at no very distant date."*

Pwllycrochan mansion was bought by John Pender, who later became Member of Parliament for Caithness, and was knighted. Thomas Hughes, a 46-years-old farmer from Maenan, bought a plot on which he built the town's first shop and dwelling, which he called Ivy House, being a translation of the name of his original family home, Plas Iorwg, at Llanrwst. The house still stands, at the top of Ivy Street - the borough's only "street," which took its name from Ivy House. Thomas Hughes's grandson, Thomas Arthur Hughes, became mayor of Colwyn Bay in 1942, and died in office.

Gradually a village began to grow between the railway station and Ivy House, and in October 1871 the town's first hotel was opened, with the pioneering name of Colwyn Bay Hotel. With it came the first section of the now splendid promenade. Not to be confused with the former Hotel 70° which was built at Penmaenhead in 1971, at a cost of £230,000 (and sold for £147,000 in 1976), and which was renamed Colwyn Bay Hotel in 1994, the original hotel of that name was at the junction of Marine Road and the promenade, with its own private path to the railway station.

Mr Pender visited his new village on 18 March 1872, which was declared a public holiday. When he arrived at the railway station a band struck up with *See the conquering hero comes*, and as he emerged from the station he was saluted by a salvo of artillery, and welcomed by a reception committee headed by the Vicar of Llandrillo-yn-Rhos, the Rev. William Venables Williams (who remained in office from 1869 until 1900). A contemporary record of the visit[4] tells of Mr Pender's inspection of:

"the building operations that are at present going on for the beautifying of this charming watering place, which every year, as it becomes better known, is being more largely patronised by visitors. So great indeed has been the increase in visitors that it was deemed necessary to build another hotel."

Three years later Mr Pender sold his land, most of it to a Manchester syndicate, and it was from that date Colwyn Bay grew rapidly as a holiday resort. Two famous public schools, Penrhos College (for girls) and Rydal were established in the town in 1880 and 1890 respectively (and merged in 1995). By 1901 the population had grown to 8,689,[5] an unusual feature of the growth being the absence of any industry to sustain it. Half the population comprised a readily recognisable class of people who had no need to work, while the other half serviced their needs and those of the summer influx of visitors. It was a convenient economic balance which then worked very well, though incomprehensible in relation to today's expectations.

Now with a population of 25,576, Colwyn Bay no longer has an obviously affluent layer of idle rich, though it was very much in evidence as recently as 1959, when this manuscript was originally written. It was then commonplace to see chauffeur-driven widows being taken to the nationally famous shops which graced Station Road, or being taken for morning coffee at the Metropole Hotel, now a block of flats at the bottom of Penrhyn Road. By that time Colwyn Bay knew it could never recapture the golden age of its holiday trade, and began turning to industrial development on corporation land at Mochdre, in conjunction with a firm of industrial financiers headed by Lord Macdonald of Gwaenysgor. There was also a lot of office development in the town centre, at a time when there were still businessmen who lived in Colwyn Bay and commuted daily on their special trains, to offices in Merseyside or Manchester.

As a gesture of its confidence in the rebirth of Colwyn Bay, the borough council bought the little Repertory Theatre, on Abergele Road, in 1958. They refurbished what began as the Public Hall, the name still preserved in the original brickwork. It served as St.Paul's church from 1886-88, became the Territorial Army Drill Hall and Company HQ in 1908, the Rialto Cinema in the 1920s, was burnt down in 1930, was soon rebuilt as the New Rialto, and became Colwyn

Bay Repertory Theatre in 1937 until it closed in 1958. It reopened on 11 June 1959 as the Prince of Wales Theatre, with a performance of *Dear Delinquent*. The auditorium was again refurbished in September 1969, when the seating capacity was reduced from 516 to a more comfortable 428. Council "political correctness" required the name Prince of Wales Theatre to be replaced, in May 1991, with the exceedingly dull and uninspired Theatr Colwyn. In September 2000 a screen and cinema projector were added, at the expense of 42 more seats.

Colwyn Bay used to have several cinemas. The tiny Cosy Cinema, in Conwy Road, survived into the 1960s, largely as a venue for foreign films. The Wedgewood, in Princes Drive, began as Catlin's Arcadia Theatre, but was demolished in 1981. The Rhos Playhouse retained its attractive frontage when converted into a Co-op supermarket in 1975. The Supreme, in Old Colwyn, also became a supermarket. The Princess Cinema, in Princes Drive, was built in 1914 and a balcony was added in 1932, together with neo-Egyptian embellishments to its architecture. It had been a bingo hall for some years when converted into a pub in 1998, by which time it was a listed building. The town's 1,700-seat Odeon Cinema was one of the best classic designs of Harry Weedon, and should have been given listed building status. It opened in April 1936, closed in January 1957, reopened as the Astra cinema in 1969 and finally closed in December 1986. Demolition began a year later to make way for a block of flats.

COLWYN BAY HOTEL

Opened in October 1871, and soon to give the new town its name, the Colwyn Bay Hotel had taken two years to build. Two of the town's first residents had already built small summer residences and a private church on the site. When construction of the 92-bedroom hotel began in 1869 these buildings were designed into the Gothic complex, by Chester architect John Douglas - the houses as pump house and laundry, and the church as one of the finest kitchens in Britain. Douglas deliberately designed the complex to contain 365 windows, one for each day of the year. The pump house was used to supply sea water to the bathrooms, but only at high tide, in an era when people believed the sea to be a cure for virtually anything, including: "Cold bathing has this good alone: it makes old John to hug old Joan; and does fresh kindnesses entail on a wife tasteless, old and stale." By 1910 the hotel was advertising: "Hotel porters in blue and scarlet livery meet all trains," adding that the establishment was equipped with electric light.

During alterations in the 1950s the bell pulley system in the old church again became visible in the kitchen, and the telltale church belfry was still intact when the hotel closed for demolition in January 1974, to make way for the flats now known as Princess Court. The last public meals served at the hotel were on Christmas Day 1973; the last private function on New Year's Eve. Its residents had included Adelina Patti, David Lloyd George, Cary Grant (visiting Ingrid Bergman during the filming of *Inn of the Sixth Happiness* at Beddgelert), David Kossof, Anthony Steel, Roy Plumley, and an author whose name no-one could recall, but who used to take a first-floor suite for three months every year, together with his secretary, to write each successive novel.

Captain Philip Quellyn Roberts, the last chairman of Quellyn Roberts & Co, owners of the Colwyn Bay Hotel, carved his name on history while working at the Admiralty during World War II. One of his jobs was to allocate a number to every convoy either leaving or heading for Britain. For the hazardous convoys to Russia he chose his own initials - all were PQ going out and QP coming back. The most famous was PQ17, which sailed on 27 June 1942, with 33 merchant ships and a tanker, escorted by 21 warships, with a further two battleships, one aircraft carrier, six cruisers and 17 destroyers theoretically available to reinforce the convoy, although they failed to arrive in time. German aircraft and submarines scattered PQ17 and only ten ships reached Murmansk.

A Brief History

THE COMING OF THE RAILWAY

The birth and growth of Colwyn Bay was inevitably linked to the laying of the Chester & Holyhead Railway, which began, at Chester, on St David's Day 1845. The 60-mile Chester-Bangor section was opened to passengers on 1 May 1848, when the nearest stations to Colwyn Bay were at Conwy and Abergele. The town's first station was opened in 1849, close to the present tunnel which takes the Llanelian road down to the promenade. It was called "Colwyn."

In return for allowing the railway to cross her land, the widowed Lady Erskine (daughter of the Rev. Hugh Williams) was given her own station, called "Pwllycrochan Halt," near the present exit from the A55 expressway into Princes Drive. This was later moved to the site of the present Colwyn Bay station, originally as no more than two wooden platforms built of railway sleepers; passengers having to walk across the track to get from one to the other.

The town's finances were improved dramatically by the arrival of the railway, after the Vicar, the Rev W.Venables Williams, succeeded in having the London & North Western Railway Company fully rated in 1871, from when they had to pay £950 a mile per annum, instead of the previous £125. That resulted in the local rates (council tax) being cut from 5s 1d (25p) in the pound of rateable value in 1870, to 2s 3d (11p) in 1872.[6]

In 1906 Colwyn Bay station was enlarged to give it four platforms, and remained unchanged until reduced to its present size to make way for the A55 dual carriageway, of which the Colwyn Bay section was completed in June 1985. As recently as 1959 all four platforms were in use, with trains arriving at intervals of four or five minutes during the peak summer season.

A much-used facility at that time was the Holyhead-Crewe travelling post office, or TPO. Fully equipped as a sorting office, the Post Office section of the late evening Holyhead-London train was fitted with an external letter box aperture, in which letters carrying an extra halfpenny ($\frac{1}{2}$d) postage were cleared that night for next day delivery virtually anywhere in Britain. As many as 20 or 30 people would gather on the platform each evening to make use of this late facility. The TPO had replaced an earlier non-stop automatic pickup facility just east of the station.

Construction of the A55 dual carriageway also obliterated the last traces of the short-lived Mochdre & Pabo station, of special interest to railway historians as the location of the world's first experiment in supplying moving trains with water. Troughs were laid between the rails in 1860 and remained in use until 1871, enabling trains to scoop up the water with an enormous splash which engulfed the entire train. The original troughs were removed to Aber in 1871 and remained in use until 1962.

With little foresight as to the future development of Colwyn Bay, much of the soil for the construction of the railway embankment was scooped from the centre of what was to become the town, to create the huge bowl now containing the car park for the Bay View Shopping Centre, opened in 1987. With equal lack of foresight the railway embankment was built in such a way as to prevent any other form of development along the seafront. Before the construction of the present A55 road there were four road tunnels under the railway: (1) at Marine Road, (2) on Victoria Drive, opposite the Pier, (3) at the Dingle cul-de-sac, and (4) at Wynnstay Road. There was also a pedestrian tunnel known as the Donkey Path. With the construction of the new road Colwyn Bay retained only the Marine Road tunnel, the cul-de-sac to the Dingle and the Wynnstay Road tunnel at Old Colwyn, but the Donkey Path was converted into the present hazardous extension to Llanelian Road. The most used road, immediately east of the railway station, was converted into an obscure footpath - its original configuration, once with "excursionist" steps up to the station, can still be recognised, opposite the Pier.

Incidentally, the name Donkey Path had nothing to do with any suggested use by donkeys. It began as a footpath from Min-y-don to the beach, crossing a brook, a stile and the railway track. After a fatal accident on the railway crossing, in about 1910, it was decided to improve the path and a black donkey was raffled to provide the necessary £60. It remained an attractive and much used walk until the coming of the A55 expressway.

In July 1938 a Patriot class 4-6-0 steam locomotive was named *Colwyn Bay* and given a civic send off from Colwyn Bay station. By 1963 it had completed 1,469,953 miles and its brass nameplate was returned to the care of Colwyn Bay Borough Council when the engine was scrapped.

CREATION OF COLWYN BAY PARISH

In the face of considerable local opposition, Queen Victoria signed an Order in Council on 15 May 1893 creating the Parish of Colwyn Bay. For any study of the history of the church in Colwyn Bay it is perhaps easier to ignore local government boundaries, for no area has seen a greater upheaval of church and local government lines of demarcation.

Briefly let it be remembered that Colwyn Bay & Colwyn Urban District came into being in 1895, by consolidating the Colwyn Bay & Colwyn Local Board created in 1887 to administer a merger of what is now Colwyn Bay town centre with Old Colwyn - at that time still known as Colwyn, with the present Colwyn Bay usually known as New Colwyn. In 1923 the detached Caernarvonshire parish of Llysfaen, with boundaries dating from 1284, incorporating much of Old Colwyn, became part of Denbighshire, and was amalgamated with the Colwyn Bay & Colwyn Urban District. This title was changed in 1926 to the Urban District of Colwyn Bay. In 1927 the various parishes in the new Urban District were consolidated, for local government purposes, under the title of the Parish of Llandrillo-yn-Rhos. In 1934 the Borough of Colwyn Bay was created by merging the Urban District with the villages of Rhos-on-sea, Mochdre and Bryn-y-maen. In 1974 the Borough absorbed Abergele and the rural hinterland to create Colwyn Borough, which was merged in 1996 with Aberconwy District (a 1974 creation) to create Conwy – within which Colwyn Bay retains its postal name.

Independently of these local government changes, designed to bring about an ever-bigger administrative area for rating purposes (the equivalent of the modern council tax), there was a reverse process within the church - then the Church of England, before the 1920 disestablishment of the now autonomous Church in Wales. Several new parishes were born out of historic parishes that had existed for centuries.[7]

The ecclesiastical parish of Llandrillo-yn-Rhos (as distinct from the local government parish) has been in existence since the earliest days of the Celtic church. Llysfaen appears to have been carved out of Llandrillo in late medieval times. It was out of these (with a small portion of the parish of Llanelian) that Colwyn Parish (now Old Colwyn) was carved in 1844, with jurisdiction as far as a point near the present Eirias Park. Half-a-century later the parish of Colwyn Bay was created out of Llandrillo-yn-Rhos, so that it lay between Colwyn parish and all that was left of Llandrillo (now confined to Rhos-on-sea). In 1900 there were further changes when the new parishes of Colwyn Bay and Colwyn, together with the older ones of Llanelian and Llansanffraid (Glan Conwy) each gave up some territory to create the parish of Bryn-y-maen. Only against that background can one hope to follow the complex history of the church in the present town of Colwyn Bay.

In 1869 the Rev. William Venables Williams was appointed Vicar of Llandrillo-yn-Rhos, which had 900 inhabitants. There was no such place as Colwyn Bay, although his parish extended as far as today's Eirias Park. By 1871 the embryo of a new township was developing around the railway station, and in that year the Calvinistic Methodists began to hold meetings in a carpenter's shop, on the site of the MANWEB switch room and transformer house near the top of Ivy Street.[8] Although the carpenter's shop was owned by Abel Williams, of Llandudno, a well-known Nonconformist, the Rev. Venables Williams obtained permission to celebrate

A Brief History

This postcard shows St Paul's parish church before the addition of its tower in 1911. The gap seen to the left, in Rhiw Road, is where the present Police Station and Court were built in 1907 – the old court is now the home of the Bay of Colwyn Town Council, created in 1996

Anglican evensong there on Sunday afternoons. The first such service was on 18 June 1871, with a congregation of 70. Exactly a year later the first service was held in a mission chapel erected at a cost of £170 on the site of the present parish church of St Paul, the land having been given to the Church of England by Sir Thomas Erskine, during the original disposal of the Pwllycrochan estate in 1865. Designed by John Douglas, it was a handsome little structure built of bricks, timber and iron, and roofed with red tiles, with chairs for 220. In 1886 the New Colwyn mission chapel was burnt down (allegedly by Mochdre tithe rioters, who blamed an overheated boiler) and services continued to be held in the nearby Public Hall, on Abergele Road - now Theatr Colwyn.

Most of the present magnificent church of St Paul was consecrated on 13 July 1888. The chancel was added in 1895, and the splendid tower in 1911. It was designed by the famous Chester partnership of (John) Douglas & (D.P.) Fordham, and was the last work Douglas was to supervise, dying before the tower was completed. A west porch by W.D. Caröe was added in 1920, as a war memorial. The beautifully carved reredos was added in 1937. The church hall and vicarage, also by Douglas & Fordham, were completed in 1895. This unusual ecclesiastic group was completed in 1903 with the opening of St David's church, for Welsh services. The handsome Vicarage in the church grounds is in the process of being vacated in 2001- to free the incumbent from visiting beggars and drug addicts.

With the consecration of St Paul's in 1888, the Bishop of St Asaph, the Rt.Rev. Joshua Hughes, set about creating the new parish of Colwyn Bay. It was his intention that Venables Williams, vicar of Llandrillo, should hold both livings, but the bishop died during the negotiations. His successor, Alfred George Edwards (later to become the first Archbishop of Wales) had different ideas, under which a new vicar, independent of Llandrillo, would be installed at Colwyn Bay.

Understandably, perhaps, this move annoyed the people of Llandrillo, whose endeavours had established the new church. In April 1893 the House of Commons ordered the publication of all correspondence on the matter. This document reveals the bitterness which by then surrounded the controversy. A petition opposing the separation was signed by John Porter and Daniel Allen (churchwardens) and 582 parishioners, and sent to the Ecclesiastical Commissioners. Venables Williams also wrote a personal letter to Queen Victoria.

With greater foresight than his opponents, Bishop Edwards remained adamant that Colwyn Bay should grow as a separate parish, and the Queen signed the Order in Council. The first vicar was the Rev. Hugh Roberts. The feelings of Venables Williams are preserved in a circular letter he sent to his parishioners on 25 May 1893:

"I feel very keenly and bitterly the having to give up my ministrations at St Paul's. I think the division of the parish need not have been so cruelly and relentlessly carried out (no reasons being assigned) during my life time."

During his incumbency Venables Williams raised £20,000 within Llandrillo parish for the extension of the church and his mission. When he placed the contract for St Paul's in 1887 he mortgaged all his personal securities to the builder, to meet the first instalment. A drinking fountain (now in need of repair) on Rhos-on-sea promenade records its erection by subscription *"in recognition of the many public services rendered by the Rev. W.Venables Williams, MA Oxon, JP, during the 31 years he was Vicar of Llandrillo-yn-Rhos."*

THE FIRST POLICEMAN

Over the side door leading to the floors above Liberty's bar in Station Road there is a design carved into the stonework incorporating handcuffs and the scales of justice - a reminder that when built in 1892 it was the entrance to the town's Police Station. Paradoxically, the building briefly housed two rival massage parlours in the mid-1990s!

The first known reference to crime in Colwyn Bay occurs in the Caernarvonshire Quarter Sessions file for 14 June 1552[9], when the scattered hamlets now absorbed in the town included Rhiw and Eirias. It reads: *"Elsbeth ferch Rulinge of Rywe in the county of Denbigh, the wife of Robert ap Gruffydd, yeoman, broke and entered the house of John Conowey of the town of Eirias in the county of Caernarvon, gentleman, and stole a sheet worth 3s 4d from the said John Conowey's bed."* Her subsequent punishment is lost.

The town's most famous arrest occurred in 1880 when John Jones, better known as Coch Bach y Bala, was hunted down at the Swan Inn, Mochdre. He was the most famous Welsh burglar of his era and was also skilled at escaping from custody. In December 1879 he escaped from Ruthin Prison, while awaiting trial at Merioneth Quarter Sessions. Bala policeman William Jones eventually traced him to the Swan Inn, where he was masquerading as a wealthy gentleman. He was in bed when arrested and was sent to prison for 14 years.

Denbighshire Constabulary came into being in 1840, with one Chief Constable (salary £250 a year), two superintendents (£100), three constables at 18s a week, and a further 21 constables receiving 15s a week. (There were 20 shillings in £1). It was some years later before Colwyn Bay was allocated its first constable, whose uniform comprised a blue swallow-tailed coat with brass buttons, blue trousers with a two-inch wide red stripe down each leg, a top-hat made of patent leather decorated with whalebone, and a baton. His beat extended from Rhos-on-sea to Llysfaen and his office, in the old carpenter's shop in Ivy Street, which had formerly served as church and chapel, was shared by the Fire Brigade and the Local Government Board. Law and order in the parish of Llandrillo-yn-Rhos was under the jurisdiction of the petty sessional division of Llanrwst until 1879, when the vicar, the Rev. Venables Williams secured transfer to the care of Abergele court.

By 1892 there had been considerable expansion in the town and a Police Station was part of a new administrative centre, incorporated in the neat row of Ruabon red brick buildings erected in a field which ran down the western side of Station Road. High on the turret of the same building one can still read the inscriptions of the other occupants: Pwllycrochan Estate office, Denbighshire County Council (law and order), the National Provincial Bank of England (now the bar) and Colwyn Bay & Colwyn Local Board. At Denbighshire Quarter Sessions, in April 1898, it was decided to make Colwyn Bay a separate petty sessional division. This was followed in 1907 by the erection of the present Police Station in Rhiw Road, with an adjoining Magistrates Court - which became one of the venues of Denbighshire Quarter Sessions until as recently as October 1971. In 1972 the ancient court of Quarter Sessions was replaced by a new Crown Court, sitting at Mold. Colwyn Bay court room was closed in 1999, and the town no longer has its own Petty Sessions. The Police Station now closes in the early evening.

In July 1971 Prince Philip, Earl of Merioneth, visited Colwyn Bay to see the new £600,000 North Wales Police Headquarters then nearing completion beside Eirias Park.

THREE PIER PAVILIONS

The present Pier Pavilion at Colwyn Bay is the third structure to bear the name. The first pile for the pier was driven on 1 June 1899, and the 360 yards long, 19-34 ft wide deck, called Victoria Pier, was officially opened exactly one year later, together with an impressive 2,400 seat Pavilion, accommodating a stage 27 feet square.

"The only amusements in Colwyn Bay are two pierrot troupes and two cinematograph houses, so that the Pavilion is practically without any opposition," said general manager W.Yates Gregory, in a pre-opening leaflet inviting *"managers of theatrical touring companies, costume concert parties, solo vocalists and instrumentalists, flying matinees and other high-class attractions to submit their vacant dates."*[10]

Adelina Patti, the Spanish-born Italian soprano from Craig-y-nos, then aged 57, was engaged for the opening concert (on 2 June 1900). She and her third husband, Baron Cederstrom, were given a civic reception at the railway station, where the platform had been covered in red carpet. A banner across Victoria Drive (now reduced to a footpath), along which the prima donna's coach proceeded to the Pavilion, proclaimed: "Welcome to the Queen of Song." She sang 30 operatic roles at Covent Garden between 1861 and 1886 - with a clause in her contract excusing her from all rehearsals

Patti was no stranger to North Wales. In 1886, as the widowed Marquise de Caux contemplating her second marriage, to Covent Garden tenor Ernest Nicolini, she entered into negotiation with John Ernest Greaves, Lord Lieutenant of Caernarvonshire, to buy Dolfriog, at Nantmor,[11] but the newlyweds settled down at Craig-y-nos, north of Swansea, where she built her famous private theatre.

Neither was she any stranger to the Pavilion's orchestra and its 81-years-old volatile French conductor, Jules Prudence Riviére. He was a friend of her elder sister Carlotta, who died in 1889. Adelina had first sung with him at Llandudno Pier Pavilion, to where he was appointed musical director in 1887, when 68 years of age.[12] In 1894 Riviére ended his stormy relationship with Llandudno Pier Company and moved along the promenade to open his own Opera House - later the Hippodrome, and long known as Catlin's Arcadia when it closed in 1994. A rival pier was part of the Riviére Opera House plan, but nothing came of it, and in 1900 he fell out with the whole of Llandudno and moved over the hill, taking his entire orchestra with him to the new Colwyn Bay Pier Pavilion.[13]

This fine Pavilion, equipped with all the luxury demanded by Victorian theatregoers, was destroyed by fire in 1922. In the following year the second Pavilion, with a reduced seating

Emblazened with the name of its 81-years-old French conductor, Jules Prudence Rivière, the first Pier Pavilion opened in 1900. Rivière died six months later. It had a luxurious 2,400-seat auditorium (below) which was totally destroyed by fire in 1922

capacity of 1,500, was built, the Pier Undertaking having been acquired in that year by the Urban Council. That Pavilion was also destroyed by fire, in 1933.

The third Pavilion was opened in 1934, with only 700 seats. Built at a cost of £16,000, and lacking any architectural merit, it had the doubtful benefit of being constructed with fire-resistant materials - many of its critics believing it should suffer the same fate as its predecessors. In 1968 Colwyn Bay Borough Council sold the pier and Pavilion to Fortes, for £59,000 - of which £29,500 was used to clear the Pier Committee's debts. Until then the Pavilion had been the venue for all the town's main public functions, including the annual mayoral luncheon, and a small municipal orchestra was maintained until the end. It was also a popular venue for many national conferences. Fortes changed the Pavilion into a dance hall and bar, and built a slot-machine arcade across the pier entrance, to end the genteel family ambience which had been part of the pier for 68 years. They sold it in 1979 to a St Asaph entrepreneur, who promptly ended any hint of the Pavilion's once refined image by engaging the Ladybirds, a Danish pop group of four girls whose dress comprised boots and G-strings – and nothing else.

By 1993 the pier was closed, its buildings were boarded up and much of the decking looked dangerously rotten, prompting Colwyn Council to give planning consent for the demolition of most of the complex, including the derelict Pavilion. The work was never carried out and in 1994 the pier was bought by Mike Paxman who, in 1995, embarked upon a five-year restoration programme. Much remains to be done.

During World War II the Government ordered the removal of the pier decking seaward of the Pavilion, as an anti-invasion protection, but the pier had never been designed to receive ships and could never have been adapted for such use, being high and dry for most of each tidal cycle.

BOD ALAW SCHOOL

A link with the opening of Colwyn Bay pier is found in the name of the Welsh junior school, opposite the gates to Eirias Park. After his arrival at Llandudno in 1887 Jules Riviére built a house in Church Walks, which he called Bod Alaw - a descriptive Welsh name roughly translating as House of Song.

His eventual disenchantment with Llandudno was such that when he took his orchestra of 42 musicians over the Little Orme to the new Colwyn Bay Pavilion, in 1900, he also moved house, taking with him the name of Bod Alaw, to the road now bearing his name: Riviére's Avenue (the Welsh equivalent of Rhodfa Riviére having recently been added to the street name plate). It was in this semi-detached glazed-brick house that Colwyn Bay's Welsh-language primary school was first opened on St David's Day, 1950, taking the name of Ysgol Bod Alaw. The name was retained when the school moved into its present premises in 1972, though no one seemed aware of its origins. Riviére's original slate nameplate still adorns one of the gateposts of his old home, where he lived only a few months, dying in December 1900. He is commemorated in the west window of Llandrillo-yn-Rhos church, and is buried in the churchyard. His widow Amy Frances Riviére died in 1930, and was buried with him.

Jules Riviére's fame began in his youth after rolling on the ground with Jacques Offenbach, on the Champs Elysées, in a fight over the rights to the services of a particular singer. His many "firsts" included a Welsh promenade concert at Covent Garden in 1873, using only Welsh music and musicians, backed up by the first bilingual Welsh/English posters outside the Royal Opera House. His soloists for that historic event included Brinley Richards (composer of *God Bless the Prince of Wales*), John Thomas (Pencerdd Gwalia, harpist to Queen Victoria), Edith Wynne (soprano), Mary Davies (soprano), Lizzie Evans (contralto), Robert Rees (the tenor Eos Morlais), and Lucas Williams (baritone).[14]

RHOS PIER

The town once possessed a second pier, which accommodated small passenger steamers. Only the entrance and ticket office now survive, converted into a shopping complex at Rhos Point, Rhos-on-sea. This pier, 1,240 yards long, was second-hand when erected in 1896 by William Horton, who had just acquired the 350 acre Rhos estate. It had first been built, some five years earlier, at Douglas, Isle of Man, stretching out to sea opposite the Villa Marina. It was demolished in 1954, after being destroyed by fire a few years earlier.

A green wreck buoy, a few hundred yards out to sea, marks the remains of the 196-ton paddle steamer *Rhos Neigr*, whose dramatic sinking was watched by 75 intending passengers gathered on Rhos pier. In terms of the number of passengers affected it was the biggest maritime accident on the North Wales coast for 77 years. The remains of the paddle wheels are exposed at very low tides.

Built in 1876 as the *Prince Leopold*, for service between Southampton and the Isle of Wight, she was renamed *Rhos Neigr* when bought in 1905 by the Colwyn Bay & Liverpool Steamship Company. Horton's company was sold in 1907, and in June 1908 the *Rhos Neigr* was bought by Captain Walter Hawthorn, of Rhyl. On 20 July 1908 she was wrecked. Capable of carrying 436 passengers, she had left Llandudno pier with 80, who had paid half-a-crown (12½p) for a return trip to Blackpool. Another 75 were waiting on Rhos pier and for all these, plus a crew of 19, there were only two small lifeboats on board. Paddling a familiar course, at 10 knots, on a calm day, the steamer was midway between Llandudno and Rhos-on-sea when Captain Smallman heard "a sudden grinding noise" from somewhere below the waterline. Going below to investigate, he found water pouring into the forward half. He ordered the sealing of all bulkheads as he headed for Rhos pier, but was 350 yards short of his destination when he

Colwyn Bay's first Pier Pavilion

Still bearing her original name Prince Leopold in this picture, the old paddle steamer had been renamed Rhos Neigr when she sank off Rhos-on-sea in 1908

realised he would never make it. Slowly turning the sluggish paddler to starboard, and sounding a continuous blast of alarm on his siren, he ran his ship aground some 200 yards from the beach. The ship's lifeboats were supplemented by two from her sister paddler, the *Rhos Trevor* (originally the *Carisbrooke*, built in 1876, later the first *St Trillo*), which happened to be anchored nearby, and all the passengers were ferried ashore.

Four hours later, at 2.30 pm, the *Rhos Neigr* refloated on the rising tide and swung round a little, but at 3 pm she suddenly dropped by the bows, and as the crew abandoned ship the stern suddenly sank to the bottom, sucking down the owner, Captain Hawthorn, who was fortunate enough to be blown to the surface in an air bubble, seconds later.[15]

Captain Smallman indignantly denied he could have struck a rock off the Little Orme, and Captain Hawthorn was equally adamant that intact paddle wheels refuted the alternative suggestion of a floating baulk of timber having been driven through the hull. The mystery remains unsolved. Captain Hawthorn's fleet ceased sailing in 1911.

ST TRILLO

Early in the 6th century a young Breton monk landed on a lonely part of the shores of Wales, at Colwyn Bay. He was Trillo, one of a band of famous missionaries led by St Cadfan, who set out from the Celtic community of north-west France to evangelise Cornwall and Wales.[16] His first necessities were a roof over his head and a supply of fresh water. In the same way as Arabs of 20th century Palestine could find fresh water by sinking a well beneath a seashore cliff, at places like modern Netanya, Trillo dug his well under what we now know as Rhos Point. Over this he built his hut, or hermit's cell, and enclosed an area of land that he could farm, to sustain himself. Such an enclosure became known in Wales as a *llan*.

Although Welsh dictionaries slavishly translate *rhos* as "marsh," one should perhaps look further afield than the Welsh language, to the Arabic *ras*, Hebrew *rosh* or Gaelic *ross*, all of which mean "headland." That would give the name Llandrillo-yn-Rhos the more plausible translation of "St Trillo's enclosure on the headland."

That was the beginning of the existing St Trillo's Chapel, the smallest church in the British Isles. Little is known about St Trillo, but the practice of these Breton hermits was to work, wherever possible, with the co-operation of the local chieftain. St Trillo's landing place suggests he was aware of the fortified camp of Maelgwn Gwynedd, still identifiable (with medieval additions) at Deganwy, then the most important community in north-west Wales. Rhos Point was both sufficiently near to acquire Maelgwn's protection, and sufficiently far to avoid too much unwelcome attention from ignorant soldiers. Trillo's signature appeared on the grant which Maelgwn made to St Kentigern at the time when the See of Bangor was created. The other signatories were St Deiniol (first Bishop of Bangor), St Grwst (who established a church at Llanrwst) and Prince Rhun ap Maelgwn (i.e. son of Maelgwn), who gave his name to Caerhun, in the Conwy Valley, on the site of the Roman fort of Conovium (which had taken its name from the river Conwy, derived from the Celtic *cyn-gwy,* meaning "chief water"). With the protection of Maelgwn, St Trillo extended his mission 50 miles inland, up the Conwy Valley and into the Upper Dee Valley, to establish a community still known as Llandrillo, between Bala and Corwen.

It is presumably to the Cistercians that we owe the survival of St Trillo's chapel. His original cell would be a mud and wattle hut, perhaps protected against the north winds with a wall of stones collected off the beach. His well became a holy site and its water was used for baptisms. It was over this well that the Cistercians built a more permanent structure, which is presumably incorporated in what we see today, probably after restoration early in the 18th century, and again by William Horton after his acquisition of the Rhos Estate in 1896. The roof is a remarkable architectural feature, but dates from Horton's restoration, with further consolidation in 1935, when the chapel was re-dedicated. However the building still looks the same as when first noted by Thomas Pennant, in 1773:

"*Saw, close to the shore, the singular little building called St Trillo's Chapel. It is oblong; has a window on each side and at the end; a small door; and a vaulted roof, paved with round stones, instead of being slated. Within is a well. On a hill, about half-a-mile distant from this chapel, is the church of St Trillo, dedicated to the same saint.*"

Trillo's well is still accessible beneath the altar, and occasional services are still held there, although there is room for a congregation of only six.

RHOS FYNACH

St Trillo's original settlement, at Rhos Point, gradually became known as Rhos Fynach, meaning "monk's promontory," a description handed down through the centuries until committed to paper in the reign of Llywelyn the Great. In a charter dated 1230 Llywelyn authorised his steward, Ednyfed Fychan, to purchase "the land at Ros Venych" together with its wood, grazings, paths, waters and all easements on sea and land. Thus it was called Rhos Fynach prior to the land's becoming the property of the Cistercian monks whose abbey Llywelyn had founded at Conwy (on the site of the parish church). At about this time either Ednyfed or the monks built a farmhouse close to St Trillo's chapel.

By 1575 Rhos Fynach had lapsed into royal ownership and formed part of the Lordship of Denbigh, which Queen Elizabeth gave to Robert Dudley, Earl of Leicester. He, in 1577, sold Rhos Fynach and adjoining lands and fishing waters for 6d (2½p) to a distinguished master mariner called Morgan ab John ap David.[17] Captain Morgan was the ancestor of Thomas

A Brief History

Rhos Fynach before restoration

Parry whose initials, and date 1717, are inscribed on a tablet forming part of one of the exterior walls, presumably inserted after extensive refurbishment. It was officially listed as a building of historic or architectural importance by 1972, when its then owners, Colwyn Bay Borough Council, sought permission to demolish Rhos Fynach. Fortunately the building survived, and it is now a popular restaurant and bar, after major restoration in 1993.

FISHING WEIR

No description of Rhos Fynach would be complete without reference to the ancient fishing weir at this spot. Although it was allowed to go to ruin during the 1914-18 World War, this weir is one of the few specifically exempted from the provisions of an 1861 Act abolishing all sea fishing weirs - known as "fixed engines" - established after the Magna Charta of 1215. The case for the Rhos Fynach exemption was argued and won before a special commission that sat at Conwy in 1867.

St Trillo may have built the first weir. It was a plentiful source of food for the Cistercian monks, and was presumably the "fishing waters" mentioned in the sale of 1575. On every tenth tide the catch was given to Llandrillo-yn-Rhos church, in the proportions of three-quarters to the absent sinecure rector and one quarter to the resident vicar. This tithing was commuted to an annual payment of £640 to the Bishop of St Asaph, midway through the 19th century. The weir was a source of entertainment for visitors well into the last century, and 10 tons of mackerel were taken on a single tide in 1907. The greatest recorded catch of herrings on any one tide was 35,000. An 8-ft shark was trapped in the weir in 1865, and displayed at Llandudno market. Though no longer identifiable, the weir and its rights are vested in Conwy County Borough Council.

NONCONFORMITY

Nonconformity[18] in what became the borough of Colwyn Bay appears to date back to 1772, when a Calvinistic Methodist preacher from South Wales began holding services at Mochdre - where a chapel was built in 1778. In the actual town of Colwyn Bay the start of Nonconformity can be traced back to 1847 when regular Sunday schools were held in a thatched roof cottage known as Ty'n-y-ffordd, located in Abergele Road, opposite the present junction with Belgrave Road. The Presbyterian Sunday School at Ty'n-y-ffordd continued until work started on Hebron C.M. chapel, at Old Colwyn, in 1861. In 1871 a group of people began holding services in a carpenter's shop in Ivy Street, and shortly afterwards John Pender, purchaser of the Pwllycrochan Estate, gave land for a chapel, on condition English services were held there. This chapel opened in 1873 on Conwy Road, opposite Woodland Road West. Its services were bilingual until 1879, when the Welsh members opened their own chapel, Engedi, in Woodland Road West.

A new English Presbyterian Chapel was built at the junction of Conwy Road and Hawarden Road in 1891. The original chapel of 1873, built at a cost of £700 on a site valued at £100, was sold for £1,800 for conversion into livery stables - such was the rapid increase in land values in the new town. Hermon Chapel, Brompton Avenue, was opened in 1904. Sion Chapel had been opened in Upper Colwyn Bay in 1895, Bethlehem in Lawson Road in 1897, Rhiw Road Chapel in 1902, and Penrhyn Bay in 1906.

The first Wesleyan Methodist chapel in the area opened at Bron-y-nant, in 1809. The cause opened its first town centre chapel in Greenfield Road, in 1876, followed by Horeb, in Rhiw Road, in 1900. The Welsh Methodist Circuit also has Bethesda (Old Colwyn), Seion (Bron-y-nant) and Disgwylfa (Penmaenrhos). English Methodism in the town dates back to 1882 when the foundation stone for the ornate pseudo-episcopalian style St John's church was laid. The architect was Robert Curwen. Only the Manse, the ornate lych-gate and walls surrounding the grounds had been completed when funds ran out. The site remained in this sorry state for many years, and was known for miles around as "Wesley's Folly." In 1887 there was another stone-laying ceremony, for the church itself. It opened in the following year, complete with spire. Both within and without it could be mistaken for an Anglican church. Nant-y-glyn English Methodist church was opened in 1905. Its roof, terra-cotta tracery and Ruabon brick walls are all the same shade of red.

The Congregationalist cause was founded in the area in 1804, when services were held in an Old Colwyn cottage known as Bryn-y-gwynt. English and Welsh Congregationalists combined in 1878 to erect a corrugated iron chapel on the site of the present Union Church, in Abergele Road. In 1882 there was a formal separation of the two churches, but they continued to use the same building for another three years. The Welsh built Salem, higher up the road, in 1885, and the English proceeded to build the present Union Church.

Welsh Baptists opened a small chapel in Church Walks, Old Colwyn, in 1862. An English Baptist church was formed in 1884, using Calfaria Welsh church. In 1888 Welsh Baptists opened Tabernacl chapel, in Abergele Road, Colwyn Bay, and the English worshippers followed them from Old Colwyn, opening their own temporary chapel in 1893 in Abergele Road (near Erw Wen Road). The present Baptist building at the corner of Hawarden Road and Princes Drive was opened in 1913, after a short interim period during which services were held in the early cinema on the site of the first Presbyterian place of worship in Abergele Road. Colwyn Bay's English Baptists united with the English Congregationalists in 1946 to form the United Reformed Church.

ROMAN CATHOLICISM

Until the turn of this century Roman Catholicism in Colwyn Bay was part of the Llandudno Mission district, founded in 1868 with one priest, Father P.Mulligan, whose parish contained 27 members, dispersed between Bangor and Rhyl, and southwards to Dolgellau.[19] Mass was celebrated in a private house in Rhiw Road, and later in two hotels, and a resident priest was appointed in 1895. Three years later the foundation stone for St Joseph's church was laid by Dr Mostyn, Bishop of Menevia, and the new church opened in 1900, when it was placed in charge of the Oblates of Mary Immaculate. In 1905 the church of the Convent of Sisters of Mercy was founded in Old Colwyn. The Roman Catholic school opened in 1933.

Speaking in Welsh to a huge international congregation, including Rome's entire Diplomatic Corps (and this author, reporting for the *Daily Post*) at the Vatican's enormous St Peter's cathedral, in 1987, Pope John Paul II beatified the Venerable William Davies, of Groes-yn-Eirias, Colwyn Bay, a priest who was hanged, drawn and quartered at Beaumaris Castle in 1593. He was arrested at Holyhead while trying to escape to Ireland after his secret printing press had been discovered in a cave on the Little Orme. The cave still exists, with evidence of its 16th century use as a workshop, but access is not recommended for anyone other than properly equipped climbers. It was here that the first book in the Welsh language, a religious tract called *Y Drych Cristionogawl* (The Christian Mirror) was printed in 1585. Beatification is the first step towards canonisation as a saint of the Roman Catholic church, a process which might span several centuries.

EDNYFED FYCHAN & LLYS EURYN

Never seen by most of the residents of Colwyn Bay, the impressive ruined shell of Llys Euryn, home of Ednyfed Fychan, ancestor (via the Tudors) of the present Royal family, stands on the lower slopes of Bryn Euryn, the 429 ft high hill which dominates the town. A few yards west of the northern end of Tan-y-bryn Road, a recently erected plaque marks the start of a footpath (through a jungle of brambles) leading to the ruins.

It was on this hill that the earliest inhabitants of Colwyn Bay built their fortified camp, long before the arrival of the Romans. Their fortifications, enclosing an area of $1^{1}/_{2}$ acres, can still be traced on the summit. Numerous discoveries of Roman coins on Bryn Euryn, including an urn-full found in 1902, indicate either long-term occupation and trading by the natives or short-term Roman military use of the site.

Ednyfed Fychan's name might be translated as "Little Bold Eagle." He made an early reputation as a soldier and in his youth was reputed to have taken part in the Third Crusade. By 1210 he was a commander in the army of Llywelyn the Great and distinguished himself against the invading army of King John of England, earning himself a new coat of arms depicting the severed heads of three warriors decapitated in battle. Originally called Saxons' heads, they were later attributed to Ednyfed's crusading days and described as Saracen victims of his sword, to avoid upsetting the English court which his family was destined to rule.

In 1215 Ednyfed became the seneschal - or prime minister - to Llywelyn, and thereafter figured prominently in the affairs of Wales. He was present at Gloucester in 1218 for the signing of a treaty between Llywelyn and Henry III. Following Llywelyn's death in 1240 Ednyfed became adviser to Prince David. Ednyfed died in 1246 and was said to have been buried at Llandrillo-yn-Rhos. The eighth direct male descendant of Ednyfed became Henry VII, founder of the Tudor dynasty, thus fulfilling an ancient prophecy that a Welshman would some day sit on the throne of England.

All that remains of Llys Euryn are three walls and a massive chimney rising from a huge fire place of majestic proportions. There are no windows but a series of niches similar to the arrow-slits in older castles. Only one narrow door led into the fortified house. Holes to carry supporting beams for another storey can be seen in the walls. The second floor was equipped with four guarderobes - medieval lavatories. It was described in 1584 as Ednyfed Fychan's *"chiefest manor house ... a royal palace now decay'd for want of reparation"*[20]

One does not know how much of these particular ruins were familiar to Ednyfed, for the house remained in continuous habitation for some centuries, and would have been repaired, rebuilt or reinforced by different occupants, notably by Robin ap Gruffydd Goch, early in the 15th century. Robin's descendants took the surname of Conway, one of whom was prominent at the Battle of Bosworth. The Conways married into most of the famous families of North Wales. They sold Llys Euryn in 1629 to Sir Peter Mutton, of Llewenni and Llannerch, whose descendants appear to have abandoned the house early in the 18th century.[21]

Through a female line the land became the property of Whitehall Dod, and from him Sir Everard Cayley, whose names are preserved in Whitehall Road, Everard Road and Cayley Promenade. Whitehall Dod's initials are carved in stone plaques on the frontages of six houses in Rhos Road, two pairs dated 1857 and the third 1883. The family is also commemorated in names like Kenelm Road, Digby Road, Brewis Road, Brompton Avenue and Llannerch Road. Even St George's church, built in 1913 (with the tower added in 1965) and St George's Road, derive their names from the estate - commemorating Sir George Cayley, of Brompton-by-Sawdon, the true pioneer of aviation, who made a model glider in 1804, later developing it for a successful flight manned by his coachman.

The summit of Bryn Euryn was refortified towards the end of 1940 when the RAF occupied the hill for one of the very early radar sites, to detect German bombers heading for the port of Liverpool from the captured French air bases in Brittany. It was the RAF who built the present guide-rail to the summit, for use in the dark when walking to and from their huts lower down, of which the concrete bases still survive. One of the bored airmen shot and killed himself playing Russian roulette, a bizarre barrack room game in which each player spins a revolver chamber containing only one round (instead of six) before placing the gun to his head and squeezing the trigger.

LLANDRILLO CHURCH

Originally the mother church of a huge parish anciently known as Dinerth, the ministrations of Llandrillo-yn-Rhos are now confined to Rhos-on-sea. The present church is believed to incorporate the earlier private chapel of Ednyfed Fychan, visible in the north wall. The south aisle was added by the ladies of the Conway family, at Llys Euryn, in the 16th century. They also left money with which the unusual tower was built, matched in North Wales only by Llanbeblig church, in Caernarfon, though the Irish architectural practice of stepped battlements and watchtower were adapted in more modern form for St Paul's church, in Colwyn Bay, and later for Bryn-y-maen church, probably as a sentimental link with the mother church.

Restoration work was undertaken in 1857, when an ancient five-light stained-glass east window was demolished, only two fragments surviving, and now incorporated in the vestry window. Richard Fenton described the window in 1808 as containing Ednyfed Fychan's coat of arms of *"a chevron between three helmets,"* i.e. further sublimation of the original three Saxons' heads, via three Saracens' heads, to three helmets, as the family worked its way into the London-based Establishment. Llandudno-born artist Hugh Hughes also described the coat of arms in 1823, adding that the window contained 12 figures in different dress. Lewis, describing the window in his famous *Topographical Dictionary of Wales*, in 1848 suggested the 12 figures represented the 12 tribes of Wales, a suggestion reinforced in an 1850 observation by Sir William Glynne, that the window displayed the armorial bearings of the 12 tribes. The

A Brief History

Rustic tranquility at Rhos-on-Sea. Apart from the second (and present) Ship Inn, built in 1873, the parish church, and the old Vicarage (replaced in 1903), the scene is agricultural

present east window is an 1873 thanks offering for the recovery from illness of Edward Brookes, of Pabo.

Where Ednyfed Fychan was buried is not known. An ornately carved sarcophagus lid in the porch contains the clearly readable name of Ednyfed but is believed to relate to a pre-Reformation priest, Ednyfed ap Bleddyn, appointed in 1407. The marble altar, installed in 1948, is a memorial to William and Mary Horton. The reredos is a memorial to the dead of World War One. In 1827 a local man, Hugh Williams, was sentenced to seven years transportation to Australia for stealing the church plate.

The present Ship Inn was built in 1873 by Whitehall Dod, to replace the original inn of 1736 on the opposite side of Tan-y-bryn Road, and nearly opposite the church gates. The present vicarage was built in 1903 on land given by Sir Everard Cayley. When the houses behind the Vicarage were being built in January 1964 a perfect stone-lined well, 63 ft deep and 4 ft 6 ins in diameter, was discovered when the floor of a new integral garage, some 12 paces from the churchyard wall, collapsed overnight. The contractors filled the well and the garage was completed.

BETRAYAL OF KING RICHARD

One of the most tragic episodes in the history of the Royal family was the betrayal, at Colwyn Bay, of King Richard II, who came to the throne at the age of eleven, and died in captivity 24 years later. Richard had banished Henry Bolingbroke, Duke of Lancaster, and had seized his lands. In 1394 Richard led an army of 34,000 men on a fairly successful campaign in Ireland, culminating in a peace treaty and the knighting of the Irish chieftains. However Richard dallied in Ireland, and in his absence Bolingbroke landed in Yorkshire and enlisted the support of Percy, Earl of Northumberland, and Neville, Earl of Westmoreland.

Still in Dublin, Richard's response to Bolingbroke's march on London was to send the Earl of Salisbury to North Wales to recruit an army, with which he hoped to retain his crown. Salisbury recruited 40,000 men. They were assembled at Conwy but grew ever more restless as time went by without any sign of the King - and his promised payment. Shakespeare recorded their attitude: *"My Lord of Salisbury, we have stay'd ten days, and hardly kept our countrymen together. And yet we hear no tidings from the King; therefore we will disperse ourselves; farewell."*[22]

Despite Salisbury's plea: *"Stay yet another day, thou trusty Welshmen; the King reposeth all his confidence in thee,"* the mercenaries returned to their villages, and only a handful of troops were available to greet Richard when he arrived at Conwy, in August 1399. By that time Bolingbroke's army was nearing Chester, with the Earl of Northumberland vowing to capture the King. Northumberland placed his army in ambush at Penmaenhead and rode to Conwy with only five men.

Fortunately for history Richard was accompanied by a French knight called Creton, whose written description of subsequent events is now preserved at the British Museum. On arriving at Conwy castle Northumberland begged the King's pardon, offering peace in return for the restoration of his Lancastrian lands and office of Chief Justice of England. Left with no alternative, Richard and Northumberland went to the garrison chapel for mass and afterwards swore before the altar to keep the terms of their treaty.

Thus feeling secure, Richard and the Earl of Salisbury left Conwy with 23 followers, bound for Rhuddlan. Northumberland had travelled ahead and Creton records that as the King's party crossed over Penmaenhead they were met and surrounded by Northumberland's cavalry. *"I am betrayed,"* said the King, who was taken in captivity to Flint castle, where he later met Bolingbroke - soon to be crowned as Henry IV. Richard died mysteriously at Pontefract castle in the following year. The new King Henry rewarded Northumberland by giving him the Isle of Man, restoring him as Chief Justice of England, and appointing him constable of the castles at Chester, Flint, Conwy and Caernarfon.

ROYAL VISITS

Colwyn Bay's first royal visitor of modern times was Princess Victoria, in 1832, five years before she ascended the throne. Accompanied by her mother, the Duchess of Kent, she was returning to London by horse and carriage after a brief holiday at Plas Newydd, home of the Marquess of Anglesey - during which she had attended the National Eisteddfod at Beaumaris. The royal carriage stopped at the Ship Inn, Old Colwyn, to rest and water the horses for the long haul over Penmaenhead. It was said that during the stop the young princess was taken to nearby Maes Cadwgan farm, where she drank a glass of milk. As the carriage descended on the other side of Penmaenhead the princess was met by the same sight as that which had met Richard II in 1399 - a squadron of cavalry. They were men of the Denbighshire Yeomanry who had ridden out to escort her to Abergele, where the carriage horses were changed. A salute of 21 guns was fired from Abergele Vicarage as the party entered the town.

David, Prince of Wales, briefly visited the town on 2 November 1923, during his North Wales tour in support of the unemployed ex-Servicemen of World War I, some of whose experiences he had shared. He reigned briefly as King Edward VIII before abdicating to marry an American divorcee with whom he went into exile as the Duke of Windsor.

Queen Elizabeth II, Countess of Merioneth, accompanied by the Duke of Edinburgh, was driven through the town in 1953, during her Coronation tour of Wales. She next visited the town on 16 March 1984 to open the Royal Welch Fusiliers' new Territorial Army company drill hall in Groes Road.

David, Prince of Wales, visited Colwyn Bay in 1923, during his tour in support of umemployed ex-Servicemen of World War I

Left: The civilian in the background, with bow tie and Charlie Chaplin moustache (talking to Major Ivan Edwards Evans, a local solicitor) is Sir Henry Morris-Jones, a local GP who served in the war as a medical officer. He was elected Liberal MP for Denbighshire in 1929 and used his political influence to obtain a charter of incorporation for grouping Colwyn Bay, Llysfaen, Mochdre and Brynymaen to create the Borough of Colwyn Bay in 1934. He retired from politics in 1950 and was elected an Honorary Freeman of Colwyn Bay in 1956. He was the last surviving freeman when he died in 1972

Princess Margaret, Countess of Snowdon (sister of the Queen), was one of eight family mourners at Colwyn Bay Crematorium on 29 January 1966, for the funeral of her father-in-law, Ronald Armstrong-Jones, QC, of Plas Dinas, near Caernarfon. The other mourners were Lord Snowdon (formerly Antony Armstrong-Jones); former air hostess Mrs Jenifer Armstrong-Jones, third wife of Ronald; Tom Unite, brother of Jenifer; Viscount and Viscountess de Vesci, her being Lord Snowdon's sister Susan Anne, both being children of the Countess of Ross, the first of Ronald's wives; and the Hon. Sir Denys and Lady Buckley, her being Ronald's sister Gwendolen Jane. On their way back to Caernarfon Princess Margaret stopped briefly at the Station Hotel, Llandudno Junction, to use the toilet. Princess Margaret returned to Colwyn Bay on 12 May 1981 to open the new leisure centre in Eirias Park.

Charles, Prince of Wales, visited Colwyn Bay Civic Centre on 5 August 1969. He again visited the town on 11 July 1980, to open the new science laboratory at Penrhos College, then celebrating its centenary. The most disappointed pupil of the day was Princess Marie of Romania, aged 15, who was not among those singled out to meet the Prince. "We treat her like an ordinary pupil," said the headmaster. The Princess told the author she had not had an opportunity to meet Prince Charles since she was 10, when she was at Windsor Castle with her parents, who normally lived in Switzerland.

Prince Philip, Duke of Edinburgh and Earl of Merioneth, consort of the Queen, flew his own helicopter into Rhos-on-sea on 23 June 1965, to open (officially) Llandrillo Technical College. Next day the Duke again flew his helicopter to Colwyn Bay (from Llandudno), landing in Eirias Park to attend a rally of Denbighshire and Flintshire participants in the Duke of Edinburgh Award Scheme. Afterwards the Duke visited the Civic Centre and had lunch in a marquee at the rear. Prince Philip returned on 23 July 1971 to discuss progress on the construction of the new North Wales Police headquarters. "Meet the Joneses," said Chief Constable Philip Myers, as the Duke inspected a guard of honour of 22 constables, a sergeant and an inspector, all named Jones - with another 114 Joneses in reserve on the nominal roll. Mr Myers later became one of HM Inspectors of Constabulary and was knighted.

On 8 June 1960 the Duke of Gloucester, brother of the Duke of Windsor, visited Colwyn Bay to lay the foundation stone for the extension to the town library of 1905. He was accompanied by the Duchess of Gloucester who afterwards visited the Colwyn Bay & West Denbighshire Hospital, in Hesketh Road, while the Duke opened the new Colwyn Bay Cricket Club.

THE FLAGSTAFF - ECCENTRIC'S PARADISE

THE Welsh Mountain Zoo is far more than a collection of animals. Before becoming a zoo the 37-acre wooded Flagstaff estate was shrouded in mystery, a place rarely seen after the 1909 proclamation of the following year's National Eisteddfod at Colwyn Bay. The Gorsedd circle for that event dominates a knoll now used for falconry displays, and is just one of the zoo's many unusual facets.

When the Gorsedd returned to Colwyn Bay in 1910 Archdruid Dyfed apologised for the circle's distance from the pavilion.[23] "The Gorsedd events of Eisteddfod week will therefore be held on Rydal fields," he said, adding: *"But the stones placed for last year's proclamation at Y Fanerig will remain for ever, a memorial to the Colwyn Bay National Eisteddfod."* Fanerig is a translation that has probably not been heard since, for what older residents still describe as The Flagstaff, a name dating from 1887, when Mochdre tithe rioters used it to signal the approach of police and troops.

It was in the 1890s that Dr Walter Whitehead, of Manchester, then in his 50s, thought he had found himself a bride and set about planning a home for her on the 37-acre Flagstaff estate. Professor Thomas H.Mawson, designer of some of the world's most famous gardens, and his architectural partner Dan Gibson, were commissioned to develop the site. Their 1898 plan shows a large house at the end of a 400-yards long drive. Although the drive and gardens are still there, the house was never built. Legend has it that when the bride-to-be was brought to survey the site of her future home she was frightened by the eeriness of the remote and lonely spot, and fled back to the more familiar streets of Manchester. For whatever reason, Dr Whitehead never married and never built his mansion. Instead he moved into the gatehouse, now the zoo office, the only part built of Gibson's grand plan. Mawson said in his memoirs that Dr Whitehead swindled them of their fees.

The Italian gardens, rockeries and lily ponds were designed by a Llandudno Junction gardener, William Lee, who spent 27 years on the estate after Dr Whitehead's death in 1913. A plaque on the bridge over Lee's lily pond commemorates the zoo's founder, Robert Jackson, who was killed in 1969 when a tree fell on him while he was fishing.

Another feature one does not expect to find in a zoo is the doctor's tomb. Not very obvious, it is beside the path beyond the present penguin pool. It records he was president of the BMA in 1903 and was nearly 73 when he died. The tomb contains a casket of his ashes together with those of a nameless eccentric German, who shared Whitehead's home in the gatehouse, and predeceased him. The German's ashes were originally kept in a marble urn in Dr Whitehead's study. A similar urn was made for the doctor's ashes after his death.[24] The men built what was meant to represent the bridge of a ship, complete with portholes, wall bunks and mast - and a large wine cellar. Wearing sailor's caps, they would spend hours together, surveying the then very busy Liverpool Bay with telescopes. Part of their fantasy survives in what is now the Lookout Cafe.

Colwyn Bay Borough Council bought the estate for £8,500 in 1955, using it as a nursery and public park. In 1962 it was leased to the Jackson family for conversion into the Welsh Mountain Zoo, which opened in the following year.

COLWYN BAY AT WAR

Colwyn Bay's biggest contribution to World War II was in providing a home for the Ministry of Food but the town's war began on 2 September 1939, some 24 hours before Britain formally declared war on Germany. On that day thousands of pathetic Liverpool children arrived by train, each with a bag of belongings and a cardboard box containing a gas mask - in which the principal filters were made of deadly asbestos! The children were dispersed throughout the borough, and Blackburn House School, from Liverpool, was integrated with the local grammar school. They had been evacuated as a precaution against enemy air attack, an eventually that did not occur until the following year - by which time many of the children had returned to Liverpool. Never very popular in certain parts of the town, most of the remainder were moved elsewhere, to make room for civil servants.

A battalion of the Royal Welch Fusiliers also arrived on the same day, apparently with orders to requisition anything green - they took possession of all parks, bowling greens and playing fields as potential tent sites. Sentries were posted at the gates of Eirias Park while their comrades were taught obsolete strategy within.

Then came the blitzkrieg and the evacuation from Dunkirk, and the raising of the Local Defence Volunteers, or LDV, later renamed Home Guard. Each volunteer was equipped with a Canadian rifle which he kept propped in a corner in his home, usually with a full magazine of bullets. It was the period of the Fifth Column scare and a genuine belief that the Netherlands had been captured by German paratroopers disguised as nuns. In those days all nuns wore gowns down to their feet and many an innocent sister was followed home to her convent by a suspicious Home Guardsman - whose brief instruction leaflet told them how to say "Hands

Spitfire P8529 was named "Borough of Colwyn Bay" in recognition of the town's investment in National Savings during Wings for Victory week, It crashed in Scotland during a training flight in 1943

The former infantry Drill Hall in Princes Drive — a couple of hundred yards west of the artillery drill hall.

up!" in German. The story is told of one Old Colwyn nun who had a difficult time explaining why she obeyed such a command; it just so happened that German was one of the many languages in which she was fluent.

As a precaution against invasion and enemy seizure of the BBC's facilities, with which to begin controlling the country, a secret studio was built on the first floor, first room on the right, of 5 Penrhyn Buildings, Princes Drive. It would have been linked, in an emergency, to one of the BBC's stock of portable "H Group" low power (100 W) transmitters, with an aerial hidden in the roof. The author, who spent the early war years with the BBC, rediscovered the studio, still with microphone suspended from the ceiling, in 1969 when the local Liberals rented the room as their office for the 1970 general election. They removed the baffle screening and re-equipped the glass fronted control room as a kitchen.

With more psychology than sense the decking was removed from Colwyn Bay Pier, but only from beyond the licensed bar. With that done Colwyn Bay could sit back, confident that an invasion had been thwarted. It never seemed to occur to anyone that while no ship could ever tie up at the pier, the two miles of flat beaches either side might have been designed for a landing. The Pier Pavilion served as an Army gymnasium during the winter but was released each summer for holiday variety shows.

Colwyn Bay was never bombed deliberately but it was straddled with a stick of bombs jettisoned from a damaged Heinkel 111 on its death dive towards the Conwy Valley. These bombs exploded at intervals through the full length of the town but each one fell on open ground, and there were no casualties. Drifting sea mines caused many scares, and buildings along the seafront would be evacuated as the progress of each one was observed. Some were exploded by rifle fire, and others drifted ashore where they were defused.

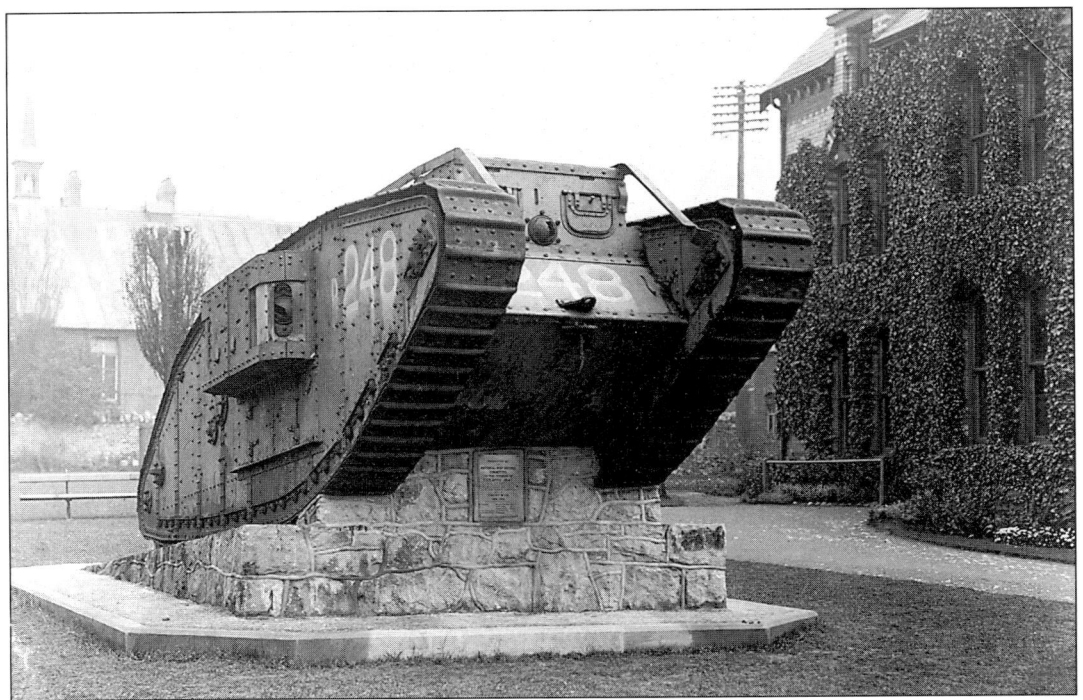

A specimen of the world's first tank — a relic of World War I. It stood beside the then Town Hall, at the junction of Coed Pella Road and Conway Road, from 1920 to 1937.

Colwyn Bay Civil Defence Corps never lacked volunteers who regularly relieved their colleagues during the sustained attack on Liverpool, then the country's main port for the vital Battle of the Atlantic. The local Auxiliary Fire Service also went to Liverpool to support their city colleagues.

Slaters garage, in Conwy Road, was used for the assembly of thousands of Jeeps, the versatile military vehicle whose original name (now a manufacturer's registered trade name) was simply a corruption of the American Army letters GP, an abbreviation of "general purpose." The finished vehicles were parked in long lines all over the town, awaiting collection for shipment and transportation across the world.

After Pearl Harbor a thousand men of the United States army requisitioned several houses around the then Odeon cinema, now replaced by flats at the junction of Conway Road and Marine Road. They also established a tented camp on fields behind the Glyn estate. In those days the 1,700-seat Odeon was packed with two shows a night and three on Saturdays - but none on Sundays.

MINISTRY OF FOOD

The nation's remarkably successful food rationing system during World War II was operated from Colwyn Bay by an army of 5,000 clerks. When rationing began in January 1940 the Ministry was comfortably ensconced in London, with little apparent threat from the enemy, for the BBC broadcast with daily monotony: "All is reported quiet on the Western Front." Neither were the rations of that phoney war period any great hardship, with weekly allowances of 4 ozs of bacon or ham, 12 ozs of sugar and 4 ozs of butter. Meat rationing followed in March, controlled by price instead of weight, with a weekly allowance of 1s 10d (9p in today's money), soon cut to 1s 1d, so that people could choose between quality and quantity, with no restrictions on offal. That was at a time when beef cost 1s a pound (i.e. 11p per kilogram). Later the rations were drastically reduced.

In April 1940 Lord Woolton, a non-political businessman, was appointed Minister of Food - and a month later the world was overwhelmed by Hitler's blitzkrieg and premature surrender of a bellicose France and its useless army. While the British Expeditionary Force was being rescued from the beaches of Dunkirk, Lord Woolton sent his requisitioning officers to Colwyn Bay to prepare for a very long and hungry war.

They first took over the Colwyn Bay Hotel, to serve for the duration of the war as national headquarters of the Ministry of Food. They seized Rydal School (which was evacuated to the Sychnant Pass) and Penrhos College (evacuated to Chatsworth House, in Derbyshire). They also took over 35 hotels and a shop and maisonette block. People remember train loads of thick brown government linoleum arriving in the town, some of which can still be recognised on the floors of long-since derequisitioned buildings.

By the end of June everything was ready and the whole of the Ministry of Food was evacuated to Colwyn Bay, complete with countless tons of cabinets containing a file on every person resident in the British Isles. Billeting officers knocked on doors, forcing families to give up their spare accommodation to the civil servants. St Enoch's hotel was converted into a transit hostel for men awaiting a billet - far enough away from the women's hostel at Plas-y-coed, in The Dingle. Staff canteens were opened in the Queen's Hotel (now a nursing home in Old Colwyn), the Metropole, (now flats in the town centre), and the Pwllycrochan Hotel (which now houses Rydal junior school).

There was never any need to turn the girls out of Penrhos College where, after the conversion of one fine room into the town's biggest bar, the rest of the school was used as an oversized staff club. Even the rooms used as headquarters for the 11th Denbighshire (Ministry of Food)

Battalion of the Home Guard were little more than an elitist extension of the social club, in which much-emphasised ranks like captain and major were related to the man's rank in the Ministry rather than any military prowess.

Lord Woolton kept aloof from the Ministry's social scene at Colwyn Bay and took a bedroom for the duration of war at the Station Hotel, conveniently opposite Llandudno Junction station, to facilitate his frequent rail journeys to London, where he had retained a small office. He would also travel by train to his Colwyn Bay office, linked by a special trackside short-cut path to the station.

If enemy action had severed the national telephone links, instructions for any sudden change or reduction in individual food rations would have been despatched from Colwyn Bay by carrier pigeon, to various strategic centres. The wartime pigeon loft survived until 1975, behind the now-demolished Colwyn Bay Hotel. This reliance on pigeon power led to a strange military expedition in 1941, when a hand-picked posse of men from the Ministry of Food Home Guard, armed with shotguns and a couple of rifles, were taken to the Great Orme, at neighbouring Llandudno, to hunt down and eliminate one of Britain's rarest birds - the peregrine falcon. Great Orme falcons were the finest in the land, and the source of the royal hunting cast kept by Queen Elizabeth I and her successors. According to the famous laws of Prince Hywel Dda (circa AD 940) the chief falconer was fourth in rank in his court. Unfortunately the peregrine's favourite food was a tasty pigeon.

Food rationing continued for some years after the war, but the Ministry gradually drifted back to London after 1945. The once mighty legion of ration administrators was down to a mere 130 when the last department - the Bakery Finance Division - left the town on 29 September 1956.

COLWYN BAY'S OWN REGIMENT

In 1946 the Honorary Freedom of the Borough of Colwyn Bay was granted to the 61st (Caernarvon & Denbigh Yeomanry) Medium Regiment, Royal Artillery, who occupied one of two drill halls then in Princes Drive. Long since disbanded, this Territorial Army regiment traced its traditions back to 1795, via the Wrexham Yeomanry Cavalry of that year; renamed Denbighshire Yeomanry Cavalry in 1820; Denbighshire Hussars in 1885; 24th Denbighshire Yeomanry Battalion Royal Welch Fusiliers in 1916; 61st (Caernarvon & Denbigh Yeomanry) Medium Brigade, Royal Garrison Artillery in 1920; and 61st (Caernarvon & Denbigh Yeomanry) Medium Regiment, RA, in 1939. In its infantry role during World War One the regiment was awarded eight battle honours: Egypt 1916-17, Gaza, Jericho, Tel Asur, Jerusalem, Palestine 1917-18, France & Flanders 1918, and Ypres 1918.

Shortly after the regiment was given the Freedom of the town, for its service at Dunkirk, Normandy and Western Europe in World War Two, it was merged with the 69th (Caernarvon & Denbigh Yeomanry) Medium Regiment, to become 361 (Caernarvon & Denbigh Yeomanry) Medium Regiment, RA, which in 1956 was merged with 384 (Royal Welch Fusiliers) Light Regiment, RA, to form 372 (Flintshire & Denbighshire Yeo) Light Regiment, RA, now disbanded. Colwyn Bay was the headquarters of both the 61st and 361st Regiments.

Colwyn Bay had also been the home, since 1908, of a company of the 4th Battalion, Royal Welch Fusiliers, who occupied the other drill hall in Princes Drive. This latter unit had regimental traditions dating back to 1689, via the Denbighshire Rifle Volunteer Corps of 1860, which became the 1st Volunteer Battalion RWF in 1884. On the formation of the Territorial Army, in 1908, it was renamed the 4th (Denbighshire) Battalion RWF. It was one of the first TA units to land in France in November 1914, and gained its first battle honour - Givenchy - in January 1915. In 1939 the 8th Bn RWF was formed out of the 4th. It fought with the 53rd Welsh Division from Normandy into Germany, and was in Hamburg on the day the German army surrendered. From 1971 the local infantry traditions were preserved within the 3rd (Volunteer) Bn, RWF, with a new drill hall in Groes Road – now part of the new pan-Wales Royal Welch Regiment, founded in 1999 by merging the Territorial Army units of both the Royal Welch Fusiliers (23rd Foot) and the Royal Regiment of Wales (24th/41st Foot). There is no Regular Army equivalent of the Royal Welch Regiment.

THE ERA OF THE TRAMS

To the strains of Auld Lang Syne and a cacophony of motor horns, fireworks and hand-bells, the last tram of Llandudno & Colwyn Bay Electric Railway Ltd (also the last company-owned tram in Britain) left Llandudno for Colwyn Bay at 10.30 pm on Saturday 24 March 1956.

It was an open-top double-deck ex-Bournemouth 1925 type, carrying 50 invited passengers, among whom the author was privileged to be present. The company secretary, Mr D.Baker, told the guests, during a reception at the Imperial Hotel, prior to the last journey, that the trams had carried more than 130 million passengers, an average of 2,653,061 per year.

"Unfortunately the popularity of the trams has waned during the winter months, and the fall in revenue has made it necessary to change to buses," he said, adding that the Light Railway Transport League had raised £10,000 towards a fund designed to persuade the company to retain the trams. The last fare-paying passenger tram ran a few minutes before the final car, and enthusiasts fought for a place. This was a single-deck type, which was stripped of seats, destination boards, straps, signal bells and other souvenirs by the time it arrived at Colwyn Bay.[25] Next day the remaining trams at the Rhos-on-sea depot were sold for £150 each, two being bought by the British Transport Commission Museum, in Norwood.

The present concrete surface in Penrhyn Avenue, Rhos-on-sea, is a memorial to that weekend. Fearing the company would simply abandon its track (which it did for the most part), Colwyn Bay Borough Council had demanded that in terminating its service the company should either pay compensation for reinstatement or leave the track-bed in its original state. The discussions had been exceedingly acrimonious and the company had the last laugh, by tearing the rails and sleepers out of Penrhyn Avenue, which had been a field when the track was laid. The company's dramatic gesture made the road quite unusable and concrete was the quickest solution.

The colourful history of the Colwyn Bay trams began in 1894, when many companies were formed in quick succession, with the declared aim of providing a more direct link with Llandudno than that provided by the London & North Western Railway Company, via Llandudno Junction. These companies went into liquidation almost as quickly as they were formed. One, the Llandudno & Colwyn Bay Light Railway Company obtained a Light Railway Order in 1898 and got as far as placing a contract for the Llandudno-Rhos section, of what was envisaged as a 21-mile track to Prestatyn, but the work was never commenced. In 1906 the Llandudno & Colwyn Bay Electric Traction Company Ltd was formed and began laying track in Llandudno. It was superseded in the same year by the Caernarvonshire Electric Traction Syndicate Ltd, who proposed extending the route to Deganwy. Both companies collapsed.

Undaunted, Llandudno & District Electric Tramway Construction Company Ltd was also formed in 1906, with the intention of running both passenger and goods vehicles. They laid nearly five miles of 3ft 6ins gauge track from Llandudno's West Shore to Rhos-on-sea, and carried their first passengers on 19 October 1907. The company had acquired a fleet of 14 single-deck 42-seat cars - one of which was still in use on the day the trams stopped running in 1956. The Board of Trade required special braking arrangements to be fitted to these trams because of the potential hazard of the 1:11 gradient over the Little Orme.

These cars were painted maroon and cream, changed in 1931 to green and cream, to avoid confusion with the maroon and cream livery which the predatory London, Midland & Scottish

A Brief History

Original 1907 tram cars are seen in the views (left) — on Penrhyn Hill, on the Upper Cayley Promenade, and at Penrhynside - and above, showing the car on what is now the down lane of Penrhyn Hill. The up lane was excavated out of the rock in 1921, between the tram track and the ancient horse track, which still exists.

Railway Company had imposed on a rival bus company (Crosville) in which it had acquired a financial stake.

In 1907 the company began extending its track from Rhos-on-sea to the top of Station Road, in Colwyn Bay. This was a major factor in the development of the town. It is now difficult to appreciate that the area surrounding the tram sheds, in Penrhyn Avenue, was then known as the Klondyke. In November of that year a Board of Trade inquiry was held at Colwyn Bay to hear the company's case for extending its service to the Queen's Hotel, Old Colwyn. The main objection was the narrowness of the road, but the service commenced on 26 March 1915. This extension remained in use until 21 September 1930, when the route was terminated at the top of Greenfield Road. The company changed its name in 1909.

One of the most popular features was the open "toast-rack" class of car, each seating 70 passengers, introduced at the end of World War One, and which remained in use until 1955. The conductor collected his fares by walking up and down a footboard running the full length of the car, on the outside – in those carefree days before the Health & Safety Executive.

It was not until 1930 that the local authorities gave permission for a limited tram service on Sundays - after a well attended public meeting had voted in favour of a limited Sunday bus service proposed by Crosville Motor Services Ltd. A year later the company prepared plans to meet the omnibus competition with trolley-buses, but abandoned the scheme because of the cost of surfacing considerable sections of track running on grassland.

Second-hand single-deck cars from Accrington were introduced in 1932, and open top double-deckers from Bournemouth in 1936. Before the double-deck cars could be put into use the Board of Trade ruled that a wind-speed gauge should be erected on the exposed coastal strip between Rhos-on-sea and Penrhyn Bay (the present high sea wall not being built until 1955). Whenever the wind speed reached 50 mph all upper deck passengers had to be moved downstairs.

Wartime evacuation of the Ministry of Food to Colwyn Bay and Inland Revenue to Llandudno gave the trams a much-needed boost, and with an eye to further improvement the company bought two streamlined all-metal double-deckers from Darwen Corporation in 1946. Alas the Board of Trade ruled they could not be used either on Penrhyn Hill or the exposed coastal section at Penrhyn Bay, and the cars were sold 18 months later.

The trams were replaced by second-hand double-deck well-worn buses in 1956, and the company was immediately forced into operating an uneconomic 10-minute service to match the competition of a fleet of brand new buses put on the route by the then nationalised giant Crosville Motor Services Ltd - to whom the Llandudno & Colwyn Bay Electric Railway Company sold its stage carriage licences for £40,000 in May 1961, before going into liquidation in November of that year.

RHOS TOLLGATE

Writing to the author in 1959, Mr D.R.Baker, company secretary of Llandudno & Colwyn Bay Electric Railway, said: *"This company has never achieved financial success and it has almost never paid a dividend to its shareholders. But over the years it has maintained a valuable public service, looked after its staff and met its obligations."*

He was defending the company's operation of a tollgate at the Rhos-on-sea end of the coast road beside the golf course, along which the trams used to run. The tollgate's origins are recalled in the name of a nearby house - The Old Budget Gate. Local landowner William Horton was a well-known litigant, who had allowed the tram company to lay its track along the shore in 1907. This also created an unsurfaced track which the new motorcars and other traffic began using as a free alternative to the parallel toll road (Llandudno Road) leading to Penrhyn Bay – where the present beauty salon occupies the site of the old toll-bar and petrol shop.

We know the coastal alternative was already a well-established route from a 1687 law suit concerning the ancient tidal port of Aber Cerrig Gwynion - now in the garden of Odstone, the house on Rhos-on-sea golf course. The suit was caused by the erection of a bridge across the neck of the harbour, which would then have been the outlet for the Afon Ganol. Thus an obvious time-honoured right of way existed long before Horton bought the land, but he cared little for such niceties. A plaque in the garden of Odstone reminds us it was from Aber Cerrig Gwynion that Prince Madoc of Gloddaeth sailed in 1170, with his ships *Corn Gwynant* and *Pedr Sant,* to land at Mobile, Alabama, and thus discover America 322 years before the better publicised voyage of Christopher Columbus - though the Norwegians say the Vikings got there long before Madoc.

In 1908 David Lloyd George introduced his Old Age Pensions Act which provided five shillings (25p) a week for the over-seventies, with $37^{1}/_{2}$p for couples. When asked how he proposed to finance the pensions Lloyd George replied: *"I have no nest-eggs. I am looking for someone else's hen-roost to rob next year."* Horton retaliated against the anticipated increased taxes by erecting what he called his Budget Gate, and declaring: *"Lloyd George is not going to rob my nest!"* He sold the road, complete with tollgate, to the tram company in 1911. The company continued to collect the toll until it went into liquidation in 1961. The liquidators continued to collect the tolls until 1963 when Llandudno Urban Council and Colwyn Bay Borough Council combined to buy the 570 yards of road and give it its first proper surface.

When the toll house - still with its Board of Trade 1936 anemometer - was demolished in 1963 its notice board displayed the charges, demanding a penny for passage with a perambulator, light handcart or pedal-cycle, although pedestrians and cyclists had been able to avoid paying since 1956 by walking along the footpath incorporated in the sea wall. Cars were charged a shilling (5p), as was a cart drawn by one horse, but a two-horse cart was charged $7^{1}/_{2}$p.[26]

LLANELIAN

Not quite within the grasp of Colwyn Bay's urban sprawl, the ancient village of Llanelian manages to retain its rural identity. It was originally part of Llandrillo parish. Its first name, recorded as long ago as 1291, was the township of Bodlennyn, and its church is dedicated to St Hilary (or Eleri), yet its name centres upon St Elian - for all the wrong reasons.

Tradition has it that having taken ill while walking just north of the present village, in the ancient township of Eirias, Elian prayed for water, and a spring appeared. In gratitude Elian prayed that henceforth this well might be the means of granting the wishes of any who asked in faith. But man may wish for good or evil, and Ffynnon Elian came to be known the length and breadth of Wales as a very efficient cursing well.

The reputed properties of the well were known to Pennant in 1773, when he recorded that he had himself been threatened with a curse. The ritual involved writing the name of the person to be cursed on a piece of slate, lead or a pebble. The person buying the curse stood with this beside the well while the "priest" read passages from the Scriptures and took up a small quantity of water. Some of this was drunk by the "curser" and the remainder tossed over the sorcerer's shoulder. The ritual was repeated three times while the person desiring the curse muttered his imprecations. At the end of the ceremony the marked object was thrown into the well.[27]

By 1818 the local sorcerer was charging a shilling for a curse, and ten shillings for removing it - and was jailed for a year at Mold assizes, for obtaining money by false pretences. The well was said to be worth £300 a year in fees. There were similar prosecutions in 1820 and 1823, and the Rector destroyed the well in 1829, although the site was used for cursing as recently as 1871, and is still shown on the Ordnance Survey.

The village centrepiece is its church, restored in 1859. It comprises two parallel naves, one medieval, the other more recent - note the different styles in the two east windows. That on the south nave is in memory of John Wynn, of Coed Coch, who died in 1862; that on the north nave in memory of his wife Mary (co-heiress of John Holland), who died in 1844. The crosses were added to the gable ends in 1931. Tombstone inscriptions date from 1587 and include several of the Holland family, beginning in 1612 with Humphrey, son of Pyers Holland, founder of Kinmel.

To reach the church one has to walk across the neat little courtyard of the White Lion Inn, which is very old, though probably some 900 years younger than claimed on one of its walls! Its most famous licensee was John Parry, the bard, who was born at the nearby Y Wern, in 1770. His best-known poem was *Myfyrdod Mewn Mynment*, likened to a Welsh equivalent of Thomas Grey's *Elegy written in a country churchyard*. He was buried in Llanelian churchyard in 1820.

On the opposite side of the courtyard there is a store room for the inn, in a well-built adaptation of the old school, built in 1865 by John Lloyd Wynn, of Coed Coch, and endowed in perpetuity with the £154 proceeds of a bazaar held at Coed Coch, and invested in Delhi Railway 5% stock! Just off the square, across the road from the White Lion, Llan farm (once known as Hên Siop, or Old Shop) still has its thatched roof. Some of its internal walls (under the stairs) are of wattle and daub construction.

The benevolent influence of the Coed Coch estate (into which the Hollands married) is to be seen in the many date stones bearing the initials "CC" - though the Wynns sold the freeholds relatively recently to pay death duties. Many people remember when the then landlord, Miss Margaret "Daisy" Brodrick and her agent used to visit the White Lion every six months, to collect the rents from her tenants.

COED COCH

Architectural authors disagree as to the origins of Coed Coch. Elizabeth Beazley and Peter Howell say the elegant Grecian villa was built in 1795, to the design of Henry Hakewell, whose work includes St Peter's church in London's Eaton Square.[28] Edward Hubbard says: "With a foundation stone of 1804 in the cellar, it is unlikely to be the 'Villa in North Wales' which [Hakewell] exhibited at the Royal Academy in 1795."[29] There were alterations in the 1930s to the design of Sir Clough Williams-Ellis, who denied responsibility for the removal of the Greek Doric portico.

John Wynn (1776-1862) was the father of John Lloyd Wynn (1807-1887), who was the father of Major-General Edward William Wynn, whose widow Anne (daughter of H.R.Hughes, of Kinmel, and his wife Florentia Emily Liddell), married, secondly, the Hon. Laurence Alan Brodrick (died 1915). Florentia Liddell (1853-1909) was a great-granddaughter of Sir Henry George Liddell, who was also the grandfather of the Very Rev. Henry George Liddell, Dean of Christ Church, Oxford - father of Alice, of Wonderland fame.

Keith Gaskell founded Heronwater School at Coed Coch in 1941. It was a prep school for 80 boys. The stable block was converted into an unusual school chapel in 1962. Dr Fisher, the then Archbishop of Canterbury, used to spend his summer holidays at the school in the 1950s, wearing non-clerical casual clothing - to the dismay of the then incumbent of Llanelian church, where Dr Fisher preferred to worship, occupying the seat immediately beneath the pulpit.

Miss Margaret "Daisy" Brodrick, daughter of Anne Brodrick, inherited the use and income of Coed Coch, and continued to use the estate for the development of her famous stud of Welsh ponies. With her stud groom, John Jones, she began selective buying in 1924, gradually breeding the distinctive Coed Coch stock. When Miss Brodrick died, in 1962, the entailed estate passed to her stepbrother Lt-Colonel Edward Wynn (son of the General), who acquired a hefty overdraft to buy the ponies that grazed upon it. When the colonel died in 1977 the estate remained within the family, but the ponies, being his personal property, had to be sold to pay some of the death duties. There were 220 ponies in the 1978 auction, which raised £184,453, with several horses going to Australia, Canada and the United States.

Coed Coch became known as Living Waters in 1980, when it was used as a Christian centre for residential courses or simply for group use as a base for exploring the countryside, but has recently closed.

BETWS-YN-RHOS

Betws-yn-Rhos is as near a perfect village as one could ever expect to find. It straddles a couple of horrendous bends never intended for modern traffic, though once forming part of the main road from Chester to Conwy ferry, via Denbigh, Henllan and Glanconwy corner. Since 1985 the former parish has been united ecclesiastically with Llanelian, to form one rectorial benefice.

The Wheatsheaf was the official coaching stop during the 18th century, though the building is much older. Its present name is derived from the coat of arms of the Oldfield family, who lived at Ffarm, the big manor house to the rear. The Wheatsheaf used to be licensed as the

Beehive, though known locally simply as Dafarn Uchaf (Upper Tavern) to distinguish it from Dafarn Isaf (Lower Tavern) at the bottom of the hill.

Equally old, Dafarn Isaf was licensed as the Saracen's Head – another mutation of severed Saxon heads from the wars between the Welsh and the English. More recently Dafarn Isaf has been known as Llais Afon (Voice of the River) where a former nurse gave Betws-yn-Rhos an enviable catering reputation during her 16-year incumbency, from which she retired some years ago. The singing river still runs past the restaurant and under the main street, the general consensus being that its name is probably Afon Fedw.

Despite the traffic hazards, modern motor coaches visit the village in the summer for tourists to watch the hour being struck on the dual-purpose church bell, suspended between two mini-towers over the western entrance. A quixotic creation of architect John Welch, and looking like a poor man's do-it-yourself Neuschwanstein, the belfry-cum-clock-tower is served both by a tolling rope and a complex hinged mechanism linked to the 1877 clock - which keeps time.

Built during 1838-39, the church still displays its 1853 seating plan in the porch, to provide an interesting social study. The Coed Coch and Ffarm families glowered at each other from inward facing pews on either side of the tiny chancel, with their respective servants in the front rows of the forward facing pews. In the Victorian pecking order the Vicarage family were two rows behind the Coed Coch servants, and the Vicarage servants yet a further seven rows to the rear. The church's east window is inscribed in memory of Mary (died 1844), wife of John Wynn, of Coed Coch (not to be confused with Mary, wife of John Lloyd Wynn, of Coed Coch, son of Mary).

Betws-yn-Rhos was the birthplace in 1871 (at Gwyndy Ucha) of journalist, author and poet Professor T.Gwynn Jones. He had little formal education but was a natural writer and spent 19 years in journalism before becoming a cataloguer at the National Library of Wales, an opening from which he moved into the academic world, being appointed to the Gregynog chair of Welsh literature, at the University College of Wales, Aberystwyth, in 1919.

BRYN-Y-MAEN

Bryn-y-maen, still a quiet rural backwater though part of the borough of Colwyn Bay since 1934, was the magnanimous creation of a woman born into poverty at a lonely cottage half-a-mile away. Little now remains of Rhwng-y-ddwyffordd (meaning "between the two roads") in which Eleanor Jones was born in 1826.

She was the seventh daughter of a couple who earned their daily bread bartering candles, made with rushes collected by the children. But the children's education was not neglected for they walked five miles a day to and from Llansanffraid Glan Conwy, to attend Bryn Rhys School. (The author's own poor ancestors were instrumental in founding this small school, after draining the duck pond, which was the only site offered when they petitioned the squire of Bryn Eisteddfod estate).

At 12 years of age Eleanor became a servant at the home of industrialist John Frost, whose wife set about re-educating her. In 1863 Eleanor, then 37, married the heir, Charles Frost, 32, and by 1874 they were living at Min-y-don Hall, Old Colwyn, the impressive former home of Richard Butler Clough. They travelled widely, including a pilgrimage to Palestine from where they returned with enough Jordan water to re-baptise all their young relatives.

When Charles Frost died in 1896, leaving everything to his widow, Eleanor inherited the extensive Bryn-y-maen farmland which overlooked her birthplace, and on which she decided to build a memorial church as the centre for a new community. She engaged famous Chester architect John Douglas to design what we should now be calling Christ Church - instead of its better-known sobriquet "Cathedral in the hills." Douglas also designed the Vicarage, across

Christ Church, Bryn-y-maen was designed by John Douglas, principal designer of St Paul's, and dedicated in 1897 in memory of Charles Frost, of Min-y-don

the road, and a house for the widowed Mrs Frost, which she called Bryn Eglwys (Church Hill).

Her beautiful church interior is unusual in being bereft of memorial inscriptions, though a discreet plaque, some 4 x 3 inches, has crept into the porch to record a 1983 legacy. Only at the rear of the church, beneath the east window, does one find the modest inscription: *"Built to the honour and glory of God and to the memory of Charles Frost, by Eleanor his widow. May 4th AD 1897."* This was the foundation stone laid by Eleanor, whose church opened $2^{1}/_{2}$ years later, when she moved into Bryn Eglwys, which still bears her initials and date over the doorway. She also provided the embryo community with a church hall. Eleanor died in 1902, and lies buried beside her husband in a fenced off grave behind the church - her details being barely readable on the granite memorial, although she left a maintenance bequest for the church.

MIN-Y-DON

Richard Butler Clough (1781-1844) mentioned above, was the uncle of Anne Jemima Clough (1820-92), a pioneer of education for women and founder principal of Newnham College, Cambridge, and her brother Arthur Hugh Clough (1819-61), the poet. All three made their home at Min-y-don at different times. A.H.Clough was a friend of Matthew Arnold and Tennyson.

St Catherine's church, Old Colwyn, was dedicated to St Catherine of Alexandria in honour of Catherine Clough who, with her husband Richard, was largely responsible for the erection of the church in 1837, on land given by John Lloyd Wynn, of Coed Coch. Colwyn parish did not exist at that time and St Catherine's was a chapel of ease of Llandrillo. Catherine was the daughter of Richard's uncle, the Rev. Roger Butler Clough (1759-1833).

After Richard Clough's death in 1844, Min-y-don passed out of the family, who had been in financial difficulty ever since their Denbigh bank (founded in 1794 by Roger) failed in 1814. The family repaid all their debts by 1820. The family was descended from Sir Richard Clough, of Denbigh, who died in 1570, having amassed a fortune as a merchant in Antwerp. He built Plas Clough, Denbigh and died in Hamburg. He was the second of the four husbands of the notorious Catrin o'r Berain (Llanefydd). His title came from a visit to Jerusalem, where he was appointed a Knight of the Holy Sepulchre.

Min-y-don Hall, parts of which dated back 300 years, was demolished in 1940 to make way for houses which retain the street name. The last occupiers were Major and Mrs Marle, from 1919 to 1937. Their oldest deeds for Min-y-don showed it as Colwyn Farm "situated midway between Abergele and Conway River."

STATION ROAD

Colwyn Bay's now somewhat depressed Station Road was once the Mecca of North Wales shoppers seeking elegance and quality. It was in decline by 1961 when three architects - Sir Clough Williams-Ellis (of Portmeirion fame), Leonard Moseley and S.Powell Bowen - proposed a £7,000 rescue, based on the 1958 co-ordinated face-lift that had given new life to Norwich's Magdalen Street. All that came of the Colwyn Bay plan was the unnecessary 1964 removal of an interesting and historic drinking fountain and gas lamp standard, at the top of the hill, presented in 1895 by John Porter, the town's principal architect. It went to improve two-way traffic flow, but the road was semi-pedestrianised in 1988.

Central Hotel, at the top of the road, was originally the Station Hotel, being visible across the open field separating it from the railway station at the bottom of the hill. Next is an 1892 example of Porter's work (in association with Lawrence Booth and Thomas Chadwick) - a row of nine shops in glazed red brick, eight with peaked gables and the ninth with a tower, all built by Edward Foulkes.

The original Victorian canopy of W.H.Smith & Son still contains stained-glass representations of Chaucer, Shakespeare, Dante and Dickens. High on one of the gables is a reminder that it was once the Post Office. Colwyn Bay's original postal address was "near Conway." The first Post Office was in a small shop in Conwy Road, from where a lone postman covered an area extending from Llysfaen to Mochdre. It was also located first in Abergele Road and in 1904 in Penrhyn Road, moving in 1926 to a neo-Georgian building in Princes Drive, which closed in 1994 when postal facilities were moved into the new Safeways shop. Most important of all the Station Road inscriptions are those on the tower of the town's old administrative centre, already discussed earlier in this book, now known as Liberty's, a public house.

At the bottom of the road the attractive clock tower was erected in 1989, in memory of an adventurous local man who died at the age of 34. Tragically, another memorial plaque had to be added to the base in memory of a craftsman who was fatally injured in a fall while erecting the clock. It stands outside the corner shop once known as Uxbridge House, the road's first grocer. Boots is a 1979 replacement for a once-famous draper's shop, Neville & Co. Even more famous was the big furniture shop of Daniel Allen, in mock-Tudor style. It closed in 1971 when the founder's grandson said he would not ruin the family's reputation by selling the inferior products of modern manufacturers.

The attractive Peacocks store, at the top of the road, was once the most famous shop of all, with a reputation stretching the length and breadth of North Wales. It was designed in 1933 by local architect and honorary Freeman of the Borough Sidney Colwyn Foulkes (son of Edward, the builder), for William S.Wood - whose monogram survives in the bronze flower boxes at first floor level.

J. R. Jones's shop at Lancaster House in Abergele Road, Colwyn Bay

In stark contrast to most Colwyn Bay architecture, William S. Wood's store was designed in 1933 by future freeman of the borough Sidney Colwyn Foulkes

A Brief History

A good example of the town's once famous cast-iron pavement canopies adorned The Regent (above) at the corner of Conwy Road and Llewelyn Road. Williams's livery stables (below), next-door-but-one to the Public Hall (now Theatr Colwyn,) in Abergele Road, advertised "pony carriages with or without drivers". J.R Jones, the saddler, is seen next-door

COLWYN, U.S.A.

Few people are aware that simultaneously with the growth of Colwyn, North Wales, another borough of the same name was developing 3,200 miles away, in the Commonwealth of Pennsylvania, USA.

William J. O'Neill, Burgess (Mayor) of Colwyn, USA, told the author in 1958 that his town had derived its name from its Welsh parent. William Penn sold a plantation to a cousin, Peter Elliott, and this land later became subdivided into several farms. It was among these farms, southwest of Philadelphia, in the county of Delaware, that a community began to grow.

This development began in 1890, and within two years the new township was big enough for incorporation as a borough. The community was first called Darby Level, being a breakaway from Darby Town, now situated south of the borough, from which the farmers believed they were not getting a fair return for their taxes, and would do no better if they merged with rival Darby Borough, to the north.

The new borough was incorporated under the name of Molendale, a big estate in the town, but within a few weeks a public meeting was held at Mrs Woodhead's store to choose a new name. Various names were chalked on a blackboard, borrowed from the local one-room school. Morgan Williams, an immigrant from Colwyn, North Wales, added the name "Colwyn" to the board, and this won the vote. He was well known for his singing abilities and a prominent member of the choir at the first Presbyterian church built in Darby.

Colwyn expanded rapidly and was linked by a tram to Philadelphia (a 35-minute journey) and by a railway (12 minutes). In 1897 two rooms were added to the school. In 1900 a two-storey eight-room school was built, being replaced in 1932 by a new 12-room school. In 1903 the first Fire Company was formed, a wholly volunteer unit which, in 1958, had 200 members with two motorised pumps, supported by the Ladies Auxiliary Fire Company. The fire station was incorporated in the Town Hall, together with the police and the civic administration. The building also contained an indoor pistol and rifle range for the use of club members who were all sworn in as Special Police Officers.

By 1958 the borough had a population of 2,900, with 800 houses, a school, two churches (Presbyterian and Baptist), and four factories (making bronze castings, air conditioning plant, wood tanks and soap). This little community was served by four locally printed newspapers (one morning, one evening, one Sunday and one weekly).

THE NATIONAL EISTEDDFOD

The National Eisteddfod visited Colwyn Bay in 1910 and 1947, and was held in 1995 at Abergele in the greater Borough of Colwyn. The Gorsedd circle for the 1910 event can be seen within the grounds of the Welsh Mountain Zoo; the 1947 circle is in Eirias Park. Having used the circle for the 1909 proclamation ceremony, the Archdruid Dyfed declared it too far from the town for the actual eisteddfod and convened all the 1910 Gorsedd events on Rydal fields. The Eisteddfod Pavilion was a magnificent wooden structure containing 10,000 comfortable seats and a stage for 500.

The 280-page 1910 programme reads like a preview of the *Dictionary of Welsh Biography*. The overall event president was Sir J.Herbert Roberts, MP for West Denbighshire, with Sir Thomas Marchant Williams, barrister and author in the role of chairman of the Council of the National Eisteddfod Association. Day presidents included the Hon.Laurence Brodrick, of Coed Coch; Major-General Sir Ivor Herbert, MP, later Lord Treowen; the Rt.Rev. Alfred George Edwards, Bishop of St Asaph, later the first Archbishop of Wales; David Lloyd George, MP for Caernarvon Boroughs (which included Llandudno Urban District); and Sir J.Pritchard Jones, the Newborough-born draper who made a fortune in London as founder managing director of

Dickins & Jones, in Regent Street, and paid for the building of the Pritchard Jones Hall at the University College of North Wales (at a cost of £17,000). Presidents of various subsidiary events within the eisteddfod included O.M.Edwards, the first chief inspector of schools in Wales, who was knighted in 1916; and Sir William Preece, the Caernarfon inventor of wireless communication, who gave the young Marconi his first job in Britain.

The eisteddfod choir of 265 was recruited from a wide area, and conducted by the famous John Williams, of Caernarfon. One of the three platform accompanists was T.Osborne Roberts, later to marry the winner of the contralto solo competition, Maggie Jones, better known by her subsequent professional name of Leila Megane.

A profit of £208 was declared after paying the £3,329 which the 1910 eisteddfod had cost. This compared with £335 in London the previous year and £905 at Carmarthen in the following year.

Colwyn Bay had been chosen as the venue for the 1941 National Eisteddfod but because of World War Two it was made into a brief radio-only event, which was broadcast from a church hall at Old Colwyn. When the National Eisteddfod proper returned to Colwyn Bay in 1947 the local president was Professor T.Gwynn Jones, who was born at Betws-yn-Rhos. The day president for the opening session was R.O.F.Wynne, of Garthewin, who was not then known to have stored the petrol and syringes used by the three Welsh Nationalists who set fire to the contractor's stores during the building of RAF Penrhos in 1936,[30] later standing bail for one of the accused, Saunders Lewis.

The 1947 eisteddfod made a profit of £732 on an expenditure of £3,924. Some of the profit was used to establish an outstanding Welsh section, in a separate room at Colwyn Bay library, and some to provide a set of wrought-iron gates, incorporating eisteddfodic symbols, for Eirias Park. The Welsh library was broken up as a separate entity after the 1974 reorganisation of local government. At about the same time the gates were nearly destroyed during the widening of the entrance into the park. Having watched these gates being made by D.J.Williams and his son Harold at the famous Brunswick Ironworks, behind the old Herald Office, at Caernarfon, the author campaigned for their preservation and they were re-hung as ornamental railings inside the gateway. In their final stage of construction at Caernarfon they were too big for the ironworks and were completed outside, in St Helen's Road.

THE MOCHDRE TITHE WAR

In 1886 the farmers of Mochdre petitioned the Ecclesiastical Commissioners for a 25% reduction in their tithe charges, a tax which the church had levied since medieval times, ostensibly to maintain the services of a priest. In practice many beneficiaries were absentee rectors who lived in comfort off the tithes, a small portion being used to pay someone else to perform a few duties as a "perpetual curate" or "vicar" (from the Latin *vicarius,* meaning substitute). Some places had additional vicarial tithes.

Even where the rector, vicar or perpetual curate conscientiously carried out his church duties there was much resentment among the Nonconformist farmers of Victorian Wales at having to pay a cash commutation, based on an earlier calculation of a tenth of their production, to maintain the Church of England. Mochdre was part of Llandrillo-yn-Rhos where the Rev.Venables Williams reported he had received an anonymous threat to blow up his vicarage, if the farmers' demands were not met. His Mission Room at Colwyn Bay was burnt down on 31 October 1886.[31]

In 1887 the Chester office of the Ecclesiastical Commissioners rejected the Mochdre demands and served notice on farmers in arrears - each for an average of £11. Some paid but the holders of Glanywern, Tanrallt Isa, Tanrallt Ucha, Cefngarlleg and Mynydd stood firm. On 24 May a

Rhyl shoemaker was paid to guide the bailiffs through Mochdre. The party was challenged but the shoemaker said he and his friends were on their way to Penmaenmawr to seek work, and they were allowed through the road block. Too late, the farmers discovered their true errand, by which time the bailiffs had got away with two cows seized from each of the five farms. It was the area's first distraint for non-payment.[32]

With most of the farmers refusing to pay the additional vicarial tithe, pickets were posted throughout the area and three flagstaffs were erected on high ground above the hamlet to enable warnings to be signalled to Old Colwyn, Pydew and Glanconwy if the bailiffs were sighted. One of these flagstaffs is remembered to this day in the name of its location, Flagstaff, now the home of the Welsh Mountain Zoo.

On 16 June 1887 the Army was called out to help Denbighshire Constabulary restore law and order. A special train stopped at the level crossing near where the Mochdre and Pabo railway station was later built, and 76 policemen and 76 Militiamen in their scarlet tunics alighted, marching across growing corn to reach the village.

Flags were hoisted on the hill above, horns were sounded and one gunshot was heard as the troops headed up Chapel Street, towards the old mill, where the protesters seemed to have congregated. A large number of curious but peaceful inhabitants followed the troops, whose first call was at Mynydd farm. When negotiations with the farmer failed to resolve the issue the police began to withdraw, but while in retreat some of the police turned to confront an estimated 250 followers. The whole thing flared up into a riot, with stones and staves used against the police, who responded with their truncheons. The farmer at Mynydd was persuaded

This picture encapsulates the scene of the Mochdre tithe war of 1886. The tenant of Glanywern, of which only the gates survive, was one of the firt to refuse to pay his tithe

to pay his tithe and the police moved on, into the teeth of another barrage of stones and sticks. The Riot Act was read at Felin gate. The wounded were carried into Y Felin where their wounds were bandaged.

All the tithes were eventually recovered and the grievance rumbled on. An 1891 Act made the tithe payable by the landowner, but in practice it was still the tenant who paid. The Welsh tithe ended in 1920 with the Disestablishment of the Church in Wales. It ended in England in 1996 under the provisions of the Tithe Redemption Act, 1936.

THE CONGO INSTITUTE

ONE of the lesser-known aspects of explorer H.M.Stanley's life was his involvement with the Congo Training Institute, founded at Colwyn Bay by the Reverend William Hughes, a man banished from all the standard Welsh biographical reference works. William Hughes was born in 1855 on a farm at Rhoslan, near Criccieth. He was ordained from Llangollen Baptist College in 1882 and accepted by the Baptist Missionary Society for service in the Congo. *"Soon after my arrival ... I found it would be impossible to get proper hold of the young people without separating them as much as possible from former friends, old superstitions and other injurious influences,"* wrote Hughes in his 1892 handbook.[33] To achieve this, he proposed returning to Wales with some African acolytes, and his scheme was given impetus in 1885 when, in failing health, he was advised by Stanley's doctor (a fellow Welshman) that survival depended upon his leaving the Congo. During a hundred miles river trip to the coast he was nursed by two Congolese boys, Nkanza and Kinkasa, who remained with him until all three arrived at Liverpool in September.

Hughes took them with him to his sister at Llanelian, where they lived on charity and money collected at lectures, such as that advertised to take place at the Baptist Chapel, Water Street, Rhyl, in 1886 when William Hughes was still described as a missionary. The speaker was to be accompanied by *bechgyn duon* (black boys), who would sing in Welsh, English and their native language. They also sold photographs of themselves. In 1887 Hughes was appointed pastor of the Welsh Baptist churches at Old Colwyn and Llanelian, followed in 1888 by the additional care of Tabernacle, built at Colwyn Bay in that year.[34]

Hughes never ceased to proclaim his dream and in 1889 the committee of the Congo Training Institute met for the first time, at Llandudno, under the presidency of Alderman Richard Cory, of Cardiff. The others present at that first meeting were T.T. Marks, of Llandudno; Principal Gethin Davies, of Llangollen Baptist College; Simon Jones, Wrexham; W. S. Jones, Chester, and the Reverend W. Ross, ex-Congo, with William Hughes as secretary.

The brave pioneering idea had by then crystallised into a scheme whereby young Congolese boys would be brought to Colwyn Bay for a Christian education coupled with a craft apprenticeship, later to return to their own people as self-supporting missionaries. The Elder Dempster shipping company had agreed to transport the students free of charge between Africa and Liverpool (from where the Liverpool & North Wales Steamship Co, following their formation in 1891, provided free passages to Llandudno pier). In April 1890 the committee were able to meet in their new Congo House, in Nant-y-glyn Road.

In July Hughes told his committee that H.M. Stanley had promised to visit North Wales to deliver a lecture in support of the Institute.

"His promise alone has already been the best advertisement we have had to our work, and it has been the means of drawing the attention of many new friends to the scheme. If the rumour has done so much, what will the visit do? I feel sure it will set the whole thing going with a fresh life and energy; it will immortalise a plan that is destined to have a great future before it," reported Hughes.

Stanley's promised visit took place on 15 June 1891 when he was cheered all the way from Caernarfon railway station to the town's enormous 1877 Eisteddfod pavilion (demolished in 1962). There he praised the work of the Institute to an audience of 4,000, telling them one student, who had been trained as a carpenter, had already returned to the Congo where he had commenced to preach.

An interesting sequel occurred at Bangor on the following day when a correspondent of the Welsh-language newspaper Yr *Herald Gymraeg* went to the railway station to catch a glimpse of the explorer. Looking through the carriage window he saw that Stanley was reading that morning's *Herald Gymraeg* containing a report of the Caernarfon meeting. "Who now will deny he is a Welshman?" wrote the correspondent. Stanley's ability to read Welsh, even after many years in the United States, would make sense, for Welsh was the natural first language of his childhood and teenage years in Denbigh, St.Asaph and Tremeirchion.

Stanley's influence was emphasised a month later when William Hughes received a letter from the Brussels palace of Leopold II, King of the Belgians, stating: *"I have the honour to make known to you that the King accedes to the request which was addressed to him in your name by Mr. H. M. Stanley, consenting to grant his patronage to the establishment founded at Colwyn Bay under the title of Congo House Training Institute for African. Students. Accept, sir, the assurance of his very distinguished patronage."*

From Switzerland, on 17 Jul 1891, Stanley wrote to Hughes stating he too had received a letter from Leopold. *"You are thus permitted by His Majesty's gracious permission to use his name as patron of your very interesting institution. I hope that the promise of usefulness and good which I have seen, and which recommends itself to the gracious notice of His Majesty, will be realised,"* wrote Stanley.

Subscriptions for what gradually changed its name to the African Institute shot up from £88 in 1889 to £476 in 1891. In 1892 Hughes relinquished his three pastorates to apply all his time to the Institute. However, he was dogged by misfortune. His daughter Edith died on 13 March 1893, aged 6 months. His wife Katie died on 20 August 1894, aged 33, and his elder daughter, also named Katie, died on 24 May 1909 aged 22 years. In 1908 he was chosen by public acclaim to take on the task of honorary secretary for the National Eisteddfod which was held at Colwyn Bay in 1910, and for which he was listed as a guarantor.

Disaster came swiftly after the notorious journalist Horatio Bottomley heard a whisper of scandal which resulted in a *John Bull* story with accompanying street poster: "Black Baptist's brown bastard" – an alliteration which told the whole story. Hughes made the mistake of suing a man who thrived on litigation, and lost the day and his credibility at Ruthin Assizes. Subscriptions for the Institute dried up immediately and the last of the Africans were sent home in 1911. Hughes was declared bankrupt in the following year, losing the last shreds of his reputation at a humiliating and searching public examination at Bangor. With a couple of notable exceptions, his beloved Baptists hastened to distance themselves from him, and the Welsh Establishment expunged his name. William Hughes died a lonely broken man, at Conwy Workhouse, on 28 January 1924, and was buried at Old Colwyn. The two Congolese pioneers Nkanza and Kinkasa also lie in the Old Colwyn cemetery, along with several other young African students struck down by European infections.

Notes in the Text

NOTES FOR BOOK 1 – *COLWYN BAY, ITS ORIGIN AND GROWTH*

1 TSt.A. Vol.1, p 202.
2 Par. p 39.
3 The title survives in the Welsh word *Rhaglaw,* meaning "governor" or "lieutenant." (IWJ).
4 Porter, p 108.
5 Cal,of Inq. 9 Ed.III (No.617).
6 Pen. Vol.3, p 146.
7 Porter, p 08.
8 NWWN, 16 Dec 1943,
9 HNW. Vol.1, p 444.
10 Parry, pp 157-159.
11 J.E.Morris, *The Welsh Wars of King Edward I*, p 139
12 The change was correct Welsh orthography for "Pool of the cauldron." (IWJ).
13 They have not been apparent at Rhos-on-Sea since the beach level rose after the building of the new stone breakwater in 1982. (IWJ).
14 Lleweny MSS. 3-45, NLW.
15 A.H.Dodd, HSCym. 1942, pp 34-35.
16 Cal.SP.Dom. Chas I, cccxci, 105.
17 Ellesmere MSS, ix 7420, Huntingdon Library.
18 NWP. 25 Oct 1923.
19 Land & Sea, p 168.
20 Coastline, p 186.
21 Itin. p 89
22 TstA. Vol III, p 210.
23 HSCym.
24 ED(D) pp 196-7.
25 ibid p 194.
26 Ibid p 203.
27 Ven.Wms. p 11.
28 Ibid p 10.
29 Ven.Wms p 11
30 Rhos Abbey Hotel was demolished in 2001, to make way for flats. (IWJ).
31 ED(F) pp 441-2.
32 ED(D) pp 198-9.
33 *Handbook of the Vale of Clwyd*, 1857.
34 ED(D) pp 375-6.
35 Par. p 40.
36 ED(D) p 198.
37 Field Club, Vol X, pp 70-1.
38 Ibid.
39 ED(D) pp 198-9.
40 Aber, p 115.
41 HNW Vol I, pp 145-6.

42 Ibid.
43 ED(D) p 376.
44 Segontium, the Roman fort at Caernarfon, was garrisoned until at least AD 394. (IWJ).
45 Pen. Vol 3, p 145.
46 *The Lives of the British Saints*, Gould & Fisher, Vol IV, pp 263-4.
47 Aber. P 118.
48 Heywood's *Illustrated Guide to Colwyn Bay.*
49 Arch.Camb. 1893 p 275.
50 Report AM. par 312.
51 E.A.Lewis, *The decay of tribalism in North Wales.*
52 JELl, Vol II, pp. 684-5.
53 Ped. p 290.
54 Cal.Inq. 10 Ed II, p 413, No. 617.
55 Arch.Camb. (1846) p 339.
56 Pen. Vol II, p 111.
57 Arch.Camb.
58 Cal.Inq. (1) Misc (1219-1397) No. 1024.
59 Cal.Pat. Ed.I (1272-1281) p 334-5.
60 Cal.Pat. (1281-1292) 13 Ed.I, p 149.
61 Arch.Camb. 1846, p 339.
62 Cal.Inq. 9th Ed.II, No.617, p 413.
63 Cal.Pat. II Ed.I (1283), p 82.
64 Frank Almoigne = The Prince retains no jurisdiction over the land but assigns it to ecclesiastical authority.
65 Welsh Assize Roll, p 111.
66 Glanville R.J.Jones, *The Military Geography of Gwynedd in the 13th century*, unpublished thesis UCW.
67 Goronwy Edwards, *A Calendar of Unpublished Correspondence concerning Wales*, HLS No.2, p 40.
68 Ibid.
69 Cal.Inq, Misc.1, p 343, No. 1149.
70 Par. p 40.
71 *The decay of tribalism in North Wales*, Cym. 1902-3.
72 Maenan remained part of Caernarvonshire until the 1974 reorganisation of local government. The first Assistant Bishop of the new Church in Wales, in 1920, was given the title Bishop of Maenan. (IWJ).
73 Cym. 1902-3) p 47.
74 *Black Prince's Register*, Pt.III, Chester, pp 350-2.
75 Parry, pp 206-7, quoting British Museum translation, by Webb, of original MS.
76 Cal.Pat.R. 21 Hy VII, Pt.2, p 471.
77 Early Chancery Proceedings, Abstract C1/913/27.
78 Exchequer Bills and Answers, W.112/59/22.
79 Exchequer Proceedings, H&LS.
80 Exchequer Bills & Answers, E.112/59/33.
81 HLS No.4, 59/33.
82 CWP 427.
83 CWP 435.
84 CWP 510.
85 CWP 528.
86 CWP 718.
87 WstA p 246.
88 CWP 362, 364.
89 CWP 162.
90 The Venerable William Davies was beatified at the Vatican in 1987. (IWJ).
91 Pedigrees, p 259.
92 Star Chamber Proiceedings, St.Ch.5.
93 The hotel was demolished in 2001. (IWJ).
94 St.Ch.Pr., Bundle J.18/1 (Eliz) Caernarvon.

Notes in the text

95 Frank Price Jones, UCNW Bangor, subsequently suggested this probably referred to the "nine houses" talogion had to build for their lord, according to the Laws of Hywel Dda. (IWJ).
96 Translations from unpublished thesis by Abraham Jenkins, University of Wales.
97 Mostyn MSS, No.219, NLW.
98 Arch.Camb III, iii 40.
99 Glanville R.J.Jones, unpublished thesis, *The Military Geography of Gwynedd in the 13th Century,* p 98 UCW.
100 Pedigrees p 290, footnote.
101 History of Aberconwy, p 41.
102 Ifan Llwyd, Mostyn MSS, No.219, NLW.
103 Lloyd, *History of Powys Fadog* (1887). Vol.VI, Pedigrees.
104 *The Mostyns of Mostyn,* p 76.
105 Cal.Pat.R, Hy VII (1494-1509) p 15.
106 Arch.Camb. 1869, p 16.
107 E. Gwynne Jones. *Exchequer Proceedings (Equity) concerning Wales.*
108 Quarter Sessions, 1/2/172, Caernarvonshire County Archives.
109 Ven.Wms p 33.
110 CWP 171.
111 Ibid. 2851.
112 E.Gwynne Jones, *Catholic Recusancy in the Counties of Denbigh,* etc, 1945, p 120.
113 A Margaret Conway was buried in 1654.
114 Porter, Appendix 2.
115 Gwysaney Papers, No.762, UCNW.
116 J.Bernard Burke, *A Genealogical History of the House of Gwysaney,* 1847, pp 41-4, 63-5.
117 Schedules of Deeds and Documents deposited at NLW by Philip Tatton Davies-Cooke, 1942, No.389.
118 The surrounding Glyn farm land is in the process of being developed as a housing estate in 2001 – Glyn itself being preserved as a registered building. (IWJ).
119 CWP.
120 CWP 774.
121 Arch.Camb, June 1926, The Old Poor Law in North Wales.
122 A.H.Dodd, *The Rise of the North Wales Coastal Resorts* (Handbook, NUT Conference, Llandudno, 1939. p.77).
123 Ven.Wms. p.31.
124 CWP No.1223.
125 CWP No.1475.
126 Ind.Rev. p.123.
127 Ha.Exe. pp 61-2.
128 Holyhead Road Reports, 1818-22, p 568.
129 *Third Report from Select Committee on Holyhead Roads,* 1922, p 556.
130 Porter, p 57.
131 Ald.D.O.Williams, notes.
132 A General View of Agriculture and Domestic Economy in North Wales. P 459.
133 T.Parry & T.M.Jones, *Methodistiaeth yn Nosbarth Colwyn Bay.*
134 After which James Frost moved into Min-y-Don. (IWJ).
135 TStA. Vol.III, p199.
136 *Memories of Frances Ridley Havergal,* by Her Sister.
137 HNW, Vol.2, p 320.
138 The strip of land at Llandrilo-yn-Rhos which contained Rhos Fynach and Rhyd, being in Caernarvonshire, was included in Eirias Township, which was also part of Caernarvonshire.
139 NWP Incorporation Supplement, 20 Sept 1934.
140 *Rydal School -1885-1935,* p 17.
141 WCP, 7 Jul 1907. The station was much reduced in size and two platforms and two tracks were removed in 1982, to make way for the present A55 road. Once again it is "a primitive affair of two platforms" unmanned in the evening and with indifferent lighting which may be worse than that noted in 1889. (IWJ).
142 A "Ship" is mentioned in the 1821 Llandrillo parish census.

143 Now Queen's Court Nursing Home. (IWJ).
144 Lhwyd mentions a Ffynnon Owen in1699, p 40.
145 NWP (1924).
146 Telford, p 579.
147 Porter, p 26.
148 NWC 26 Oct 1850.
149 This refers to the original Colwyn Bay Hotel, closed in 1973 and demolished to make way for flats. (IWJ).
150 Caernarvon & Denbigh Herald, 23 Mar 1872.
151 Porter pp 102-3.
152 Porter, p 62.
153 The County Building in Rhiw Road was reduced to a part-time police office in the mid-1990s. (IWJ).
154 Only the circular base stone survives in 2001, and that is loose and damaged, and a few inches away from its original position. It is inscribed: "This fountain was presented to the ratepayers of the Urban District Council of Colwyn Bay and Colwyn, by the Rev. Thomas Parry, BA, Llys Aled, Colwyn Bay, to commemorate the completion of the Promenade. December 1897." (IWJ).
155 The municipal electricity undertaking was nationalised at just about the time N. Tucker was writing, and Colwyn Bay became part of the National Grid. (IWJ).
156 Now flats at the bottom of Penrhyn Road. (IWJ).
157 At the official Inquiry into the Tithe Disturbances the commissioners noted that the fire occurred before the demand for a tithe reduction had been made. (IWJ).
158 Reprinted in NWWN Jubilee Supplement, 23 Feb 1939.
159 *Report of an Inquiry into Disturbances connected with the Levying of Tithe Rentcharge in Wales*, 1887.
160 Called *Theatr Colwyn* in 2001, but there are proposals to revert to the former name of Prince of Wales Theatre adopted in 1959. (IWJ).
161 Demolished to make way for flats c.1995. (IWJ).
162 The Penrhos College buildings are scheduled for demolition in 2001, to make way for a housing estate.(IWJ).
163 Became Vicar of Llandrillo in 1855 (IWJ).
164 TStA Vol.III, pp 199-202.
165 Norman Tucker's father. (IWJ).
166 This was opposite the present HSBC. (IWJ).
167 In Ivy Street. (IWJ).
168 Since replaced with a purpose-built café. (IWJ).
169 Destroyed by arson in the 1990s. (IWJ).
170 *Report on the State of Education in Wales*, Vol. III, p 59. This inquiry by a team of barristers, who attributed all the failings in the schools of Wales to "the language of slavery" (i.e. Welsh), has gone down in history as *Brad y Llyfrau Gleision*, meaning Treason of the Blue Books. (IWJ).
171 Ibid. pp 286,282,198,201.
172 Demolished to make way for flats in the mid 1990s. (IWJ).
173 Rosa Hovey, *Penrhos 1880-1930*.
174 Penrhos College merged with Rydal School in 1995, and the college's furnishings were auctioned in 2001, ready for the buildings to be demolished to make way for a housing estate. (IWJ).
175 The Colwyn Bay buildings having been requisitioned by the Government. (IWJ).
176 i.e. in 1951. (IWJ)
177 John Porter's drinking fountain was removed for no good reason in 1964. (IWJ).
178 Now NatWest Bank. (IWJ).
179 Opposite the present HSBC, which still bears the original legend North & South Wales Bank. (IWJ).
180 Built by J.Roberts, of Llandudno, in 1903. (IWJ).
181 From the Official Guide of the Colwyn Bay & Liverpool Steamship Company, 1904, p 55.
182 Destroyed to make way for a box-like amusement arcade when the Council sold the pier in 1979.(IWJ).

Notes in the text

183 Later ordained a priest of the Anglican Communion. He died in 1970 as Vicar of Sandbach. (IWJ).
184 The Council vacated these offices in 1964, and moved into Glan-y-don, a former mental home. (IWJ).
185 Now Queen's Court Nursing Home. (IWJ),
186 It was actually a Farman biplane. The pilot had taken off from Blackpool, and his arrival at Rhos-on-Sea established a new international record for the longest oversea flight, of 63 miles. (IWJ).
187 The memorial was moved to Queen's Gardens (Rydal Gardens), beside Conwy Road, when the Council Offices closed in 1964. (IWJ).
188 Closed in 1994 when the Post Office moved into Safeways shop, in the Bay View shopping centre. (IWJ).
189 A local government parish, not ecclesiastical. (IWJ).
190 Officially renamed Queen's Gardens, in commemoration of the Coronation of Queen Elizabeth II in 1953, but still better known under its original name. (IWJ).
191 i.e. Colwyn Bay Urban District became the Borough of Colwyn Bay, which remained the local authority until the 1974 reorganisation of local government. (IWJ)
192 Near the junction of Colwyn Crescent and Penrhyn Avenue. Boarded up in 2001, in anticipation of sale as a housing site. (IWJ).
193 Arch.Camb. III, iii.40.
194 WStA. Vol.1. p 324. The walls were again whitewashed in 2000. (IWJ).
195 TstA, Vol III, p 210.
196 The old parish church of Caernarfon. (IWJ).
197 Fen.T. p 201.
198 Arch.Camb. 1,iii. 275.
199 TstA. Vol.III, p 213.
200 And again restored and re-roofed in 2000. (IWJ).
201 HNW, Vol.I, p 360.
202 Possibly Dinerth.
203 Ven.Wms. p 35.
204 In January 1964 a stone-lined well, 63ft deep and 4ft 6ins across, appeared overnight under the collapsed floor of a garage of a new housing estate being developed in the old Vicar age orchard, some 10 yards from the churchyard wall. The builders filled the well and completed the house. (IWJ).
205 Guide. Colwyn Bay &Liverpool Steamship Co., 1904, p 19.
206 TstA, Vol.III, p 224.
207 Baring-Gould and Fisher, Vol. II, p 246.
208 Arch.Camb, 1884, p 103.
209 TstA, Vol. III, p 224.
210 Extracts from MS of Rev. T.Llechid Jones, at UCNW, Bangor.
211 But not until 29 September. (IWJ).
212 Field Club, Vol. IX, p 23.
213 Lewis, Topographical Dictionary, Vol. 1, 1833.
214 Rev.Griffith Williams, *Llanelian yn Rhos, an outline of the chief characteristics of the Church*, 1940.
215 TstA, Vol, III, p 215.
216 i.e. he had a coat of arms. (IWJ).
217 Baring-Gould and Fisher. Vol.II, p 440.
218 Hd.Exe. pp. 63-65.
219 *Parochialia*. Arch.Camb. Sup't. 1909, p 36.

NOTES FOR BOOK TWO: *A 21st CENTURY OVERVIEW*

1 Thomas Pennant, *Tours in Wales*, (1778).
2 Edmund Hyde Hall, *A description of Caernarvonshire, 1809-1811*, (1952).
3 He meant "theatre," of course (an "amphitheatre" is round or oval).
4 *Caernarvon & Denbigh Herald*, 23 March 1872.
5 The census returns, following the 1895 creation of the urban district, were: 1901 - 8,576; 1911 - 12,630; 1921 - 21,566; 1931 - 21,566; 1951 - 22,276; 1961 - 23,201; 1971 - 25,564; 1981 - 26,278; 1991 - 25,576.
6 Rev. D.R.Thomas, *A History of the Diocese of St Asaph*, 1874.
7 Rev.W.Venables Williams, *An archaeological history of Llandrillo-yn-Rhos*, c.1893; Rev. W.Hugh Rees, *Parish of St.Paul, Colwyn Bay*, 1953; Norman Tucker, *Colwyn Bay, its origins and growth*, 1953.
8 Parch. T.Parry a Parch. T.M.Jones, *Methodistiaeth yn Nosbarth Colwyn Bay*, 1909.
9 W.Ogwen Williams, Calendar of the *Caernarvonshire Quarter Sessions Records, Vol.1, 1541-1558* (1956).
10 Promotional leaflet by the Victoria Pier & Pavilion Company (Colwyn Bay) Ltd, 1899.
11 Ivor Wynne Jones, *Eagles do not catch flies*, 1986.
12 Ivor Wynne Jones, *Llandudno, Queen of the Welsh Resorts*, 1975.
13 Ivor Wynne Jones, *Llandudno's operatic tradition*, 1979.
14 Jules Riviére, *My musical life and recollections*, 1893.
15 Ivor Wynne Jones, *Shipwrecks of North Wales*, 1973 and 2001.
16 E.G.Bowen, *The settlements of the Celtic saints in Wales*, 1956.
17 Rev. D.R.Thomas, *A History of the Diocese of St Asaph*, 1874.
18 Parch. T.Parry a Parch. T.M.Jones, *Methodistiaeth yn Nosbarth Colwyn Bay*, 1909; A.H.Williams, *Welsh Wesleyan Methodism 1800-1858*, 1935.
19 Ivor Wynne Jones, *Llandudno, Queen of the Welsh Resorts*, 1975.
20 David Powel, *Historie of Cambria, now called Wales*, 1584.
21 Norman Tucker, *The Conways of Bryn Euryn*, 1966.
22 *Richard II*, 1597.
23 *Rhaglen Swyddogol Eisteddfod Frenhinol Genedlaethol Cymru*, 1910.
24 William Lee, in information given to the author in 1955. He said he transferred the two urns from an earlier tomb to the present structure while working for the estate's then owner, C.H.Mitchell.
25 Such archives as were available at the Rhos-on-sea depot, mainly the company scrap book and a few loose papers, were secured by the author and deposited at Caernarvonshire Record Office, under archive file reference: XM 1213/236.
26 Ivor Wynne Jones, *Llandudno, Queen of the Welsh Resorts*, 1975.
27 Samuel Lewis, *A topographical dictionary of Wales*, 1848
28 Beazley & Howell, *The Companion Guide to North Wales*, 1975.
29 Edward Hubbard, *The buildings of Wales: Clwyd*, 1986.
30 Information given to the author by R.O.F.Wynne and first published in the *Daily Post* on 20 October 1977 in a series of features entitled "Head of the family." Mr Wynne died in 1992.
31 Note from Frank Price Jones, UCNW, to Norman Tucker, amending p.176 of *Colwyn Bay, its origins and growth*, after using the *Baner* to interpret "evidence question 3993" put to the Rev. Venables Williams at the 1887 Tithe Inquiry.
32 *Llandudno Advertiser*, 4 June 1887.
33 Rev.W.Hughes, *Dark Africa and the way out*, 1892
34 Ivor Wynne Jones and Lucy M.Jones, *H.M.Stanley and Wales*, 1972

ABBREVIATIONS USED FOR THE NOTES NUMBERED IN THE TEXT

Aber.	Williams, (Rev. R.) The history and antiquities of the town of Aberconwy and its neighbourhood, 1835.
Arch.Camb.	Archaelogia Cambrensis
Coastline.	Ashton (W.), Evolution of a coastline, 1920.
CHS.	Caernarvonshire Historical Society Transactions.
Cal.Ch.R.	Calendar of Charter Rolls
Cal.of Inq.	Calendar of Inquisitions.
Cal.Pat.	Calendar of Patent Rolls.
Cal.SP.Dom.	Calendar of State Papers: Domestic.
CWP.	Calendar of Wynn Papers. 1926.
ED.(D).	Davies (Rev. Canon Ellis). The pre-historic and Roman remains of Denbighshire. 1929.
ED.(F).	Ibid. The pre-historic and Roman remains of Flintshire, 1949.
Fen.T.	Fenton (Richard). Tours in Wales, 1804-1813). (Arch. Camb. Supplement). 1917.
Field Club.	Llandudno, Colwyn Bay and District Field Club Proceedings.
Gould & Fisher.	Baring-Gould (S.) and Fisher (J.) Lives of the British Saints, 4 vols. 1907.
Ha.Exc.	Halliwell (J.R.) Notes of family excursions in North Wales, 1860.
HLS.	Wales: University. Board of Celtic Studies History and Law Series.
HNW.	Lowe (W. B.) Heart of Northern Wales. 2 vols. 1912
HSCym.	Honourable Society of Cymmrodorion. Transactions.
Ind.Rev.	Dodd (A. H.) The Industrial Revolution in North Wales, 1933,
Itin. Leland	Itinerary in Wales of John Leland in or about the years 1536-153,9 edited by Lucy T. Smith. 1906.
JELI.	Lloyd (J. E.) A History of Wales. 2 vols. 1912.
Land.	Ashton (W.) The Battle of land and sea. 1909.
Lewis.	Lewis (Edward). Topographical dictionary of Wales. 2 vols. 1833.
NLW.	National Library of Wales.
NWP.	North Wales Pioneer.
NWWN.	North Wales Weekly News.
Par.	Lhwyd (Edward). Parochialia, edited. by R. H. Morris. (Arch. Camb Suppt)1909-1911.
Parry.	Parry (Edward). Royal visits and progresses to Wales, 1880.
Ped.	Griffith (J. E.) Pedigrees of Anglesey and Caernarvonshire families, 1914.
Pen.	Pennant (Thomas). Tours in Wales. 3 vols, 1883.
Porter.	Porter (George). Colwyn Bay before the houses came, 1938.
Report AM.	Report of the Royal Commission on Ancient and Historical Monuments: County of Denbigh, 1914.
St.Ch.Pr.	Star Chamber Proceedings, edited. by Ifan ab Owen Edwards. Board of Celtic Studies: History and Law Series, (No. 1). 1929.
Telford	Life of Thomas Telford, civil engineer, written by himself ... edited. by John Rickman.
TSt.A.	Thomas (D.R.) History of the Diocese of St. Asaph, 3 vols, 1908-13.
UCW.	University College of Wales
Ven.Wms.	Venables-Williams (W.), An archaeological history of Llandrillo-yn-Rhos and the immediate neighbourhood, 1898.
WCP.	Welsh Coast Pioneer.
WStA.	Willis (Browne). Survey of St. Asaph. 2 vols, 1801

Index

A
A55 dual carriageway 102, 205
Abbey Road 20
Aber Cerrig Gwynion 18, 21, 230
Aberconwy Abbey 14, 19, 20, 37, 45, 174
Abergele Road 84, 117, 119, 122, 144, 235, 236
Aberhod 17, 39, 128, 148, 159, 167, 170, 178
Aethelstan 31
Afon Colwyn 10
Afon Ganol 19-21, 78, 79, 167
Afonrhiw 78
African Institute, see Congo Institute 242
Alhstan 31
Allanson Road 99
Allen, Daniel 208, 235
Allen, Edward 138
arbutus tree 116
auction of 1875, 118
aviation 162, 165, 218

B
Baldwin 10
Banastre, Robert 40
Bangor, Bishop of 11, 27, 56
banks 123, 136, 209
Baptists 136, 145, 241
Barlow, Sir John 110
Barton, Sir William 145
Bath-house 128, 148, 159
bathing place 194
Bay View Shopping Centre 100, 205
BBC 225
Beach Road 81, 88
beacons 56
Beech Holme 141

Beehive 233
Belgrave Road 88, 143
Bethesda Chapel 83, 104, 108, 140
Bethlehem chapel 142, 143, 145
Betws-yn-Rhos 74, 182, 232
Bevan, George 165
Bijou Pavilion 165
Black Cat 99
Black Death 45
Black Prince 46
Blackburn House School 223
Blacksmith 143
Blue Bell Inn 99, 160
Board School 118, 126, 133, 148
Bod Alaw School 211
Bodrhydden 41
Bodlondeb 115, 117
Bodysgallen 75
Borough of Colwyn Bay 202, 206
Booth, Lawrence 118, 235
Bottomley, Horatio 242
Bowen, S.Powell 235
Boulger, Rev. John 139
brewery 112
Brewis Road 218
brick-works 122
British Legion Club 114
British School 110
Brodrick, Anne 232
Brodrick, Laurence 238
Brodrick, Margaret "Daisy" 232
Brompton Avenue 164, 218
Bron Derw 123
Bron-y-Nant 119, 140, 161, 165
Bryn Dinerth 84, 177, 178
Bryn Eglwys 234

Bryn Euryn 12, 19, 27, 36, 39, 115, 154, 164, 165, 167, 178, 217
Bryn Rhys School 233
Bryn yr Odin 32, 183
Bryn-y-Gwynt 89, 108, 144
Bryn-y-maen 11, 32, 139, 206, 233
Bryndinerth 99, 170
Brynffanigl 34, 183
Bryntirion 94
Bulkeley, Thomas 67
Butler, William 186
Byron, Colonel Gilbert 75

C
Cae Calch 187
Cae Eithin 84
Cae Rodin 187
Cae Sam 100
Calvinistic Methodists 88, 143
Cath Ddu 99
Cath Goch 99
Cath Wyn 99
Conway, Catherine 69
Catlin's Arcadia Theatre 204
Catrin o'r Berain 72, 235
causeway 19, 21
Cayley Arms 99, 160, 162
Cayley Estate 62, 129, 178
Cayley, Sir Everard 176, 177, 218, 219
Cayley, Sir George 218
Cefn-Ffynnon 84
Cefngarlleg 239
Central Hotel 123, 125, 235
Central School 152
Chadwick, Thomas 235
Chapel Street 133, 240
Charter of Incorporation 165
Christ Church 139, 233

Index

Church in Wales 206
Church Walks 110, 143
Cil Cow, 115
Cil-llidiau 10
Cilgwyn 84, 86, 88, 92, 177
cinemas 141, 142, 145, 153, 203, 204, 226
Cistercians 30, 36, 57, 214
Civil War 75
Clock House 122
Clough, Anne Jemima 89, 234
Clough, Arthur Hugh 89, 234
Clough, Catherine Butler 140
Clough, Rev. Roger Butler 234
Clough, Richard Butler 88, 98, 139, 233, 234
Clough, Sir Richard 235
Clwyd river 13, 32
coaching 153, 232
Coch Bach y Bala 208
Coed Coch 31, 88, 108, 139, 194, 197, 231-234, 238
Coed Pella Hotel 114
Coed Pella Road 114, 161
coins 14, 77
Colwyn 10, 12, 50, 86, 88, 92, 116, 177, 202
Colwyn Avenue 145
Colwyn Bay 12, 125, 126, 202, 207
Colwyn Bay & Colwyn Urban District 153, 164, 206
Colwyn Bay & Liverpool Steamship Company 212
Colwyn Bay & West Denbighshire Hospital 164, 222
Colwyn Bay and Pwllycrochan Estate Company 118, 126
Colwyn Bay Cricket Club 222
Colwyn Bay Gas Company 129
Colwyn Bay Hotel 102, 113-116, 118, 136, 203, 204, 226
Colwyn Bay parish 177, 206
Colwyn Bay station 205
Colwyn Bay Water Works Company 126
Colwyn Farm 89
Colwyn Fawr 81, 82, 106
Colwyn Parish 177, 206
Colwyn Station 116
Colwyn stream 10, 82, 100, 104, 105

Colwyn, U.S.A. 238
Combermere Lodge 160, 162
Congo Institute 132, 133, 241
Congregationalism 144
Conway Road 124, 153
Conway Rural Sanitary Authority 126
Conway, David Lloyd 66
Conway, Edward 12, 54, 66, 67
Conway, Elizabeth 186
Conway, Evan ap John 55
Conway, Harry 69
Conway, Hugh 54, 57, 65, 67, 173
Conway, Huw 37, 60
Conway, John 67, 111
Conway, Lowry 66
Conway, Margaret 173
Conway, Reinallt 67
Conway, Rheinallt 19, 68
Conway, Robert 67, 69, 111, 174
Conway, Sir Henry 41
Conway, Sir John 41
Conway, William 66
Conway Union 119, 125
Conwy 13, 40
Conwy and Colwyn Bay Joint Water Supply Board, 129
Conwy Castle 12, 15, 46
Conwy County Borough 202, 215
Conwy river 18, 45
Conwy Road 123, 125, 142, 235
council offices 123, 161
County Buildings 123
County Court 162
Cowlyd 126, 164
Craig-y-don 20
Creuddyn 11, 21, 35, 41, 43, 45, 170
Crevecoeuer, Sir Hugh 41
Crevequer, John de 41
Crevequer, Robert de 41, 43
Crevequer, Sir Robert de 40
Crosville Motor Services Ltd 230
cursing well 143, 196, 231
Cymryd 31

D
Dafarn Isaf 233
Dafarn Uchaf 233
Dafydd ap Jenkin 65
David, Prince of Wales 220

Davies, Daniel 88
Davies, Mutton 68
Davies, Principal Gethin 241
Davies, Robert 19, 68, 69
Davies, Venerable William 217
Davies, William 56
de Montfort, Eleanor 42
Denbighshire County Council 209
Denbighshire Quarter Sessions 209
Denbighshire Yeomanry 220
Dew, William 115, 118, 202
Digby Road 218
Dinerth 11, 13, 19, 76, 86, 90, 167, 171, 177, 182, 218
Dinerth Road 39, 170, 173
Dingle 78, 83, 122, 127, 205, 226
Dinglewood field. 162
Dinglewood School 138
Disgwylfa 140
Disserth 65
Dod, Whitehall 62, 77, 99, 115, 178, 218
Dol ddu 84, 103
Dolwen 11, 12, 81
Dolwyd 80
Donkey Path 102, 110, 205
Douglas, John 116, 118, 119, 204, 207, 233, 234
Drill Hall 203, 157, 162, 220, 224, 227, 228
drinking fountain 127, 153, 161, 208
Duchess of Gloucester 222
Dudley, Robert 58, 214
Duke of Gloucester 222
Dyfed, Archdruid 238
dyke 18

E
Eagles 81, 82, 114, 165, 178, 191
Earl of Chester 40
Earl of Leicester 53, 58, 66
Earl of Northumberland 46, 219
East Parade 102, 152
East Promenade 128, 130, 136
Ebenezer Chapel 88, 106
Ednyfed Fychan 33, 34, 62, 119, 170, 217
education 146
Edward I, 11, 15, 40, 42

Edwards, O.M. 239
Edwards, Rt.Rev. Alfred George 238
Edwards, Thomas Charles 142
Edwin 32
Egbert, King 31, 171
Eirias 21, 69, 86, 88, 89, 92, 125, 170, 177
Eirias Dingle 14, 82, 100, 136
Eirias Park 163-165, 202, 206, 238, 239
Eirias stream 66, 78
electricity 123, 130, 162, 164
Elizabeth II, 220
Ellesmere Road 159
Elwy Road 177
Engedi 136, 142, 143
English Baptist 145
English Congregational Church 136
English Methodism 141
English Presbyterian 136
English Wesleyans 141
erosion 18
Erskine Arms 115
Erskine Road 145
Erskine Villa 114, 122
Erskine, Captain David 112
Erskine, David 111
Erskine, Lady [Jane Silence] 99, 100, 111, 112, 202
Erskine, Sir David 88, 98, 112
Erskine, Sir Thomas 112, 118, 119, 207
Everard Road 218

F
Fairy Glen 103, 161
Felin 135
Felin Eithin 108
Fern Bank 142
ferry 12, 78, 79, 82, 112, 191
Festival of Britain 7
Fferm 182, 232
Ffordd Bont Sych 108
Ffynnon Elian 84, 231
fire brigade 123, 131
Flagstaff 135, 154, 162, 222, 240
food rationing 226
"Forty-five" rebellion 74
Foulkes, Edward 141, 235
Foulkes, Robert 21
Foulkes, Sidney Colwyn 235

Four Crosses 80-82, 84, 88
Frongoch 110
Frost, Charles 233, 234
Frost, Eleanor 139, 140
Frost, John 233
Furnace 95

G
Garthewin 88
gas works 83, 129
Gegin 108
George, David Lloyd 162, 204, 230, 238
Giraldus Cambrensis 10
Gilbertville 135, 148
Gildas 10, 27
Glan Aber 150, 161
Glan Conwy Corner 19, 82
Glan-y-Don 81, 84, 103, 167, 170
Glan-y-Mor 84
Glan-y-Wern 178
Glanymor Road (Beach Road) 106, 108
Glanywern 239
Gloddaeth 50, 75, 80, 85
Glyn 69, 71, 84, 89, 175, 178, 197, 226
Glyndwr revolt 35
Gorsedd circle 113, 222, 238
Graianllyn 12, 64, 135, 174, 191
Graig 88
Grammar School 152
Grant, Cary 204
Green Bank 108
Greenfield Road 122, 141, 154, 229
Griffith de Colwyn 195
Griffith Goch 64
Groes 164
Groes Bach 82, 89, 110
Groes Bridge 81, 153, 165
Groes Fawr 47, 89
Groes Mill 48
Groes Road 78, 81, 228
Groes stream 126
Groes-yn-Eirias 14, 57, 78, 79, 82, 178, 217
Groesffordd 12, 80
Gronw ap Heilyn 35, 41-43, 48, 62
Gruffydd Goch 32
Gruffydd Llwyd 35
Guardians of the Poor 123

Gweirglodd Isallt 183
Gwydir 80
Gwysaney 68

H
Hafod Euryn 175
Hafodunos 81, 108
harbour 18
Havergal, Frances Ridley 89
Hearth Tax 72, 188
Hebron Chapel 142, 143
Henry III, 40
Henry VII, 37, 217
Hermon 142, 143
Heronwater School 232
Hesketh Road 222
Higher Grade School 151
Hillside Road 123
Holland, David 54, 57
Holland, Foulk 53
Holland, Humphrey 194
Holland, Hugh 57, 184
Holland, Hugh Gwyn 57
Holland, Jane 111
Holland, Morgan 66
Holland, Robert 53
Holland, Thomas 194, 195
Holland, William 54, 111
Hookes, William 67
Horeb 140
Horton, Mary 219
Horton, William 145, 165, 167, 177, 212, 214, 219, 230
Hovey, Rosa 148, 149
Hughes, Hugh 60, 173, 218
Hughes, Leonard 163
Hughes, Thomas 113, 116, 203
Hughes, Rev. William 133, 241
Hydropathic Establishment 136, 148, 149

I
Ievan ap Robert 65
Ifores Gwynedd 113
Imperial Hotel 123, 136, 157
Independent Chapel 136
Ingleside 150
Iron Church 137, 138
Isallt 80
Isolation Hospital 161
Ivy Cottages 113
Ivy House 113, 116, 122, 143, 203
Ivy Street 113, 116, 131, 142, 164, 206, 208

Index

J
John, Augustus 163
Johnson, Dr. Samuel 77, 81
Jones, Anne 140
Jones, Dr. T.Gwynn 103, 233
Jones, Eleanor 233
Jones, Professor T.Gwynn 239
Jones, Sir J.Pritchard 238
Jones, Rev. J. D. 116
Julius Agricola 202

K
Kenelm Road 218
Kingfisher 99
King's Road 150
Kinmel 57, 231

L
Lacy, Henry de 41
Lancaster House 236
Lansdowne Road 150
Lawson Road 145
Leila Megane 239
Leland, John 10
Lhwyd, Edward 10
Liberty's bar 208
library 222
Liddell, Alice 157, 232, 239
Little Orme 56, 217
Llais Afon 233
Llan Farm 197
Llanddulas 74, 186
Llanddulas stream 78
Llandrillo Church 38, 71, 115, 167, 170-172, 211, 215, 218
Llandrillo Technical College 222
Llandrillo-yn-Rhos 13, 21, 56, 74, 76, 86, 88, 119, 125, 164, 167, 170, 177, 214, 217
Llandudno & Colwyn Bay Electric Railway Ltd 228
Llandudno Junction 126
Llandudno Road 19, 84
Llanelian 10, 56, 68, 71, 74, 76, 142, 143, 193, 231, 241
Llanelian Road 106
Llangynfryn 181
Llangystennin 165
Llannerch 66, 68, 218
Llannerch Road 147, 161, 185, 218
Llanrhos Road 19
Llansanffraid Glan Conwy 12, 18, 56, 65, 165, 233, 240

Llawr Pentre 105, 107, 108
Lletty'r Dryw 84, 89, 103
Llewelyn Road 237
Llywelyn the Great 14, 19, 20, 34, 37, 57, 214, 217
Llowarch ap Bran 35
Lloyd, Abraham 118
Lloyd, Hugh 54
Lloyd, Meredith 69
Llwydcoed 11, 49, 86, 91, 94, 177
Llyn Dolddu 108
Llys Euryn 10, 32, 36, 39, 60, 65, 115, 165, 167, 170, 173, 217
Llysfaen 10, 11, 13, 16, 21, 31, 40, 42, 43, 45, 51, 54-56, 71, 74, 76, 84, 86, 88, 110, 147, 164, 165, 181, 186, 188, 206
Llysfaen Road 82
Llywelyn ap Griffith 40, 42
Local Board 123, 126, 206, 209
London Road 114
Longueville, Sir Thomas 41
Loraine, Robert 162
Lord Byron 75
Lord Colwyn 163, 164
Lord Mostyn 178
Lord Woolton 226
Lordship of Denbigh 12, 43, 45, 54, 66
lych-gate 71, 175, 190

M
Madoc Gloddaeth 50, 230
Madoc Rebellion 35, 43
Maelgwn Gwynedd 10, 19, 27, 214
Maen Rhys 17
Maen-y-Hensor 17
Maes Cadwgan 84, 107, 108, 220
Maes Mawr 53
Maes y gaer 178
Maescadwgan 89
Magistrates Court 209
Mair Glan Conway 113
Marchudd ap Cynan 33, 34, 64
Marchweithian 72
Marine Drive 156
Marine Hotel 17
Marine Path 127
Marine Road 100, 114, 118

Marks, T.T. 241
Marl Hall 184
Marle, Major 235
marsh 18, 69
Maternity and Child Welfare Centre 165
Mawson, Thomas H. 222
Meifod 84, 103, 193
Metropole Hotel 203, 226
Mews 124, 153
Militia 87, 94, 95, 133, 240
Mill 48, 50, 66, 88, 89, 108, 110, 115, 126, 133, 135, 178, 240
Min-y-don 84, 89, 164, 183, 233, 234
Minafon 89, 140
Miners' Arms 110
Ministry of Food 223, 226
Minydon 98, 108, 110, 139, 140, 165, 170
mission chapel 119, 122, 133, 138, 207
Mobile, Alabama 230
Mochdre 11, 18, 21, 50, 76, 86, 88, 91, 133, 143, 177, 191, 239
Mochdre and Pabo railway station 102, 133, 205, 240
Monaville 164
monolith 17
Montacute, William de 43, 45, 51
Moon's 136
Moranedd 99, 160
Morfa 16, 19, 21, 67, 171
Morfa Inn 108
Morfa Rhuddlan 13
Morfa Road 19
Morgan ab John 178, 214
Morgan ab John ap David 58
Moriah 142
Moseley, Leonard 235
Mostyn Road 132
Mostyn, Colonel Roger 75
Mostyn, Robert 69
Mostyn, Sir Roger 55, 69, 78, 80
Mountain View 82, 191
Mutton, Sir Peter 19, 68, 218
Myddelton, Captain Will 57
Mynydd 133, 239, 240

N
Nant 88, 161
Nant Uchaf 84
Nant-y-Glyn 14, 84, 141
Nant-y-glyn Road 133, 241
National Eisteddfod 113, 162, 222, 238
National School 88, 110, 140, 146, 151, 170
National Telephone Company 153
Nazareth 88, 143
Neville & Co 235
New Colwyn 10, 119, 125, 206
Newnham College 89, 234
Nonconformity 216

O
Oaklands 123
Oakwood Park 151
Oblates of Mary Immaculate 140
Odstone 19, 230
Oldfield, Rev. Edward 182
Old Budget Gate 230
Old Colwyn 10, 16, 18, 83, 141, 240
Old Highway 14, 15, 71, 78-82, 191
Old Price 82, 112, 167
ornamental fountain 124
Owain Glyndwr 38, 47, 64
Owen, Robert 55
Owen, Sir John 75

P
Pabo 173, 219
Pant Glas 71
Pant-y-gloch 88
Parc 84
Parciau 89, 103, 106
Park Road 145
Parochial Board 126, 129
Parry, Rev. Thomas 122, 123, 163
Parry, Thomas 58, 116
Parry-Evans, J.L. 58
Payne, Rev. F. 148, 150
Patti, Adelina 156, 204, 209
Pen Geulan 84
Pen-y-bryn 84, 89, 102
Pen-y-coed 102
Pen-y-corddin Mawr 14
Pen-y-dorlan 115, 122
Pen-y-groes 115
Pen-y-Maes 122
Pender, John 116, 118, 203
Pender, Sir John 115
Pendorlan 84, 154
Pendre 108
Penffordd 108
Penmaen Head 11, 13, 40, 43, 51, 81, 83, 100, 102, 108, 220
Penmaen View 116
Penrhos College 135, 136, 148, 149, 203, 222, 226
Penrhos Lodge 114
Penrhos Road 148
Penrhyn Avenue 20, 145, 165, 167, 228
Penrhyn Bay 19, 20, 164, 230
Penrhyn Creuddyn 19, 34, 68, 75
Penrhyn Isaf farm 84
Penrhyn Marsh 75, 169
Penrhyn Road 119, 122, 154, 203
Pentre Gwyddel 186
Pentre Isa 103
Pentre-uchaf 84
Penybryn 108
Penycefn 187
Penygraig Cottages 108
Peulwys 54, 110, 186
Peulwys Lane 80, 103
pier 127, 135, 154, 164, 209, 226
Pier Pavilion 154, 165
pigeon loft 113, 227
pinfold 108
Plough 100
pirates 59
plague 56
Plas Clough 235
Plas Iolyn 14, 57
Plas Isa 68
Plas Llewelyn 194
Plas Nant 64
Plas Newydd 71
Plas yr Esgob 11, 181
Plas-y-coed 226
Plas-yn-Llysfaen 112
Plastirion 165
Plough 110, 178
Plough Cottages 106
Plough Terrace 162, 183
police 89, 97, 123, 133, 207, 208, 240, 222
Pont-y-groes-yn-Eirias 122
popish recusants 74
Poplas 86, 115
population 74, 86, 87, 123, 126, 139, 159, 171, 188, 203
Porter, George 115
Porter, John 111, 116, 118, 122, 123, 125, 153, 164, 208, 235
Post Office 78, 84, 125, 153, 164, 191, 205, 235
PQ17 204
Presbyterian Church 122, 124, 141
Preece, Sir William 239
Price, Captain Thomas 14, 57
Price, John 112
Price, Rev. James 112
Prince of Wales 11, 164, 220, 222
Prince of Wales Theatre 204
Prince Philip 209, 222
Princes Drive 132, 145, 159, 164, 205, 235
Princess Court 204
Princess Margaret 222
Princess Marie of Romania 222
Princess Victoria 84, 110, 220
printing press 56
promenade 18, 116, 125, 127-130, 135, 136, 154, 159, 161, 163, 203, 218
Public Hall 135, 157, 203, 207, 237
Pugh, Captain Robert 75
Pugh, Robert 56
Pugh, William 19
Puleston, Sir John 67
Pwll-y-crochan Isaf 115
Pwllycrochan 14, 16, 66, 69, 88, 98, 109, 111, 170
Pwllycrochan Avenue 112
Pwllycrochan Estate office 209
Pwllycrochan Halt 100, 205
Pwllycrochan Hotel 100, 114, 116, 118, 136, 226
Pwllycrochan Isa 143
Pwllycrochan Woods 15, 112, 126, 161
Pydew 240
Pyers Conway 67
Pyers Holland 231

Q
Quay 19, 20, 167
Queen's Hotel 110, 162, 226, 229

R
RAF 218
railway 20, 21, 84, 88, 100, 115, 122, 123, 177, 203, 205, 206
Ramsbottom, John 102
Raynes quarries 187
Red Lion 100, 108, 178
Rees, Henry 143
Repertory Theatre 135, 203, 204
reservoir 126
Rhianfa 161
Rhiw 11, 12, 48, 50, 66, 84, 86, 90, 111, 115, 126, 177
Rhiw Bach 114, 115
Rhiw Bella 143
Rhiw Ganol 84
Rhiw Mawr 115
Rhiw Road 123, 140, 142, 143
Rhiwledyn 56
Rhodri Mawr 31
Rhos 13, 42
Rhos Abbey Hotel 58, 167, 168
Rhos Estate 214
Rhos Farm 178
Rhos Fynach 20, 35, 36, 57, 59, 94, 167, 170, 171, 178, 214, 215
Rhos Goch 32
Rhos Golf Links 20, 162
Rhos Neigr 212
Rhos Pier 58, 153, 167, 212
Rhos Playhouse 204
Rhos Point 212
Rhos promenade 168
Rhos Quarry 119
Rhos Quay 167
Rhos Recreation Ground 165
Rhos Road 9, 21, 39, 79, 84, 88, 99, 125, 141, 161, 167, 169, 218
Rhos tollgate 230
Rhos Trillo 167
Rhos-on-Sea 16, 125, 167
Rhos-on-Sea Congregational Church 145
Rhos-on-sea golf course 169, 230
Rhoslan 114
Rhuallt 83, 110
Rhuddlan Castle 15
Rhwng-y-ddwyffordd 233
Rhyd Farm 21, 84, 169, 178
Rhyd-y-cerrig-gwynion 18, 21, 230
Rhyd-y-Foel 14, 80, 181
Rhydgwynt 111
Rhys ap Gruffydd Goch 12
Rhys ap Gruffydd, Lord 35
Rhys Fawr, Sir 66
Richard ap Howel 65
Richard II, 46, 202, 219
Rifle Volunteers 154
Rising Gull 20, 167, 175
Rising Sun 21, 82, 87, 115, 175
River Colwyn 107
Riviére, Jules Prudence 156, 209, 211
Riviére's Avenue 211
Roberts, Abel 142, 143
Roberts, Captain Philip Quellyn 204
Roberts, Sir J.Herbert 238
Roberts, T.Osborne 239
Robin ap Griffith Goch 35, 60, 65, 218
Roman Catholicism 140, 217
Rose Cottage 116, 133
Rose Place 106
Ross, Reverend W. 241
Royal Artillery, 61st (C&D Yeo) Med. Regt, 227
Royal Hotel 116, 117, 136
Royal Visits 220
Royal Welch Fusiliers 87, 157, 162, 220, 225, 227
Royal Welch Regiment 228
Rydal fields 238
Rydal public gardens 165
Rydal School 100, 148, 150, 203, 226

S
Sale of 1865, 111, 114, 143, 202
Salem Chapel 144
Salusbury, Catherine 195
Salusbury, Harry 55
Salusbury, Henry 55
Salusbury, Sir John 55
Salusbury, Thomas 65
Salusburys of Lleweny 54
Salvation Army 145
Saracen's Head 233
Sarn-y-Mynach 19, 80
Saxon ring 171
Saxons 30
Schools 96, 147, 152, 188, 193
Sea Shore Road 114
Sea View Crescent 113, 116, 122
Sea View Road 122
Sea View Terrace 100, 122
Seafield Road 14
Seaview Road 117
Secondary Modern School 152
Seion 140, 143
semaphore station 84, 188
sewerage 161, 164
Ship Inn 21, 39, 77, 82, 84, 97, 100, 108, 110, 219, 220
Sion 142
Sir Tudor ab Ednyfed 43
Sisters of Mercy 140
smithy 47, 88, 161
Society of Friends 145
Spitfire 224
Sr Thomas Prendergast 184
St Catherine's Church 106, 234
St David's church 139, 207
St Deiniol 214
St Elian 193, 231
St Enoch's hotel 226
St George's church 177, 218
St George's Road 218
St Hilary 193, 231
St Trillo 20, 27, 28, 33, 169, 171, 213-215
St Andrew's Church 139
St Asaph, Bishop of 11, 16, 43, 55, 95, 207, 215, 238
St Catherine's Church 84, 88, 104, 139, 164
St Cynfryn's 181
St John's Church 135, 136, 140-142, 164
St Joseph's Church 140
St Paul's Church 113, 119, 136-138, 207
Steel, Anthony 204
Stanley, H.M. 241
Stanley, Sir Henry M. 133
Station Hotel 122, 123, 125, 235
Station Road 82, 108, 113, 116, 119, 122, 124, 125, 148, 203, 209, 235
stocks 78, 192
storm of 1606, 17
street lighting 129

Suetonius Paulinus 10, 202
Suffragettes 162
Sun Bach cottage 108
Sun Inn 100, 108
Sunday School 88
sundial 76, 184
Swan Inn 82, 178, 191, 208
Swift, Dean 77

T
Tabernacl Chapel 145, 241
Tai-newyddion 108
tailors 88
Tan Lan Estate 164
Tan y Dderwen 194, 195
Tan-y-bryn Bridge 161
Tan-y-bryn Hotel 146
Tan-y-bryn Road 39, 88, 125, 146, 173
Tan-y-Lan 10
tank 225
Tanllan 84
Tanrallt Isa 239
Tanrallt Ucha 239
Tanybont Cottages 108
Tanybryn Cottages 108
Tanybryn Road 170
Tanycoed 164
Telford, Thomas 82
tennis courts 132
Territorial Army 162, 227
Teyrdan 31, 194
The Jungle 88
The Parade 116, 148
The Rough 89
Theatr Colwyn 204, 237
tithe rioters 222
Tithe War, 133, 239
toll-bar 19, 116, 119, 230
Town Hall 225
traffic 130
trams 161, 162, 228
travelling post office 205
Treaty of Aberconwy 42, 44
Trebwll 67
trees 116, 131, 186
Tu Hwnt i'r Afon 84, 89, 103, 106
Tucker, Norman 7
Tudors 37, 53, 61
turnpike 77, 78, 80, 106, 114, 116, 122, 125, 167, 183
Twnan 11, 108, 197
Ty Fry 84, 169

Ty Groes 103
Ty Gwyn 68, 94
Ty Mawr 76, 80, 84, 108, 186, 187
Ty Newydd 84, 89, 178
Ty'-n-y-Ffordd 141
Tyddyn Du 67
Ty'n y Caeau 84
Ty'n y Coed 143
Ty'n-maes 122
Ty'n-y-ffordd 115, 122, 143
Ty'n-y-Maes (Dinglewood) 115

U
Union Church 145
United States army 226
Urban District of Colwyn Bay and Colwyn 45, 123, 126, 129, 153, 164, 206
Urdd 165
Uwchdulas 11
Uxbridge House 235

V
Vaughan, Captain Henry 71
Vaughan, Henry 71, 175
Vaughan, John 71, 186
Vaughan, Major Henry 71
Vaughan, Margaret 69
Vaughan, Sir William 55, 75
Vavghan, Thomas 186
Verbrugghen, Henri 156
Vicarage 39
Vicar's Road 19
Victoria Drive 156
Victoria Park 154
Victoria Pavilion 156
Volunteers 156, 162
Vychan, Hugh 67

W
Walshaw Avenue 113, 150
war memorial 164
water 125, 126, 161, 188
water troughs 102
Wayside 164
Weedon, Harry 204
weir 30, 57, 99, 169, 170, 178, 215
Welsh Baptist churches 145, 241
Welsh Calvinistic Methodists 141, 142
Welsh Congregational 144
Welsh Independents 88
Welsh Methodists 136, 140

Welsh Mountain Zoo 222, 238, 240
Wern cottage 113
Wesley, Rev. John 77
Westwood Terrace 122
Wheatsheaf 232
wheelwright 107
Whitaker, Oldham 89, 140
White Horse 82, 191
White Lion Inn 74, 193, 195, 197, 231
Whitehall Road 84, 99, 218
Whitehead, Dr Walter 222
Williams, Abel 206
Williams, Archbishop John 75
Williams, Colonel Thomas Peers 115
Williams, General Owen 20
Williams, John 239
Williams, Morgan 238
Williams, Rev. Hugh 111
Williams, Rev. W. Venables 116, 118, 119, 123, 133, 135, 161, 173, 203, 205
Williams, Robert 111
Williams, Thomas Peers 178
Williams-Ellis, Sir Clough 235
Wood, William S. 235
Woodland Road West 142, 143, 159
World War II 223
wreck buoy 212
Wynn Gardens 163, 164
Wynn, Brownlow 115
Wynn, John 231, 232
Wynn, John Lloyd 139, 195, 231, 232, 234
Wynn, Major-General Edward William 232
Wynn, Mary 174
Wynn, Sir John 54, 67, 80
Wynn, Sir Watkin Williams 163, 184
Wynne, Colonel Hugh 75
Wynne, General 88, 108
Wynne, R.O.F. 239
Wynns of Gwydir 54
Wyrion Eden 49

Y
Y Llan 187
Y Wern 231
YMCA 162
Ysgubor Newydd 197